The
Eclectic
Gourmet
Guide to
Chicago

Also available from MENASHA RIDGE PRESS

The Eclectic Gourmet Guide to Los Angeles,
  by Colleen Dunn Bates

The Eclectic Gourmet Guide to New Orleans,
  by Tom Fitzmorris

The Eclectic Gourmet Guide to San Francisco & the Bay Area,
  by Richard Sterling

The Eclectic Gourmet Guide to San Diego,
  by Stephen Silverman

The Eclectic Gourmet Guide to Washington, D.C.,
  by Eve Zibart

The Eclectic Gourmet Guide to Atlanta,
  by Jane Garvey

The Eclectic Gourmet Guide to Chicago

2nd Edition

Camille Stagg

MENASHA
RIDGE
PRESS

Menasha Ridge Press, Inc.
P.O. Box 43673
Birmingham, Alabama 35243

Cover and text design by Suzanne Holt

Cover art by Michele Natale

ISBN 0-89732-326-2

Manufactured in the United States of America

10 9 8 7 6 5 4 3 2 1

Second Edition, First Printing

Distributed by The Globe Pequot Press

CONTENTS

acknowledgments

A special thank you to the many people who assisted with the research and compilation of this book, including those who shared their restaurant experiences. Special thanks to the crack team of Medill School of Journalism students and recent graduates who assisted with gathering the current restaurant data for the first book edition: Meg McGinity, American and seafood restaurants; Greg Henkin, steak and German restaurants; Andrea Sachs, French and vegetarian restaurants; and Sarah Stirland, from Hong Kong, Asian cuisine, and many others. Many thanks to Rummana Hussain, whose Indian heritage, knowledge of Middle Eastern cuisines, and journalistic skills were invaluable as she worked with me to the final deadline on all editions. Ritu Upadhyay also deserves thanks for her contribution to the book's early editions and for sharing information on Indian culture. A special note of gratitude to Lyle Sinrod Walter (M.S., Medill School of Journalism; certificate, L'Academie de Cuisine, Bethesda, Maryland), whose knowledge of cuisines, languages, and journalism helped immensely. Thanks also to Maya Norris of Hawaii, who put in long hours to help complete the second printing while earning her master's, and then assisted with the second edition. And thanks to sophomore Jennifer Wielgus, who assisted with the same edition of this book.

Thanks to several for their help with the initial book: Joan Hersh, owner of A Matter of Course catering; Robert Rohden, president of Laser List Chicago, wine consultant, and computer consultant; John Davis, owner and president of several companies, including A Taste of California, the largest wine mail-order business in the United States; Lucia de la Cruz, a bilingual friend who lived in Spain, for Spanish vocabulary advice;

Lowell B. Komie, for his counsel and dining reports; Kay Komie and Ann Lee, for their Hyde Park restaurant recommendations; Mel Markon, former restaurateur, for his restaurant suggestions; Toshihiko Sawada, former director of the Japan National Tourist Organization, for sharing his expertise on his native cuisine; Yong-Ku Hwang, director of the Korea National Tourist Organization, for his Korean restaurant suggestions; and to Jasmine Fernandez, a Wright College student who assisted with galleys for this edition.

And a very special thank you to my dining companions for both editions, including my mother, Jeanette Stagg, who instilled in me a love of food and cooking; Jim White, Dallas broadcaster and food lover, whose articulate critiques breathed life into the original project; Ed Jarratt, who is without food prejudices and is willing to try anything once—even czarnina; to B. C. Kent, whose knowledge of fish (and penchant for catfish) and fondness for desserts helped immeasurably; to Lyle Sinrod Walter, who assisted with communicating in Thai for that cuisine category; to Rummana Hussain and Maya Norris, for opinions of several places we tried; to Phyllis Magida, who accompanied me in sampling vegetarian food; to Julie Youngs, a frequent diner-about-town who assisted in many ways; to Martin Gaspar, attorney, for his sharing various restaurant experiences; to Meryl and Richard Cannon, for their input on northwest suburban restaurants; and to journalist Gary Moore, for sharing his Hispanic expertise regarding Mexican cuisine.

Thansk also to publisher Bob Sehlinger and his cheerful staff at Menasha Ridge Press, especially associate publisher Molly Merkle, managing editors Holly Cross and Chris Mohney, copy editor Annie Long, and fact checker Tiffany Prewitt for their continuing support and teamwork.

About the Author

Camille Stagg is a food and travel writer and editor with more than 25 years of experience in the journalism and consulting profession. Her work for over 12 years as food editor for the *Chicago Sun-Times* won awards for excellence in food journalism. She was also food editor of *Cuisine* magazine, has appeared regularly on television and radio including WBBM News Radio and FM 100, and is the author of several books, including the culinary troubleshooting reference, *The Best of The Cook's Advisor.* Her latest cookbook, *Cooking with Wine* (Time-Life), was released in August 1997. She appeared on leading television and radio shows during national media tours with her first best-selling book, *The Cook's Advisor.*

Ms. Stagg has directed a cooking school and teaches numerous seminars and classes at Wright College and College of DuPage, among other places. She develops recipes for A Taste of California, a wine-of-the-month club with more than 50,000 members, and conducts an annual ethnic wine dinner program with that organization. Her recipes appear in the second edition of *A Taste of California: Tenth Anniversary Cookbook,* which pairs dishes with varietal wines. She has contributed to numerous publications in the United States and abroad, such as *The Washington Post, The Boston Globe, Wine Spectator, Bon Appetit,* and *Irish Tatler* in Dublin. Ms. Stagg has served as dining critic for the *Chicago Sun-Times,* Pulitzer-Lerner Newspapers, *Inside Chicago* magazine, *Talking to the Boss, Chicago Social,* and currently for Copley Chicago Newspapers, including *Fox Valley Villages* 60504 and the *Napierville Sun.* Her travel assignments focusing on cuisine and culture have taken her to Europe, Australia, North Africa, Hong Kong, Canada, the Caribbean, Mexico, and most of the United States. She holds a B.S. in food science and journalism from the University of Illinois and has studied cooking with experts in the U.S. and abroad.

GEttiNG iT RiGHt

A lot of thought went into this guide. While producing a dining guide may appear to be a straightforward endeavor, I can assure you that it is fraught with peril. I have read dining guides by authors who turn up their noses at anything except four-star French restaurants (of which there are a whole lot fewer than people think). Likewise, I have seen a guide that totally omits Thai and Indian restaurants—among others—because the author did not understand those cuisines. I have read guides absolutely devoid of criticism, written by "experts" unwilling to risk offending the source of their free meals. Finally, I've seen those books that are based on surveys and write-ins from diners whose credentials for evaluating fine dining are mysterious at best and questionable at least.

How, then, do you go about developing a truly excellent dining guide? What is the best way to get it right?

If dining guides are among the most idiosyncratic of reference books, it is primarily because the background, taste, integrity, and personal agenda of each author are problematical. The authors of most dining guides are vocational or avocational restaurant or food critics. Some of these critics are schooled professionals, with palates refined by years of practical experience and culinary study; others are journalists, often with no background in food criticism or cooking, who are arbitrarily assigned the job of reviewing restaurants by their newspaper or magazine publisher (although it *is* occasionally possible to find journalists who are also culinary professionals). The worst cases are the legions of self-proclaimed food critics who mooch their way from restaurant to restaurant, growing fat on free meals in exchange for writing glowing reviews.

Ignorance of ethnic cuisine or old assumptions about what makes for haute cuisine particularly plague authors in cities without much ethnic variety in restaurants, or authors who have been writing for years about the same old, white-linen, expense-account tourist traps. Many years ago in Lexington, Kentucky, for example, there was only one Chinese restaurant in town and it was wildly successful—in spite of the fact that it was Chinese in name only. Its specialty dishes, which were essentially American vegetable casseroles smothered in corn starch, were happily gobbled up by loyal patrons who had never been exposed to real Chinese cooking. The food was not bad, but it was not Chinese either. Visitors from out of town, inquiring about a good local Chinese restaurant, were invariably directed to this place. As you would expect, they were routinely horrified by the fare.

And, while you might argue that American diners are more sophisticated and knowledgeable nowadays than at the time of the Lexington pavilion, the evidence suggests otherwise. In Las Vegas, for instance, a good restaurant town with a number of excellent Italian eateries, the local Olive Garden (a chain restaurant) is consistently voted the city's best Italian restaurant in a yearly newspaper poll. There is absolutely nothing wrong with the Las Vegas Olive Garden, but to suggest that it is the best Italian restaurant in the city is ludicrous. In point of fact, the annual survey says much more about the relative sophistication of Las Vegas diners than it does about the quality of local Italian restaurants.

But if you pick up a guide that reflects the views of many survey respondents, a *vox populi* or reader's choice compendium, that is exactly the problem. You are dependent on the average restaurant-goer's capacity to make sound, qualitative judgments—judgments almost always impaired by extraneous variables. How many times have you had a wonderful experience at a restaurant, only to be disappointed on a subsequent visit? Trying to reconcile the inconsistency, you recall that on your previous visit, you were in the company of someone particularly stimulating, and that perhaps you had enjoyed a couple of drinks before eating. What I am getting at is that our reflections on restaurant experiences are often colored by variables having little or nothing to do with the restaurant itself. And while I am given to the democratic process in theory, I have my doubts about depending entirely on survey forms that reflect such experiences.

There are more pragmatic arguments to be made about such eaters' guides as well. If you cannot control or properly qualify your survey respondents, you cannot ensure their independence, knowledge, or critical sensitivity. And, since literally anyone can participate in such surveys, the ratings can be easily slanted by those with vested interests. How many bogus responses would it take to dramatically upgrade a restaurant's rating in a survey-based, big-city dining guide? Forty or even fewer. Why? Because the publisher receives patron reports (survey responses, readers' calls) covering more restaurants than can be listed in the book. Thus the "voting" is distributed over such a large number of candidate restaurants that the median number of reports for the vast majority of establishments is 120 or fewer. A cunning restaurant proprietor who is willing to stuff the ballot box, therefore, could easily improve his own rating—or lower that of a competitor.

So my mission in the *Eclectic Gourmet Guides* is to provide you with the most meaningful, useful, and accessible restaurant evaluations possible. Weighing the alternatives, I have elected to work with culinary experts, augmenting their opinions with a carefully qualified survey population of totally independent local diners of demonstrated culinary sophistication. The experts I have sought to author the *Eclectic Gourmet Guides* are knowledgeable, seasoned professionals; they have studied around the world and written cookbooks or columns, and they closely follow the development of restaurants in their cities. They are well versed in ethnic dining, many having studied cuisines in their native lands. And they have no prejudice about high or low cuisine. They are as at home in a Tupelo, Mississippi, catfish shack as in an exclusive French restaurant on New York's Upper East Side. Thus the name *Eclectic Gourmet*.

Equally important, I have sought experts who make every effort to conduct their reviews anonymously, and who always pay full menu prices for their meals. We are credible not only because we are knowledgeable, but also because we are independent.

You, the reader of this *Eclectic Gourmet Guide,* are the inspiration for and, we hope, the beneficiary of our diligence and methodology. Though we cannot evaluate your credentials as a restaurant critic, your opinion as a consumer—of this guide and the restaurants within—is very important to us. Please tell us about your dining experiences and let us know whether you agree with our reviews.

Eat well. Be happy.

Bob Sehlinger

‡ dininq in chicaqo

Chicago, in my opinion, is the dining mecca of the United States—certainly in terms of ethnic diversity. It's no longer the "Second City." Even a well-known New York critic wrote several years ago that Chicago was the most exciting city for dining. Most experts agree that it is one of the best places for cuisine quality and variety. New York, still deemed number one by many, excels in a variety of ethnic cuisines as well. However, dining in Chicago is less of a hassle—not as crowded and certainly less costly. This heartland city has not only caught up to but surpassed most other key cities in the dining arena.

O'Hare International Airport, the busiest airport in the world, provides a port of entry for the best fresh seafood and other products to be flown in regularly from around the globe. In fact, even though it's in the Midwest, Chicago has a wider assortment of fresh seafood than many coastal cities. And because Chicago is a key convention town, it features many restaurants and hotels for diners demanding the best quality.

At last count, Chicago had about 6,000 restaurants in the city, and about 2,000 of those hold liquor licenses. Including Chicago, Cook County boasts approximately 9,000 food service establishments, according to the Illinois Restaurant Association. No one can give an exact count of restaurants in this vast suburbia. To select just 220 or so of the best of these was no easy task. The restaurants profiled reflect a balance of cuisines, styles, geographic locations, price, and the popular as well as the hidden gems. Numerous fine restaurants are not included here, but that

4

doesn't mean they are unworthy. Some are quite new and need a chance to settle in; others were in the process of change at press time; some will be covered in subsequent editions of this book.

Burgeoning Neighborhoods

Particularly hot neighborhoods for new restaurants include the following: River North, with its art galleries and antique shops, is home to **Brasserie Jo, Crofton on Wells, Hudson Club,** and **Wildfire** (see profiles).

The gentrified diagonal Near North Clybourn Corridor: **Goose Island Brewing** (1800 North Clybourn Avenue; (312) 915-0071) makes great seasonal beers and serves appropriate fare. **Bistro Ultra** (2239 North Clybourn; (773) 529-3300), opened in 1997, is intimate (55 seats), smartly decorated with fine art Belle Epoque posters on exposed brick walls, and serves some exceptional fare, including bay scallops Provençale, Lake Superior grilled whitefish, and Don Juan's Rack (of lamb). Prices are modest, service is professional, and it's worth seeking out.

The booming United Center neighborhood—Madison from the stadium to Halsted Street: the new **Carmichael's Chicago Steak House** (1052 West Monroe Street; (312) 433-0025), is one of just several restaurants in the Chicago area offering certified Black Angus beef, with steaks char-broiled; other bonuses include fresh seafood, a complimentary valet, a large courtyard, a pianist nightly, and a free shuttle bus to hotels for groups. A hotspot: **Thyme** serves French regional Mediterranean-influenced food created by John Bubala (464 North Halsted; (312) 226-4300). Fairly new is **Flat Top Grill,** an American stir-fry that allows diners to create their own stir-fry meals (see profile).

Navy Pier's grand opening was in 1995: **Riva,** serving seafood, steak, and pasta, is an anchor restaurant there (see profile). **Joe's B-Bop Cafe & Jazz Emporium** (see profile), operated by Wayne Segal (who also operates **Jazz Showcase,** founded over 50 years ago by his father, Joe) and the Chicago Restaurant Corporation, has a bandstand and a menu featuring barbecue-style foods. In 1998, **Bubba Gump Shrimp Co. Restaurant & Market** opened, fashioned after the hit film *Forrest Gump* and specializing in shrimp dishes (700 East Grand Avenue (312) 595-5500).

Randolph Market: **Vivo** (Italian, 838 West Randolph, (312) 733-3379), **Marché** (French/American brasserie, 833 West Randolph; (312) 226-8399), and the latest by the same owners, **Red Light** (Pan-Asian, especially Chinese and Thai with Malaysian and Vietnamese elements, 820

West Randolph; (312) 733-8880), provide a good dining mix. Newcomers include **Bluepoint** (oysters, seafood, and sushi, 741 West Randolph, (312) 207-1222); **Millennium** (steak house, 832 West Randolph; (312) 455-1400); **Toque,** (816 West Randolph; 666-1100) a chic, graceful place with delicious food, such as house pâté, terrine and cured salmon with caviar, crème fraîche and cucumber relish and brioche, and vanilla-scented duck breast ; and **Blackbird** (619 West Randolph; (312) 715-0708), a hot restaurant with highly recognized chef Paul Kahan. In 1999, he was named one of the ten best new chefs by *Food & Wine* magazine; he turns out seasonal American food with French inspiration.

Wicker Park/Bucktown, one of the top three artist communities in the United States: **ConFusion** (1616 North Damen Avenue; (773) 772-7100), serves fusion cuisine in a lovely outdoor garden. One of the co-owner chefs at ConFusion opened **Feast** (1835 West North Avenue; (773) 235-6361), a neighborhood restaurant with a lush garden, serving global cuisine. A recent addition is **Cafe Matou** (1846-n-48 North Milwaukee Avenue; (773) 384-8911), serving traditional French cuisine in a casual setting. **Club Lucky** in Bucktown (1824 West Wabansia; (773) 244-2003), serves traditional Italian fare in a family style. **Soul Kitchen** (see profile) features a fine mix of Soul, Southwestern, Creole, and Caribbean cuisines.

Halsted Street, which was called First Street in earlier times, continues to be "restaurant row," with many good dining spots on the same block, especially north from North Avenue. Printer's Row in the south downtown area developed several years ago and seems well anchored with some stable restaurants. Some restaurants recently opened in Chinatown, and several years ago Greektown got a few new faces. The "Little Saigon" or "New Asia" area at North Argyle Street and Sheridan Road is home to a few good storefront restaurants and ethnic shops. And West Devon Avenue has several special street signs designating its diverse ethnicity. Some of the best Indian restaurants are found from 2300–2600 West Devon Avenue, and new ones keep popping up.

There are great Italian shops and restaurants along the middle section of North Harlem Avenue, in the Norridge, Harwood Heights and River Grove area, such as **Rex Italian Foods** delicatessen and café (4431 North Harlem Avenue in Norridge; (708) 457-0177) and **Vince's Italian Restaurant** (4747 North Harlem Avenue in Harwood Heights; (708) 867-7770).

The western and southwestern suburban area has developed so much in the past several years that it is called a "boom town." New additions duplicating city restaurants in Naperville in that area are **La Sorella de**

Francesca (18 West Jefferson Street; (630) 961-2706), **Rosebud Café** (see profile), and **Mongolian Barbecue** (see profile). This suburban area is considered to be the fastest-growing community in the United States.

Except for the bastions of old Italian neighborhoods such as the Heart of Italy (near Midway Airport—see profile of **Bruna's Ristorante**) and Taylor Street (see profiles of **Tuscany** and **Tufano's**), and several fine restaurants here and there, the South Side is sparse as a dining zone (Zone 7). **Chesden's** (4465 South Archer; (773) 247-2400), dates back to the mid-1940s and serves good, straightforward Italian fare. The Hyde Park area around the University of Chicago, however, is an enclave of some nice restaurants, including **Piccolo Mondo** (1642 East 56th Street; (773) 643-1106); **Lulu's** (1333 East 57th Street; (773) 288-2988), an offshoot of Lulu's in Evanston (see profile); **Pizza Capri** (1501 East 53rd Street; (773) 324-7777), a branch of the one in Lincoln Park; **Thai 55th** (1607 East 55th Street; (773) 363-7119); **Medici's on 57th** (1327 East 57th Street; (773) 667-7394), a famous coffeehouse; and **Valois Restaurant** (1518 East 53rd Street; (773) 667-0647), a popular cafeteria. **Jackson Harbor Grill** (6401 South Coast Guard Drive; (773) 288-4442), in an old Coast Guard House on South Lake Shore Drive, is a new summertime restaurant operated by the Chicago Park District and Mary Ellen Diaz, chef of North Pond Cafe (see profile).

Much new restaurant activity has recently occurred in the north and northwest suburbs, too. Highwood (in the North Shore), anchored by generations-old Italian establishments, has diversified. **Carlos'** (see profile) in adjacent Highland Park, **Gabriel's Restaurant, Froggy's French Café, Del Rio,** and **Pappagallo's** can all be found here (see profiles), and now the area supposedly boasts more restaurants per capita than almost any other suburb in the country.

The Rosemont area near O'Hare offers a good assortment of restaurants because many conventions and business meetings are held there. The Westin Hotel O'Hare (6100 North River Road; (847) 698-6000) has two good restaurants: **The Benchmark,** featuring bistro-style atmosphere with French influence in dishes, and **The Bakery Café,** serving casual American cuisine. The Hotel Sofitel (5550 North River Road; (847) 678-4488) also has two restaurants: **Chez Colette,** a charming French brasserie with a fireplace, and the fine dining of **Le Cafe de Paris,** which offers a unique très-French menu with waiter and maître d' speaking only French on Thursday and Friday evenings; reservations requested, (847) 928-6950). For other noteworthy restaurants in this area, see profiles of **Carlucci** (Rosemont), **Harry Caray's,** and **Pazzo's Cucina Italiana.**

Connoisseurs with cars seeking unusual places with exceptional wine lists will not mind the 30- or 45-minute trip to 1776 in Crystal Lake (take Northwest Tollway to Randall Exchange, (815) 356-1776) for unusual regional American food, including midwestern (plenty of game). Also worth the drive are **Courtwright's** in Willow Springs, 302 **West** in Geneva, and **Bistro Banlieue** in Lombard (see profiles). **D & J Bistro** (466 South Rand Road; (847) 438-8001) in Lake Zurich serves mostly French fare. And certainly the well-established **Le Vichyssois** in Lakemoor, **Montparnasse** in Naperville, and **Le Titi de Paris** in Arlington Heights are three of the best suburban French restaurants (see profiles). **Tallgrass** in Lockport is a great destination for New French cuisine (two prix fixe menus; see profile).

Downtown Chicago amazingly continues to build and develop areas such as Cityfront, Navy Pier, the River East Plaza, and the planned East River area. The relocated **Palm Restaurant** (see profile), now in the Swissôtel Chicago hotel, has one of the best views of the new golf course (to the east) and of Navy Pier. Chicago's South Loop is being developed, and **Gioco** (1312 S. Wabash; (312) 939-3870), serving rustic Italian cuisine, including seafood, prime beef, veal, homemade pastas and wood-fired thin-crust pizza, opened in October, 1999, leading the way for the dining scene there. The mastermind behind this new place is Jerry Kleiner (Kleiner Design), who pioneered Randolph Street Market District with Vivo (1991), Marché (1994), and Red Light (1996), with co-owner Howard Davis.

Hotel Dining

Hotel dining is better than ever; executive chefs allot large budgets for the best ingredients and can concentrate on their kitchens, unlike the owner-chefs running independent places. Also, since hotels must attract a local clientele to survive and competition is fierce, they've really improved their dining act in the past several years. Hotel dining has become a destination, and it's often complemented by live music in a nearby lounge. Many hotels have made their restaurants more casual and lower priced.

Examples of luxury hotels with top-notch dining options are The Ritz-Carlton (see profiles of **The Dining Room** and **The Café**), Four Seasons Hotel (see profile of **Seasons Restaurant**), The Drake Hotel (see profile of **Cape Cod Room**), The Fairmont Hotel at Grant Park (see profile of **Entre Nous**), and Westin Hotel River North (formerly Nikko) on the Chicago River (**Celebrity Café** has a nice Sunday brunch, and there's a new **Hana Lounge Sushi Hut**). Swissôtel Chicago has the charming **Konditorei** (bakery), **Cafe Suisse** (serving daily buffet breakfasts and lunches), and **Palm Restaurant** (see profile). I also recommend cuisine at the Omni Ambassador East (see profile of **The Pump Room**) and the Hyatt on Printer's Row (see profile of **Prairie**). The Hotel Inter-Continental features the casual **Amber.** The Westin Hotel recently underwent a $6.5 million renovation and enlarged and combined the previous restaurant and bar into **The Chelsea Restaurant and Bar,** an American bistro with innovative American cuisine.

Other noteworthy hotel dining: The Regal Knickerbocker Hotel's new **Nix** (a restaurant serving fusion cuisine—here Asian/American with some southwestern influences); Sutton Place Hotel 's **Whiskey Bar and Grill** serves modern American cuisine, and is owned by Randy Gerber, Cindy Crawford's husband; Midland Hotel (**Exchange Restaurant,** fine dining; and **Ticker Tape Bar & Bistro**); the Renaissance Chicago Hotel (**Cuisines** (see profile) and **Great Street Restaurant and Bar**); and the Palmer House Hilton (**French Quarter** and **Big Downtown Chicago**). The hotel recently opened the high-tech Hilton TeleSuite, offering life-size video teleconferencing. This special dining conference room allows diners to do virtual conferencing while "sharing" a meal with business colleagues, family, or friends. In addition to Chicago's Palmer House Hilton, TeleSuite systems are in the Waldorf-Astoria in New York City, the Hilton Capital & Towers in Washington D.C., and the Hilton Beverly Hills in California. Call (800) 955-9400 for reservations.

There are even more dining-destination hotels: Chicago Hilton and Towers (see profile of **Kitty O'Shea's**); Chicago Marriott Downtown (Allie's Bakery and JW's Steakhouse are being merged into a new bistro interior); Sheraton Chicago Hotel and Towers (**Streeterville**); The Tremont Hotel (see profile of **Iron Mike's Grille**), and across the street, the Whitehall Hotel (**Whitehall Place Restaurant**—a bistro with multicultural cuisine and a nice Sunday brunch); and the Claridge Hotel's **Foreign Affairs** is aptly named for the international cuisine, including great marlin steak Balsamico and seafood ravioli. And this list is not comprehensive!

Celebrity Restaurants

This is a big sports city, so naturally a few athletes, coaches, and announcers own restaurants. Some, like Ditka's (which was overpriced) and Red Kerr's (which was good), have closed. Others, such as **Harry Caray's** (see profile) and **Michael Jordan's** (soon to be Sammy Sosa's), offer good food and service. Former Bears Coach Mike Ditka (recently fired by the New Orleans Saints) combined forces with restaurateur Joe Carlucci and opened **Iron Mike's Grille** in The Tremont Hotel (see profile). There are numerous restaurant hangouts around the ballparks, and some of the food service within the parks is noteworthy. Food service at both Comiskey Park, home of the Chicago White Sox, and Wrigley Field, home of the Chicago Cubs, is managed by Levy Restaurants and is excellent. Entertainment celebrities, political figures, and other VIPs have their favored haunts as well, and many are included in this guide. **The Pump Room, Cape Cod Room,** and **Spiaggia** are three examples; a longtime standby is **Eli's, the Place for Steak** (see profiles).

New-age Cuisine

Food is more enlightened today—lighter, with flavoring coming from fresh herbs, spices, infused oils, vinaigrettes, and wines, and from healthful cooking methods like grilling, flat-top grilling, roasting in wood-burning ovens, and slow simmering. Sure, restaurant icons still offer some old-guard, flour-thickened sauces with cream and butter, but they are usually enjoyed only occasionally. Most day-to-day eating is geared to feeling fine, and that means lower fat (less meat and fried fare), higher carbohydrates (grains, veggies, and fruit), and less sodium and sugar. New-age cuisine leans in the direction of natural and organically grown foods, produce that is not genetically altered, chemical-free ingredients, line-caught fish, and vegetarian fare. Chefs proudly promote vegetarian specialties and menus, and more businesspeople are ordering these items for lunch with mineral water instead of the steaks and martinis they downed years ago. However, history repeats itself, and we're seeing a comeback of steak places and martini bars, touting their special flavors and concoctions that sell for a whopping $6–9 a drink!

New-age Dining Style

There is a tendency for restaurant interiors to be casual and more homey these days, bringing some comfort and a nurturing environment to our dining-out experiences—much needed in our fast-paced, high-stress lives. Food at such places is appropriately simple and home-style. The modern, spacious, minimalist, clean look is also very "in."

Smoking has become a more important health and social issue, and in Chicago all restaurants must set aside a minimum of 30 percent of their active dining room for nonsmokers. Restaurants that wish to establish larger nonsmoking sections have the option of certifying a minimum of 50 percent of their space as nonsmoking. Once a minimum is decided upon, it must be maintained until the next license renewal. More restaurant owners are opting for smoke-free dining rooms with smoking only in the bar areas. Establishments may also select to be 100 percent smoke-free, and several enlightened owners have banned smoke from their places entirely. The designated nonsmoking area must be contiguous. Bars and meeting rooms for private functions are exempt. Sign postings with specific wording designated by the city are required.

The cigar craze was launched by a cigar magazine and backed by the tobacco industry, and many restaurants, seeking to please all customers, have beckoned to gimmicky "cigar dinners" and cigar lounges. The latest reports indicate that this fad is thankfully waning.

Trends

Cooking in open kitchens, such as grilling and baking in wood-fired ovens, is growing in popularity. Diners enjoy watching the cooks prepare their food. Stir-fry and flat-top grill places are a rage spreading quickly in both the city and suburbs. The magical formula tends to be as follows: First, the customer selects preferences from a vast raw buffet of vegetables, meats, poultry, seafood, and sauces, and combines them in a bowl. Second, the contents of the coded bowl are cooked by the staff for all to watch, and within minutes the dish is ready to eat. Some aspects of the process may vary with the restaurant (the combination of self-serve and service, the number of helpings, etc.), but the concept is the same. The food is fresh, tends to be healthful, and is served quickly.

Cuisines that are hot: Spanish cuisine made a splash here in the years following 1992, the year commemorating the 500th anniversary of the discovery of America, the Barcelona Summer Olympics, and Expo '92 in Seville. Spain's tapas and the sampling or "tasting" style has spread from the host cuisine to others, so we now see American and eclectic tapas.

Nuevo Latino is a new wave, with restaurants such as **Nacionale** 27 (325 West Huron; (312) 664-2727), representing the cuisines of 27 Spanish-speaking nations, and **Mas** (1670 West Division Street in Wicker Park; (773)276-8700), serving classic Latin cuisine inspired by South and Central America as well as Portugal and Spain.

Pan-Asian restaurants, especially noodle shops and places serving wraps, are growing. Fusion cuisine, often East-West of some sort, is adopted by many chefs today, and restaurants like **Nix** in the Regal Knickerbocker Hotel, **ConFusion** (1616 North Damen Avenue; (773) 772-7100) in Wicker Park, and **Madame B** (3441 North Halsted Street; (773) 248-4040) on the mid-north side are devoted to this cuisine.

Mediterranean and Italian cuisines continue to be popular. Recently more French bistros and brasseries and Louisiana and South American places have appeared. Two completely new cuisines recently opened on North Sheridan Road: **Tibet Cafe** (3913 North Sheridan Road, (773) 281-6666), and next door is a place **Ofie** (3911 North Sheridan Road; (773) 248-6490).

We've seen a glut of bagel shops, and what I predicted happened; it came down to the survival of the fittest (see "Best Bagels" below). And after all our new coffee houses, I also predicted that soon we'll see more tea cafes and tea houses. That is beginning to happen. Besides the lovely afternoon teas served in hotels, the **Big Bowl Cafés** (see profile) are featuring extraordinary fine teas and currently are the only restaurants in the city creating custom whole leaf blends in partnership with Imperial Tea Court (served at all four Big Bowl locations).

In the heartland, chefs take pride in seeking out small, quality purveyors and changing their menus to utilize the freshest of seasonal ingredients. Wine lists have improved dramatically, and many have become user friendly. Restaurants are giving customers more options, and many offer half-portions when possible. Some places even offer half-glasses of wine so people can do more tastings. More wine bars have sprung up and more restaurants are adding "wine bar" to their name. One good example is **Cyrano's Bistrot & Wine Bar** (see profile).

Tourist Places

There are many places that tourists, for one reason or another, have heard about and want to try. Some, like **The Pump Room, Michael Jordan's Restaurant** (soon to be Sammy Sosa's), and **Iron Mike's Grille,** are excellent or very good. Others are less so, and many are overpriced. Some of the following may offer good food and unique atmosphere, but overall they do not merit full profiles:

Dick's Last Resort

435 East Illinois Street   (312) 836-7870

This River East Plaza spot attracts tourists who shop in the building and see the riverfront. It's fine for simple American fare and music (especially for young groups), but not as a dining destination.

Ed Debevic's Short Order Deluxe

640 North Wells Street   (312) 664-1707

Typical American diner food in a fun atmosphere.

Gene & Georgett

500 North Franklin Street   (312) 527-3718

Considered by many steak-lovers to be a great place, although inconsistent food and service, crowded conditions, and dated decor prevent a recommendation.

Greek Islands Restaurant

200 South Halsted Street   (312) 782-9855

A popular, large Greektown favorite that is attractive and serves decent Greek food. Unfortunately, much of it is kept on a steam table. Several other nearby restaurants are profiled in this guide.

The Hard Rock Cafe

63 West Ontario Street   (312) 943-2252

Good American/ethnic food and glitzy presentations; decibel level has been lowered to a comfortable level.

Rainforest Cafe

605 North Clark Street   (312) 787-1501

(also one in Woodfield Mall, Schaumberg)

Their trademark motto: A Wild Place To Shop and Eat. Garish exterior. Gimmicky decor, but kids love it. Attractive, good fare. This theme restaurant has won awards like "Retailer of the Year" but it's pricey for the quality. You pay for the pizazz—smart retailer!

Three Happiness

2130 South Wentworth Avenue   (312) 791-1228

Bustling, popular Cantonese and dim sum place; good, authentic food, if you don't mind crowds. Reservations accepted weekdays.

New and Changing Places

Here are just a few of the new places that opened or changed in the past 18 months or so. They show great promise for future editions:

A La Turka   *Turkish*

Adobo Grill *Mexican*

Bistrot Margo *Neo-classic French bistro*

Bricks *Pizza and beer*

The Capital Grille *New York–style steak house*

Carpaccio (Palatine) *Italian*

Cheesecake Factory *Eclectic American* John Hancock Building

The Chicago Firehouse Restaurant *Classic American*

ConFusion *Fusion*

Cy's Steak & Chop House *Steak house*

Emil's *American* "Flavors of Italian and Fall" promotion in November, reflecting themes of the November operas at the Lyric Opera next door.; thoughtful progressive wine list; popular for pre-opera dinners.

Fahrenheit *Creative New American*

Fuzio *Global Fusion/Universal Pasta*

Grace *American* Robust flavorings, domestic artisan products and full wines set the tone here.

The Grill Room *Midwestern Chophouse/wine bar* Loop

Japoni Santa *Franco/Japanese* Lincoln Park

mk *New American* Michael Kornick-style

Madam B *Pacific Rim*

Malz *Pre-Hispanic Mexican* Division and Damien, Wicker Park area

M-Cafe *Eclectic* Museum of Contemporary Art

Nicolina's Cucina *Italian/Seafood* NBC Tower

Nix (Regal) *Fusion* Knickerbocker Hotel

Phoenix *Chinese* Chinatown

Okno *New American* Hip Wicker Park restaurant with chic interior.

RL *Italian* Designer Ralph Lauren's first restaurant; chic Jazz night, the first Thursday of each month, transforms the restaurant into a nightclub atmosphere. From 8 p.m.; plush and expensive.

Slicker Sam's On Halsted *Immigrant Italian* is how they define it, which translates to simple and hearty. Run by the same family that owns Slicker Sam's in Melrose Park, this one is a touch more urbane for the city slickers.

Southern Roots   *Southern*

Tizi Mellou   *French Moroccan*   Named for a Moroccan mountain, this place includes a round communal dining room where diners sit on poufs and banquettes and can eat with their hands in traditional Moroccan style.

Tomboy   *Eclectic*

Triple Crown Seafood   *Cantonese/Seafood*   Chinatown

Vegetarian Garden   *Vegetarian Chinese*   Chinatown

Recommended New Restaurants

Aubriot   *French*   Excellent simple cuisine in this charming location at 1962 North Halsted Street owned by a young couple. Try braised leeks in truffle vinaigrette; potato-wrapped goat cheese with Romaine and sourdough crouton; roasted rabbit loin with chives, sage, and thyme veal reduction; pan-seared sea bass with seafood emulsion and root vegetable puree; special salmon with lettuce sauce; and great wines, including some from Austria. Soufflé of the day is usually light, yet voluptuous.

Bistrot Zinc/Café Zinc   *French*   Excellent bistrot fare at two locations, at 3443 North Southport and the newer one downtown at 1131 North State Parkway; the greatest is the pissaladiere caramelized onion tart, flavored with miso, olives, and thyme.

Blackbird   *Seasonal American with French inspiration*   Hot spot with good food by an award-winning chef, Paul Kahan; drab, austere decor and ugly sidewalk cafe that's depressing.

Bluepoint   *Oyster bar/seafood/sushi bar*   Large space; good seafood; music some nights.

Buca Di Beppo   *Italian, family style*   Huge portions; good for groups. 3 locations: Chicago, Wheeling, and Lombard.

Cafe Matou   *Traditional French*   Good cooking; can be noisy inside; great outdoor garden in summer.

The Clubhouse   *Contemporary American classics*   Oak Brook

Club Macanudo   *New American with French influence*   Very good food, beautiful presentations. Try giant diver scallop Medallion au gratin, Colorado Rack of Lamb, and signature warm chocolate truffle infused with rum. Nightly live jazz and dessert tastings. Closed Sunday.

Fog City Diner   *American Diner*   By the same owners as Fog City Diner in San Francisco; great oyster shooters; assorted crostini, sandwiches and entrees at low prices for downtown.

Foreign Affairs   *International*   Claridge Hotel

Hacienda Tecalitlan   *Mexican*   Elaborate, large interior that resembles a courtyard in Mexico.

Harvest on Huron   *New American*

Jaipur Palace   *Authentic Royal Indian*   Good luncheon buffet.

McCormick & Schmick's Seafood Restaurant   *Seafood*   Large, well-run place that became popular from the start. Wonderfully prepared, fresh seafood.

Meritage   *Pacific Northwest, Asian influences*

Millennium   *Steak and seafood*   Good restaurant in the Randolph Market area.

Mio Mezzo and Kinzie Market   *Italian*   Kinzie Market is a European-style gourmet shop/cafe. Excellent Italian fare, including pastas, salads, pastries.

Nacional 27   *Nuevo Latino*   Recognizing the culinary specialties of 27 Latino countries, this Lettuce Entertain You restaurant celebrates the ingredients and flavors of the southern hemisphere. Late-night menu and dancing. Friday and Saturday evenings.

P. F. Chang's China Bistro   *Contemporary Chinese*   Bustling; good food and wine list, inconsistent service.   Downtown and Northbrook locaitons.

Plaza Tavern   *American*   A chic 1940s-style supper club with music. Creative, wonderful dishes; good wines. Complimentary parking.

Pollo Rey   *Mexican*   Quick, full-service.   Wrigleyville

Red Rock Grill   *Texan*   Spicy or not, the food is good and the interior attractive.

Red Light   *Pan-Asian*   Some of the best example of this type of cuisine; new chef has changed menu somewhat.   Randolph Market

Rhapsody   *Regional American with European influences*

Rocco's Ristorante   *Italian*   Good food and wine in a friendly, Gold Coast–upscale neighborhood bar environment.

Savarin   *French*   Excellent cuisine by fine chef John Hogan.

Smith & Wollensky   *Steak and seafood*

Tavern on Rush   *American steakhouse*

The Shark Bar   *Southern*   Good cooking and a great top deck with a view of downtown Chicago.

Taza's Marinated, grilled Amish chicken; one of the best fast-food places downtown.

Thyme *French/regional Mediterranean-influenced* Inspired cuisine by John Bubala, such as steamed black mussels with fennel, thyme, and oven-roasted tomatoes, and spit-roasted rabbit ragout with lavender and sherry.

Tru *Progressive French* This is one of the most special of fine dining places to open in the city recently. Tru is an acronym that represents chef owners Rick Tramonto and unlimited. It's a joint venture between Tramonto, his pastry chef wife Gale Gand, and Richard Melman, chairman of the board and founder of Lettuce Entertain You Enterprises. It's understated simplicity in style, with superb service and delicious creations presented artistically. Emphasis is on prix fixe tasting menus or multi-coursed collections. Ultra sophisticated with prices to match.

Established Restaurants, Especially Recommended

Julie Mai's Le Bistro *French/Vietnamese* Good French Vietnamese cooking; new menu. Now featuring music in renovated Shangri-La Room on weekends.

Les Nomades *French* Chef Roland Liccioni and pastry chef/manager wife Mary Beth operate this intimate fine dining establishment on the Gold Coast.

Mambo Grill *Latino* Festive casual decor and boldly flavored favored food at this River North spot. Recommended: artichokes de carne, tortilla de canarone, and halibut empanisado de platano.

Monastero's *Italian* Family-run business; good food, hearty servings and live operatic music; annual grape stomping contests; lively and fun; popular for private parties.

Nick & Tony's *Home-style Italian* Hearty cooking; generous portions; good service; comfortable setting.   Two locations

Palette's *American* A lovely, elegant, colorful interior with dishes that are culinary works of art; try potato crab cakes, rack of lamb, and banana sandwich with ice cream. Designed in the visionary style of Heinz Kern, with murals and sculptures by artist Boban Ilic. Live music nightly.

Patrick and James' *American with a French twist* Excellent service, comfortable ambience and good food.   Glencoe

Plentywood Restaurant *American/Midwestern* Chef John Draz prepares Midwestern American (contemporary farm-style) food.   Bensenville

Quincy Grille   *Regional American*   Situated on the Chicago River, this is one of the most aesthetic dining rooms for a fine lunch (or dinner on Lyric Opera nights) with a lovely riverscape. Talented Chef Jason Tsoris creates many specialties around fresh fish, since he deals directly with fishermen. Recommended are his citron-cured salmon with Sonoma goat cheese appetizer, grilled Key West shrimp, sashimi tuna steak with Dijon crust, clam risotto, grilled Maine salmon with marinated peppers and cilantro with shallot Chardonnay cream, grilled bluefin marlin from Hawaii, and the veal shank was incredible, too. Intelligent American wine list, including 1997 Benziger Fume Blanc and 1998 Clos du Bois Chardonnay.

Rhumba   *Brazilian*   Good food; late night female impersonator entertainment not for everyone.

Texas Star Fajita Bar   *Texan*   Excellent fajitas and other Texas fare in a bar.

Tibet Cafe   *Tibetan*   Unique and charming, this tiny gem, owned by a former Tibetan monk, serves delicious momos (dumplings) and stir-fried food in a serene environment with butter sculptures and background chanting tapes.

Trattoria No. 10   *Contemporary Italian Classics*   This is a well-established, family-run restaurant that is consistently excellent. In the lower level of 10 North Dearbown.

Trocadero Bistro & Bar   *Bistro Fare*   Named for a Metro stop in Paris, this is mainly French fare including bouillabaisse and French onion soup. Some Italian specialties, such as potato gnocchi and tomato tortellini, sneak in too. Good food and service.

Vinci   *Authentic Northern Italian*   About nine years old in 2000, this restaurant continues to be a favorite. Chef-owner Paul LoDuca turns out consistently fine regional Italian dishes, such as the best polenta con funghi (grilled polenta with portobello and cremini mushrooms in porcini broth); garganelli pasta tossed with shrimp, calamari, spinach, and tomato in white wine broth; and marinated hen, grilled under a hot brick, with robust roasted potatoes, garlic, and rosemary. Great wine list. Beautiful, upscale, artistic interior.

Zealous   *New American*   Boldly flavored and creative food by talented chef-owner Michael Taus; excellently run restaurant.   Relocated from Elmhurst to downtown Chicago.

More Recommendations

◆ Best Bagels

Einstein Bros. Bagels
44 East Walton (Gold Coast) (312) 943-9888
949 West Diversey Parkway (773) 935-9888
About 30 locations; bagels made on premises. Favorites include
cinnamon-raisin, blueberry, spinach-herb, and sundried tomato.

Kaufman's Bagel and Delicatessen
4905 West Dempster Street, Skokie (847) 677-9880
Old-fashioned Jewish deli–style bagels.

Upper Crust Bagels
835 Waukegan Road (just north of Deerfield Road), Deerfield
(847) 405-0805
Kettle-boiled, New York–style, hand-rolled bialys; specialty sandwiches; flavored cream cheese; lox; smoked fish; and deli fare.

◆ Best Bakeries

Allegretti's Bakery
7717 West Lawrence Avenue, Norrige (708) 453-4412

Ambrosia Euro-American Patisserie
710 West Northwest Highway, Barrington (847) 304-8278

Blind Faith Cafe and Bakery
525 Dempster Street, Evanston (847) 328-6875
3300 North Lincoln Avenue (773) 871-3820

The Corner Bakery
516 North Clark Street (312) 644-8100
Union Station, Adams Street Concourse, 210 South Canal Street
(312) 441-0821
Water Tower Place, Mezzanine, 835 North Michigan Avenue
(312) 335-3663
Sante Fe Building, 224 South Michigan Avenue (at Jackson
Boulevard) (630) 431-7600
Oakbrook Center, Route 83 at 22nd Street, Oak Brook
(630) 368-0505
1901 East Woodfield Road, Schaumburg (847) 240-1111

Eli's Cheesecake World
6701 West Forest Preserve Drive (773) 736-3417.
The 56 varieties of Eli's cheesecakes are sold and served here in the
retail shop and cafe. Outdoor cafe in summer. Newly expanded
to include smoothies, various coffee drinks, cookies, scones,
blueberry cream cheese muffins, and more. New flavors of
cheesecake: banana fusion, chocolate sundae, and totally turtle.

Foodstuffs
2106 Central Avenue, Evanston (847) 328-7704
338 Park Avenue, Glencoe (847) 835-5105

Great Harvest Bread Co.
2120 Central Street, Evanston (847) 866-8609
846 West Armitage Avenue (773) 528-6211

Konditorei
Swissôtel Chicago, 323 East Wacker Drive (312) 565-0565
Wonderful European breads.

Nancy's Bakery
7645 West Montrose Avenue, Norridge (708) 452-9878

Sicilian Bakery
4632 North Cumberland Avenue (773) 589-2602

◆ Best Barbecue and Ribs

Gayle Street Inn
4914 North Milwaukee Avenue   (773) 725-1300
Baby-back ribs.

Hecky's BBQ
1902 Green Bay Road, Evanston   (847) 492-1182
Rib tips and chicken wings.

Joe's B-Bop
600 East Grand Avenue, Navy Pier   (312) 595-5299

Leon's Bar-B-Q
8249 South Cottage Grove Avenue   (773) 488-4556
1158 West 59th Street   (773) 778-7828
1640 East 79th Street   (773) 731-1454

Mama Luci's
416 North State Street   (312) 527-5230

Miller's Pub
134 South Wabash Avenue   (312) 645-5377

N. N. Smokehouse
1465–67 West Irving Park Road   (773) TNT-4700

Robinson's No. 1 Ribs
655 West Armitage Avenue   (312) 337-1399
Ribs and chicken.
Smoke Daddy
1804 West Division Street   (773) 772-MOJO
Specialties: Three kinds of ribs; ribs sampler and smoked sweet potato.
Live blues, jazz Monday–Saturday; live mambo Wednesday.
Twin Anchors Restaurant and Tavern
1655 North Sedgwick Street   (312) 266-1616
In business for over 60 years.

◆ Best Beer Lists

Big Bar
Hyatt Regency, 151 East Wacker Drive (312) 565-1234
Cork & Carry
10614 South Western Avenue (773) 445-2675
Seventy varieties, twelve on tap.
Goose Island Brewing Company
1800 North Clybourn Avenue (312) 915-0071
Healy's Westside
7217 West Madison, Forest Park (708) 366-HARP
Hopcats Brew Club
2345 North Clybourn Avenue (773) 868-4461
Jameson's Tavern
118 South Clinton Street (312) 876-0016
Joe Bailly's
10854 South Western Avenue (773) 238-1313
Millrose Brewing Company
45 South Barrington Road, South Barrington (847) 382-7673
Quigley's
43 East Jefferson Street (630) 428-4774
Ranalli's
1925 North Lincoln Avenue (312) 642-4700
Red Lion Pub
2446 North Lincoln Avenue (773) 348-2695
One of the best selections of English beers.
Resi's Bierstube
2034 West Irving Park Road (773) 472-1749
Perhaps the oldest beer garden in the city; 60 imports—6 on tap.

◆ Best Breakfasts

Ann Sather
929 West Belmont Avenue (773) 348-2378
5207 North Clark Street, Andersonville (773) 271-6677
2665 North Clark Street, Lincoln Park (773) 327-9522

Army & Lou's
422 East 75th Street (773) 483-3100

The Corner Bakery
516 North Clark Street (312) 644-8100
Union Station, Adams Street Concourse, 210 South Canal Street
(312) 441-0821
Water Tower Place, Mezzanine, 835 North Michigan Avenue
(312) 335-3663
Sante Fe Building, 224 South Michigan Avenue (at Jackson
Boulevard) (630) 431-7600
Oakbrook Center, Route 83 at 22nd Street, Oak Brook
(630) 368-0505
1901 East Woodfield Road, Schaumburg (847) 240-1111

Egg Harbor Cafe
512 North Western Avenue, Lake Forest (847) 295-3449

Elaine's
Ontario Center Building, 448 East Ontario Street (312) 337-6700
Formerly Elaine and Ina's.

Heaven on Seven
111 North Wabash Avenue (312) 263-6443

Iron Mike's Grille
100 East Chestnut (312) 587-8989

Lou Mitchell's
565 West Jackson Boulevard (312) 939-3111

Mrs. Park's Tavern
198 East Delaware Place (312) 280-8882

The Pump Room
Omni Ambassador East Hotel, 1301 North State Parkway
(312) 266-0360

Seasons Restaurant
Four Seasons Hotel, 120 East Delaware Place at Michigan Avenue
(312) 280-8800, ext. 2134

3rd Coast
1260 Dearborn Street (312) 649-0730

◆ Best Brunches

Bistro 110
110 East Pearson Street (312) 266-3110
New Orleans–style jazz brunch on Sunday.

Blue Mesa
1729 North Halsted Street (312) 944-5990
New Mexican cuisine and Sunday brunch.

Celebrity Cafe
Westin Hotel River North, 320 North Dearborn Street
(312) 744-1900
Sunday brunch.

Cité
Top of Lake Point Tower (world's tallest residential building),
70th floor, 505 North Lake Shore Drive (312) 644-4050
Sunday champagne brunch.

The Dining Room
The Ritz-Carlton Chicago, 160 East Pearson Street
(312) 266-1000
Exquisite and extensive Sunday brunch.

Four Farthings Tavern & Grill
2060 North Cleveland Avenue (773) 935-2060
Newly expanded Sunday buffet brunch.

Hong Min
221 West Cermak Road, Chinatown (312) 842-5026
Saturday and Sunday brunch.

House of Blues
329 North Dearborn Street (312) 527-2583
Sunday gospel brunch; seatings at 10 a.m., 12:15 p.m., and 2:30 p.m.

Joe's B-Bop
600 East Grand Avenue, Navy Pier (312) 595-5299
Sunday jazz brunch.

The Pump Room
Omni Ambassador East Hotel, 1301 North State Parkway
(312) 266-0360
Sunday brunch.

Seasons Restaurant
Four Seasons Hotel, 120 East Delaware Place at Michigan Avenue
(312) 280-8800
Sunday brunch.

The Signature Room at the Ninety-Fifth

John Hancock Center, 95th floor, 875 North Michigan Avenue
  (312) 787-9596

Elegant Sunday buffet champagne brunch with live music and an
  excellent panoramic city view.

◆ Best Burgers and Sandwiches

Abbey Pub

4320 West Grace (773) 463-5808

Arturo Express/Turano Baking Co.

919 North Michigan Avenue (312) 251-2250

980 North Michigan Avenue (312) 222-1525

Billy Goat Tavern

430 North Michigan Avenue (312) 922-6847

Hackney's

1514 East Lake Avenue, Glenview (847) 724-7171

1241 Harms Road, Glenview (847) 724-5577

Known for burgers and fried onion loaf. Other suburban locations:
  Wheeling, LaGrange, and Lake Zurich.

Iron Mike's Grille

100 East Chestnut (312) 587-8989

John Barleycorn Memorial Pub, Inc.

658 West Belden Avenue (773) 348-8899

Bar food, good burgers and sandwiches, salads; classical music and
  art slides. Nice garden.

Kasia's Deli & Catering

2101 West Chicago Avenue (773) 486-6163

Polish fare.

Kitty O'Shea's

720 South Michigan Avenue, Chicago Hilton & Towers
  (312) 922-4400

Louisina Kitchen

2666 North Halsted Street (773) 529-1666

Sunday jazz brunch.

Magnum's Steak & Lobster

225 West Ontario (312) 337-8080

Moody's

5910 North Broadway (773) 275-2696

24

Muskie's

2870 North Lincoln Avenue (773) 883-1633

963 West Belmont Avenue (773) 477-1880

This place has a 50s theme and turns out good charburgers, charbroiled chicken, and vegetarian sandwiches.

P. J. Clarke's

1204 North State Parkway (312) 664-1650

◆ Best Coffees and Desserts

Cafe Express

615 Dempster Street, Evanston (847) 864-1868

Cafe Express South

500 Main Street, Evanston (847) 328-7940

The Corner Bakery

516 North Clark Street (312) 644-8100

Union Station, Adams Street Concourse, 210 South Canal Street
(312) 441-0821

Water Tower Place, Mezzanine, 835 North Michigan Avenue
(312) 335-3663

Sante Fe Building, 224 South Michigan Avenue (at Jackson
Boulevard) (630) 431-7600

Oakbrook Center, Route 83 at 22nd Street, Oak Brook
(630) 368-0505

1901 East Woodfield Road, Schaumburg (847) 240-1111

Eli's Cheesecake World

6701 West Forest Preserve Drive (773) 736-3471

Jazz and Java

3428 South King Drive (312) 791-1300

Live jazz Friday and Saturday; offers soups, sandwiches, and salads.

Jillian's Coffee House & Bistro

674 West Diversey Parkway (773) 529-7012

Soups, quiches, salads, sandwiches, desserts, wine, beer, and coffee
drinks.

Lutz's Continental Cafe and Pastry Shop

2458 West Montrose Avenue (773) 478-7785

Peet's Coffee & Tea

1000 West North Avenue, (312) 475-9782

1622 Chicago Avenue, Evanston (847) 864-8413

236 South Washington Avenue, Naperville (630) 718-1799

◆ Best Cornbread

Bandera
535 North Michigan Avenue (312) 644-FLAG
Made in an iron skillet.
Joe's B-Bop
600 East Grand Avenue, Navy Pier (312) 595-5299
Louisina Kitchen
2666 North Halsted Street (773) 529-1666
Sunday jazz brunch.
Redfish and The Voodoo Lounge
400 North State Street (312) 467-1600
Moist inside, crusty outside.

◆ Best Delis

Bagel Restaurant and Deli
3107 North Broadway   (773) 477-0300
50 Old Orchard Shopping Center, Skokie   (847) 677-0100
Manny's Coffee Shop and Deli
1141 South Jefferson   (312) 939-2855
Since 1942. Great corned beef and pastrami sandwiches.
Szynanski Deli
6016 West Irving Park Road   (773) 202-0886
Polish deli, bakery and grocery.

◆ Best Hot Dogs

Gold Coast Dogs
418 North State Street (312) 527-1222
25 South Franklin Street (312) 939-2624
Vienna beef dogs; friendly service; also great burgers. Other locations include Northwestern Atrium, (312) 879-0447, or Union
Station, (312) 258-8585.
Portillo's Hot Dogs
100 West Ontario Street   (312) 587-8910
Steamed Vienna beef dogs served Chicago style in poppyseed buns.
Wiener Circle
2622 North Clark (773) 477-7444

Tasty Dawg
1041 Rohlwing Road, Elk Grove (847) 593-3294

◆ Best Picnic Meals

Ann Sather
929 West Belmont Avenue (773) 348-2378
5207 North Clark Street, Andersonville (773) 271-6677
2665 North Clark Street, Lincoln Park (773) 327-9522
Open daily; 24-hour advance notice required. Box lunches created from choice of sandwiches, salads, and desserts.

Cobey Foods and Catering
1712 North Wells Street, Old Town (312) 397-0090
Mostly French cuisine with international influences; numbered box lunches can be customized; 24-hour advance notice for large orders.

Mario's Ristorante
21 West Goethe (312) 944-0199
Will pack anything from the menu to go for picnics.

Sopraffina
10 North Dearborn Street (312) 984-0044
Italian. Create your own menu; 24-hour notice required.

Tutto Pronto
401 East Ontario Street (312) 587-7700
Italian food and wine shop with deli.

◆ Best Pizza

Bacino's (several locations)
Bacino's of Lincoln Park, 2204 North Lincoln Avenue
(773) 472-7400
Good stuffed and heart-healthy pizza.

Bertucci's Brick Oven Pizza
675 North LaSalle Street (312) 266-3400
Three other new locations in suburbs. More thick-crust pizza pie.

California Pizza Kitchen
414 North Orleans Street (312) 222-9030
Call about other locations. Thin-crust/gourmet.

Edwardo's Natural Pizza Restaurant

1212 North Dearborn Street (312) 337-4490

521 South Dearborn Street (312) 939-3366

Call for other locations.

Father & Son Pizza

645 West North Avenue (312) 654-2550

2475 North Milwaukee (773) 252-2620

Giovanni's Pizza

6823 West Roosevelt Road, Berwyn (708) 795-7171

Mama Luci's

416 North State Street (312) 527-5230

O Famé

750 West Webster Avenue (773) 929-5111

Good thin-crust, pan, or Chicago-style pizzas; they also have a full
  menu.

The Original Gino's East

1321 West Golf Road, Rolling Meadows (847) 364-6644

Rated number one in the nation by *People* magazine editors.

Pat's Pizzeria & Ristorante

3114 North Sheffield Avenue (773) 248-0168

211 North Stetson (312) 946-0732

Named the number one thin crust pizza by the *Chicago Tribune* and
  the *Chicago Sun-Times.*

Pizzeria Uno

29 East Ohio Street (312) 321-1000

Pizzeria Due

619 North Wabash Avenue (312) 943-2400

Both Uno and Due serve Chicago-style, deep-dish pizza.

Suparossa

7309 West Lawrence Avenue, Harwood Heights (708) 867-4641

Newest locations: 210 East Ohio Street and another in Woodridge.
  Call for other locations. Original stuffed pizza—the award-
  winning lasagna pizza stuffed with ricotta and spinach is a
  favorite. The new wood-fired oven pizzas are great appetizers.

◆ Best Wine Bars

Bin 36
339 North Dearborn (312) 755-WINE
Cru Cafe & Wine Bar
888 North Wabash Avenue (312) 337-4001
Geja's Cafe
340 West Armitage Avenue (773) 281-9101
This fondue cafe was the city's first wine bar. It's very romantic
  with live guitar.
Hudson Club
5504 North Wells Street (312) 467-1947
Large list of wines by the glass—over 100. A wine-oriented
  restaurant.
Madison's (Italian steak house)
1330 West Madison Street, United Center area (312) 455-0099
More than 20 wines by the glass. Good wine list.
Meritage Cafe and Wine Bar
2118 North Damen Avenue (773) 235-6434
Narcisse Champagne Salon & Caviar Bar
710 North Clark Street (312) 787-2675
New champagne and caviar bar with light fare.
Pops for Champagne
2934 North Sheffield Avenue (773) 472-1000
Adjacent Star Bar does monthly tastings. Call (312) 472-7272.
Rush
948 West Armitage Avenue (773) 871-8123
French/Italian food; international wines.
Webster's Wine Bar
1480 West Webster Avenue (773) 868-0608
Long list of wines by the glass or two-ounce tastes; complemen-
  tary, healthful, simple foods.

‖ understanding
‖ the ratings

We have developed detailed profiles for what we consider the best restaurants in town. Each profile features an easy-to-scan heading that allows you to check out the restaurant's name, cuisine, star rating, cost, quality rating, and value rating quickly.

Star Rating.   The star rating is an overall rating that encompasses the entire dining experience, including style, service, and ambience in addition to the taste, presentation, and quality of the food. Five stars is the highest rating possible and connotes the best of everything. Four-star restaurants are exceptional, and three-star restaurants are well above average. Two-star restaurants are good. One star is used to connote an average restaurant that demonstrates an unusual capability in some area of specialization, for example, an otherwise unmemorable place that has great barbecued chicken.

Cost.   Beneath the star rating is an expense description that provides a comparative sense of how much a complete meal will cost. A complete meal for our purposes consists of an entree with vegetable or side dish, and choice of soup or salad. Appetizers, desserts, drinks, and tips are excluded.

Inexpensive	$16 and less per person
Moderate	$17–29 per person
Expensive	$30–40 per person
Very Expensive	$40 or more per person

Quality Rating. Below the cost rating appear a number and a letter. The number is a quality rating based on a scale of 0–100, with 100 being the highest (best) rating attainable. The quality rating is based expressly on the taste, freshness of ingredients, preparation, presentation, and creativity of food served. There is no consideration of price. If you are a person who wants the best food available and cost is not an issue, you need look no further than the quality ratings.

Value Rating. If, on the other hand, you are looking for both quality and value, then you should check the value rating, expressed in letters. The value ratings are defined as follows:

A Exceptional value, a real bargain
B Good value
C Fair value, you get exactly what you pay for
D Somewhat overpriced
F Significantly overpriced

Locating the restaurant

Just below the restaurant name is a designation for geographic zone. This zone description will give you a general idea of where the restaurant described is located. For ease of use, we divide Chicago into 11 geographic zones.

Zone 1.	North Side
Zone 2.	North Central/O'Hare
Zone 3.	Near North
Zone 4.	The Loop
Zone 5.	South Loop
Zone 6.	South Central/Midway
Zone 7.	South Side
Zone 8.	Southern Suburbs
Zone 9.	Western Suburbs
Zone 10.	Northwest Suburbs
Zone 11.	Northern Suburbs

If you're on Michigan Avenue and intend to walk or take a cab to dinner, you may want to choose a restaurant from among those located in Zone 4. If you have a car, you might include restaurants from contiguous zones in your consideration.

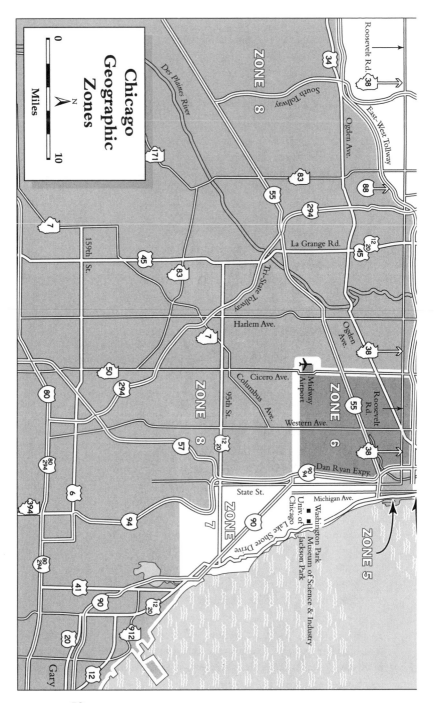

Chicago Geographic Zones

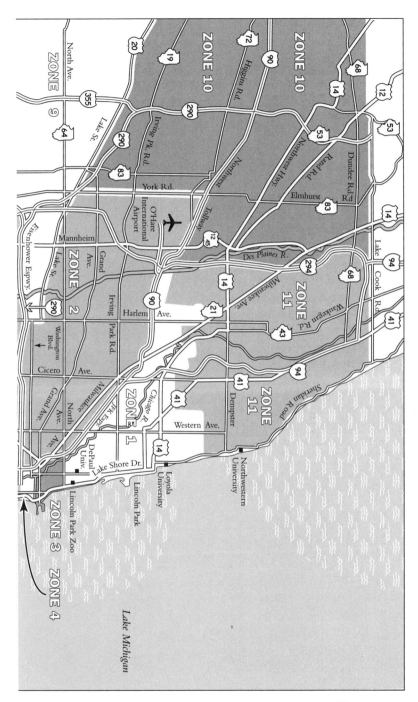

33

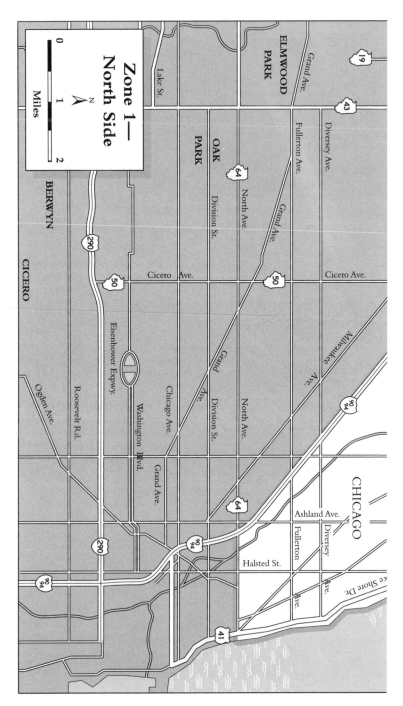

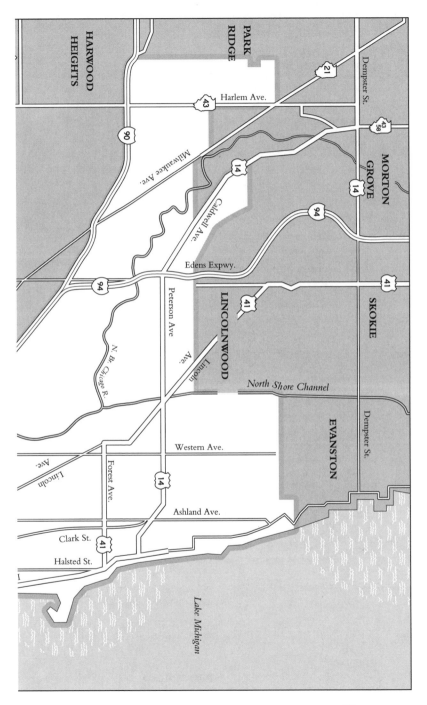

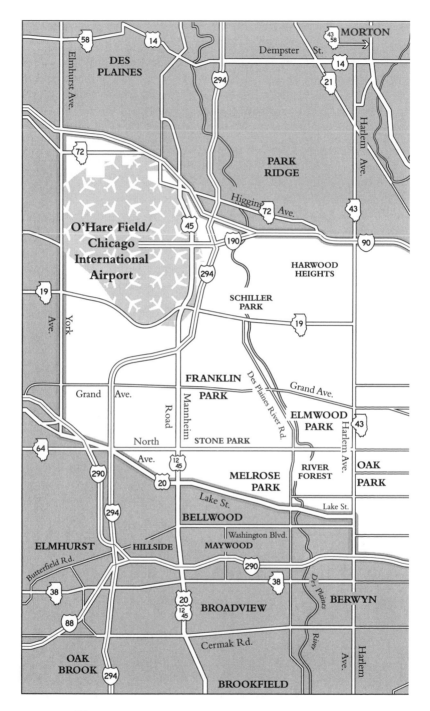

Zone 2—
North Central/
O'Hare

N

0   1   2
Miles

GROVE
SKOKIE
Dempster St.

EVANSTON

Edens Expwy.

Caldwell Ave.

LINCOLNWOOD

Shore Channel

North

Western Ave.

Ashland Ave.

Lake
Michigan

Peterson Ave.

North Br.

Lincoln Ave.

Chicago River

Foster
Ave.

Ashland Ave.

Clark St.

Lincoln Ave.

Halsted St.

Milwaukee

CHICAGO

Ave.

Diversey   Ave.

Diversey Ave.

Fullerton   Ave.

Fullerton Ave.

Milwaukee Ave.

Halsted St.

North Ave.

Grand

Division St.

Ave.

Cicero

Chicago Ave.

Grand Ave.

Ave.

Washington

Eisenhower

Blvd.

Expwy.

Roosevelt Rd.

CICERO

Ogden Ave.

Ave.

Ashland

Michigan Ave.

MLK, Jr. Dr.

Cermak   Rd.

Archer Ave.

Halsted Ave.

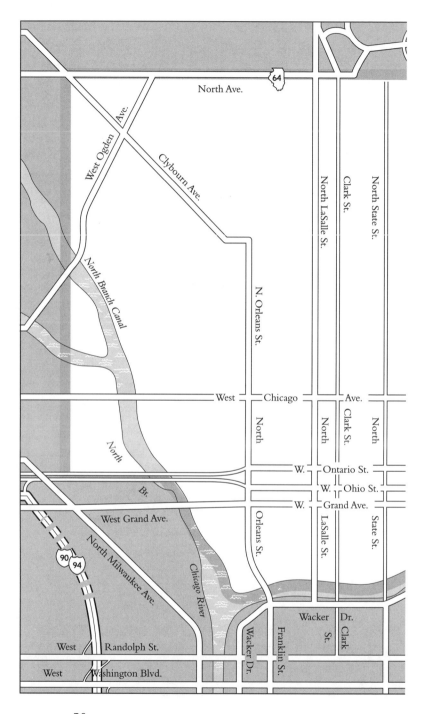

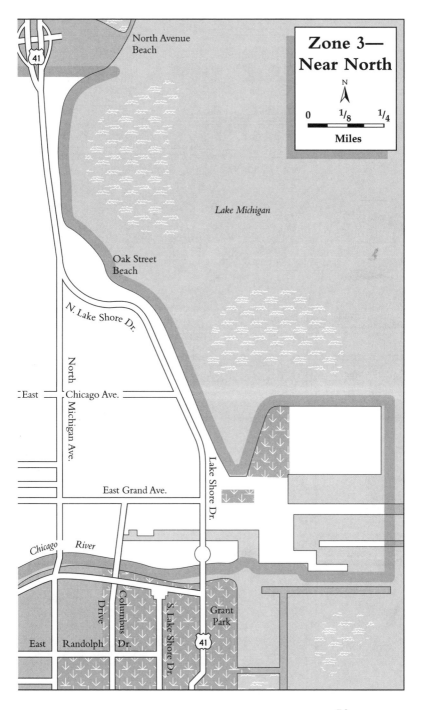

Zone 3—
Near North

N

0   1/8   1/4

Miles

North Avenue
Beach

Lake Michigan

Oak Street
Beach

N. Lake Shore Dr.

North Michigan Ave.

East Chicago Ave.

East Grand Ave.

Lake Shore Dr.

Chicago River

Drive

Columbus Dr.

S. Lake Shore Dr.

Grant Park

East Randolph

41

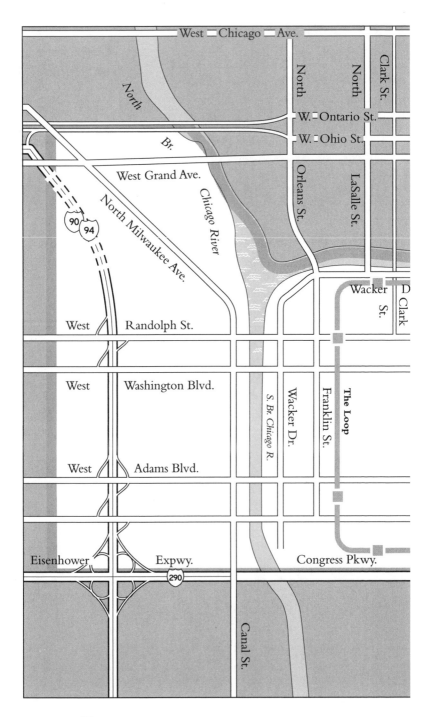

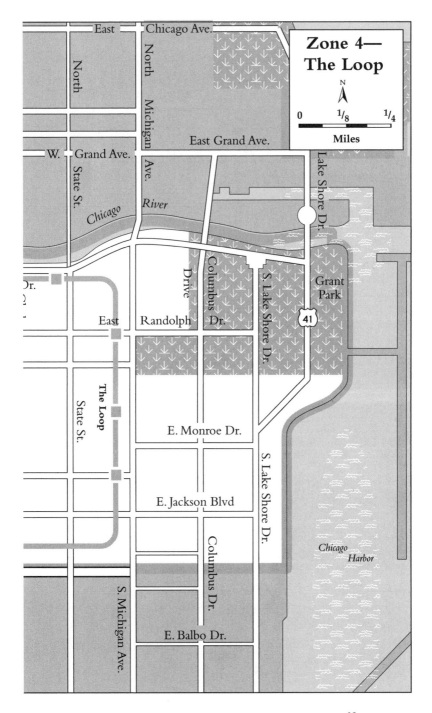

Zone 4—
The Loop

N

0   ⅛   ¼

Miles

East Chicago Ave.

North

North

North Michigan Ave.

East Grand Ave.

W. Grand Ave.

State St.

Chicago River

Lake Shore Dr.

Columbus Drive

S. Lake Shore Dr.

Grant Park

41

East Randolph Dr.

The Loop

State St.

E. Monroe Dr.

E. Jackson Blvd

S. Lake Shore Dr.

Chicago Harbor

Columbus Dr.

S. Michigan Ave.

E. Balbo Dr.

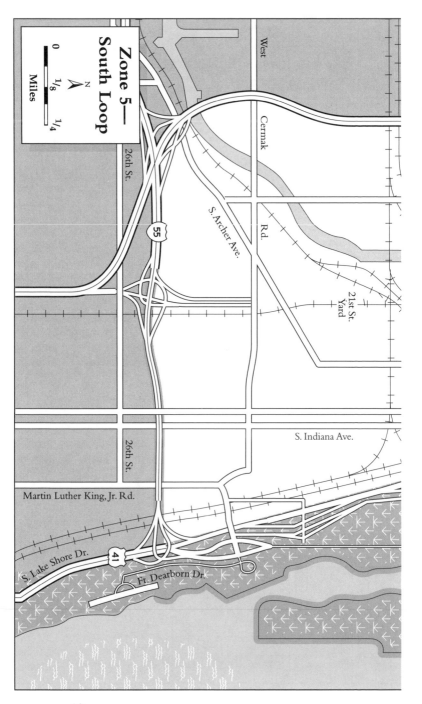

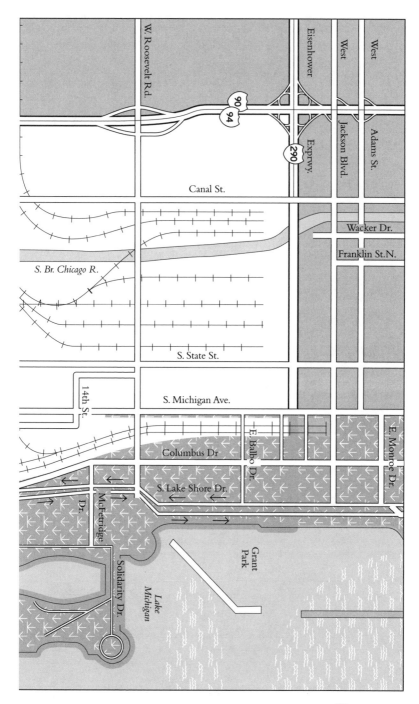

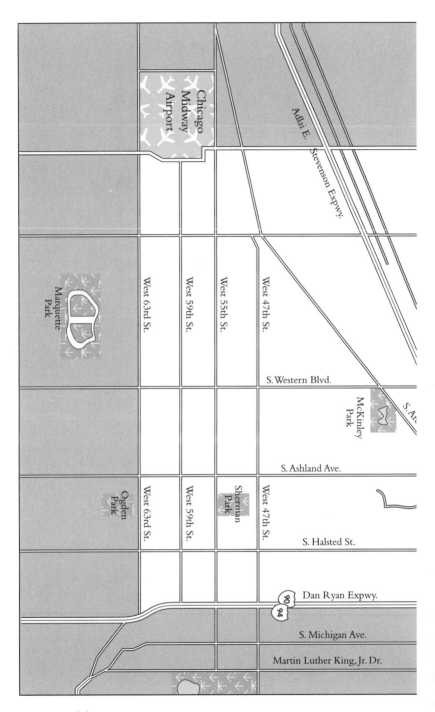

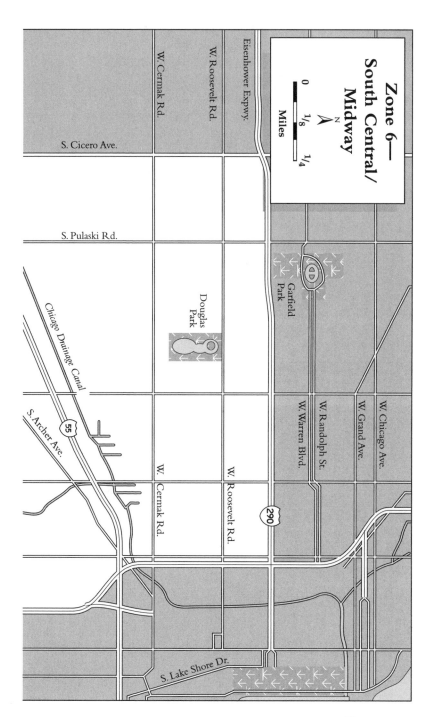

**Zone 6—
South Central/
Midway**

N

0   1/8   1/4
Miles

Eisenhower Expwy.

W. Cermak Rd.

W. Roosevelt Rd.

S. Cicero Ave.

S. Pulaski Rd.

Garfield
Park

Douglas
Park

Chicago Drainage Canal

S. Archer Ave.

55

W. Cermak Rd.

W. Roosevelt Rd.

290

W. Warren Blvd.

W. Randolph St.

W. Grand Ave.

W. Chicago Ave.

S. Lake Shore Dr.

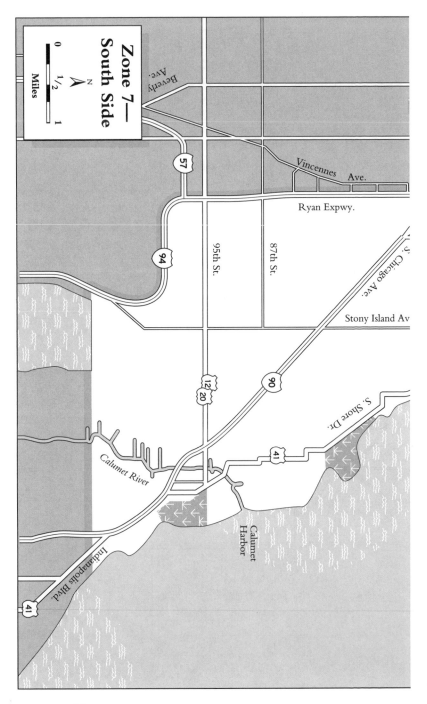

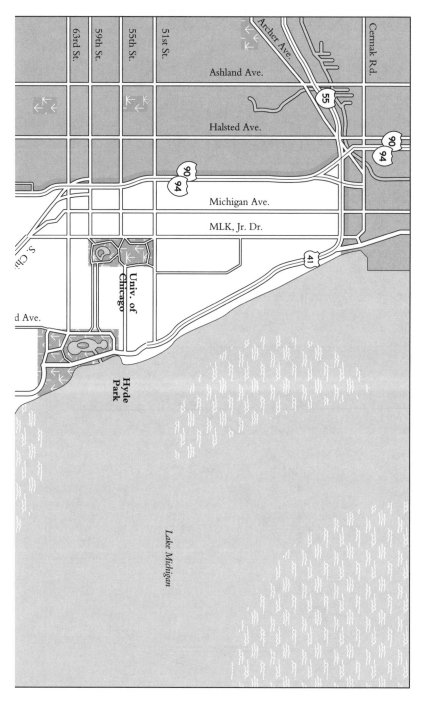

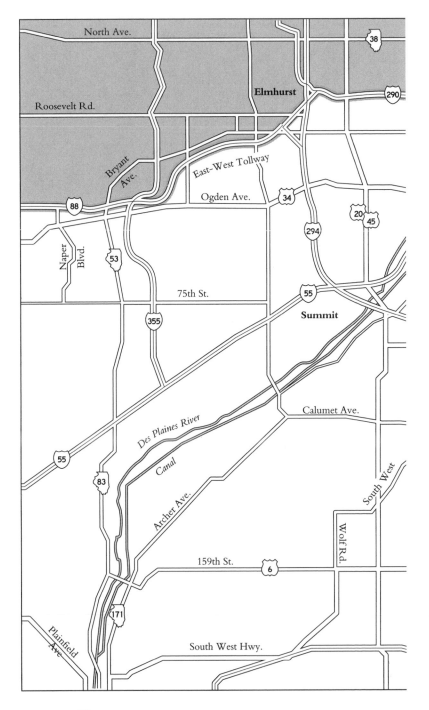

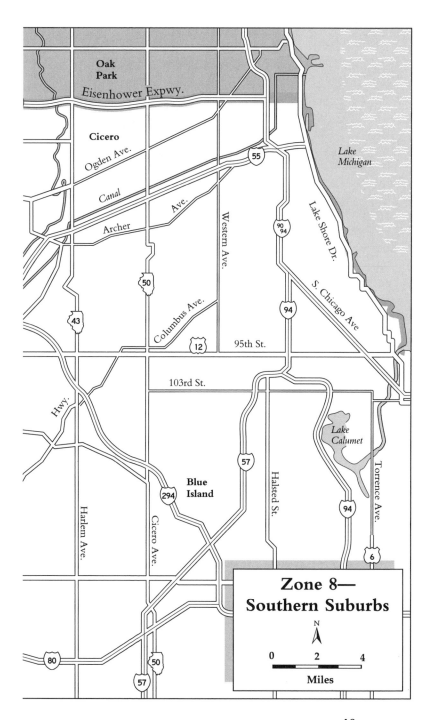

Oak
Park

Eisenhower Expwy.

Cicero

Ogden Ave.

Canal

Archer   Ave.

Western Ave.

Lake Shore Dr.

Lake
Michigan

55

90
94

94

S. Chicago Ave.

50

43

Columbus Ave.

12

95th St.

103rd St.

Hwy.

Lake
Calumet

57

Halsted St.

294

Blue
Island

94

Torrence Ave.

Harlem Ave.

Cicero Ave.

6

80

50

57

**Zone 8—
Southern Suburbs**

N

0   2   4

Miles

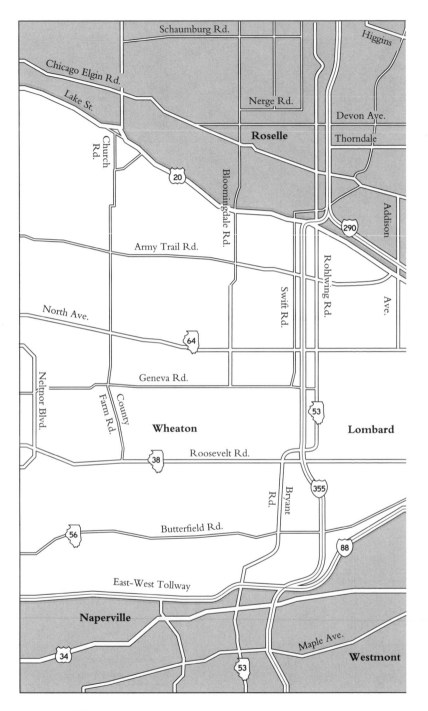

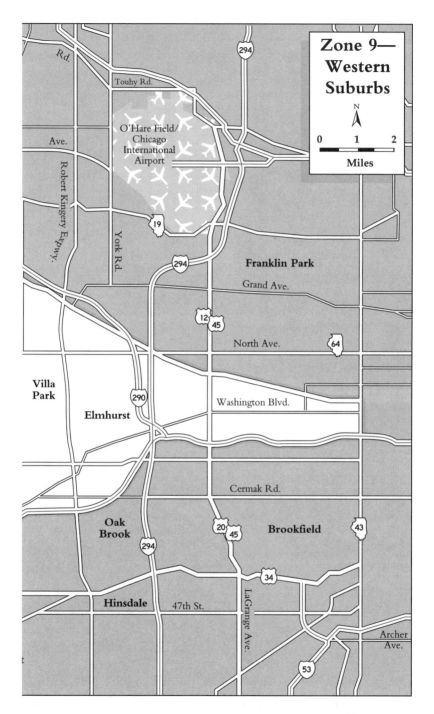

Zone 9—
Western
Suburbs

N

0   1   2

Miles

Rd.

294

Touhy Rd.

O'Hare Field/
Chicago
International
Airport

Ave.

Robert Kingery Expwy.

York Rd.

19

294

Franklin Park

Grand Ave.

12 45

North Ave.

64

Villa
Park

290

Washington Blvd.

Elmhurst

Cermak Rd.

Oak
Brook

20 45

Brookfield

43

294

34

Hinsdale   47th St.

LaGrange Ave.

Archer
Ave.

53

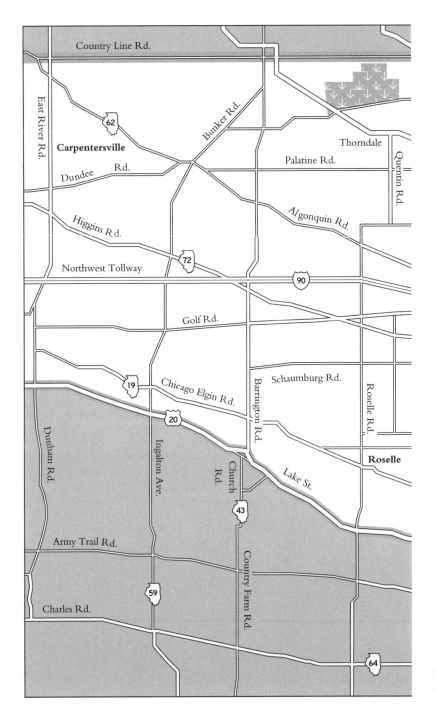

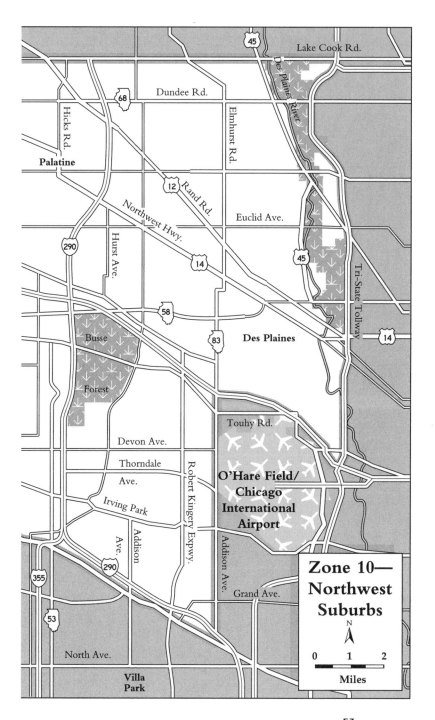

Zone 10—
Northwest
Suburbs

N

0   1   2

Miles

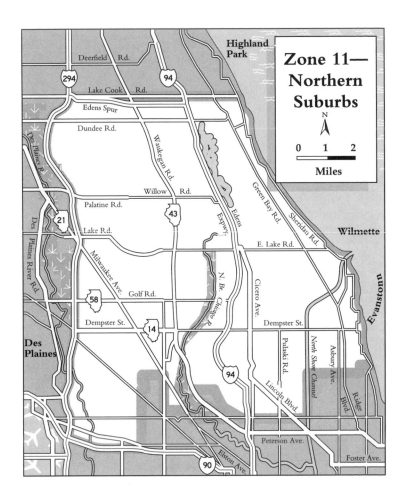

Zone 11—
Northern
Suburbs

N

0   1   2
Miles

Highland
Park

Deerfield Rd.

294

94

Lake Cook Rd.

Edens Spur

Dundee Rd.

Des Plaines Rd.

Waukegan Rd.

Willow Rd.

Palatine Rd.

43

21

Lake Rd.

Des Plaines River Rd.

Milwaukee Ave.

58

Golf Rd.

Dempster St.

14

Des
Plaines

Edens Expwy.

Edens

Green Bay Rd.

Sheridan Rd.

Wilmette

E. Lake Rd.

N. Br. Chicago R.

Cicero Ave.

Dempster St.

Evanston

94

Pulaski Rd.

North Shore Channel

Asbury Ave.

Ridge Blvd.

Lincoln Blvd.

Peterson Ave.

90

Elston Ave.

Foster Ave.

OUR pick of THE bEST Chicago RESTAURANTS

Because restaurants open and close all the time in Chicago, we have confined our list to establishments with a proven track record over a fairly long period of time. Newer restaurants (and older restaurants under new management) are listed but not profiled. Those newer or changed establishments that demonstrate staying power and consistency will be profiled in subsequent editions.

The list is highly selective. Noninclusion of a particular place does not necessarily indicate that the restaurant is not good, but only that it was not ranked among the best in its genre. Note that some restaurants appear in more than one category. Detailed profiles of each restaurant follow in alphabetical order at the end of this chapter. Also, we've listed the types of payment accepted at each restaurant using the following codes:

AMEX	American Express
CB	Carte Blanche
D	Discover
DC	Diners Club
MC	MasterCard
VISA	VISA

A NOTE AbouT spElliNg

Most diners who enjoy ethnic restaurants have noticed subtle variations in the spelling of certain dishes and preparations from one menu to the next. A noodle dish found on almost all Thai menus, for example, appears in one restaurant as *pad thai,* in another as *Phat Thai,* and in a third as *Phad Thai.*

This and similar inconsistencies arise from attempts to derive a phonetic English spelling from the name of a dish as pronounced in its country of origin. While one particular English spelling might be more frequently used than others, there is usually no definitive correct spelling for the names of many dishes. In this guide, we have elected to use the spelling most commonly found in authoritative ethnic cookbooks and other reference works.

We call this to your attention because the spelling we use in this guide could be different from that which you encounter on the menu in a certain restaurant. We might say, for instance, that the *tabbouleh* is good at the Pillars of Lebanon, while at the restaurant itself the dish is listed on the menu as *tabouli.*

Restaurants by Cuisine

Name	Star Rating	Price Rating	Quality Rating	Value Rating	Zone
American					
Seasons Restaurant	★★★★★	Mod/Exp	99	C	3
Spago	★★★★½	Mod/Exp	94	B	3
Spago Grill	★★★★	Mod/Exp	94	B	3
The Pump Room	★★★★	Exp	93	C	3
The Cafe	★★★★	Mod	92	B	3
Iron Mike's Grille	★★★½	Mod/Exp	90	C	3
Oceanique	★★★½	Mod/Exp	88	C	11
Harry Caray's	★★★½	Mod/Exp	86	C	4
The Mity Nice Grill	★★★½	Inexp/Mod	86	C	3
Wild Onion	★★★½	Inexp/Mod	85	B	1
Walker Bros. Original Pancake House	★★★	Inexp	88	B	10,11
Don Roth's in Wheeling	★★★	Mod	84	C	10
Wildfire (Russell Bry's)	★★★	Inexp/Mod	84	C	3
Ann Sather	★★★	Inexp	83	B	1
Big Shoulders	★★★	Inexp	82	B	1
foodlife	★★★	Inexp	82	C	3
R. J. Grunts	★★★	Inexp	82	A	1
American Brasserie					
Le Francais	★★★★★	V Exp	99	C	10
Brasserie T	★★★½	Inexp/Mod	90	B	11
American Ethnic					
Zinfandel	★★★★	Mod	91	C	1
American Stir-Fry					
Flat Top Grill	★★★	Inexp	85	B	2,3,11
Argentinian					
Tango Sur	★★½	Inexp/Mod	78	B	1
Asian Grill					
Mongolian Barbeque	★★★½	Inexp	85	B	1,8
Bakery Cafe					
Corner Bakery	★★★½	Inexp/Mod	90	B	4
Barbecue					
Joe's B-Bop Cafe	★★★½	Inexp/Mod	90	B	3

Name	Star Rating	Price Rating	Quality Rating	Value Rating	Zone
Barbecue *(continued)*					
N. N. Smokehouse	★★★	Inexp/Mod	82	B	1
Cajun/Creole					
Louisiana Kitchen	★★★½	Inexp/Mod	91	B	1
Carzz Grilleria	★★★½	Inexp/Mod	88	B	8
Maple Tree Inn	★★★½	Inexp/Mod	88	B	8
Heaven on Seven	★★★½	Inexp	86	B	4
Caribbean					
Carzz Grilleria	★★★½	Inexp/Mod	88	B	8
Julio's Latin Cafe	★★★	Mod	83	C	10
El Dinamico Dallas	★★½	Inexp	79	B	1
Chinese					
Szechwan East	★★★★	Mod	92	C	3
Ben Pao, Chinese Restaurant and Satay Bar	★★★½	Inexp/Mod	90	B	3
Emperor's Choice	★★★½	Inexp/Mod	88	B	5
Mandar Inn	★★★½	Inexp/Mod	88	C	5
Mei-Shung Chinese Restaurant	★★★½	Inexp	87	B	1
Hong Min Restaurant	★★★	Inexp/Mod	85	B	5,8
Szechwan Restaurant	★★★	Inexp/Mod	83	C	3
Continental					
Hudson Club	★★★★½	Mod	95	B	1
Biggs	★★★★	Mod	90	C	3
Cité	★★★★	V Exp	89	D	1
Skadarlija	★★★	Mod	84	B	1
Creative American					
Courtwright's	★★★★½	Mod/Exp	96	B	8
Mrs. Park's Tavern	★★★½	Inexp/Mod	89	C	3
Dim Sum					
Hong Min Restaurant	★★★	Inexp/Mod	85	B	5,8
Eclectic					
Green Dolphin Street	★★★	Mod/Exp	91	C	1
Gateway Bar & Grill	★★★	Inexp/Mod	85	B	1

Name	Star Rating	Price Rating	Quality Rating	Value Rating	Zone
Ethiopian					
Mama Desta's Red Sea Ethiopian Restaurant	★★★	Inexp	86	B	1
Addis Adeba	★★★	Inexp	84	C	1
Filipino					
N. N. Smokehouse	★★★	Inexp/Mod	82	B	1
Pampanga Restaurant	★★½	Inexp	77	B	1
Fondue					
Geja's Cafe	★★★½	Exp	90	B	1
French					
Everest	★★★★★	Exp	98	C	4
Vong	★★★★½	Mod/Exp	97	C	4
Carlos'	★★★★½	Mod/Exp	96	C	11
Le Vichyssoise	★★★★½	Mod	95	B	10
Entre Nous	★★★★½	Mod	90	C	4
Gabriel's Restaurant	★★★★	Mod/Exp	93	C	11
The Pump Room	★★★★	Exp	93	C	3
Brasserie Jo	★★★★	Inexp/Mod	92	B	3
L'Olive Cafe	★★★★	Inexp	92	A	1
Le Colonial	★★★½	Mod	88	C	1
Oceanique	★★★½	Mod/Exp	88	C	11
Wild Onion	★★★½	Inexp/Mod	85	B	1
La Crêperie	★★½	Inexp/Mod	80	A	1
French Bistro					
Kiki's Bistro	★★★★	Inexp/Mod	94	C	3
Mossant	★★★★	Mod	94	C	4
Bistro Banlieue	★★★★	Inexp/Mod	83	B	8
Mon Ami Gabi	★★★½	Mod	92	C	1
Cyrano's Bistrot & Wine Bar	★★★½	Inexp/Mod	90	B	3
Bistro 110	★★★½	Mod	86	C	3
Fusion					
Trio	★★★★★	Exp/V Exp	98	C	11

Name	Star Rating	Price Rating	Quality Rating	Value Rating	Zone
German / American					
Golden Ox	★★★★	Mod	90	C	1
The Berghoff	★★★½	Inexp	88	B	4
Mirabell Restaurant	★★★½	Inexp/Mod	88	B	2
Hans' Bavarian Lodge	★★★	Inexp/Mod	80	B	10
Greek					
The Parthenon	★★★★½	Inexp/Mod	95	B	4
Papagus Green Taverna	★★★★	Mod	90	C	3,6
Mykonos	★★★½	Inexp/Mod	92	B	11
Roditys	★★★	Mod	89	B	4
Santorini	★★★	Inexp/Mod	89	C	4
Pegasus Restaurant and Taverna	★★★	Inexp/Mod	83	C	4
Healthy Cuisine					
Earth	★★★½	Mod/Exp	90	C	3
Indian					
Indian Garden	★★★★	Inexp/Mod	94	C	8
Klay Oven	★★★★	Mod	94	B	4
Bukara	★★★½	Mod	80	C	3
Viceroy of India	★★★	Inexp/Mod	84	B	1,9
Sher-A-Punjab	★★★	Inexp	82	B	1
Chowpatti Vegetarian Restaurant	★★★	Inexp	80	B	10
Irish Pub					
Kitty O'Shea's	★★★	Inexp	81	B	5
Italian					
Va Pensiero	★★★★½	Mod	96	C	11
Spiaggia	★★★★½	Mod/Exp	95	C	3
Vivere (Italian Village)	★★★★½	Mod	95	C	4
Campagnola	★★★★	Inexp/Mod	94	B	11
Mangia Italiano Ristorante	★★★★	Inexp	94	B	2
Gabriel's Restaurant	★★★★	Mod/Exp	93	C	11
Caliterra	★★★★	Mod	92	B	3
Cuisines	★★★★	Inexp/Mod	92	B	4

Restaurants by Cuisine (continued)

Name	Star Rating	Price Rating	Quality Rating	Value Rating	Zone
Italian (continued)					
Coco Pazzo	★★★★	Mod	91	C	4
Trattoria Gianni	★★★★	Inexp/Mod	91	C	1
La Strada	★★★★	Mod/Exp	90	C	4
Trattoria Parma	★★★★	Inexp/Mod	89	B	3
Carlucci	★★★★	Mod	88	C	2
Cafe Luciano	★★★½	Inexp/Mod	96	C	3,11
Cafe Spiaggia	★★★½	Mod	89	C	3
Cucina Roma	★★★½	Inexp/Mod	89	B	8
Pane Caldo	★★★½	Inexp/Mod	89	D	3
The Primavera Ristorante	★★★½	Inexp/Mod	88	C	4
Bice Ristorante	★★★½	Mod/Exp	87	D	3
Harry Caray's	★★★½	Mod/Exp	86	C	4
Wild Onion	★★★½	Inexp/Mod	85	B	1
Bacino's Trattoria	★★★	Inexp/Mod	84	B	8
La Bocca della Verità	★★★	Inexp/Mod	84	B	1
Pappagallo's	★★★	Inexp/Mod	84	B	11
Red Tomato	★★★	Inexp	84	B	1
Tuscany	★★★	Mod	84	C	5
Del Rio	★★★	Inexp/Mod	83	B	11
Rosebud Cafe	★★★	Inexp/Mod	83	C	5
Francesco's Hole in the Wall	★★★	Inexp/Mod	83	B	11
Filippo's	★★★	Inexp/Mod	82	C	1
Mia Francesca	★★★	Inexp/Mod	82	B	1
Maggiano's Little Italy	★★★	Mod	81	C	4,8,11
Bruna's Ristorante	★★★	Inexp/Mod	80	B	5
Cafe Borgia	★★½	Inexp/Mod	78	B	8
Tufano's (Vernon Park Tap)	★★½	Inexp/Mod	76	C	5
Japanese					
Kuni's	★★★★½	Inexp/Mod	96	C	11
Yoshi's Cafe	★★★★	Inexp/Mod	94	B	1
Sai Cafe	★★★½	Inexp/Mod	91	B	1
Katsu Japanese Restaurant	★★★½	Inexp/Mod	90	B	1
Akai Hana	★★★½	Inexp/Mod	88	C	11
Shilla	★★★½	Mod	86	C	1
Hatsuhana	★★½	Inexp/Mod	76	C	3

Name	Star Rating	Price Rating	Quality Rating	Value Rating	Zone
Korean					
Woo Lae Oak	★★★★	Inexp	94	C	3
Korean Garden	★★★½	Inexp/Mod	88	B	8
Shilla	★★★½	Mod	86	C	1
Bando	★★★	Inexp/Mod	83	C	1
Amitabul	★★½	Inexp	80	B	1
Laotion					
Nhu Hoa Cafe	★★★½	Inexp/Mod	89	B	1
Lebanese					
Olive Branch	★★★	Inexp	85	B	3
Mediterranean					
Cuisines	★★★★	Inexp/Mod	92	B	4
Mexican					
Topolobampo	★★★★½	Mod	95	C	4
Frontera Grill	★★★★	Inexp	93	B	4
Don Juan	★★★½	Inexp	93	B	1
Chapultepec	★★★½	Inexp/Mod	90	B	3
Twisted Lizard	★★★½	Inexp	87	B	1
¡Salpicón!, A Taste of Mexico	★★★½	Inexp/Mod	85	C	3
El Tipico	★★½	Inexp	79	B	1,11
Midwestern					
Prairie	★★★★½	Mod/Exp	95	C	5
erwin	★★★★	Inexp/Mod	94	B	1
Moroccan					
L'Olive Cafe	★★★★	Inexp	92	A	1
New American					
Charlie Trotter's	★★★★★	V Exp	99	C	1
Spruce	★★★★½	Inexp/Mod	94	B	3
Hudson Club	★★★★	Mod	95	B	1
Printer's Row	★★★★	Mod	95	B	5
erwin	★★★★	Inexp/Mod	94	B	1
Park Avenue Cafe	★★★★	Mod/Exp	94	C	3
North Pond Cafe	★★★★	Mod	92	B	1

Name	Star Rating	Price Rating	Quality Rating	Value Rating	Zone
New American (continued)					
one sixtyblue	★★★★	Mod/Exp	92	C	2
302 West	★★★★	Mod	92	C	9
The Signature Room at the 95th	★★★★	Mod/Exp	90	C	3
Crofton on Wells	★★★½	Mod	91	B	3
Jack's	★★★½	Mod	90	B	1
Elaine's	★★★½	Inexp/Mod	89	B	3
The Greenery	★★★½	Mod/Exp	88	C	10
Jilly's Cafe	★★★½	Inexp/Mod	85	B	11
Blackhawk Lodge	★★★	Mod	82	C	3
Hubbard Street Grill	★★★	Inexp/Mod	81	C	4
New French					
Tallgrass	★★★★★	V Exp	98	C	8
The Dining Room	★★★★★	Mod/Exp	97	C	3
Le Titi de Paris	★★★★½	Mod/Exp	97	C	10
Ambria	★★★★½	Mod/Exp	96	C	1
Montparnasse	★★★★½	Mod/Exp	95	C	8
Yoshi's Cafe	★★★★	Inexp/Mod	94	B	1
Yvette	★★★½	Inexp/Mod	85	C	3
Froggy's French Cafe	★★★	Mod	84	B	11
New Italian					
Bella Vista	★★★½	Inexp/Mod	86	C	1
Via Veneto	★★★½	Inexp	85	B	1
Pazzo's Cucina Italiana	★★½	Inexp/Mod	79	C	2,8
Northern Californian					
Caliterra	★★★★	Mod	92	B	3
Pan-Asian					
Stir Crazy	★★★½	Inexp	88	B	9
Lulu's	★★★	Inexp	85	B	11
Big Bowl Cafe	★★★	Inexp	84	B	3
Persian					
Pars Cove	★★★½	Inexp	89	B	1
Reza's	★★★½	Inexp/Mod	89	C	1,3
Cy's Crab House	★★★	Inexp/Mod	84	B	1

Name	Star Rating	Price Rating	Quality Rating	Value Rating	Zone
Polish					
Lutnia Continental Cafe	★★★½	Inexp/Mod	87	C	2
Home Bakery	★★½	Inexp	77	B	2
Russian					
Russian Tea Time	★★★★	Mod	93	C	4
Seafood					
Nick's Fishmarket	★★★★½	Mod/Exp	95	D	2,4
Shaw's Crab House and Shaw's Blue Crab Lounge & Oyster Bar	★★★★½	Mod	95	C	4
Don's Fishmarket and Tavern	★★★★	Inexp/Mod	93	B	11
Cape Cod Room	★★★★	Mod/Exp	91	C	3
Palm Restaurant	★★★★	Mod/Exp	87	C	4
Catch 35	★★★½	Mod/Exp	93	C	4
Riva	★★★½	Mod/Exp	90	C	3
Cy's Crab House	★★★	Inexp/Mod	84	B	1
Bob Chinn's Crab House	★★★	Mod	82	B	10
Shaw's Seafood Grill	★★★	Mod	80	C	11
Serbian					
Skadarlija	★★★	Mod	84	B	1
Southern					
Army & Lou's	★★★★	Inexp/Mod	90	B	7
House of Blues	★★★½	Inexp/Mod	90	B	3
Joe's B-Bop Cafe	★★★½	Inexp/Mod	90	B	3
Carzz Grilleria	★★★½	Inexp/Mod	88	B	8
Soul Kitchen	★★★	Inexp/Mod	84	C	2
Stanley's Kitchen & Tap	★★½	Inexp	79	A	1
Southwestern					
Blue Mesa	★★★★	Inexp/Mod	89	B	1
Twisted Lizard	★★★½	Inexp	87	B	1
Spanish					
Meson Sabika's Tapas Bar Restaurant	★★★★	Mod	93	C	8
Emilio's Tapas Chicago	★★★★	Mod	91	C	1

64

Name	Star Rating	Price Rating	Quality Rating	Value Rating	Zone
Spanish (continued)					
Brios	★★★★	Mod/Exp	90	C	3
Cafe-Ba-Ba-Reeba!	★★★½	Mod	87	C	1
Cafe Iberico Tapas Bar	★★★½	Inexp/Mod	87	B	3
Steak					
Gibson's Steakhouse	★★★★½	Mod/Exp	94	C	3
Chicago Chop House	★★★★	Mod	94	C	3
Morton's of Chicago	★★★★	Exp	93	C	2,3,8,10
Ruth's Chris Steakhouse	★★★★	Mod/Exp	93	B	4
Kinzie Street Chophouse	★★★★	Mod	91	B	4
Lawry's The Prime Rib	★★★★	Mod	90	B	3
Palm Restaurant	★★★★	Mod/Exp	87	C	4
Riva	★★★½	Mod/Exp	90	C	3
The Saloon	★★★½	Mod/Exp	89	C	3
Eli's, the Place for Steak	★★★½	Mod/Exp	88	C	3
Swedish					
Ann Sather	★★★	Inexp	83	B	1
Thai					
Vong	★★★★½	Mod/Exp	97	C	4
Arun's	★★★★½	Mod/Exp	95	C	1
P. S. Bangkok	★★★	Inexp	84	A	1
Siam Cafe	★★★	Inexp	84	A	1
Vegetarian					
Reza's	★★★½	Inexp/Mod	89	C	1,3
Olive Branch	★★★	Inexp	85	B	3
Karyn's Fresh Corner	★★★	Inexp	84	C	1
Blind Faith Cafe	★★★	Inexp	82	B	1,11
Chowpatti Vegetarian Restaurant	★★★	Inexp	80	B	10
Amitabul	★★½	Inexp	80	B	1
Vietnamese					
Pasteur	★★★★	Inexp/Mod	92	B	1
Nhu Hoa Cafe	★★★½	Inexp/Mod	89	B	1
Le Colonial	★★★½	Mod	88	C	1

Restaurants by Star Rating

Name	Cuisine	Price Rating	Quality Rating	Value Rating	Zone
Five-Star Restaurants					
Charlie Trotter's	New American	V Exp	99	C	1
Le Francais	American Brasserie	V Exp	99	C	10
Seasons Restaurant	American	Mod/Exp	99	C	3
Everest	French	Exp	98	C	4
Tallgrass	New French	V Exp	98	C	8
Trio	Fusion	Exp/V Exp	98	C	11
The Dining Room	New French	Mod/Exp	97	C	3
Four-and-a-Half-Star Restaurants					
Le Titi de Paris	New French	Mod/Exp	97	C	10
Vong	Thai/French	Mod/Exp	97	C	4
Ambria	New French	Mod/Exp	96	C	1
Carlos'	French	Mod/Exp	96	C	11
Courtwright's	Creative American	Mod/Exp	96	B	8
Kuni's	Japanese	Inexp/Mod	96	C	11
Va Pensiero	Italian	Mod	96	C	11
Arun's	Thai	Mod/Exp	95	C	1
Hudson Club	New American/ Continental	Mod	95	B	1
Le Vichyssoise	French	Mod	95	B	10
Montparnasse	New French	Mod/Exp	95	C	8
Nick's Fishmarket	Seafood	Mod/Exp	95	D	2,4
The Parthenon	Greek	Inexp/Mod	95	B	4
Prairie	Midwestern	Mod/Exp	95	C	5
Shaw's Crab House and Shaw's Blue Crab Lounge & Oyster Bar	Seafood	Mod	95	C	4
Spiaggia	Italian	Mod/Exp	95	C	3
Topolobampo	Mexican	Mod	95	C	4
Vivere (Italian Village)	Italian	Mod	95	C	4
Gibson's Steakhouse	Steak	Mod/Exp	94	C	3
Spago	American	Mod/Exp	94	B	3
Spruce	New American	Inexp/Mod	94	B	3
Entre Nous	French	Mod	90	C	4

66

Restaurants by Star Rating (continued)

Name	Cuisine	Price Rating	Quality Rating	Value Rating	Zone
Four-Star Restaurants					
Printer's Row	New American	Mod	95	B	5
Campagnola	Italian	Inexp/Mod	94	B	11
Chicago Chop House	Steak	Mod	94	C	3
erwin	New American/ Midwestern	Inexp/Mod	94	B	1
Indian Garden	Indian	Inexp/Mod	94	C	8
Kiki's Bistro	French Bistro	Inexp/Mod	94	C	3
Klay Oven	Indian	Mod	94	B	4
Mangia Italiano Ristorante	Italian	Inexp	94	B	2
Mossant	French Bistro	Mod	94	C	4
Park Avenue Cafe	New American	Mod/Exp	94	C	3
Spago Grill	American	Mod/Exp	94	B	3
Woo Lae Oak	Korean	Inexp	94	C	3
Yoshi's Cafe	New French/ Japanese	Inexp/Mod	94	B	1
Don's Fishmarket and Tavern	Seafood	Inexp/Mod	93	B	11
Frontera Grill	Mexican	Inexp	93	B	4
Gabriel's Restaurant	French/Italian	Mod/Exp	93	C	11
Meson Sabika's Tapas Bar Restaurant	Spanish	Mod	93	C	8
Morton's of Chicago 2,3,8,10	Steak	Exp	93	C	
The Pump Room	French/American	Exp	93	C	3
Russian Tea Time	Russian	Mod	93	C	4
Ruth's Chris Steakhouse	Steak	Mod/Exp	93	B	4
Brasserie Jo	French	Inexp/Mod	92	B	3
The Cafe	American	Mod	92	B	3
Caliterra	Italian/Californian	Mod	92	B	3
Cuisines	Italian/ Mediterranean	Inexp/Mod	92	B	4
L'Olive Cafe	French/Moroccan	Inexp	92	A	1

Name	Cuisine	Price Rating	Quality Rating	Value Rating	Zone
Four-Star Restaurants *(continued)*					
North Pond Cafe	New American	Mod	92	B	1
one sixtyblue	New American	Mod/Exp	92	C	2
Pasteur	Vietnamese	Inexp/Mod	92	B	1
Szechwan East	Chinese	Mod	92	C	3
302 West	New American	Mod	92	C	9
Cape Cod Room	Seafood	Mod/Exp	91	C	3
Coco Pazzo	Italian	Mod	91	C	4
Emilio's Tapas Chicago	Spanish	Mod	91	C	1
Kinzie Street Chophouse	Steak	Mod	91	B	4
Trattoria Gianni	Italian	Inexp/Mod	91	C	1
Zinfandel	American Ethnic	Mod	91	C	1
Army & Lou's	Southern	Inexp/Mod	90	B	7
Biggs	Continental	Mod	90	C	3
Brios	Spanish	Mod/Exp	90	C	3
Golden Ox	German/American	Mod	90	C	1
La Strada	Italian	Mod/Exp	90	C	4
Lawry's The Prime Rib	Steak	Mod	90	B	3
Papagus Green Taverna	Greek	Mod	90	C	3,6
The Signature Room at the 95th	New American	Mod/Exp	90	C	3
Blue Mesa	Southwestern	Inexp/Mod	89	B	1
Cité	Continental	V Exp	89	D	1
Trattoria Parma	Italian	Inexp/Mod	89	B	3
Carlucci	Italian	Mod	88	C	2
Palm Restaurant	Steak/Seafood	Mod/Exp	87	C	4
Bistro Banlieue	French Bistro	Inexp/Mod	83	B	8
Three-and-a-Half-Star Restaurants					
CafeLuciano	Italian	Inexp/Mod	96	C	3,11
Catch 35	Seafood	Mod/Exp	93	C	4
Don Juan	Mexican	Inexp	93	B	1
Mon Ami Gabi	French Bistro	Mod	92	C	1
Mykonos	Greek	Inexp/Mod	92	B	11

68

Name	Cuisine	Price Rating	Quality Rating	Value Rating	Zone
Three-and-a-Half-Star Restaurants					
Crofton on Wells	New American	Mod	91	B	3
Louisiana Kitchen	Cajun/Creole	Inexp/Mod	91	B	1
Sai Cafe	Japanese	Inexp/Mod	91	B	1
Ben Pao, Chinese Restaurant & Satay Bar	Chinese	Inexp/Mod	90	B	3
Brasserie T	American Brasserie	Inexp/Mod	90	B	11
Chapultepec	Mexican	Inexp/Mod	90	B	3
Corner Bakery	Bakery Cafe	Inexp/Mod	90	B	4
Cyrano's Bistrot & Wine Bar	French Bistro	Inexp/Mod	90	B	3
Earth	Healthy Cuisine	Mod/Exp	90	C	3
Geja's Cafe	Fondue	Exp	90	B	1
House of Blues	Southern	Inexp/Mod	90	B	3
Iron Mike's Grille	American	Mod/Exp	90	C	3
Jack's	New American	Mod	90	B	1
Joe's B-Bop Cafe	Barbecue/ Southern	Inexp/Mod	90	B	3
Katsu Japanese Restaurant	Japanese	Inexp/Mod	90	B	1
Riva	Seafood/Steak	Mod/Exp	90	C	3
Cafe Spiaggia	Italian	Mod	89	C	3
Cucina Roma	Italian	Inexp/Mod	89	B	8
Elaine's	New American	Inexp/Mod	89	B	3
Mrs. Park's Tavern	Creative American	Inexp/Mod	89	C	3
Nhu Hoa Cafe	Vietnamese/ Laotion	Inexp/Mod	89	B	1
Pane Caldo	Italian	Inexp/Mod	89	D	3
Pars Cove	Persian	Inexp	89	B	1
Reza's	Persian/Vegetarian	Inexp/Mod	89	C	1,3
The Saloon	Steak	Mod/Exp	89	C	3
Akai Hana	Japanese	Inexp/Mod	88	C	11
The Berghoff	German/American	Inexp	88	B	4
Carzz Grilleria	Cajun/Creole/ Southern/Caribbean	Inexp/Mod	88	B	8

Name	Cuisine	Price Rating	Quality Rating	Value Rating	Zone
Three-and-a-Half-Star Restaurants (continued)					
Eli's, the Place for Steak	Steak	Mod/Exp	88	C	3
Emperor's Choice	Chinese	Inexp/Mod	88	B	5
The Greenery	New American	Mod/Exp	88	C	10
Korean Garden	Korean	Inexp/Mod	88	B	8
Le Colonial	French/Vietnamese	Mod	88	C	1
Mandar Inn	Chinese	Inexp/Mod	88	C	5
Maple Tree Inn	Cajun/Creole	Inexp/Mod	88	B	8
Mirabell Restaurant	German/American	Inexp/Mod	88	B	2
Oceanique	French/American	Mod/Exp	88	C	11
The Primavera Ristorante	Italian	Inexp/Mod	88	C	4
Stir Crazy	Pan-Asian	Inexp	88	B	9
Bice Ristorante	Italian	Mod/Exp	87	D	3
Cafel berico Tapas Bar	Spanish	Inexp/Mod	87	B	3
Cafe-Ba-Ba-Reeba!	Spanish	Mod	87	C	1
Lutnia Continental Cafe	Polish	Inexp/Mod	87	C	2
Mei-Shung Chinese Restaurant	Chinese	Inexp	87	B	1
Twisted Lizard	Southwestern/ Mexican	Inexp	87	B	1
Bella Vista	New Italian	Inexp/Mod	86	C	1
Bistro 110	French Bistro	Mod	86	C	3
Harry Caray's	American/Italian	Mod/Exp	86	C	4
Heaven on Seven	Cajun/Creole	Inexp	86	B	4
The Mity Nice Grill	American	Inexp/Mod	86	C	3
Shilla	Korean/Japanese	Mod	86	C	1
¡Salpicón!, A Taste of Mexico	Mexican	Inexp/Mod	85	C	3
Jilly's Cafe	New American	Inexp/Mod	85	B	11
Via Veneto	New Italian	Inexp	85	B	1
Wild Onion	American/ Italian/French	Inexp/Mod	85	B	1
Yvette	New French	Inexp/Mod	85	C	3
Bukara	Indian	Mod	80	C	3

Name	Cuisine	Price Rating	Quality Rating	Value Rating	Zone
Three-Star Restaurants					
Green Dolphin Street	Eclectic	Mod/Exp	91	C	1
Roditys	Greek	Mod	89	B	4
Santorini	Greek	Inexp/Mod	89	C	4
Walker Bros. Original Pancake House	American	Inexp	88	B	10,11
Mama Desta's Red Sea Ethiopian Restaurant	Ethiopian	Inexp	86	B	1
Flat Top Grill	American Stir-Fry	Inexp	85	B	2,3,11
Gateway Bar & Grill	Eclectic	Inexp/Mod	85	B	1
Hong Min Restaurant	Chinese/Dim Sum	Inexp/Mod	85	B	5,8
Lulu's	Pan-Asian	Inexp	85	B	11
Mongolian Barbeque	Asian Grill	Inexp	85	B	1,8
Olive Branch	Lebanese/ Vegetarian	Inexp	85	B	3
Addis Adeba	Ethiopian	Inexp	84	C	1
Bacino's Trattoria	Italian	Inexp/Mod	84	B	8
Big Bowl Cafe	Pan-Asian	Inexp	84	B	3
Cy's Crab House	Seafood/Persian	Inexp/Mod	84	B	1
Don Roth's in Wheeling	American	Mod	84	C	10
Froggy's French Cafe	New French	Mod	84	B	11
Karyn's Fresh Corner	Vegetarian	Inexp	84	C	1
La Bocca della Veritá	Italian	Inexp/Mod	84	B	1
P. S. Bangkok	Thai	Inexp	84	A	1
Pappagallo's	Italian	Inexp/Mod	84	B	11
Red Tomato	Italian	Inexp	84	B	1
Siam Cafe	Thai	Inexp	84	A	1
Skadarlija	Serbian	Mod	84	B	1
Soul Kitchen	Southern	Inexp/Mod	84	C	2
Tuscany	Italian	Mod	84	C	5
Viceroy of India	Indian	Inexp/Mod	84	B	1,9
Wildfire (Russell Bry's)	American	Inexp/Mod	84	C	3
Ann Sather	Swedish/American	Inexp	83	B	1

Name	Cuisine	Price Rating	Quality Rating	Value Rating	Zone
Three-Star Restaurants *(continued)*					
Bando	Korean	Inexp/Mod	83	C	1
Del Rio	Italian	Inexp/Mod	83	B	11
Francesco's Hole in the Wall	Italian	Inexp/Mod	83	B	11
Julio's Latin Cafe	Caribbean	Mod	83	C	10
Pegasus Restaurant and Taverna	Greek	Inexp/Mod	83	C	4
Rosebud Cafe	Italian	Inexp/Mod	83	C	5
Szechwan Restaurant	Chinese	Inexp/Mod	83	C	3
Big Shoulders	American	Inexp	82	B	1
Blackhawk Lodge	New American	Mod	82	C	3
Blind Faith Cafe	Vegetarian	Inexp	82	B	1,11
Bob Chinn's Crab House	Seafood	Mod	82	B	10
Filippo's	Italian	Inexp/Mod	82	C	1
foodlife	American	Inexp	82	C	3
Mia Francesca	Italian	Inexp/Mod	82	B	1
N. N. Smokehouse	Barbecue/Filipino	Inexp/Mod	82	B	1
R. J. Grunts	American	Inexp	82	A	1
Sher-A-Punjab	Indian	Inexp	82	B	1
Hubbard Street Grill	New American	Inexp/Mod	81	C	4
Kitty O'Shea's	Irish Pub	Inexp	81	B	5
Maggiano's Little Italy	Italian	Mod	81	C	4,8,11
Bruna's Ristorante	Italian	Inexp/Mod	80	B	5
Chowpatti Vegetarian Restaurant	Indian/Vegetarian	Inexp	80	B	10
Hans' Bavarian Lodge	German/American	Inexp/Mod	80	B	10
Shaw's Seafood Grill	Seafood	Mod	80	C	11
Two-and-a-Half-Star Restaurants					
Amitabul	Korean/Vegetarian	Inexp	80	B	1
La Crêperie	French	Inexp/Mod	80	A	1
El Dinamico Dallas	Caribbean	Inexp	79	B	1
El Tipico	Mexican	Inexp	79	B	1,11
Pazzo's Cucina Italiana	New Italian	Inexp/Mod	79	C	2,8

Name	Cuisine	Price Rating	Quality Rating	Value Rating	Zone
Two-and-a-Half-Star Restaurants					
Stanley's Kitchen & Tap	Southern	Inexp	79	A	1
Cafe Borgia	Italian	Inexp/Mod	78	B	8
Tango Sur	Argentinian	Inexp/Mod	78	B	1
Home Bakery	Polish	Inexp	77	B	2
Pampanga Restaurant	Filipino	Inexp	77	B	1
Hatsuhana	Japanese	Inexp/Mod	76	C	3
Tufano's (Vernon Park Tap)	Italian	Inexp/Mod	76	C	5

Restaurants by Zone

Name	Star Rating	Price Rating	Quality Rating	Value Rating
Zone 1—North Side				
◆ *American*				
Big Shoulders	★★★	Inexp	82	B
R. J. Grunts	★★★	Inexp	82	A
◆ *American Ethnic*				
Zinfandel	★★★★	Mod	91	C
◆ *American/Italian/French*				
Wild Onion	★★★½	Inexp/Mod	85	B
◆ *Argentinian*				
Tango Sur	★★½	Inexp/Mod	78	B
◆ *Asian Grill*				
Mongolian Barbeque	★★★	Inexp	85	B
◆ *Barbecue/Filipino*				
N. N. Smokehouse	★★★	Inexp/Mod	82	B
◆ *Cajun/Creole*				
Louisiana Kitchen	★★★½	Inexp/Mod	91	B
◆ *Caribbean*				
El Dinamico Dallas	★★½	Inexp	79	B
◆ *Chinese*				
Mei-Shung Chinese Restaurant	★★★½	Inexp	87	B
◆ *Continental*				
Cité	★★★★	V Exp	89	D
◆ *Eclectic*				
Green Dolphin Street	★★★	Mod/Exp	91	C
Gateway Bar & Grill	★★★	Inexp/Mod	85	B
◆ *Ethiopian*				
Mama Desta's Red Sea Ethiopian Restaurant	★★★	Inexp	86	B
Addis Adeba	★★★	Inexp	84	C

Restaurants by Zone (continued)

Name	Star Rating	Price Rating	Quality Rating	Value Rating
◆ *Filipino*				
Pampanga Restaurant	★★½	Inexp	77	B
◆ *Fondue*				
Geja's Cafe	★★★½	Exp	90	B
◆ *French Cafe*				
La Crêperie	★★½	Inexp/Mod	80	A
◆ *French Bistro*				
Mon Ami Gabi	★★★½	Mod	92	C
◆ *French/Moroccan*				
L'Olive Cafe	★★★★	Inexp	92	A
◆ *French/Vietnamese*				
Le Colonial	★★★½	Mod	88	C
◆ *German/American*				
Golden Ox	★★★★	Mod	90	C
◆ *Indian*				
Viceroy of India	★★★	Inexp/Mod	84	B
Sher-A-Punjab	★★★	Inexp	82	B
◆ *Italian*				
Trattoria Gianni	★★★★	Inexp/Mod	91	C
La Bocca della Veritá	★★★	Inexp/Mod	84	B
Red Tomato	★★★	Inexp	84	B
Filippo's	★★★	Inexp/Mod	82	C
Mia Francesca	★★★	Inexp/Mod	82	B
◆ *Japanese*				
Sai Cafe	★★★½	Inexp/Mod	91	B
Katsu Japanese Restaurant	★★★½	Inexp/Mod	90	B
◆ *Korean*				
Bando	★★★	Inexp/Mod	83	C
◆ *Korean/Japanese*				
Shilla	★★★½	Mod	86	C

Name	Star Rating	Price Rating	Quality Rating	Value Rating

Zone 1—North Side *(continued)*

◆ *Korean/Vegetarian*

| Amitabul | ★★½ | Inexp | 80 | B |

◆ *Mexican*

| Don Juan | ★★★½ | Inexp | 93 | B |
| El Tipico | ★★½ | Inexp | 79 | B |

◆ *New American*

Charlie Trotter's	★★★★★	V Exp	99	C
North Pond Cafe	★★★★	Mod	92	B
Jack's	★★★½	Mod	90	B

◆ *New American/Continental*

| Hudson Club | ★★★★½ | Mod | 95 | B |

◆ *New American/Midwestern*

| erwin | ★★★★ | Inexp/Mod | 94 | B |

◆ *New French*

| Ambria | ★★★★½ | Mod/Exp | 96 | C |

◆ *New French/Japanese*

| Yoshi's Cafe | ★★★★ | Inexp/Mod | 94 | B |

◆ *New Italian*

| Bella Vista | ★★★½ | Inexp/Mod | 86 | C |
| Via Veneto | ★★★½ | Inexp | 85 | B |

◆ *Persian*

| Pars Cove | ★★★½ | Inexp | 89 | B |

◆ *Persian/Vegetarian*

| Reza's | ★★★½ | Inexp/Mod | 89 | C |

◆ *Seafood/Persian*

| Cy's Crab House | ★★★ | Inexp/Mod | 84 | B |

◆ *Serbian/Continental*

| Skadarlija | ★★★ | Mod | 84 | B |

◆ *Southern*

| Stanley's Kitchen & Tap | ★★½ | Inexp | 79 | A |

Name	Star Rating	Price Rating	Quality Rating	Value Rating
◆ *Southwestern*				
Blue Mesa	★★★★	Inexp/Mod	89	B
◆ *Southwestern/Mexican*				
Twisted Lizard	★★★½	Inexp	87	B
◆ *Spanish*				
Emilio's Tapas Chicago	★★★★	Mod	91	C
Cafe-Ba-Ba-Reeba!	★★★½	Mod	87	C
◆ *Swedish/American*				
Ann Sather	★★★	Inexp	83	B
◆ *Thai*				
Arun's	★★★★½	Mod/Exp	95	C
P. S. Bangkok	★★★	Inexp	84	A
Siam Cafe	★★★	Inexp	84	A
◆ *Vegetarian*				
Karyn's Fresh Corner	★★★	Inexp	84	C
Blind Faith Cafe	★★★	Inexp	82	B
◆ *Vietnamese*				
Pasteur	★★★★	Inexp/Mod	92	B
◆ *Vietnamese/Laotian*				
Nhu Hoa Cafe	★★★½	Inexp/Mod	89	B

Zone 2—North Central/O'Hare

Name	Star Rating	Price Rating	Quality Rating	Value Rating
◆ *American Stir-Fry*				
Flat Top Grill	★★★	Inexp	85	B
◆ *German/American*				
Mirabell Restaurant	★★★½	Inexp/Mod	88	B
◆ *Italian*				
Mangia Italiano Ristorante	★★★★	Inexp	94	B
Carlucci	★★★★	Mod	88	C
◆ *New American*				
one sixtyblue	★★★★	Mod/Exp	92	C

Name	Star Rating	Price Rating	Quality Rating	Value Rating

Zone 2—North Central/O'Hare *(continued)*

◆ *New Italian*

| Pazzo's Cucina Italiana | ★★½ | Inexp/Mod | 79 | C |

◆ *Polish*

| Lutnia Continental Cafe | ★★★½ | Inexp/Mod | 87 | C |
| Home Bakery | ★★½ | Inexp | 77 | B |

◆ *Seafood*

| Nick's Fishmarket | ★★★★½ | Mod/Exp | 95 | D |

◆ *Southern*

| Soul Kitchen | ★★★ | Inexp/Mod | 84 | C |

◆ *Steak*

| Morton's of Chicago | ★★★★ | Exp | 93 | C |

Zone 3—Near North

◆ *American*

Seasons Restaurant	★★★★★	Mod/Exp	99	C
Spago	★★★★½	Mod/Exp	94	B
Spago Grill	★★★★	Mod/Exp	94	B
The Cafe	★★★★	Mod	92	B
Iron Mike's Grille	★★★½	Mod/Exp	90	C
The Mity Nice Grill	★★★½	Inexp/Mod	86	C
Wildfire (Russell Bry's)	★★★	Inexp/Mod	84	C
foodlife	★★★	Inexp	82	C

◆ *American Stir-Fry*

| Flat Top Grill | ★★★ | Inexp | 85 | B |

◆ *Barbecue/Southern*

| Joe's B-Bop Cafe | ★★★½ | Inexp/Mod | 90 | B |

◆ *Chinese*

Szechwan East	★★★★	Mod	92	C
Ben Pao, Chinese Restaurant & Satay Bar	★★★½	Inexp/Mod	90	B
Szechwan Restaurant	★★★	Inexp/Mod	83	C

Name	Star Rating	Price Rating	Quality Rating	Value Rating
◆ *Continental*				
Biggs	★★★★	Mod	90	C
◆ *Creative American*				
Mrs. Park's Tavern	★★★½	Inexp/Mod	89	C
◆ *French*				
Brasserie Jo	★★★★	Inexp/Mod	92	B
◆ *French Bistro*				
Kiki's Bistro	★★★★	Inexp/Mod	94	C
Cyrano's Bistrot & Wine Bar	★★★½	Inexp/Mod	90	B
Bistro 110	★★★½	Mod	86	C
◆ *French/American*				
The Pump Room	★★★★	Exp	93	C
◆ *Greek*				
Papagus Green Taverna	★★★★	Mod	90	C
◆ *Healthy Cuisine*				
Earth	★★★½	Mod/Exp	90	C
◆ *Indian*				
Bukara	★★★½	Mod	80	C
◆ *Italian*				
Spiaggia	★★★★½	Mod/Exp	95	C
Trattoria Parma	★★★★	Inexp/Mod	89	B
Cafe Luciano	★★★½	Inexp/Mod	96	C
Cafe Spiaggia	★★★½	Mod	89	C
Pane Caldo	★★★½	Inexp/Mod	89	D
Bice Ristorante	★★★½	Mod/Exp	87	D
◆ *Italian/Northern Californian*				
Caliterra	★★★★	Mod	92	B
◆ *Japanese*				
Hatsuhana	★★½	Inexp/Mod	76	C
◆ *Korean*				
Woo Lae Oak	★★★★	Inexp	94	C

Name	Star Rating	Price Rating	Quality Rating	Value Rating

Zone 3—Near North *(continued)*

◆ *Lebanese / Vegetarian*

Olive Branch	★★★	Inexp	85	B

◆ *Mexican*

¡Salpicón!, A Taste of Mexico	★★★½	Inexp/Mod	85	C
Chapultepec	★★★½	Inexp/Mod	90	B

◆ *New American*

Spruce	★★★★½	Inexp/Mod	94	B
Park Avenue Cafe	★★★★	Mod/Exp	94	C
The Signature Room at the 95th	★★★★	Mod/Exp	90	C
Crofton on Wells	★★★½	Mod	91	B
Elaine's	★★★½	Inexp/Mod	89	B
Blackhawk Lodge	★★★	Mod	82	C

◆ *New French*

The Dining Room	★★★★★	Mod/Exp	97	C
Yvette	★★★½	Inexp/Mod	85	C

◆ *Pan-Asian*

Big Bowl Cafe	★★★	Inexp	84	B

◆ *Persian / Vegetarian*

Reza's	★★★½	Inexp/Mod	89	C

Seafood

Cape Cod Room	★★★★	Mod/Exp	91	C

◆ *Seafood / Steak*

Riva	★★★½	Mod/Exp	90	C

◆ *Southern*

House of Blues	★★★½	Inexp/Mod	90	B

◆ *Spanish*

Brios	★★★★	Mod/Exp	90	C
CafeIberico Tapas Bar	★★★½	Inexp/Mod	87	B

Name	Star Rating	Price Rating	Quality Rating	Value Rating
◆ *Steak*				
Gibson's Steakhouse	★★★★½	Mod/Exp	94	C
Chicago Chop House	★★★★	Mod	94	C
Morton's of Chicago	★★★★	Exp	93	C
Lawry's The Prime Rib	★★★★	Mod	90	B
The Saloon	★★★½	Mod/Exp	89	C
Eli's, the Place for Steak	★★★½	Mod/Exp	88	C

Zone 4—The Loop

Name	Star Rating	Price Rating	Quality Rating	Value Rating
◆ *American/Italian*				
Harry Caray's	★★★½	Mod/Exp	86	C
◆ *Bakery Cafe*				
Corner Bakery	★★★½	Inexp/Mod	90	B
◆ *Cajun/Creole*				
Heaven on Seven	★★★½	Inexp	86	B
◆ *French*				
Everest	★★★★★	Exp	98	C
Entre Nous	★★★★½	Mod	90	C
◆ *French Bistro*				
Mossant	★★★★	Mod	94	C
◆ *German/American*				
The Berghoff	★★★½	Inexp	88	B
◆ *Greek*				
The Parthenon	★★★★½	Inexp/Mod	95	B
Roditys	★★★	Mod	89	B
Santorini	★★★	Inexp/Mod	89	C
Pegasus Restaurant and Taverna	★★★	Inexp/Mod	83	C
◆ *Indian*				
Klay Oven	★★★★	Mod	94	B
◆ *Italian*				
Vivere (Italian Village)	★★★★½	Mod	95	C

81

Name	Star Rating	Price Rating	Quality Rating	Value Rating
Zone 4—The Loop *(continued)*				
Coco Pazzo	★★★★	Mod	91	C
La Strada	★★★★	Mod/Exp	90	C
◆ *Italian*				
The Primavera Ristorante	★★★½	Inexp/Mod	88	C
Maggiano's Little Italy	★★★	Mod	81	C
◆ *Italian/Mediterranean*				
Cuisines	★★★★	Inexp/Mod	92	B
◆ *Mexican*				
Topolobampo	★★★★½	Mod	95	C
Frontera Grill	★★★★	Inexp	93	B
◆ *New American*				
Hubbard Street Grill	★★★	Inexp/Mod	81	C
◆ *Russian*				
Russian Tea Time	★★★★	Mod	93	C
◆ *Seafood*				
Nick's Fishmarket	★★★★½	Mod/Exp	95	D
Shaw's Crab House and Shaw's Blue Crab Lounge & Oyster Bar	★★★★½	Mod	95	C
Catch 35	★★★½	Mod/Exp	93	C
◆ *Steak*				
Ruth's Chris Steakhouse	★★★★	Mod/Exp	93	B
Kinzie Street Chophouse	★★★★	Mod	91	B
◆ *Steak/Seafood*				
Palm Restaurant	★★★★	Mod/Exp	87	C
◆ *Thai/French*				
Vong	★★★★½	Mod/Exp	97	C
Zone 5—South Loop				
◆ *Chinese*				
Emperor's Choice	★★★½	Inexp/Mod	88	B

Name	Star Rating	Price Rating	Quality Rating	Value Rating
Mandar Inn	★★★½	Inexp/Mod	88	C
◆ *Chinese/Dim Sum*				
Hong Min Restaurant	★★★	Inexp/Mod	85	B
◆ *Irish Pub*				
Kitty O'Shea's	★★★	Inexp	81	B
◆ *Italian*				
Tuscany	★★★	Mod	84	C
Rosebud Cafe	★★★	Inexp/Mod	83	C
Bruna's Ristorante	★★★	Inexp/Mod	80	B
Tufano's (Vernon Park Tap)	★★½	Inexp/Mod	76	C
◆ *Midwestern*				
Prairie	★★★★½	Mod/Exp	95	C
◆ *New American*				
Printer's Row	★★★★	Mod	95	B

Zone 6—South Central/Midway

Name	Star Rating	Price Rating	Quality Rating	Value Rating
◆ *Greek*				
Papagus Green Taverna	★★★★	Mod	90	C

Zone 7—South Side

Name	Star Rating	Price Rating	Quality Rating	Value Rating
◆ *Southern*				
Army & Lou's	★★★★	Inexp/Mod	90	B

Zone 8—Southern Suburbs

Name	Star Rating	Price Rating	Quality Rating	Value Rating
◆ *Asian Grill*				
Mongolian Barbeque	★★★	Inexp	85	B
◆ *Cajun/Creole*				
Maple Tree Inn	★★★½	Inexp/Mod	88	B
◆ *Cajun/Creole/Southern/Caribbean*				
Carzz Grilleria	★★★½	Inexp/Mod	88	B
◆ *Chinese/Dim Sum*				
Hong Min Restaurant	★★★	Inexp/Mod	85	B

Name	Star Rating	Price Rating	Quality Rating	Value Rating
Zone 8—Southern Suburbs (continued)				
◆ *Creative American*				
Courtwright's	★★★★½	Mod/Exp	96	B
◆ *French Bistro*				
Bistro Banlieue	★★★★	Inexp/Mod	83	B
◆ *Indian*				
Indian Garden	★★★★	Inexp/Mod	94	C
◆ *Italian*				
Cucina Roma	★★★½	Inexp/Mod	89	B
Maggiano's Little Italy	★★★	Mod	81	C
Bacino's Trattoria	★★★	Inexp/Mod	84	B
Cafe Borgia	★★½	Inexp/Mod	78	B
◆ *Korean*				
Korean Garden	★★★½	Inexp/Mod	88	B
◆ *New French*				
Tallgrass	★★★★★	V Exp	98	C
Montparnasse	★★★★½	Mod/Exp	95	C
◆ *New Italian*				
Pazzo's Cucina Italiana	★★½	Inexp/Mod	79	C
◆ *Spanish*				
Meson Sabika's Tapas Bar Restaurant	★★★★	Mod	93	C
◆ *Steak*				
Morton's of Chicago	★★★★	Exp	93	C
Zone 9—Western Suburbs				
◆ *Indian*				
Viceroy of India	★★★	Inexp/Mod	84	B
◆ *New American*				
302 West	★★★★	Mod	92	C

Name	Star Rating	Price Rating	Quality Rating	Value Rating
◆ *Pan-Asian*				
Stir Crazy	★★★½	Inexp	88	B
Zone 10—Northwest Suburbs				
◆ *American*				
Walker Bros. Original Pancake House	★★★	Inexp	88	B
Don Roth's in Wheeling	★★★	Mod	84	C
◆ *American Brasserie*				
Le Francais	★★★★	V Exp	99	C
◆ *Caribbean*				
Julio's Latin Cafe	★★★	Mod	83	C
◆ *French*				
Le Vichyssoise	★★★★½	Mod	95	B
◆ *German/American*				
Hans' Bavarian Lodge	★★★	Inexp/Mod	80	B
◆ *Indian/Vegetarian*				
Chowpatti Vegetarian Restaurant	★★★	Inexp	80	B
◆ *New American*				
The Greenery	★★★½	Mod/Exp	88	C
◆ *New French*				
Le Titi de Paris	★★★★½	Mod/Exp	97	C
◆ *Seafood*				
Bob Chinn's Crab House	★★★	Mod	82	B
◆ *Steak*				
Morton's of Chicago	★★★★	Exp	93	C
Zone 11—Northern Suburbs				
◆ *American*				
Walker Bros. Original Pancake House	★★★	Inexp	88	B

Name	Star Rating	Price Rating	Quality Rating	Value Rating
Zone 11—Northern Suburbs *(continued)*				
◆ *American Brasserie*				
Brasserie T	★★★½	Inexp/Mod	90	B
◆ *American Stir-Fry*				
Flat Top Grill	★★★	Inexp	85	B
◆ *French*				
Carlos'	★★★★½	Mod/Exp	96	C
◆ *French/American*				
Oceanique	★★★½	Mod/Exp	88	C
◆ *French/Italian*				
Gabriel's Restaurant	★★★★	Mod/Exp	93	C
◆ *Fusion*				
Trio	★★★★★	Exp/V Exp	98	C
◆ *Greek*				
Mykonos	★★★½	Inexp/Mod	92	B
◆ *Italian*				
Va Pensiero	★★★★½	Mod	96	C
Campagnola	★★★★	Inexp/Mod	94	B
Cafe Luciano	★★★½	Inexp/Mod	96	C
Pappagallo's	★★★	Inexp/Mod	84	B
Del Rio	★★★	Inexp/Mod	83	B
Francesco's Hole in the Wall	★★★	Inexp/Mod	83	B
Maggiano's Little Italy	★★★	Mod	81	C
◆ *Japanese*				
Kuni's	★★★★½	Inexp/Mod	96	C
Akai Hana	★★★½	Inexp/Mod	88	C
◆ *Mexican*				
El Tipico	★★½	Inexp	79	B
◆ *New American*				
Jilly's Cafe	★★★½	Inexp/Mod	85	B

Restaurants by Zone (continued)

Name	Star Rating	Price Rating	Quality Rating	Value Rating
◆ *New French*				
Froggy's French Cafe	★★★	Mod	84	B
◆ *Pan-Asian*				
Lulu's	★★★	Inexp	85	B
◆ *Seafood*				
Don's Fishmarket and Tavern	★★★★	Inexp/Mod	93	B
Shaw's Seafood Grill	★★★	Mod	80	C
◆ *Vegetarian*				
Blind Faith Cafe	★★★	Inexp	82	B

Addis Abeba

Zone 1   North Side
3521 North Clark Street
(773) 929-9383

Ethiopian	
★ ★ ★	
Inexpensive	
Quality 84	Value C

Reservations:	Required on weekends
When to go:	Weekdays are less crowded
Entree range:	$8.50–10
Payment:	All major credit cards
Service rating:	★ ★ ★
Friendliness rating:	★ ★ ★
Parking:	Street, three garages nearby
Bar:	Full service
Wine selection:	Italian, American, and Ethiopian
Dress:	Casual
Disabled access:	Yes, including rest rooms
Customers:	Mostly locals, ethnics; a few tourists
Dinner:	Monday–Thursday, 5–10 P.M.; Friday and Saturday, 5–11 P.M.; Sunday, 4–10 P.M.

Atmosphere/setting: Clean, well-lit setting filled with exotic artifacts of Ethiopia, including paintings and handwoven straw baskets. African tablecloths with ivory and black batik prints add to the ethnic aura.

House specialties: Fosolia (string beans, onions, and carrots cooked in tomato sauce) is exceptional; other vegetarian dishes of lentils, chickpeas, and mushrooms, seasoned with exotic spices, are equally zesty; savory doro tibs (breast of chicken stir-fried in Ethiopian herb butter and garlic) comes mild or spicy, as do many other entrees.

Other recommendations: Spicy appetizers such as the sambussa, jalapeño, and lentil "egg roll" will tingle your taste buds; katenya (spinach and cheese blended with spiced butter and cardamom, rolled up in injera, the spongy, sour bread) is another superb, tangy treat.

Summary & comments: Ethiopian dishes, most of which are saucy, are served on communal platters, from which customers dip them with injera. If you're eating with friends, it is a great idea to order the vegetarian, meat, veg-meat, or seafood and meat combinations so you can sample the wide array of succulent dishes available at Addis Abeba.

Akai Hana

Zone 11　　Northern Suburbs	Japanese
3217 West Lake Avenue, Wilmette	★★★½
(847) 251-0384	Inexpensive/Moderate
	Quality 88　　Value C

Reservations:	Accepted for 6 or more
When to go:	Before 6 P.M.
Entree range:	$10–14. Sushi combination boxes: lunch, $7.75–16; dinner, $15–16
Payment:	All major credit cards
Service rating:	★★★½
Friendliness rating:	★★★★
Parking:	Free
Bar:	Wine and beer
Wine selection:	Average for Japanese restaurant: limited—sake, some American
Dress:	Casual
Disabled access:	Yes
Customers:	Locals, including Japanese professionals who settled in the area
Lunch/Dinner:	Monday–Thursday, 11:30 A.M.–10 P.M.; Friday and Saturday, 11:30 A.M.–10:20 P.M.; Sunday, 11:30 A.M.–9:20 P.M.

Atmosphere/setting: Bright and bustling; white tablecloths with wooden accents. Recently added 50 more seats.

House specialties: Sushi combination boxes; sautéed giant clam. Salmon teriyaki is one of the best dishes. Extensive appetizer list includes some very native Japanese items, such as fried shrimp heads.

Other recommendations: Teriyaki preparations; combo plates. Green tea ice cream is a refreshing finish.

Summary & comments: This restaurant grew from a grocery and became an instant success, and it recently expanded again. The North Shore was lacking a good Japanese restaurant, and this place filled the niche. The success of Akai Hana is a good start toward expanding suburban culinary horizons beyond French, Italian, and American.

Ambria

	New French
	★★★★½
	Moderate/Expensive
	Quality 96 Value C

Zone 1   North Side
Beldon Stratford Hotel,
   2300 North Lincoln Park West
(773) 472-0076

Reservations:	Required
When to go:	Early on weeknights; late on weekends
Entree range:	$19.50–29.95
Payment:	All major credit cards
Service rating:	★★★★
Friendliness rating:	★★★★
Parking:	Valet, $6
Bar:	Full-service, dining bar for customers only
Wine selection:	Award-winning; 570 international, $15–1,500; 5 by the glass, $8–12
Dress:	Dressy; jacket required, tie optional—no denim or sneakers
Disabled access:	Wheelchair accessible
Customers:	Sophisticated, international and upscale local
Dinner:	Monday–Thursday, 6–9:30 P.M.; Friday, 6–10 P.M.; Saturday, 5:30–10:30 P.M.

Atmosphere/setting: Deep-toned woods, ultrasuede banquettes, and crystalline-etched glass with art nouveau architectural touches; tiny shaded lamps on each table; massive flower-filled urns. This place resembles an old mansion or club from the 1900s; murals and elegant fixtures; fashionable decor and ambience.

House specialties: Roasted New York State foie gras with caramelized apples; loin of lamb with sweet mini-peppers and rosemary infusion; fillet of Casco Bay cod in rice paper with lobster-paprika sauce; mango parfait with berries.

Other recommendations: Baby pheasant, foie gras, wild mushrooms, and thyme broth; a symphony of market vegetables and grains; soufflé du jour.

Summary & comments: Well-established (17-plus years) this crème de la crème of French restaurants is one of the top-shelf places within the Lettuce Entertain You Enterprises group. Longtime chef-owner Gabino Sotelino maintains fine quality here, using his solid culinary skills to produce French cuisine légère with Italian and Spanish influences. The menu has been simplified over the years. Lovely presentations. Some minor flaws occasionally in food and service, but overall, a very reliable place.

Honors/awards: Four-star rating from *Chicago* magazine, *Chicago Tribune,* and *Mobil Travel Guide;* five diamonds from AAA; Award of Excellence for its wine cellar from *Wine Spectator.*

Amitabul

Zone 1   North Side
3418 North Southport
(773) 472-4060

Korean/Vegetarian	
★★½	
Inexpensive	
Quality 80	Value B

Reservations:	Accepted any time for any number
When to go:	Weekdays after 3 P.M. are less crowded
Entree range:	$5.50–7.99
Payment:	AMEX, VISA, MC
Service rating:	★★★
Friendliness rating:	★★★★
Parking:	Street
Bar:	Wine and microbrew beer
Wine selection:	Small selection of 5-7 wines, including sake and nine-grain wine
Dress:	Casual
Disabled access:	Yes
Customers:	Diverse; no age gap, couples, singles and committed vegetarians
Lunch/Dinner:	Daily, 11 A.M.–9:30 P.M.

Atmosphere/setting: A contemporary, simple decor with wood and plants; beamed ceilings with lighting behind trellis work; clean design gives a purifying feeling; Buddhist meditative music.

House specialties: Mandoo can do (12 Korean-style egg rolls); entrees of Amitabul bi-bim-bop (various steamed vegetables and roots over steamed brown rice served with zesty plum sauce and spicy brown rice miso); Buddha bop (steamed brown rice with chestnuts, dates, red beans, and barley over various vegetables); Amitabul original, a vegan item served in a small or large portion (whole wheat pancakes with vegetables and white or brown rice); attractive jade maki, (rice rolls with avocado, cucumber and spinach); and a potent ginger tea, good iced.

Other recommendations: Real vegan egg roll (seems to be a misnomer, but these egg rolls are egg-and-dairy-free); Buddha's three luck dish (steamed zucchini, green beans, wild sesame leaves, and lotus roots with mild apple sauce served over steamed brown rice cakes); heavenly nirvana (flavorful salad with tofu, seaweed, vegetables, and sweet apple or apple pear).

Summary & comments: Amitabul in Korean terms means "awakening," which is appropriate for this type of spiritual, healthful, vegan vegetarian food. Some dishes are spicy, and others are a bit too bland, but they can be enlivened with the sauces on the table—hot or sweet.

ANN SATHER

Zone 1 North Side	Swedish/American (diner-style)
929 West Belmont Avenue, Lakeview	★★★
(773) 348-2378	Inexpensive
Zone 1 North Side	
5207 North Clark Street, Andersonville	Quality 83 Value B
(773) 271-6677	

Zone 1   North Side
5207 North Clark Street, Andersonville
(773) 271-6677

Zone 1   North Side
2665 North Clark Street, Lincoln Park
(773) 327-9522

Reservations:	Accepted for 6 or more
When to go:	Monday, Tuesday, and Wednesday
Entree range:	$7.95–11.95
Payment:	VISA, MC, AMEX
Service rating:	★★★★
Friendliness rating:	★★★★½
Parking:	Lot (Belmont); street (Lincoln Park); call for details (Andersonville)
Bar:	Full service, including Swedish beer and cocktails such as glögg and Simply Swedish (Absolut on the rocks)
Wine selection:	6 American choices at the reasonable price of $3 a glass or $12 a bottle
Dress:	Casual
Disabled access:	Yes (Lakeview and Lincoln Park); no (Andersonville)
Customers:	Neighborhood regulars, families, singles, seniors
Open:	Daily, 7 A.M.–10 P.M.; breakfast served all day; lunch/dinner starts at 11 A.M.; Lincoln Park location does not serve dinner

Atmosphere/setting: Hand-painted Scandinavian murals grace the walls. The original Lakeview location has six rooms on two levels. The third and newest Lincoln Park cafe is the tiniest. All the locations are homey and welcoming— you'd be secure in taking your mother or children there. Andersonville designates the downstairs a nonsmoking area on weekends, 9:30 A.M.–2 P.M.

House specialties: For dinner, Swedish sampler (roast duck with lingonberry glaze, meatballs, potato sausage, sauerkraut, and brown beans); broiled salmon with mustard dill sauce; Swedish meatballs. Lunch items include grilled chicken breast sandwich; burgers of several styles (avocado Swiss, blue cheese);

(continued)

veggie burger; and cold sandwiches: chef's market ham, roast turkey, or roasted beef tenderloin served on choice of bread (Swedish limpa, rye) with trimmings. A variety of enticing salads include shrimp and seafood, stuffed tomato, and citrus chicken. For breakfast, don't miss the signature large cinnamon rolls or the Swedish pancakes with lingonberries.

Other recommendations: For dinner, Swedish sirloin steak with onions; roast loin of pork with celery dressing and gravy; Swedish potato sausage; Lake Superior whitefish broiled with lemon and tartar sauce; hot peach cobbler with ice cream; Swedish spritzer. Lunch: vegetarian chili and daily homemade soup. Breakfast: Swedish waffles with the option of ice cream and strawberries.

Summary & comments: The only restaurant serving Swedish specialties at meals other than breakfast, and dinner items come in two sizes and prices, diner-style. Complete meals include a starter, an entree, two sides, and a dessert; light meals include a light portion entree and two sides. The menu prices appear to be yesterday's, so dining here is a great value today. This Swedish diner founded by Ann Sather in 1945 was bought by current owner Tom Tunney. Very comfortable for dining alone. Friendly, nurturing staffers welcome customers of any age—kids get complimentary kiddy cocktails and rainbow sherbet.

Honors/awards: Voted best breakfast in the Midwest, January 1994, by *CBS This Morning.*

Army & Lou's

Zone 7   South Side
422 East 75th Street
(773) 483-3100

	Southern
	★★★★
	Inexpensive/Moderate
	Quality 90 Value B

Reservations:	Accepted any time for any size group
When to go:	Weekdays after lunch rush
Entree range:	$6.95–22.95
Payment:	VISA, MC, AMEX; no checks
Service rating:	★★★★
Friendliness rating:	★★★★
Parking:	Lot next door
Bar:	Full service
Wine selection:	About 12 selections by the glass only; reasonably priced; mostly Californian
Dress:	Casual
Disabled access:	Yes
Customers:	From all over the area; many out-of-state visitors
Open:	Wednesday–Monday, 9 A.M.–10 P.M.

Atmosphere/setting: Bright, cheerful, and comfortable with light-colored sponged walls and a rotating art exhibit from the gallery across the street featuring African and Haitian art. Tablecloths and flowers. Nonsmoking dining room.

House specialties: Fresh farm-raised catfish steaks and catfish fillet; half a fried chicken (juicy, not greasy); award-winning seafood gumbo; U.S. prime kosher short ribs of beef jardinière; meaty baby-back ribs with zesty barbecue sauce.

Other recommendations: Chicken gumbo; New England clam chowder; fried jumbo oysters; fried jumbo shrimp; cornbread stuffing; peach cobbler; sweet potato pie.

Summary & comments: This popular South Side restaurant is celebrating its 55TH anniversary in 2000. Original recipes are used but have been adjusted to be lower in sodium and fat. The food is excellent, the servers charming and friendly, and the place comfortable, so it's no wonder that the regulars keep returning. The place swells on Sunday after church, and politicians and community groups keep the private room busy. Children's menu available.

ARUN'S

Zone 1   North Side
4156 North Kedzie Avenue
(773) 539-1909

Thai
★★★★½
Moderate/Expensive
Quality 95   Value C

Reservations:	Required
When to go:	Dinner
Entree range:	$13.95–23.95
Payment:	Major credit cards
Service rating:	★★★★★
Friendliness rating:	★★★★½
Parking:	Street
Bar:	Full service, including Thai and Japanese beers
Wine selection:	International—about 2 dozen Austrian, French, Italian, and Californian, $18–46; by the glass, $5
Dress:	Casual; mostly chic and business attire
Disabled access:	Yes
Customers:	Local and out-of-town, professionals, couples
Dinner:	Tuesday–Thursday, 5–9 P.M.; Friday and Saturday, 5–10 P.M.; Sunday, 5–9 P.M.

Atmosphere/setting: Colorful exterior. Beautifully appointed, multi-level interior with a small, museum-like front alcove devoted to antiques and exquisite art, includign a new mural in the foyer. The narrow upper dining area has open windows with a view into the lower dining room. Colorful authentic art and other Thai artifacts adorn the intimate rooms. The kitchen has recently been enlarged. The owner's brother, an artist/architect, did much of the work, and the owner's paintings decorate the rest rooms.

House specialties: Khao kriab (steamed rice dumplings filled with shrimp, chicken, chili, shallot, and a tangy sweet-sour vinaigrette); picturesque golden baskets (flower-shaped, bite-sized pastries filled with a mixture of shrimp, chicken, sweet corn, and shiitake mushrooms, garnished with intricately carved vegetable baskets); three-flavored red snapper (crisply fried whole fish with traditional Bangkok-style three-flavored tamarind sauce: spicy, sweet, and sour).

Other recommendations: Siamese dumplings (delicate rice dumplings with minced shrimp, chicken, sweet daikon turnips, peanuts, chopped chiles, cilantro, and lettuce); chicken coconut soup; summer salad (seasonal) with mint, sprouts, and fish cake slices; gingery veal with lemongrass and miso (no veal in Thai history—the owner created this); the popular roast duck with French fried chutney

(continued)

in raspberry-peach sauce, with scallion pancake rolls; meefun delight (soft-fried noodles with shrimp, chicken, and scallion). Desserts are delightful: seven-layer rice custard (alternating colors of white, pink, and pale green) steamed from a mixture of rice flour and coconut milk; traditional Thai dessert platter, with daily specials and fruit sorbets. End with a wonderful elixir of lemongrass, water, and tiny fruit balls, which is purifying and serves as a digestive.

Summary & comments: This magnificently decorated restaurant serves appropriately exquisite food. Chef-owner Arun Sampanthavivat has refined traditional Thai cuisine and elevated Thai cooking to a new fine dining plateau. The menu reveals the use of chiles, but the food doesn't cause burns and tears if you're cautious about eating the peppers. The flavor nuances are more herbal, spicy, sweet, and sour. Arun loves to carve the intricate vegetable baskets that garnish plates, and spends about two hours daily on this task. To be able to spend more time managing the business, he's appointed five chefs, including his brother Akanit and husband-wife team Art and Saiyud Lee, to run the kitchen. The higher prices here are understandable once you taste the results of this labor-intensive cuisine.

Honors/awards: Four stars from *Mobil Travel Guide,* 1997; chef was named Best Chef in the Midwest by the James Beard Foundation, 1997; AAA four stars for five consecutive years

BACINO'S TRATTORIA

	Italian/American
Zone 8 Southern Suburbs	★★★
1504 North Naper Boulevard,	Inexpensive/Moderate
Tower Crossing Shopping Center,	
Naperville	Quality 84 Value B
(630) 505-0600	

Reservations:	Friday and Saturday for parties of 6 or more
When to go:	Weekends and evenings
Entree range:	$7.50–14.95 or market prices
Payment:	Major credit cards
Service rating:	★★★½
Friendliness rating:	★★★★
Parking:	Mall parking lot
Bar:	Full service
Wine selection:	Extensive; from $4.25 a glass and $14 a bottle
Dress:	Casual
Disabled access:	Yes, except for upper level and roof deck
Customers:	Professionals and families; mostly local
Lunch:	Monday–Friday, 11 A.M.–4 P.M., pasta bar ($7.95) 11 A.M.–2 P.M.; Saturday, noon–4 P.M.
Dinner:	Monday–Thursday, 4–10 P.M.; Friday and Saturday, 4 P.M.–midnight; Sunday, 3–10 P.M.

Atmosphere/setting: Painted pillars; whimsical geometric shapes; unique fireplace with painted marble tiles; hand-painted walls.

House specialties: Gorgonzola salad with watercress; bruschetta; cavatappi con pollo e spinaci (corkscrew pasta with chicken and spinach Alfredo); Heart Healthy spinach pizza; tiramisu; semifreddo (light almond semifrozen cream).

Other recommendations: Artichoke hearts baked with mascarpone; grilled portobellos; grilled calamari; pollo e verdure gourmet pizza (grilled chicken, mushrooms, etc.); pasta trio of angel hair with marinara, fettuccine with Parmesan cream sauce, and cavatappi with pesto; garganelli al granchio e rucola (tube-shaped egg pasta, crab meat, shrimp); profiteroles filled with vanilla ice cream.

Entertainment & amenities: Various bands play Thursday; jazz on Saturday.

Summary & comments: Owners Linda and Dan Bacin created this trattoria in Naperville to offer diners a greater variety of chef's selections, as well as America's First Heart Healthy pizza. The Roof Top Cafe is open during warmer months with its own menu and bar; it features an herb garden and a huge mural of classic buildings and scenes of Italy. A popular all-you-can-eat lunch pasta bar features 4 pastas, 3–4 sauces, and about 20 different ingredients cooked to order.

Bando

	Korean
Zone 1 North Side	★★★
2200 West Lawrence Avenue	Inexpensive/Moderate
(773) 728-7400	Quality 83 Value C

Reservations:	Accepted
When to go:	Any time
Entree range:	$9.95–12.95
Payment:	All major credit cards accepted
Service rating:	★★★
Friendliness rating:	★★½
Parking:	Free indoor parking; outdoor parking available
Bar:	Full service
Wine selection:	American; affordable
Dress:	Casual; some people dress up for special occasions
Disabled access:	Yes
Customers:	Local ethnic and American
Open:	Daily, 11 A.M.–10 P.M.

Atmosphere/setting: Spacious, splashy, split-level dining room with bottom-vented, built-in grills at the tables.

House specialties: Bulgoki (barbecue beef), gahl-bee (barbecue-beef short ribs), dahk bulgoki (sliced, boneless barbecue chicken), and spicy barbecue pork, all marinated, with grilled onions and mushrooms; kim chee; pan-fried, egg-battered oysters and butterfly shrimp.

Other recommendations: Spicy seafood casserole with noodles; catfish and red snapper, each prepared two ways; buckwheat noodles with sliced beef, cucumber, and a mild sauce.

Entertainment & amenities: Grilling your own dinner at your table.

Summary & comments: This Korean restaurant with large banquet facilities is popular with the Korean community. At times, there seems to be a language problem: some staffers speak and understand minimal English. The food is mainly authentic, although certain dishes are milder for American tastes. Japanese tempura and some Chinese-influenced dishes are on the menu too. Included with dinners are soup, rice, and numerous sides, Korean-style. Fresh fruit and ginseng tea make a nice finish.

Bella Vista

Zone 1   North Side
1001 West Belmont Avenue
(773) 404-0111

New Italian
★★★½
Inexpensive/Moderate

Quality 86   Value C

Reservations:	Recommended
When to go:	Weeknights
Entree range:	$8–18
Payment:	All major credit cards
Service rating:	★★★★
Friendliness rating:	★★★★
Parking:	Valet, $5
Bar:	Full service, a good beer list
Wine selection:	300 international, $19–150; substantial Italian, $4.25–9.75 a glass; reserve list on main list
Dress:	Casual
Disabled access:	Yes
Customers:	Professionals, couples, families with children
Lunch:	Monday–Saturday, 11:30 A.M.–5 P.M.; pasta bar ($7.95), 11:30 A.M.–2:30 P.M.
Dinner:	Monday–Thursday, 5–10 P.M.; Friday and Saturday, 5 P.M.– midnight; Sunday, 4–9 P.M.

Atmosphere/setting: The name "beautiful view" says it well—a stunning multilevel, colorful interior and elegant, award-winning architecture in the former Belmont Trust and Savings Bank (1929). Exquisite hand-painted walls, walk-through wine cellar, 30-foot ceiling.

House specialties: Antipasto del giorno with seasonal oak-roasted vegetables, seafood salad, and shrimp risotto; gourmet wood-fire pizzas; linguine alla Putanesca; free-form lamb and potato torta (grilled loin layered with potato "sheets").

Other recommendations: Oak-roasted calamari with purple potatoes and wilted arugula; Gorgonzola salad with endive, watercress, and red wine vinaigrette.

Entertainment & amenities: Architectural tours of the restaurant. Special dinners held around winemakers and menus from films such as *Big Night*.

Summary & comments: The architecture and interior design are a feast for the eyes, and the dishes are colorful and intricately presented. The Bella Vista Cafe, a more casual bar room, serves the same menu as the dining room. Owners Dan and Linda Bacin added the pasta bar at lunch, based on its success at their Bacino Trattoria (see Summary & comments, page 96).

Ben Pao, Chinese Restaurant & Satay Bar

	Chinese
	★★★½
Zone 3 Near North	Inexpensive/Moderate
52 West Illinois	
(312) 222-1888	Quality 90 Value B

Reservations: Recommended, especially 7:30–9 P.M.
When to go: Any time; before 7 P.M. for dinner
Entree range: $7.95–14.95
Payment: Major credit cards
Service rating: ★★★★½
Friendliness rating: ★★★★½
Parking: Valet, $5
Bar: Full service; microbrewed and Asian beers
Wine selection: About 25 selections; 15 by the glass; affordable;
                        Japanese Kinsen plum wine; two chilled sakes
Dress: Casual
Disabled access: Yes
Customers: Professionals, tourists, suburbanites, locals
Lunch: Monday–Friday, 11:30 A.M.–2 P.M.
Dinner: Monday–Thursday, 5–10 P.M.; Friday and Saturday,
                        5–11 P.M.; Sunday, 4–9 P.M.

Atmosphere/setting: Ben Pao's exquisite interior was designed with harmony and balance in accordance with traditional Feng Shui philosophy. The stunning entryway is flanked by two granite columns with water rippling down.

House specialties: Satays, including tamarind chicken, five-spice shrimp, ginger portobello, lamb, vegetable, and Mongolian beef. Black-peppered scallops; good luck shrimp dumplings; Hong Kong spicy eggplant; Teh's curried noodles; soongs (wok-seared fillings such as chicken or vegetables); tea-smoked half duck; Tony's amazing chicken; pan-fried wrinkled string beans. Mango-vanilla swirl cheesecake; triple chocolate treasure; coconut tapioca custard.

Other recommendations: Orange-peel beef; Shanghai peanut noodles; "fiery" Szechuan noodles; "crispy garlic tofu." Pineapple-ginger float; chocolate spring rolls.

Entertainment & amenities: Outdoor cafe; Autumn Moon Festival; Chinese New Year celebration.

Summary & comments: Lettuce Entertain You Enterprises' first venture into Chinese restaurants, Ben Pao is unique in Chicago for its harmonious mix of the traditional and the adventurous. It features Chicago's first satay bar; these grilled-to-order skewers are great as an appetizer or a light bite. Carryout and delivery available.

THE BERGHOFF

Zone 4 The Loop	German/American
17 West Adams Street	★★★½
(312) 427-3170	Inexpensive
	Quality 88 Value B

Reservations:	Recommended for 5 or more
When to go:	Avoid lunch and early dinner if you're in a rush
Entree range:	Lunch, $8–12; dinner, $9–17
Payment:	VISA, MC, AMEX
Service rating:	★★★½
Friendliness rating:	★★★★
Parking:	Discount in nearby garages after 4 P.M.
Bar:	Full service; The Berghoff's own regular and dark beer
Wine selection:	Extensive; inexpensive house wines
Dress:	Summer, casual; winter, dressier
Disabled access:	Yes, including rest rooms
Customers:	Locals, including a loyal German clientele; some tourists
Lunch/Dinner:	Monday–Thursday, 11 A.M.–9 P.M.; Friday, 11 A.M.–9:30 P.M.; Saturday, 11 A.M.–10 P.M.

Atmosphere/setting: Turn-of-the-century building; old paintings; lots of wood in the spacious dining room. Rathskeller downstairs serves lunch.

House specialties: Good traditional German specialties: sauerbraten and Wiener Schnitzel; seafood such as fillet of sole. Daily specials include some German items, such as Schlachtplatte (bratwurst, "Kasseler Rippchen," and smoked Thuringer with kraut). Creamed herring and chilled smoked salmon are two nice appetizers.

Other recommendations: Seafood de Jonghe; veal medallions; chicken schnitzel; broiled swordfish steak; Black Forest torte.

Summary & comments: The menu proudly states, "family operated since 1898," when Herman Joseph Berghoff opened his cafe as a showcase for his celebrated Dortmunder-style beer. The Berghoff, which turned 100 in April 1998, is a Chicago landmark because of the good-quality food, fine Berghoff beer and bourbon, low prices, old-world atmosphere, and efficient service. The management has modernized the menu to satisfy current desires for lighter fare. The delicious, textured bread is made from the brewery side products (hops, etc.), and loaves are sold to carry home. This place is a great success story, serving 2,000 a day in the street-level dining room and downstairs for lunch. Private parties and catering are available.

BICE RISTORANTE

Zone 3   Near North
158 East Ontario Street
(312) 664-1474

Italian
★★★½
Moderate/Expensive
Quality 87   Value D

Reservations:	Required on weekends
When to go:	Wednesday, Thursday, and Sunday
Entree range:	$14–26
Payment:	All major credit cards except D
Service rating:	★★★½
Friendliness rating:	★★★
Parking:	Valet
Bar:	Full service
Wine selection:	On the costly end; 110 selections; $25–300 a bottle; 8 by the glass, exclusively Italian and Californian cabernet sauvignon, $10
Dress:	Moderately casual to dressy; shorts discouraged
Disabled access:	Wheelchair; no rest room access
Customers:	Professionals, Italians; diverse and sophisticated
Lunch:	Monday–Saturday, 11:30 A.M.–5:30 P.M.
Dinner:	Monday–Thursday, 5:30–10:30 P.M.; Friday and Saturday, 5:30–11:30 P.M.; Sunday, 5:30–10 P.M.

Atmosphere/setting: Upscale, contemporary Italian; well-lit, fun, and lively. Bar area in front opens onto sidewalk. Recently, the Bice Grill opened adjacent to Bice. It's more casual.

House specialties: Menu changes daily. Fresh pastas; tuna carpaccio (appetizer); risotto fruitti di mare; panesotti stuffed with wild game; orange cake glazed with bittersweet chocolate.

Other recommendations: Veal Milanese; tiramisu; ice creams and sorbets. In the Bice Grill, pizza bianca (Parma ham and arugula); lasagna giardiniera (fresh vegetables); Toscano sandwich (on focaccia with grilled sausages); grilled Italian sausage.

Summary & comments: A chic place with prices to match, but the steady crowds here don't seem to care. It's a gathering spot for many of the Italian foodies. Excellent, *very* Italian food and comprehensive menu, but pricey, even for a pasta dish. Bice Grill is a welcome addition, since it offers an alternative: casual dining with lighter fare at lower prices. Service is professional and attentive at both places.

Big Bowl Cafe

Zone 3 Near North	Pan-Asian
159-½ West Erie Street	★★★
(312) 787-8297	Inexpensive
Zone 3 Near North	
6 East Cedar	Quality 84 Value B
(312) 640-8888	

Reservations:	Recommended for 5 or more
When to go:	Avoid peak lunch and dinner hours
Entree range:	$7.25–9.95
Payment:	All major credit cards
Service rating:	★★★½
Friendliness rating:	★★★★
Parking:	Valet; street; nearby lots
Bar:	*Erie:* beer, wine, and selected mixed drinks; *Cedar:* full service, good selection
Wine selection:	Changes seasonally; mostly Californian; by glass or bottle; modestly priced
Dress:	Casual
Disabled access:	Yes
Customers:	Locals, professionals, couples
Lunch/Dinner:	*Erie:* Monday–Thursday, 11:30 A.M.–10 P.M.; Friday and Saturday, 11:30 A.M.–11 P.M.; Sunday, 5–9 P.M.; *Cedar:* Sunday–Thursday, 11:30 A.M.–10 P.M.; Friday and Saturday, 11:30 A.M.–11 P.M.

Atmosphere/setting: Original, expanded Erie location has a casual interior and a sidewalk cafe (weather permitting). Cedar location features soft green and yellow accents, a modern bar, an open kitchen, and an enclosed sidewalk cafe.

House specialties: Pan-Asian creations in bowls; pot stickers; Thai-herb calamari; eight-vegetable stir-fry; Burmese curry shrimp; Asian wraps; Vietnamese noodle soup (pho); Chinese chicken salad with plum dressing and wontons; macadamia tart with coconut ice cream; ginger spice cake with crème fraîche.

Other recommendations: Indonesian satay with Thai cucumber salad; Mindful Vegetable spring roll (baked); noodle dishes; ice creams and sorbets; traditional iced tea and many special teas.

Summary & comments: Big Bowl's food is lively in Asian flavors and textures, and much of it is soothing and comforting. Leftovers can be carried out in "porta-bowls." One of the best restaurants of this genre and a top value.

Big Shoulders

Zone 1   North Side
Chicago Historical Society,
   1601 North Clark Street
(312) 587-7766 or 587-7342

American
★★★
Inexpensive

Quality 82   Value B

Reservations:	Recommended (especially for Sunday brunch)
When to go:	Lunch or Sunday brunch
Entree range:	Lunch, $5–10; no dinner
Payment:	VISA, MC, AMEX
Service rating:	★★★½
Friendliness rating:	★★★½
Parking:	Street or metered lot in park nearby
Bar:	Full service
Wine selection:	American
Dress:	Casual
Disabled access:	Yes
Customers:	Locals and visitors to the Chicago Historical Society
Brunch:	Sunday, 10:30 A.M.–3 P.M.
Lunch:	Daily, 11 A.M.–3 P.M.

Atmosphere/setting: The restaurant is a semicircle enclosed in glass and resembles a greenhouse. It features murals, a magnificent terra-cotta arch (from the bank at the Union Exchange), and high ceilings. Windows overlook a lovely garden.

House specialties: Grilled chicken Caesar salad; daily soups; Sheboygan-style bratwurst. Signature whole-wheat millet bread and jalapeño cornbread come with selections.

Other recommendations: Wild rice cakes with wild mushroom sauce; sirloin salad with asparagus, pistachios, chèvre, and sherry-mustard vinaigrette; apple-streusel pie à la mode.

Summary & comments: Named for Carl Sandburg's description of the city in his poem, "Chicago," this lovely restaurant has a special intellectual style befitting the Chicago Historical Society and what it represents. Owner Jerome F. Kliejunas has long been a proponent of additive-free, fresh, natural ingredients and smoke-free dining and states on his menus, "If the selection seems limited, it's because I believe one of the keys to maintaining my standards is to try to do a few things well." Dishes are attractively presented and freshly prepared with harmonious flavors. The short menu is appropriate for a place that no longer serves dinner. Catering is available for business meetings of 30 to weddings of 300.

Biggs

Zone 3   Near North
1150 North Dearborn Street
(312) 787-0900

Classic/Contemporary Continental	
★★★★	
Moderate	
Quality 90	Value C

Reservations:	Required
When to go:	Dinner
Entree range:	$17.95–32.95
Payment:	All major credit cards
Service rating:	★★★½
Friendliness rating:	★★★★
Parking:	Valet, $6; street and nearby lot parking
Bar:	Full service
Wine selection:	Extensive; 250 international; American, European, New Zealand, Australian, and Chilean, $19–120; 15 by the glass; reserve list of famous and first-growth Bordeaux
Dress:	Casual elegance
Disabled access:	No ramp; stairs to restaurant and rest room
Customers:	Professionals (lunch), couples (weekends)
Dinner:	Sunday–Thursday, 5–10 P.M.; Friday and Saturday, 5 P.M.–11 P.M. Bars: every day, 5 P.M.–2 A.M.

Atmosphere/setting: Exquisite, romantic setting in a Victorian mansion (built in 1874). Caviar and Martini Bar, Cigar and Cognac Bar, and outdoor cafe.

House specialties: Appetizers: Smoked Norwegian salmon with caviar dressing; escargot bourguignonne; lobster cocktail with cognac tarragon dressing; lobster bisque; Biggs salad. Entrees: sautéed whole Dover sole mèuniere; pheasant breast lightly breaded, sautéed, grilled fresh pineapple and juniper berry sauce; classic beef tenderloin Wellington, truffle sauce; roasted domestic rack of lamb, natural rosemary jus. Dessert: Biggs cigar dessert.

Other recommendations: Appetizers: grilled eggplant with goat cheese; lobster bisque; crêpes royale of lobster, bay scallops, mushrooms, and shrimp with glazed champagne sauce. Entrees: sautéed duck breast with grilled sweet potato and green peppercorn sauce; grilled double breast of chicken with light lemon butter. Desserts: white chocolate pyramid; tower of chocolate power; Bavarian cheesecake; trifle; and fresh berries sabayon. Caviar and Martini Bar serves caviar and smoked salmon. Cigar and Cognac Bar and the outdoor cafe also serve a lighter menu.

(continued)

Biggs *(continued)*

Summary & comments: The second owner of this landmark mansion was Joseph Biggs, who managed his catering business from the coach house and catered the most social parties of the day. Today, Biggs carries on the tradition and caters parties for up to 175 people. The food has maintained a high quality over the years, evolving from modern continental to classic/creative French, to a blend of the two through executive chef Robert Walsh's creative culinary touches.

Honors/awards: Five-Diamond Award, AAA.

Bistro 110

Zone 3   Near North
110 East Pearson Street
(312) 266-3110

French Bistro
★★★½
Moderate

Quality 86   Value C

Reservations:	Recommended
When to go:	Any time
Entree range:	$10–26
Payment:	All major credit cards
Service rating:	★★★½
Friendliness rating:	★★★★½
Parking:	Valet
Bar:	Full service
Wine selection:	Extensive French and domestic
Dress:	Casual
Disabled access:	Yes
Customers:	Local, professionals, tourist, shoppers, hip urbanites
Brunch:	Outdoor seating for Sunday jazz brunch, 11 A.M.–4 P.M.
Lunch/Dinner:	Monday–Thursday, 11:30 A.M.–11 P.M.; Friday and Saturday, 11:30 A.M.–midnight; Sunday, 11:30 A.M.–10 P.M.

Atmosphere/setting: Sidewalk cafe is great in summer; attractive bar area with tables near the window for view of the Water Tower; colorful murals.

House specialties: Oven-roasted whole garlic served with fresh crusty French bread; wood-roasted chicken, snapper, and other fish specials usually served with an array of roasted vegetables; onion soup; creative pastas.

Other recommendations: Clafoutis "tutti frutti" berries; chocolate mousse; crème brûlée.

Entertainment & amenities: Sunday New Orleans–style à la carte jazz brunch featuring the Grady Johnson Jazz Trio. Occasional French promotions with exchange chefs from France.

Summary & comments: Very alive, energetic bistro that is like a scene out of Paris. One of the loveliest views of the historic Water Tower. The chef, Dominique Toligne, oversees a menu with an emphasis on the bistro classics. The food is well-prepared and especially flavorful and healthful from the wood oven. Pastries for savory and sweet tarts are flaky and very French in nature. This place can reach high decibels on a bustling night.

BISTRO BANLIEUE

Zone 8 Southern Suburbs	French Bistro
44 Yorktown Convenience Center, Lombard	★★★★
	Inexpensive/Moderate
(630) 629-6560	Quality 93 Value B

Reservations:	Recommended, especially on weekends
When to go:	Any time
Entree range:	$10.95–20.95
Payment:	D, DC, MC, VISA
Service rating:	★★★★
Friendliness rating:	★★★★
Parking:	Mall lot
Bar:	Full-service
Wine selection:	Mostly French and American; from $18 a bottle
Dress:	Chic casual
Disabled access:	Partial accessibility; call first
Customers:	Local suburbanites, professionals, couples
Lunch:	Monday–Friday, 11:30 A.M.–4:30 P.M.; dinner specials at 4:30 P.M.
Dinner:	Monday–Thursday, last seating, 9 P.M., and Friday, 10 P.M.; Saturday, 5–10 P.M.; Sunday, 4–9 P.M.

Atmosphere/setting: Charming lace curtains, floral wall border murals, and light-hearted Parisian posters. A black-and-white tile floor and white paper over tablecloths give an appropriate bistro feel.

House specialties: Smoked salmon, goat cheese, and leek tart served warm, with two colorful sauces: an excellent tomato-basil blend and a tart lemon beurre blanc. Soupe a l'Oignon Gratinée (quintessential French onion soup); coquilles Saint-Jacques au poivron rouge. Steak pommes frites; ragôut d'Agneau; cassoulet. "Selection du jour" menu at both lunch and dinner. Desserts: crème brûlée, apple tarte Tatin, and bittersweet chocolate mousse with pistachio crème anglaise.

Other recommendations: Grilled duck breast and braised leg with blueberry sauce; ratatouille in puff pastry with fresh mozzarella; duck liver pâté, onion marmalade; pear, Roquefort, mixed greens; white chocolate mousse, raspberry sauce.

Summary & comments: When Bistro Banlieue opened in 1989, it was rare to find good French food in a suburban strip mall. But one visit to this charming place in Lombard convinced the skeptical gourmets. The split-level dining room is smoke-free. Thoughtfully, the menu offers both "entrees et petites entrees."

Honors/awards: Much media attention, including *Wine Spectator* "Award of Excellent," 1995, '96, '97. WBBM News Radio 78, Sherman Kaplan's rating 19.5 out of 20.

Blackhawk Lodge

Zone 3 Near North	New American
41 East Superior Street	★★★
(312) 280-4080	Moderate
	Quality 82 Value C

Reservations:	Recommended
When to go:	Any time
Entree range:	Lunch, $7.95–14.95; dinner, $12.95–23.95
Payment:	All major credit cards
Service rating:	★★★★
Friendliness rating:	★★★½
Parking:	Valet in the evenings; self-park garage nearby on Wabash south of Superior, $5 with validation
Bar:	Full service
Wine selection:	Nice American selection with most from California; some from New Mexico, Texas, Oregon, Washington, Virginia, and even Utah, $18–65 per bottle; several by the glass.
Dress:	Casual; some business and dressy
Disabled access:	Yes
Customers:	Neighborhood locals, tourists, shoppers; families
Brunch:	Sunday, 11:30 A.M.–3 P.M.
Lunch:	Monday–Friday, 11:30 A.M.–3 P.M.
Dinner:	Monday–Thursday, 5 P.M.–10 P.M.; Saturday, 5–11 P.M. (outdoor seating available)

Atmosphere/setting: Rustic yet gracious setting resembles a family vacation home. Warm and welcoming environment designed by Marve Cooper in collaboration with owners Doug Roth and Larry and Mark Levy of Levy Restaurants. The four sections of the restaurant include the entry and bar with dining seats, the main dining room (smoke-free), the porch, and the gazebo (with 50 outdoor seats). Indoor decor includes oak floors, knotty pine paneling, timber walls, wicker furniture, tapestries, and textured fabrics. Decorative appointments feature family photos and Audubon prints.

House specialties: Award-winning ribs, such as hickory-smoked Wichita baby back ribs with Blackhawk barbecue sauce; fabulous signature cheddar cheese grits with tasso ham; pureed vegetable soup; house-smoked trout Caesar salad with salmon caviar; oak-fired Arkansas half chicken over sweet potato hash

(continued)

with garlic-thyme jus. Desserts: banana pudding with caramel sauce; chocolate walnut tart with Wild Turkey Bourbon crème anglaise.

Other recommendations: Crabcakes; goat cheese soufflé; roasted rack of lamb with tomato-ancho chili sauce, potato and onion casserole; organic vegetable platter (grilled, braised, and roasted) with savory rice and quinoa. Cappuccino ice-cream pie.

Entertainment & amenities: Blue grass band at Sunday brunch. Occasional promotions, such as a weeklong special menu featuring the cuisine of Chef Mark Miller's Coyote Cafe in Santa Fe.

Summary & comments: This place suggests an era when life was easygoing and basic values centered around family and honesty. The back-to-basics cuisine with regional influences focuses on simple preparations with creative touches. New executive chef is Barry Rosenstein, who carries on the tradition here.

Honors/awards: *Chicago* magazine's 1992 Critic's Choice Award; Ribs voted second best in Chicago by the *Chicago Tribune.*

Blind Faith Cafe

	Vegetarian
	★★★
	Inexpensive
	Quality 82 Value B

Zone 11   Northern Suburbs
525 Dempster Street, Evanston
(847) 328-6875
Zone 1   North Side
3300 North Lincoln Avenue
(773) 871-3820

Reservations:	Accepted weekdays only for 4 or more
When to go:	Avoid peak mealtimes
Entree range:	$6.50–8.95
Payment:	VISA, MC, AMEX
Service rating:	★★★
Friendliness rating:	★★★★
Parking:	Street (metered)
Bar:	Wine and beer; juice bar
Wine selection:	Organic house wines, $17 average a bottle, $4 a glass
Dress:	Casual
Disabled access:	Yes
Customers:	Students and professors; the health-conscious
Open:	Monday–Saturday, 8 A.M–10 P.M.; Sunday, 8 A.M –9 P.M.

Atmosphere/setting: This bright, airy restaurant is divided into the casual dining room and the self-serve area. There's also an adjacent bakery. Colorful handmade quilts adorn the walls.

House specialties: Breakfast: chilaquiles, eggs, or sautéed tofu; homemade granola. Lunch/dinner: broccoli-shoyu-soba stir-fry; macrobiotic plate; fruit smoothie. The new Chicago location has more creative, exciting food.

Other recommendations: Breakfast: banana-almond pancakes; cinnamon-raisin French toast. Lunch/dinner: spicy seitan fajitas; black bean burrito; peanut butter–tofu–banana shake.

Summary & comments: This is one of Chicago's best-known and respected vegetarian restaurants. All the dishes are prepared with fresh, unprocessed, and mostly organic ingredients; dairy-free and low-fat alternatives are also available. You can take home baked goods such as potato-dill bread or tofu no-cheesecake, as well as traditional fare such as chunky chocolate cookies.

Blue Mesa

Zone 1 North Side	Southwestern
1729 North Halsted Street	★★★★
(312) 944-5990	Inexpensive/Moderate
	Quality 89 Value B

Reservations:	Recommended
When to go:	Any time
Entree range:	$8–13
Payment:	V, MC, AMEX, D, DC
Service rating:	★★★½
Friendliness rating:	★★★★½
Parking:	Valet, $4
Bar:	Full service
Wine selection:	Limited Spanish and American
Dress:	Casual
Disabled access:	Yes
Customers:	Mixed
Brunch:	Sunday, 11 A.M.–3 P.M.
Lunch:	Tuesday–Friday, 11:30 A.M.–2 P.M.; Saturday, 11:30 A.M.–4 P.M.; Monday, closed
Dinner:	Tuesday–Saturday, 5–10:30 P.M.; Sunday, 4–10 P.M.; Monday, closed

Atmosphere/setting: Authentic adobe restaurant with kiva fireplaces and large rounded rooms with dried chiles and native artwork. Outdoor patio.

House specialties: Enchilada del mar, a blend of shrimp, scallops, fish, corn, mushrooms, and leeks in a lobster-chipotle sauce, layered between two blue corn tortillas; blue corn tamales; chicken and steak fajitas. Sopaipillas are served with most entrees. Desserts include white chocolate quesadilla (white chocolate mousse served in a crispy cinnamon tortilla with honey-raspberry sauce) and adobe pie (coffee and chocolate Häagen-Dazs layered with fudge on an Oreo crust).

Other recommendations: Taste of Santa Fe appetizer; the Grande Platter.

Summary & comments: Blue Mesa is devoted to the unique cuisine of New Mexico, with some creative license. The cooking and atmosphere pay tribute to Santa Fe culture, which is an exciting blend of Indian and Spanish traditions. The Marienthal brothers built this gem after researching it carefully. Enjoy a drink at the lovely bar and then move to the dining room for a meal that gives a taste of historical Santa Fe right in Chicago.

Bob Chinn's Crab House

	Seafood
	★★★
	Moderate
	Quality 82 Value B

Zone 10   Northwest Suburbs
393 South Milwaukee Avenue,
    Wheeling
(847) 520-3633

Reservations:	Only for 6 or more; number system used
When to go:	Any day before 6 P.M. or after 9 P.M.
Entree range:	$9.95–34.95
Payment:	All major credit cards
Service rating:	★★★
Friendliness rating:	★★★
Parking:	Free valet
Bar:	Full service
Wine selection:	Wide range of Californian, (approximately 40)
Dress:	Casual
Disabled access:	Yes
Customers:	International, couples, families, professionals
Lunch:	Monday–Friday, 11 A.M.–2:30 P.M.; Saturday, noon–3 P.M.
Dinner:	Monday–Thursday, 4:30–10:30 P.M.; Friday, 4:30–11:30 P.M.; Saturday, 3–11:30 P.M.; Sunday, 3–10 P.M.

Atmosphere/setting: Similar to an old-fashioned crab house, except more vast and bustling. Very casual, no-frills, 650-seat eatery. Walls are adorned with memorabilia, kudos, and air-freight receipts as proof of the freshness of the supplies. Sinks are available for rinsing your hands.

House specialties: Alaskan Dungeness crab; raw bar; Kona crab steamed with garlic; variety of fresh fish.

Other recommendations: Beer-batter fried-fish sampler with dipping sauces; six-way fish special; aged steak dishes (e.g., choice center-cut strip steak).

Summary & comments: Early raw bar special offered daily is a great value and a nice appetizer while you wait for a table. Helpful, efficient staff offers quick service and instruction on how to tackle a Dungeness crab. This amazingly high-volume place (serving an average of 2,500 people a day!) maintains its high quality and fair pricing. Owner Bob Chinn and his wife, Marilyn, run this establishment with marketing savvy. Although not a relaxed environment, it's worth it for the good selection of simply prepared seafood.

Honors/awards: Silver Platter Award; Restaurant and Institutions 1993 Top Ten Independents award (serving 1,200,000 per year).

114

Brasserie Jo

Zone 3   Near North
59 West Hubbard Street
(312) 595-0800

Alsatian French	
★★★★	
Inexpensive/Moderate	
Quality 92 Value B	

Reservations:	Accepted
When to go:	Avoid peak meal times if you have no reservation
Entree range:	$10–18
Payment:	All major credit cards
Service rating:	★★★★½
Friendliness rating:	★★★½
Parking:	Valet
Bar:	Full service, including Hopla (slang in French for "fun"), an Alsatian beer made exclusively for the restaurant by Baderbrau Brewery
Wine selection:	Extensive, moderately priced regional French wine list, including some fine Alsatian selections
Dress:	Casual
Disabled access:	Yes
Customers:	Professionals, international, tourists, couples
Lunch:	Monday–Friday, 11:30 A.M.–4 P.M.
Dinner:	Monday–Thursday, 5–10:30 P.M.; Friday and Saturday, 5–11:30 P.M.; Sunday, 4–10 P.M.

Atmosphere/setting: Parisian Sam Lopata has created an authentic, comfortable brasserie with a 1940s look: marble, large mirrors, rich cherry wood, French furniture, and a custom-designed chandelier. For an exotic feel, there is also a 25-foot, glass-enclosed wintergarden with palm trees and wicker furniture.

House specialties: Onion soup gratinée in crock; croques monsieur with mesclun (baby lettuce mix) and frites (french fries); warm pretzel baguette with smoked chicken, Brie, and mesclun; Alsace cheesy sausage salad; crêpes with spinach, baked ham, blue cheese, mushrooms, and cheese; fish du jour; pâté en croute Strasbourgeoise; house salad Brasserie Jo; Brasserie steak with pommes frites; onion tart Uncle Hansi; mussels in white wine; steak tartare with pommes frites; escalope of salmon with lentils.

Other recommendations: Cod brandade; chicken ravioli; mussels in parchment; Les Plats du Jour de Jo (such as couscous, beef Wellington, duck a l'orange, or sautéed rabbit in mustard sauce); fruit tarts; homemade ice creams.

(continued)

Summary & comments: Master chef-owner Jean Joho, well known for his upscale Everest (see page 358), is from France's Alsace region, and he injects his heritage into this brasserie. Legend has it that Alsatians introduced to Paris the concept of the "brasserie," literally "brewery," but also a place for people to relax, socialize, dine, and drink into the wee hours. Thanks to Joho's dedication to authenticity and fresh ingredients, Chicagoans now have their own real brasserie, too. Brasserie Jo serves traditionally hearty food and drink. A unique touch that reflects Joho's culinary breadth is Les Plats du Jour, entree specials that change daily; many of these are traditional, complex dishes rarely seen on menus, such as cassoulet, beef Wellington, and bouillabaisse, and overall they are executed deliciously. The melt-in-the-mouth onion tart was named after his Uncle Hansi, who gave him the recipe. Managing partner Robert Vick of Lettuce Entertain You Enterprises operates the restaurant along with Joho.

Honors/awards: "Best New Restaurant" in 1995 by the James Beard Foundation; chef Joho won the 1995 Perrier-Jouet Best American Midwest Chef Award at the Fifth Annual James Beard Awards.

(continued)

Brasserie T

Zone 11　Northern Suburbs	American Brasserie
305 South Happ Road, Northfield	★★★½
(847) 446-0444	Inexpensive/Moderate
	Quality 90　Value B

Reservations:	Recommended
When to go:	Any time, but weekend nights are busy
Entree range:	$9.95–23.95
Payment:	VISA, MC, AMEX, D
Service rating:	★★★★½
Friendliness rating:	★★★★½
Parking:	Free shopping mall lot
Bar:	Full service; a collection of cognacs, brandies, and ports
Wine selection:	Well-balanced selection of international and domestic; several by the glass
Dress:	Casual
Disabled access:	Yes
Customers:	Diverse locals, young, old, and families
Open:	Monday–Thursday, 11:30 A.M.–10 P.M.; Friday, 11:30 A.M.–11 P.M.; Saturday, 11:30 A.M.–10:30 P.M.; Sunday, 4:30–9:30 P.M.

Atmosphere/setting:　Elegant mosaic marbles and slate floors, frosted glass and copper chandeliers, and an arched ceiling create a stylish yet timeless decor.

House specialties:　Mussels marinière; fish and chips (special); wood-grilled portobellos with roasted sweet corn polenta tart, mixed greens, and shaved Parmesan; Tramonto's escarole of braised white beans, Italian sausage, tomato (seasonal); goat cheese salad with warm, sliced potatoes, celery, roasted onions, smoked bacon vinaigrette; blue cheese and pear salad with French beans, grapes, spiced pecans, apple-walnut vinaigrette; Tuscan-style pizza; caramelized onion pizza (oven-roasted tomatoes, eggplant, black olives, and fontina); farfalle pasta with wild mushrooms, fresh tomatoes, Parmesan; goat cheese ravioli with Parmesan broth; fusilli with grilled chicken, asparagus, and tomato-Alfredo sauce; braised lamb shank with garlicky potato cake, roasted vegetables; wood-grilled salmon with spinach, roasted garlic mashed potatoes; osso buco (braised veal shank, chunky vegetables, saffron risotto). Not-your-usual lemon meringue pie; banana cream pie; and root beer float with Gale's cinnamon-ginger-vanilla root beer.

(continued)

Other recommendations: Wood-grilled shrimp wrapped in pancetta; tuna tartar with arugula salad and herbed flatbread (seasonal); crab cakes; "A Great Caesar Salad"; three-grain risotto with barley, wild mushrooms, and artichokes; wood-grilled pork chop with barley ragôut, sautéed cabbage, bacon, apples; porcini-crusted mahi mahi with barley ragôut and wild mushroom sauce. Profiteroles with a trio of ice creams, warm bittersweet chocolate sauce, and caramel-almond lace; sticky toffee pudding with dates, caramelized apples, butterscotch sauce, and honey ice cream; and an assortment of sorbets with seasonal fruits.

Entertainment & amenities: Outdoor cafe.

Summary & comments: Husband-and-wife owner-chefs Rick Tramonto and Gale Gand opened Brasserie T in 1995 after a dozen years of experience at some of the best restaurants in Chicago, New York, and Europe, most recently as chefs and partners of the new fine-dining Tru in downtown Chicago. Located in the popular, upscale Northfield Village Square, Brasserie T features an affordable menu that will appeal to everyone, offering tried-and-true country dishes from Europe and America that are big on hearty flavor and ample portions.

Honors/awards: In 1994, both Tramonto and Gand were named among the country's Top Ten Best New Chefs by *Food & Wine* magazine. They also received the coveted *Michelin Guide's* Red "M" after only a year at the Stapleford Park Hotel in Leicestershire, England. Their previous venture, Trio, earned *Chicago Tribune* critic Phil Vettel's first four-star rating to a new restaurant in six years. Tramonto was selected in 1995 as America's Rising Star Chef by Robert Mondavi and was nominated for the James Beard Award that same year. Pastry Chef Gand received the Robert Mondavi Award for Culinary Excellence in 1994, as well as honors for her pastries and desserts.

Brios

	Contemporary Spanish
	★★★★
	Moderate/Expensive
	Quality 90 Value C

Zone 3   Near North
10 West Hubbard Street
(312) 467-1010

Reservations:	Recommended
When to go:	Lunch or dinner, or just for tapas in the bar
Entree range:	$15–28
Payment:	AMEX, CB, DC, MC, VISA
Service rating:	★★★★½
Friendliness rating:	★★★★½
Parking:	Valet at dinner, $7
Bar:	Full service
Wine selection:	Spanish dominated list includes sherry flights and about 10 sherries. Besides 80 percent of the Spanish wines, the other 20 percent is a mix of Portuguese, French, Italian, and American. About 43 selections with brief descriptions are categorized thoughtfully from light, floral, clean to full-bodied and complex; countries of origin not listed (would be helpful).
Dress:	Business; chic casual
Disabled access:	Ring doorbell
Customers:	Mixed, all ages, professionals; and leisure diners
Lunch:	Monday–Friday, 11:30 A.M.–2:30 P.M.
Dinner:	Sunday, 5–9 P.M.; Monday–Thursday, 5–10 P.M.; Friday and Saturday, 5–11 P.M.

Atmosphere/setting: Enter up several steps into a spacious bar area with a 17-foot zinc bar, a trademark of the partners (they also own Bistrot Zinc in two locations). Castilian architecture's medieval style is contrasted with Barcelona's modern influences in the interior design. Original Spanish art, floor tiles from Seville, and furniture from Barcelona are showcased in the dining room. Smoke-free dining room with smoking permitted only at the bar.

House specialties: Entremeses: Excellent empanadillas de ternera (turnovers filled with braised veal, cabbage, watercress, aromatic crème fraîche); the classic jamon serrano con condimentos de la casa is great thin-sliced Spanish ham with an unusual almond-apple confitado, green grape escabeche, grilled country bread; sopa de ajo con pimenton ahumado (garlic-bread soup, smoked paprika,

(continued)

baked quail egg). Platos pincipales: zarzuela de mariscos (day boat scallops, fresh shrimp, mussels, clams, sofrito-shellfish cream; abadejo con vinagreta de aceitunas (crispy codfish, fresh cod brandada, green olive vinaigrette, mujol caviar); cocido brio (preserved pork, crispy duck leg, housemade chorizo sausage, salsa verde, red grape conserva). Postres: "tapas" de postres variados (assortment of dessert tapas—candied nuts, truffles, and dried fruit); caramelized oranges, chocolate sorbet, fresh fruit, and candied nuts; flan de cafe (orange, coffee and cinnamon-scented flan).

Other recommendations: Openers: Watch Hills oysters-on-the-half shell, warm cauliflower puree, Spanish chili oil. Warm baby octopus salad, lemon–anchovy vinaigrette. Platos pincipales: carrot-fennel rice, spinach, pine nuts, raisins, red wine–vinegar broth; slow-roasted salmon, white bean–celery root puree, sherried carrot juice; codillo de cordero (braised lamb shank, navarra wine, pancella, "secret celery." Postres: profiteroles rellenos de crema de vainilla con helado de caramelo (vanilla cream-filled fritters, caramel ice cream, fudge, and caramel sauce); bittersweet chocolate tart, cream sherry sabayon, fresh mint coulis.

Entertainment & amenities: Refrigerated sherry display case and imported Spanish orange juice machine; sherry flights; tapas display in bar.

Summary & comments: This contemporary Spanish newcomer offers creative versions of classic regional dishes that make up the fabric of Spain's diverse cuisine. At last, Chicago has a Spanish restaurant that is authentic and does not feature just tapas. The menu includes a line, "tapas de la casa" (daily selection of tapas), and they are also listed on the bar menu, as they are in Spain. On the dining room menu it's the entremeses, sopa y ensalada, and platos principales that get top billing. The wine list is fairly extensive in the Spanish territory with some good selections for the flavorful fare. Chef Michael Tsonton creates dishes that are lively in flavor, in keeping with the name, Brio, which means "energetic" in Spanish. Tour Merle Management, LLC, also operates two other restaurants in Chicago: Bistrot Zinc/Cafe Zinc, 3443 N. Southport and Bistrot Zinc, 1131 N. State St.—both serving French cuisine.

BRUNA'S RISTORANTE

Zone 5   South Loop
2424 South Oakley Avenue
(773) 254-5550

Italian	
★★★	
Inexpensive/Moderate	
Quality 80	Value B

Reservations:	Recommended
When to go:	Any time
Entree range:	$8.95–16.95
Payment:	VISA, MC, AMEX, DC, CB, D
Service rating:	★★★½
Friendliness rating:	★★★★½
Parking:	Street; valet on Friday and Saturday evenings
Bar:	Full service
Wine selection:	Mostly Italian, including restaurant's private label imported from Italy (Vino Nobile di Montepulciano and Chianti); $15.50–95 a bottle; some great choices by the glass, $3.50–4.50
Dress:	Casual
Disabled access:	No, but staff will assist those in wheelchairs up the 2 steps
Customers:	Diverse, professionals (lunch); mostly couples and families (dinner)
Lunch/Dinner:	Monday–Thursday, 11 A.M.–10 P.M.; Friday and Saturday, 11 A.M.–11 P.M.; Sunday, 1–10 P.M.

Atmosphere/setting: Old-world style with original, oil-painted murals; ceramics; casual, warm look.

House specialties: Pastas (e.g., Luciano's fusilli, various ravioli, tortellini alla Bolognese); Bruna's veal scaloppine; shrimp fra diavolo (spicy shrimp with linguine and piquant tomato sauce); chicken limone.

Other recommendations: Desserts including tiramisu and fruit tart.

Summary & comments: Owner Luciano Silvestri is on hand to direct the operation and has a keen pride in his wine cellar and the recipes he brings back from his biannual trips to Italy. He and his wife, Ilona, bought this restaurant from the original owner in 1981; it has been open since 1933—the oldest restaurant in the Heart of Italy, a close-knit Italian community on the near Southwest Side. The cooking here is full flavored and well prepared, and is served with style.

BUKARA

Zone 3   Near North
2 East Ontario Street
(312) 943-0188

Indian	
★★★½	
Moderate	
Quality 80	Value C

Reservations:	Recommended
When to go:	Any time
Entree range:	$8–25
Payment:	All major credit cards
Service rating:	★★★★
Friendliness rating:	★★★½
Parking:	Discount with validation at garage at 10 East Ontario
Bar:	Full service, including Taj Mahal beer
Wine selection:	Fairly extensive; mixed
Dress:	Moderately casual, business
Disabled access:	Yes, including rest rooms
Customers:	Diverse, professionals
Lunch:	Monday–Friday (buffet available for $7.95), 11:30 A.M.–2:15 P.M.; Saturday and Sunday, noon–2:45 P.M.
Dinner:	Sunday–Thursday, 5:30–9:30 P.M.; Friday and Saturday, 5:30–10:30 P.M.

Atmosphere/setting: Handsomely appointed, classy interior with visible tandoor kitchen. Newly built, comfortable Uncle Phil's Global Bar features 42 beers from 22 nations and international music.

House specialties: Marinated fresh seafood, poultry, and meats roasted in tandoors; sikandari raan (whole leg of lamb); tiger prawns Bukara; dal Bukara (black lentils); and roti (whole-wheat bread).

Other recommendations: Spiced cottage cheese–stuffed bread; roomali (plain wheat bread); shish kebab (skewered, charcoal-grilled, cumin-flavored, minced lamb); flavorful kulfi gulabi dessert, an exotic pudding of dates, almonds, and milk.

Summary & comments: The ancient nomad cooking of the Indian sub-continent was introduced at this restaurant several years ago. To be authentic, no utensils are used. Eating with your hands as the nomads did is sensuous and fun, although they weren't seated in such an elegant atmosphere. There's an Indian saying, "Eating with utensils is like making love through an interpreter." Sauces are well spiced, and, although some tandoori meats can be on the dry side, most are delectable. Catering is available.

122

The Cafe

Zone 3 Near North	American/International
The Ritz-Carlton,	★★★★
160 East Pearson Street	Moderate
(312) 266-1000	Quality 92 Value B

Reservations: Recommended
When to go: Weekends are the busiest
Entree range: $11–28; most lunch entrees $14–19.50
Payment: All major credit cards
Service rating: ★★★★½
Friendliness rating: ★★★★★
Parking: Ask about reduced parking fee
Bar: Beer and wine selections
Wine selection: Extensive selections of Californian, French, and
                        Italian wines by the bottle or glass
Dress: Casual to dressy
Disabled access: Yes, entrance and main floor seating
Customers: Professionals, locals, and hotel guests, including
                        many celebrities
Open: Monday–Thursday, Sunday 6:30 A.M.–11:30 A.M.;
                        Friday and Saturday, 6:30 A.M.–midnight

Atmosphere/setting: In an open alcove of the spectacular 12th-floor hotel lobby. Marble-topped oak cafe tables, botanical Wedgwood china, glistening sterling silver flatware, and fresh flowers; colorful art on walls.

House specialties: "Heartland Breakfast" that includes juice, two eggs over easy, homemade chicken or country sausage, Mom's hash browns, toasted bread, and coffee ($15.50). For lunch and dinner, specialties include chilled, grilled vegetable antipasto mozzarella di bufala, triple-decker turkey club sandwich, and dairy-free vegetarian lasagna. Signature dessert: Varying flavored crème brûlée.

Other recommendations: Daily specials: a wonderful corn chowder or grilled salmon entree with vegetables. Caesar salad comes as an appetizer, entree, and with grilled chicken breast. Pumpkin risotto with porcini mushrooms. Hearty side orders: mashed Idaho potatoes and roasted garlic and Parmesan bread. Desserts rotate; the peach cobbler is noteworthy.

Summary & comments: This cafe offers a fine dining experience with china and silver, top-quality food and service, and beautiful surroundings for the price. Special menus occasionally celebrate a Chicago Art Institute exhibit, such as "Michelangelo and His Influence"; for that occasion, Michelangelo-inspired Italian recipes by cookbook author Giuliano Bugialli were featured.

Honors/awards: See profile of The Dining Room.

Cafe-Ba-Ba-Reeba!

Zone 1 North Side	Spanish/Tapas
2024 North Halsted Street	★★★½
(773) 935-5000	Moderate
	Quality 87 Value C

Reservations:	Recommended; not accepted for patio
When to go:	Early or late to avoid waits
Entree range:	Tapas, $1.95–5.95; paella, $10.95
Payment:	All major credit cards
Service rating:	★★★½
Friendliness rating:	★★★½
Parking:	Valet, $4
Bar:	2 bars seat 170 people
Wine selection:	120 Spanish, a few American, $8–45; 4 by the glass; sangría, sherries, and Spanish liquors
Dress:	Casual, dressy
Disabled access:	Wheelchair accessible; call ahead
Customers:	Young and lively; students, professionals, tourists
Lunch:	Tuesday–Friday, 11 A.M.–2:30 P.M.; Saturday, 11:30 A.M.–3 P.M.
Dinner:	Monday–Thursday, 5:30–11 P.M.; Friday and Saturday, 5:30 P.M.–midnight; Sunday, noon–10 P.M.

Atmosphere/setting: Upbeat, vibrant interior with vivid Mediterranean colors. Murals of Spain, with a gallery of Spanish artists. Garden patio.

House specialties: Tapas: patatas con aioli (garlic potato salad); terrine of grilled eggplant; bambas a la parrilla (grilled shrimp brochette); paella Valenciana (Spanish saffron-rice, chicken, pork, seafood, green beans, and tomatoes); Fideua de mariscos (cazuela of lobster, shrimp, and monkfish baked with saffron broth and angel hair pasta); sautéed octopus; vieiras a la parrilla (grilled sea scallops).

Other recommendations: Calamares a la plancha (fresh grilled squid); champinones rellenos (mushrooms stuffed with spinach, manchego cheese, and red-pepper sauce); black bean soup with chorizo; flan de la casa; tarta de almen dras y fruta (fresh seasonal fruit and almond pastry cream in an almond-rum crust).

Summary & comments: This was the first Spanish restaurant to introduce the "little plate" concept. This lively, large place with a menu to match has a clientele that seems to continue to grow. Sample several tapas items to create a full meal—it's fun to share—or choose from the traditional Spanish dishes in larger portions.

CAFE BORGIA

Zone 8   Southern Suburbs
17923 Torrence Avenue, Lansing
(708) 474-5515

	Italian
	★★½
	Inexpensive/Moderate
	Quality 78 Value B

Reservations:	No
When to go:	Weekday evenings often less busy
Entree range:	$12.95–16.95
Payment:	All major credit cards
Service rating:	★★★
Friendliness rating:	★★★½
Parking:	Free lot or street
Bar:	Some beer and wine
Wine selection:	Limited
Dress:	Casual, but dressier on weekends
Disabled access:	Entrance, no; rest rooms, yes
Customers:	Professionals, students, couples, families
Lunch/Dinner:	Sunday–Thursday, 11 A.M.–11 P.M.; Friday and Saturday, 11 A.M.–midnight

Atmosphere/setting: Informal; granite tables with wrought-iron bases; expanded back room with bay window. Pastel-colored outdoor patio; mural of Italian scenes.

House specialties: Cream of eggplant and roasted red pepper soup; linguine pescatore with calamari, bay scallops, and mussels in a red or white sauce; tender steamed baby clams in garlic, lemon, and oil sauce; stuffed eggplant with prosciutto and mozzarella, baked in a tomato-cream sauce; zuccotto (layered sponge cake soaked in Marsala and brandy, filled with whipped cream, hazelnuts, and almonds, and topped with chocolate and raspberry sauces).

Other recommendations: Roasted lamb shank, rosemary jus, with roasted potatoes and onions; veal-spinach cannelloni; four cheese–stuffed chicken breast; tiramisu.

Summary & comments: The simple Roman cooking here is aggressively flavored by innovative chef-owner Mike Jesso. Major triumphs are his favorites: such as the cream of eggplant and roasted red pepper soup and tender baby clams, above. This well-established place is one of the best restaurants on the South Side and has a loyal following.

Cafe Iberico Tapas Bar

Zone 3   Near North
739 North LaSalle Street
(312) 573-1510

Spanish/Tapas
★★★½
Inexpensive/Moderate

Quality 87   Value B

Reservations:	Required Sunday–Thursday; not accepted on weekends
When to go:	Before 6:30 P.M. or after 8:30 P.M.
Entree range:	$7.50–17.95; tapas, $3.50–4
Payment:	VISA, MC, D, AMEX
Service rating:	★★★½
Friendliness rating:	★★★½
Parking:	Valet
Bar:	Full service
Wine selection:	Spanish; some nice selections, including sangría
Dress:	Casual
Disabled access:	Yes, including rest rooms
Customers:	Diverse, many Latin Americans and Europeans
Lunch/Dinner:	Monday–Thursday, 11:30 A.M.–11 P.M.; Friday and Saturday, 11:30 A.M.–1:30 A.M. and Sunday, noon–11 P.M.

Atmosphere/setting: Authentic touch of Spain: a tapas bar that has been recently expanded with 85 extra seats; a dining room with checkered table cloths, wall murals, and wine bottles on ceiling racks; the rustic bodega (wine cellar room) downstairs; and a newly built deli and ceramics shop.

House specialties: Paella estilo Iberico; gazpacho Andaluz. Tapas include grilled octopus with potatoes and olive oil; Spanish cured ham, Manchego cheese, and toasted tomato bread; tortilla Española. Specials include hard-to-find fish cheeks with baby eels. Poached pears with wine and ice cream.

Other recommendations: Shrimp with wine and garlic sauce; croquetas de pollo (chicken croquettes), a home-style dish; stuffed eggplant with goat cheese; crema Catalana for dessert.

Summary & comments: Just north of downtown, this popular place has expanded by adding a bodega complete with wood-burning oven. Authentic atmosphere, cuisine, and wines make this one of the best tapas places in the city, especially for the prices. Spanish food conveys passionate regionalism and culinary traditions, and it's possible to experience a good sampling of that here.

Cafe Luciano

Zone 3 Near North	Italian
871 North Rush Street	★★★½
(312) 266-1414	Inexpensive/Moderate
Zone 11 Northern Suburbs	Quality 96 Value C
2676 Green Bay Road, Evanston	
(847) 864-6060	

Reservations:	*Chicago:* recommended; *Evanston:* only for large groups on Friday and Saturday
When to go:	*Chicago:* before 7 P.M.; *Evanston:* before 5 P.M.
Entree range:	*Chicago:* $10–18.95; *Evanston:* $10–16.95
Payment:	All major credit cards (AMEX not accepted at Evanston location)
Service rating:	★★★★
Friendliness rating:	★★★★½
Parking:	*Chicago:* street, city lots, valet after 5 P.M.; *Evanston:* free valet
Bar:	Full service
Wine selection:	Moderate, mostly Italian
Dress:	Casual
Disabled access:	*Chicago:* no; *Evanston:* yes
Customers:	Mostly local
Lunch/Dinner:	*Chicago:* Monday–Thursday, 11:30 A.M.–10 P.M.; Friday and Saturday, 11:30 A.M.–11 P.M.; Sunday, noon–10 P.M.
	Evanston: Sunday–Thursday, 5–10 P.M.; Friday and Saturday, 5–11 P.M.

Atmosphere/setting: Homestyle Italian bistro setting; rustic walls and wooden floors; very colorful vines, paintings, and trims on marbled beige walls. Outdoor seating in Chicago; desserts displayed in Evanston location, which is also smoke-free.

House specialties: Rigatoni country-style; giambotta (hearty mix of chicken, sweet sausage, onions, sweet peppers, mushrooms, and potatoes sautéed in light olive oil and white wine sauce); eggplant Parmigiana alla Luciano. Appetizers: roasted peppers; polenta con funghi; mussels alla Luciano.

Other recommendations: Farfalle alla Stefano (porcini mushrooms, asparagus, peas, and onions in a light tomato sauce with a touch of cream, tossed with bowtie pasta); seafood pomodoro (in zesty marinara sauce over linguini); desserts (change often; many homemade).

(continued)

Entertainment & amenities: Chicago: piano in evenings from 7 p.m. to closing.

Summary & comments: The classic Italian cooking here has bold, lively flavors and is presented beautifully. The chef has a good sense of marrying ingredients properly. Menu has "Luciano Lite" offerings—lower in calories, fat, and sodium. Hearty portions, a good wine selection, a casual atmosphere, and friendly and efficient service combine to make the Evanston location so successful that it expanded within one year. Menus and decor similar at other locations. Owning company Café Concepts substituted Cucina Roma, an Italian bistro, for Cafe Luciano in Westmont, and opened another in Naperville.

Cafe Spiaggia

Zone 3   Near North
980 North Michigan Avenue
(312) 280-2755

Italian
★★★½
Moderate
Quality 89   Value C

Reservations:	Required
When to go:	Any time
Entree range:	$13.50–22.50
Payment:	Major credit cards
Service rating:	★★★★
Friendliness rating:	★★★★½
Parking:	Validated in garage next door; call for directions
Bar:	Full service
Wine selection:	Italian; bottles, $22–49; a few by the glass, $6–10
Dress:	Casual; chic
Disabled access:	Yes
Customers:	Tourists, conventioneers, and local residents
Lunch:	Wednesday–Sunday, 11:30 A.M.–2 P.M.
Dinner:	Monday–Thursday, 5:30 P.M.–9 P.M.;
	Friday–Sunday, 5:30 P.M.–10 P.M

Atmosphere/setting: Decor was inspired by fifteenth-century Italian frescos from a castle in Mantua, Italy. Great view of North Michigan Avenue.

House specialties: Pasticcio di salmone all'erba cipollina (demi-smoked salmon mousse); prosciutto d'anitra (duck prosciutto with zucchini salad); ravioli di ricotta con porcini (ricotta-filled ravioli with imported porcinis); gnocchi alla crema di pomodoro con speck (potato gnocchi in a creamy sauce with smoked prosciutto); tortellini pasticciati al ragu (classic handmade filled pasta with meat sauce); trancio di salmone con funghi (wood-roasted salmon with wild mushrooms); cotolette di vitello alla Milanese (pan-fried veal cutlet on mixed greens); tiramisu; and bavarese alla noce di cocco (coconut Bavarian cream).

Other recommendations: Prosciutto e melone (imported Italian Parma, San Daniele, and Carpegna prosciutto with melon); pomodoro, cipolla, e Gorgonzola (tomato, red onion, and Gorgonzola); and quaglia ripiena con polenta (wood-roasted quail with Italian sausage stuffing on creamy polenta with mushrooms).

Entertainment & amenities: Live piano music in the formal dining room.

Summary & comments: The menu reflects cuisine from all regions of Italy with chef Bartolotta's modern interpretation.

Honors/awards: Chef Bartolotta has won many awards, including the James Beard Foundation's Best Midwest Chef in 1994.

129

CALITERRA

Italian/Northern Californian

★★★★

Moderate

Quality 92   Value B

Zone 3   Near North
Wyndham Chicago,
  633 North Saint Clair Street
(312) 274-4444

Reservations:	Recommended
When to go:	Breakfast, lunch, dinner or in between; week-nights tend to be less busy
Entree range:	$15–23; 5-course tasting menu, $55 (entire table must order)
Payment:	VISA, MC, AMEX, DC
Service rating:	★★★★½
Friendliness rating:	★★★★½
Parking:	Valet; nearby lot; limited street parking
Bar:	Full; large hardwood bar in comfortable lounge area
Wine selection:	A book of 7 pages of Italian and American varietals, categorized smartly by helpful headings such as "Crisp, Lean, Refreshing Whites" and "Weighty, Powerful Reds." There are sections for "Meritage," "Champagne and Sparkling" and six flights, including "The Cal-Ital Flight." based on Italian grapes grown in California. Bottle prices start at $24; many in the $30s.
Dress:	Chic, upscale casual; business
Disabled access:	Complete
Customers:	Sophisticated locals and travelers; professionals for business meals; groups of friends or couples; fans of Chef John Coletta
Breakfast:	Daily, 6:30–11 A.M.
Lunch:	Daily, 11:30 A.M.–5 P.M.
Dinner:	Daily, 5–11 P.M.

Atmosphere/setting: Planned to incorporate both Californian and Italian elements, Bogdanow Partners Architects of New York designed the 4,500-square-foot space to develop this concept. Features include a display kitchen, two walls of glass windows, and a lovely hardwood bar. Lots of space between tables.

House specialties: Starters: crisp Santa Barbara shrimp "cigars" with mustard

(continued)

fruits, seasonal vegetable slaw, aged Balsamic syrup; ahi tuna tartar with avocado, cucumber, and Sterling caviar; soft shell crab in crisp rice flakes with tiny white asparagus salad (summer); summer pea "cappuccino" with white truffle oil; Sonoma duck ravioli with oven-dried tomato, baby arugula, and cannellini beans. Entrees: a stand-out porcini-crusted halibut with vegetable "Giardiniera" and thyme-infused zucchini broth; Sonoma lamb loin with barley caponata risotto, black trumpet mushrooms, and fennel emulsion; grilled aged angus sirloin of beef, onion marmalade, lemon-pepper Parmesan fries and red bell pepper aioli. Desserts: beautiful with multiple parts are twin mocha-mascarpone cannoli with espresso ice cream and almonds (instead of the traditional pistachios); profiteroles with trio of ice creams and glazed banana-walnut sundae; parfait of white chocolate mousse with blood orange slices, orange sorbet, pistachio wafer.

Other recommendations: Brick oven pizzas; grouper cheeks in a "cioppino" broth with sea beans and lemon aioli; diver scallops with carrot-ginger emulsion and chili sambal oil. Entrees: cod with braised field greens, exotic tomato vinaigrette (summer); grilled pork Fiorentina with summer vegetables and fork-mashed Yukon gold potatoes. Dessert: fresh fruit "minestrone" with vanilla ice cream.

Entertainment & amenities: Watching the chef and his staff in the open display kitchen.

Summary & comments: Truly an international, award-winning chef, John Coletta returned to Chicago after globe-trotting with renewed energy and inspiration to open this California-Italian restaurant in the Wyndham Chicago. One of Chicago's best new ventures, Caliterra has become an instant favorite of many connoisseurs, who appreciate the chef's talents and love the spacious, comfortable atmosphere and the knowledgeable service. The name was inspired as much by their focus on Cal-Ital wines as on their cuisine.

Honors/awards: Numerous for the world-class chef John Coletta, among them he was a Bocue d'Or finalist in 1994; member of the U.S. Gold Medal Team Culinary Olympics, 1992; recipient of individual Gold Medal in Culinary Olympics, 1984; named one of America's Top 15 Rising Star Chefs in 1995 PBS television series.

Campagnola

Zone 11   Northern Suburbs
815 Chicago Avenue, Evanston
(847) 475-6100

Italian	
★★★★	
Inxpensive/Moderate	
Quality 94 Value B	

Reservations:	Accepted
When to go:	Early or late dinner
Entree range:	$9.95–21.95
Payment:	VISA, MC
Service rating:	★★★★
Friendliness rating:	★★★★½
Parking:	Street parking available
Bar:	Full service
Wine selection:	Italian; $3.50–5 a glass and $14–36 a bottle
Dress:	Casual
Disabled access:	Yes
Customers:	Largely local; couples, professionals, families
Dinner:	Tuesday–Thursday, 5:30–9:30 P.M.; Friday and Saturday, 5:30–10 P.M.; Sunday, 5–9 P.M.

Atmosphere/setting: Rustic decor with polished wood tables, chairs, and floor; exposed brick walls; creatively draped ceiling. The outdoor deck is perfect for romantic dining in summer.

House specialties: First courses: Salad of peeky-toe crab, pickled baby beets, and grilled wild leeks; grilled organic nectarines with Parma prosciutto and mascarpone; wood-fired radicchio and pancetta with marinated goat cheese. Entrees: linguine with Maine crabmeat; conchiglie (shell pasta) with Gorgonzola; Chianti-glazed duckling; pan-roasted striped bass; Verdura del Giorno, a vegan dish. Desserts: sorbetti and gelato; tiramisu; lemon tart; and chocolate budino, a baked pudding filled with melted chocolate.

Other recommendations: Roasted eggplant salad; grilled calamari; arugula with prawns; piegata folded pizza; pasta dishes; crème brûlée; plum cobbler (special).

Summary & comments: Roughly translated to "person of the countryside," Campagnola offers diners high-quality, organic ingredients, straightforward Italian cooking, and a relaxed atmosphere. Executive chef and partner Michael Altenberg and owner Steven Schwartz opened Campagnola in June 1996; they are both enthusiastic and dedicated, and it shows. Altenberg dubs his fare "clean Italian cuisine" because he uses only free-range, antibiotic-free meats and organic produce, which is virtually unprecedented among Italian restaurants.

CAPE COD ROOM

Zone 3 Near North	Seafood
The Drake Hotel, 140 Walton Place	★★★★
(312) 787-2200	Moderate/Expensive
	Quality 91 Value C

Reservations:	Required on weekends
When to go:	Monday, Tuesday, or Wednesday
Entree range:	$21–43, served with potato and vegetables
Payment:	All major credit cards
Service rating:	★★★★
Friendliness rating:	★★★★½
Parking:	Valet for hotel guests
Bar:	Full service
Wine selection:	Good assortment of champagnes and sparkling wines; imported and domestic whites and reds chosen for the seafood menu. House wines— several by the glass; imports include French, German, and Italian; bottles $23–100. The hotel's extensive reserve list also available.
Dress:	Business casual
Disabled access:	Yes, including rest rooms
Customers:	Diverse; travelers, loyal regulars, locals, professionals, single diners and couples, celebrities including Steve Lawrence, Edie Gorme, Jane Meadows, and Paul Newman, and politicos such as Mayor Richard Daley
Lunch/Dinner:	Daily, noon–11 P.M.

Atmosphere/setting: Very authentic-looking rustic Cape Cod setting with nautical decor. Charming and intimate.

House specialties: The Cape Cod's famous Bookbinder red snapper soup with sherry; New England clam chowder; bouillabaisse (with a variety of fresh-water fish and seafood); raw bar; oysters Rockefeller; halibut papillote (fillet in parchment with lobster, mushrooms, and red wine sauce); imported Dover sole and turbot; New England scrod.

Other recommendations: Smoked salmon; oyster stew; Drake stew; crab-meat à la Newburg; shrimp à la Drake (casserole with shallots and Newburg sauce, glazed with Parmesan). Desserts include key lime pie and strawberry rhubarb crumble with vanilla ice cream.

(continued)

Cape Cod Room   *(continued)*

Entertainment & amenities: Sitting at the bar to see the initials carved by celebrities who've dined here over the years. Longtime manager Patrick Bredin will gladly help interpret them.

Summary & comments: This seaworthy legend has been sailing full tilt since 1933, and at "60-something" is the city's oldest seafood restaurant. Before Shaw's Crab House, Nick's Fishmarket, and several other excellent seafood restaurants opened, the Cape Cod Room was synonymous with Chicago seafood dining. Located on the main floor of one of the city's finest hotels, it has long been a premier place for imported Dover sole and turbot, broiled New England scrod, bouillabaisse, and the famous Bookbinder red snapper soup. The raw bar continues to be a reliable source for oysters or clams on the shell and a great socializing spot for single travelers. Categorized by type of seafood as well as seafood salads, vegetables, and desserts, the menu also has a section, "From Our Broiler," offering four items from the land—steaks and lamb chops are a few alternatives to the array of items from the waters. There are the old classic lobster preparations (e.g., lobster Thermidor and à la Newburg) as well as the best— simply broiled or steamed. Other period pieces are shrimp de Jonghe, oysters Rockefeller, and clams casino.

Honors/awards: Travel Holiday Award for 40 years; Fine Dining Hall of Fame by *Nations Restaurant News*; Ivy Award by *Restaurants & Institutions Magazine*.

Carlos'

Zone 11 Northern Suburbs	French
429 Temple Avenue, Highland Park	★★★★½
(847) 432-0770	Moderate/Expensive
	Quality 96 Value C

Reservations:	Required
When to go:	Sunday and Monday
Entree range:	$27–37
Payment:	All major credit cards
Service rating:	★★★★½
Friendliness rating:	★★★★★
Parking:	Free valet
Bar:	None
Wine selection:	40-plus-page list; bottles $28–2,000; $7–12 a glass (most selections)
Dress:	Jacket required, tie optional
Disabled access:	No, but easy entrance; accessible rest rooms
Customers:	North Shore locals, professionals, couples, families
Dinner:	*Summer:* Sunday, Monday, Wednesday, and Thursday, 5–8:30 P.M. (last seating); Friday and Saturday, seatings 5–6:30 P.M. and 8:45–9:30 P.M. *Other seasons:* dinner starts at 5:30 P.M. and kitchen closes earlier, but patrons can stay as late as they like

Atmosphere/setting: Elegant, stylized fine-dining ambience: wood-paneled walls, mirrors, and Art Deco; quiet and intimate; facilities for private parties.

House specialties: Warm oysters with cucumbers; sautéed Hudson Valley foie gras; superb lobster ravioli. Sautéed soft-shell crab and stuffed roasted quail; duck breast and leg confit; rack of lamb. Desserts (change regularly): fruit tart; chocolate fantasy. Pastries and desserts are as delicious as they look.

Other recommendations: Sautéed scallops; potato-wrapped escargot. Sautéed halibut; vegetable platter; roasted loin of Jamison baby lamb; degustation menu, $70 ($100 with wine); vegetarian degustation available with advance request.

Summary & comments: The ratio of staff members to diners on a busy night is about one to three. Guests are given complimentary hors d'oeuvres to start and mignardises (tiny sweets) at the end. Carlos' continues to be one of the best fine-dining restaurants in the Chicago area.

Honors/awards: Grand Award from *Wine Spectator*; featured on PBS/WTTW's *Great Chefs of Chicago*.

Carlucci

<table>
<tr><td></td><td>Tuscan Italian</td></tr>
<tr><td>Zone 2   North Central/O'Hare</td><td>★★★★</td></tr>
<tr><td>6111 North River Road, Rosemont</td><td>Moderate</td></tr>
<tr><td>(847) 518-0990</td><td></td></tr>
<tr><td></td><td>Quality 88   Value C</td></tr>
</table>

Reservations:	Recommended
When to go:	Any time
Entree range:	$12.50–29.95
Payment:	All major credit cards
Service rating:	★★★★½
Friendliness rating:	★★★★½
Parking:	Free valet and lot
Bar:	Full service; nice selection of spirits, including single malt scotches and small-batch bourbons
Wine selection:	Extensive Italian, most of them reds, selected for the rustic food; Tuscany is the main region featured (e.g. Chianti classico riserva by Banfi and Villan Antinori). Piemonte and other regions are represented, as are Merlot, Cabernet Sauvignon, and blends. White wines, mostly Italian with domestic, including Niebaum-Coppola Bianco, Mondavi Fume Blanc, and Sterling Vineyards Chardonnay. Four French champagnes are listed among seven dry sparkling wines. There is a reserve list, magnums (such as the super Tuscan blend, "Summus" by Villa Banfi), ports and sherries. Several by the glass; fairly priced
Dress:	Well-dressed, chic casual
Disabled access:	Yes
Customers:	Professionals, travelers, couples especially in the evenings
Lunch:	Monday–Friday, 11 A.M.–2.30 P.M.
Dinner:	Monday–Thursday, 5–10 P.M.; Friday and Saturday, 5–11 P.M.; Sunday, 4:30–9 P.M.

Atmosphere/setting: Exquisite doorways, frescoes, and tiles; handsome bar area. Open kitchen with rotisserie; warm lighting from sconces; white tablecloths; colorful artifacts, foods in jars and wine bottles—very welcoming.

(continued)

House specialties: Menu comically states, "English spoken." Antipasti: melanzane piccanti con menta (grilled Japanese eggplant with spicy corn, peppers, and mint); grilled bruschetta platter with baked fresh goat cheese, pile-on relishes of olives, tomatoes, and mozzarella; wood-fired pizzas (e.g. signature festa vegetariana with grilled asparagus, red and yellow tomatoes, basil pesto, squash, and provolone). Pastas: mafaldine con funghi selvatici (wavy broad noodles with three kinds of mushrooms, Parmesan and mushroom broth); small ravioli filled with goat cheese and ricotta with shallots, pancetta, parsley, and fresh tomato. Piatti principali: roasted rack of lamb with sweet and sour pearl onions, garlic-wine sauce, and sliced potatoes; bistecca Fiorentina (16-ounce Porterhouse with canellini beans and lemon oil). Desserts: ethereal tiramisu; crispy-firm-shelled cannoli (not your usual ones); feathery chocolate cake.

Other recommendations: Antipasti: carpaccio "purses" stuffed with Parmesan and celery with mustard-chive dressing; unusual shrimp with shaved fennel, grapefruit, orange, melon, and mint; and a foreign departure from Italian is the sliced seared tuna and house-smoked salmon with couscous salad and ginger-infused oil. Pasta: hand-rolled pasta quills in traditional Bolognese meat sauce. Piatti principali: Cornish hen in clay pot roasted in wood-fired oven with potatoes, sautéed spinach, and lemon oil; spit-roasted Long Island duck glazed with honey mustard, fresh greens tossed with mustard vinaigrette. Dessert: Chianti-poached pears.

Entertainment & amenities: Complimentary shuttle from area hotels, O'Hare Airport and Expo Center to restaurant.

Summary & comments: This, the second of the Carlucci restaurants, has served excellent Tuscan cuisine since it opened about 10 years ago. The space is beautifully designed with a lovely, inviting bar area and a welcoming open kitchen with a rotisserie in the main dining room. There's lots of bustle, especially on weekends, and showmanship with grappa carts displaying the liquor infused with fruits. Well managed by the Carlucci family and partners, who train their staff well in the art of proper Italian pronunciation for the wines and dishes. Chef Luigi Negroni is adept at producing flavorful Tuscan fare, and recently introduced a new menu with chef Alfons Fonseca. Negroni clearly loves his work here and it shows on the plate. The first Carlucci on Halsted closed in early 1997 and there are plans to reopen it in a different location.

Carzz Grilleria

Zone 8   Southern Suburbs
216 South Washington Street, Naperville
(630) 778-1944

New Orleans, Southern,
and Caribbean
★★★½
Inexpensive/Moderate

Quality 88   Value B

Reservations:	Required on weekends for 4 or more
When to go:	Weeknights; weekends 5–6 P.M. or after 8 P.M.
Entree range:	$8.95–20.95
Payment:	Major credit cards
Service rating:	★★★½
Friendliness rating:	★★★★½
Parking:	Free municipal parking lot behind restaurant
Bar:	Full service
Wine selection:	Extensive American; $3.95–5.25 by the glass; $14–36 by the bottle
Dress:	Casual
Disabled access:	Yes, call ahead; one step
Customers:	Locals, suburbanites and city residents, couples
Lunch:	Tuesday–Friday, 11:30 A.M.–2:30 P.M.
Dinner:	Tuesday–Thursday, 5–9:30 P.M.; Friday and Saturday, 5–10:30 P.M.; Sunday, 4–8:30 P.M.

Atmosphere/setting: Colorful, vibrant interior. Eye-catching high, patterned tin ceiling. Whimsical mural of the grilleria's logo. Lively music.

House specialties: New beginnings combo platter (grilled wild mushrooms, Jamaican jerk wings, baked Gorgonzola bread); Southern blackened amberjack; zesty shrimp salsa with parsley-garlic fettuccine; mushrooms marinated in herbed balsamic vinegar; lobster cakes; crawfish (not crayfish here) torte. Specials such as tomato artichoke soup and Jamaican barbecue chicken.

Other recommendations: Fried Brie with raspberry-jalapeño sauce. Rib Night features barbecue baby-back ribs in seven styles, including Cajun, Jamaican, Hawaiian, mango-rum, and sun-dried cherry tomato sauce. Ultimate peanut butter pie and pumpkin cheesecake.

Entertainment & amenities: Fun promotions. On Sunday, children under age seven eat free. Wednesday is rib night; Thursday is Mardi Gras night.

Summary & comments: "Carzz" is derived from chef-owner Tom Burke's wife's name, Carla. "Car" is her nickname, and since they didn't want the name to be Car's Grilleria, the double z's were added; they stand for zest both in life and cooking. The chef has won awards for his soups. This restaurant gains momentum from the enthusiastic owners and their community involvement.

CATCH 35

Zone 4   The Loop
Leo Burnett Building,
35 West Wacker Drive
(312) 346-3500

Seafood	
★★★½	
Moderate/Expensive	
Quality 93 Value C	

Reservations:	Recommended
When to go:	Early weekdays, 5:15–6:30 P.M.
Entree range:	$16–40
Payment:	All major credit cards
Service rating:	★★★★
Friendliness rating:	★★★★½
Parking:	Valet, $7
Bar:	Full service
Wine selection:	Extensive, mostly Californian; several by the glass
Dress:	Chic casual or business; no dress code
Disabled access:	Yes
Customers:	Many from nearby ad agencies, locals, tourists
Lunch:	Monday–Friday, 11 A.M.–1:45 P.M. (after 1:45 P.M bar remains open through dinner)
Dinner:	Monday–Thursday, 5:15–10 P.M.; Friday and Saturday, 5:15–10 P.M.; Sunday, 5–9 P.M.

Atmosphere/setting: Spectacular granite lobby entryway of Leo Burnett Building; revolving piano bar with a display of enlarged award-winning ads; stunning step interior with marble walls; colorful, elegant setting.

House specialties: Menu changes daily. Typical items are grilled grouper; grilled swordfish with light cognac-avocado salsa. Appetizers include Catch's crab cake (not fried) with rémoulade sauce; Szechuan scallops; Martha's Vineyard salad; Black Island swordfish.

Other recommendations: From the wok section: stir-fried crab claws, shrimp, and scallops with a hint of tomato sauce; nice variety of oysters on the half shell. Chocolate Kahlúa mousse (served in a caramel basket); pecan tart; white chocolate cheesecake; Key lime pie; handmade cannoli.

Entertainment & amenities: Piano player and vocalists perform evenings.

Summary & comments: Nicely prepared, showy food, some with Thai influences reflecting the chef's background. Daily menu lists categories, and main-course seafood is grouped by preparation methods (baked, grilled, wok, pan-seared). Nothing is fried. Popular with the advertising agency crowd, this is an impressive restaurant for entertaining clients.

Honors/awards: Silver Platter Award.

Chapultepec

Zone 3   Near North
700 North Dearborn
(312) 787-8937

Mexican	
★★★½	
Inexpensive/Moderate	
Quality 90	Value B

Reservations:	Suggested, especially weekends
When to go:	Anytime
Entree range:	$8.50–14
Payment:	VISA, MC, AMEX, D, DC, JCB
Service rating:	★★★★
Friendliness rating:	★★★★½
Parking:	Street
Bar:	Full service; good list of fine "sipping" tequilas and several Margaritas (flavored, regular, jumbo, pitcher, or with one of the fine tequilas). Imported and domestic beers.
Wine selection:	Smart collection of Spanish, Chilean, American and several Australian; 25–30; about 15 white and red available by the glass. Fairly priced
Dress:	Casual
Disabled access:	Yes
Customers:	Mixed, Americans and ethnic, all ages. Lots of professionals. Fans of Chef Dudley.
Open:	Daily, 10 AM–10 PM

Atmosphere/setting: Enter through the bar area, then into the dining rooms. Colorful decor, some of which is from the previous restaurant. Mexican artifacts. Comfortable. Sidewalk cafe in summer.

House specialties: Entremeses: molotes de tinga (handmade corn flour turnovers filled with spiced, shredded pork-beef mixture with Mexican sausage and fire-roasted tomatoes); quesadillas capitalinas (handmade corn flour turnovers, filled with asadero cheee, epazotea and roasted chile poblano strips; epazote gives this dish a distinctive, prehispanic Mexican flavor); sopa tarasca (creamy herbed chicken soup, with toasted chile pasilla, beans, tomatoes, shreds of tortilla. Entrees: puerco en mole negro (grilled pork tenderloin with classic mole negro from Oaxaca, with epazote-flavored rice and cactus leaf); the unusual specialty, mixiote de borrego (lamb chunks marinated in guajillo-tequila sauce, seasoned with avocado leaf and orange juice, cooked in the parchment-like outer layer of maguey leaf, with salsa borracha and frijoles de la olla); excellent camarones a la Yucateca (large

(continued)

Gulf shrimps, grilled in green pumpkin seed mole, with garlicky white rice and fried plantains). Desserts: Lucious Crepas de cajeta al amor (crêpes with rare goat milk caramel sauce with fried plantains, walnuts, and orange slice garnish).

Other recommendations: Entremeses: guacamole, ripe avocado with pico de gallo relish, with totopos (tortilla chips); ensalada de jicama y nopalitos (textural salad with fresh cactus leaves, sliced jicama, with lemon, lime and orange vinaigrette). Entrees: grilled venison steak, marinated in garlic sauce, served with salsa de molcajete, black beans, Swiss chard, and red roasted potatoes; molcajetes (prehistoric stone mortar, filled with choice of grilled skirt steak, pork, venison, or chicken, served with grilled scallions, nopalitos, asadero cheese, chipotle salsa, frijole charros, and handmade tortillas); chiles rellenos (fire-roasted poblano chiles, one filled with pork and chicken, almond, walnuts and raisins, the other with asadero and fresco cheeses in ranchero sauce). New vegetarian items like cazuela de calabacitas (sautéed zucchini with fire roasted poblano peppers, chayote, roasted corn, ranchera salsa with epasote). Dessert: mousse de mango.

Entertainment & amenities: Reading the menu, which is like a culinary history book, and learning the historical background of the dishes and sauces and about some of the unusual ingredients.

Summary & comments: Chef-owner Dudley Nieto is well known as co-owner of the Chapulin (grasshopper, a universal symbol of good fortune) restaurant. Chapultepec is named for the famous park in Mexico City, and it means "mountain of the grasshoppers." This is one of the most unusual of all Mexican restaurants because it is based on historical recipes, and the menu offers bits of the fascinating background. Dudley Nieto is scholarly in his approach to cooking. He is like a professor, researching the various dishes and ingredients.

Nieto co-authored a book with history professor Bruce Kraig: *Cuisine of Hidden Mexico* (John Wiley & Sons, Inc.), and they were featured on Kraig's documentary, "Hidden Mexico," aired on public television. Nieto learned most of his cooking from his Mexican mother and Spanish father—the time-honored way recipes are passed on through generations in his native Puebla de los Angeles. Puebla's cuisine is considered to be one of the finest in Mexico because it embraces many traditions, from indigenous to foreign. Chapultepec is a unique Mexican cultural experience.

CHARLiE TROTTER'S

New American	
★★★★★	
Very Expensive	
Quality 99	Value C

Zone 1   North Side
816 West Armitage Avenue
(773) 248-6228

Reservations:	Required
When to go:	Wednesday seems to be the least crowded
Entree range:	Prix fixe tasting menu, $110
Payment:	VISA, MC, AMEX, CB, DC
Service rating:	★★★★★
Friendliness rating:	★★★★½
Parking:	Valet
Bar:	Wine only
Wine selection:	Extensive, award-winning, international list with 1,000 different wines including French, Californian, and Italian. Rich in Burgundies and Bordeaux, $40–1,000 per bottle. Choices by the glass, $9–16, change daily with the menu. Sommelier will assist customers with ordering.
Dress:	Business; jackets requested, not required
Disabled access:	Yes
Customers:	Locals, tourists, professionals
Dinner:	Tuesday–Thursday, 6–10 P.M.; Friday and Saturday, 5:15–10 P.M.; (closing hours depend on business; last seating is at 10 P.M.; occasionally open on Sunday and Monday)

Atmosphere/setting: Upscale, understated elegance in a renovated townhouse built in the 1880s. Quietly elegant contemporary dining rooms on two floors. Burgundy carpeting, cream wall covering, white linen tablecloths, china and crystal setting.

House specialties: Menu changes daily according to the season and market availability. Examples are smoked Atlantic salmon, Maine lobster, and Oestra caviar with daikon, jicama, blended horseradish, and spicy herb sauce; the unusual peeky toe crab and black striped bass with braised cardoon, spring peas, and curry emulsion; California pigeon breast with crispy polenta, braised red cabbage, shiitakes, and cumin-infused broth; Iowa lamb loin with caramelized rutabaga, braised legumes, and meat juices. Vegetarian tasting menus include dishes along the likes of warm goat cheese with bleeding heart radishes, artichokes, and

(continued)

142

roasted hickory nuts; ragout of early spring morels, fava beans, haricots verts, and baby leeks in their own juices. Some items flavored with chef's infused oils.

Other recommendations: Vanilla-yogurt, pineapple, and pink guava sorbets with lemongrass broth; desserts vary daily along with the menu.

Summary & comments: Chef-owner Charlie Trotter is extremely gifted (he's been termed a culinary genius) in creating dishes in a new realm with some-times disparate ingredients and eclectic foreign influences. Classic dish founda-tions are often given an element of surprise and become unexpected pleasures. Trotter's cooking is difficult to define since it has long had French underpinnings, uses 95% American ingredients, and is influenced by numerous foreign cuisines. It began more as experimental contemporary French and recently turned in the direction of contemporary American, and is usually wonderful. His menu reflects the produce market availability and his creative use of lesser-known and -used vegetables. The fixed degustation menu limits the diners' choices, however, and is not everyone's favored way of dining. There's no à la carte menu, but call ahead to request any special food for dietary restrictions. Trotter had his kitchen redesigned to include state-of-the art equipment. Available for special parties.

Honors / awards: AAA five diamonds; five stars from *Mobil Travel Guide*; Relais Gourmand member; *Wine Spectator* readers voted it "Best Restaurant in the U.S." and Charlie Trotter "Best Chef in the U.S."

Chicago Chop House

Zone 3   Near North
60 West Ontario Street
(312) 787-7100

Steak	
★★★★	
Moderate	
Quality 94	Value C

Reservations:	Required
When to go:	Before 7 P.M. or after 10 P.M.; lunch is less busy
Entree range:	$16–30
Payment:	All major credit cards
Service rating:	★★★★½
Friendliness rating:	★★★★½
Parking:	Valet; $6, lunch; $7, dinner
Bar:	Full service
Wine selection:	International, extensive (has own warehouse)
Dress:	Business casual
Disabled access:	No, but managers are willing to assist
Customers:	Professionals, VIPs, lots of celebrities
Lunch/Dinner:	Monday–Thursday, 11:30 A.M.–11 P.M., Friday, 11:30 A.M.–11:30 P.M.
Dinner:	Saturday, 4–11:30 P.M.; Sunday, 4–11 P.M.

Atmosphere/setting: Century-old brownstone with three floors of dining rooms and more than 1,400 historical Chicago pictures. Every Chicago mayor is on the wall—not even City Hall has that!

House specialties: U.S. prime aged steaks and prime rib; Chop House char-broiled New York strip steak, either 16- or 24-ounce; T-bone steak, 24-ounce; namesake potato pancake.

Other recommendations: Spring lamb chops; roast loin of pork chops; broiled Lake Superior whitefish with lemon butter; Russ's American fries.

Entertainment & amenities: Pianist on Monday–Friday, 5–11 P.M.; Saturday and Sunday, 6–11 P.M. A place to see VIPs.

Summary & comments: One of Chicago's best restaurants for quality steaks and chops, founded by the late well-known restaurateur, Henry Norton. It has a loyal following, especially with certain celebrities. Menu is traditional steak house–style, featuring steaks and chops, a couple of chicken items, several seafood preparations, seafood appetizers. Food is simple and properly prepared.

Honors/awards: Knife and Fork Club '91–'95. In '94 voted Number Two steak house in the United States by Tom Horan's America's Top 10 Clubs. Listed by *Gourmet* as one of top five steakhouses in Chicago. *Wine Spectator* Award for Excellence '94–'98. Zagat Award, '97 and '98.

Chowpatti Vegetarian Restaurant

	Indian/Vegetarian
	★★★
Zone 10 Northwest Suburbs	Inexpensive
1035 South Arlington Heights Road, Arlington Heights	Quality 80 Value B
(847) 640-9554	

Reservations:	5 or more only
When to go:	Any time
Entree range:	$8–18
Payment:	All major credit cards for checks over $10
Service rating:	★★★
Friendliness rating:	★★★★
Parking:	Free lot
Bar:	No liquor; juice bar with 20–25 fruit juice combinations; nonalcoholic beer
Wine selection:	None
Dress:	Casual
Disabled access:	Yes
Customers:	International, out-of-towners, couples, families
Lunch/Dinner:	Tuesday–Thursday, Sunday, 11:30 A.M.–9 P.M.; Friday and Saturday, 11:30 A.M.–10 P.M.

Atmosphere/setting: Upscale casual, spring-looking, quiet.

House specialties: Special bhel puri with dahl; basic bhel puri with whipped homemade yogurt and chopped cucumber and tomatoes; samosa with dahl (samosa topped with whipped yogurt, sweet chutney sauce, onions, and coriander); masala dosa (dosa filled with lightly seasoned onions, potatoes, tomatoes, coriander, cashews, and raisins); aloo mutter (potato chunks and pea curry).

Other recommendations: Special sev batata purl with dahl (loaded Indian nachos); grilled club pav bhaji (grilled sandwich with layers of meatless stew and cheese); aloo paratha (paratha [flaky bread made with whole-wheat flour] stuffed with mildly spiced potatoes); veg biryani (basmati rice with green beans, carrots, green peas, cashew nuts, herbs, and spices). Kulfis (homemade Indian ice cream): malai (plain), mango, kesar-pista (saffron pistachio), and chiku (exotic fruit).

Summary & comments: The building was recently remodeled with a state-of-the-art air-filtration system and lead-free dishes. Meals are low in calories, fat, and cholesterol. Family owned and run. Very health-concerned and quality-oriented owner, and it shows in the results.

Honors/awards: Voted Best Vegetarian Restaurant and third in the Healthy Menu Items category in *North Shore* magazine, 1994.

Cité

Zone 1   North Side
Top of Lake Point Tower,
    505 North Lake Shore Drive
(312) 644-4050

Continental	
★★★★	
Very Expensive	
Quality 89	Value D

Reservations:	Required (weekends book up fast; plan ahead)
When to go:	It's easier to get a reservation on weeknights
Entree range:	$23–48
Payment:	Major credit cards
Service rating:	★★★★½
Friendliness rating:	★★★★
Parking:	Building garage
Bar:	Full service
Wine selection:	Extensive; American and European wines, from $40–140 a bottle; four available by the glass
Dress:	Jackets required for men
Disabled access:	Yes
Customers:	Tourists, couples, guests of special events
Lunch:	Monday–Friday, noon–3 P.M., Sunday brunch, 11 A.M.–3 P.M.
Dinner:	Sunday–Thursday, 5–9:30 P.M.; Friday and Saturday, 5–10:30 P.M.

Atmosphere/setting: The panoramic, 70th-floor view of Chicago's skyline and lakefront fosters a heady, romantic atmosphere at Cité. Though the view alone is spectacular, Cité enhances the scene with fresh flower arrangements.

House specialties: Appetizers: sautéed wild mushrooms in puff pastry; Mediterranean tapas; shrimp coriander. Entrees (include Cité salad): grilled Norwegian salmon fillet, with raspberry champagne sauce; roast rack of spring lamb, with sweet Dijon, fresh rosemary, and pecans; baked red snapper Mediterranean in crust of aromatic vegetables. Grand Marnier soufflé and several desserts prepared tableside.

Other recommendations: Pasta primavera; classic steak Diane, flambéed tableside; daily selections from pastry trolley.

Entertainment & amenities: The spectacular panoramic view of Chicago's skyline and lakefront.

Summary & comments: As the restaurant's postcard states: "Let the skyline surround you," and indeed it does here. This is one of the greatest views of Chicago, and it's 25 floors closer to earth than The Signature Room at the Ninety-Fifth. The restaurant has had its ups and downs over the years, but lately has seemed reliable in its commitment to fine dining. A great restaurant for a special occasion: birthday guests see their name in a frame at the table.

Coco Pazzo

Zone 4   The Loop
300 West Hubbard Street
(312) 836-0900

Italian
★★★★
Moderate
Quality 91   Value C

Reservations:	Highly recommended, especially on weekends
When to go:	During the week
Entree range:	$13–30
Payment:	V, MC, AMEX, D
Service rating:	★★★★
Friendliness rating:	★★★★
Parking:	Valet; city garages nearby
Bar:	Full service, including grappa selection
Wine selection:	85 Italian selections, some French champagne, sparkling wines from California; $20–225 per bottle. By-the-glass include Eno Friuli 1996 Chardonnay; "Monte Antico" 1995 Sangiovee, and Cielo 1997 Merlot
Dress:	Chic casual to upscale, no jackets required, but many men wear them
Disabled access:	Yes
Customers:	Mostly local; professional; sophisticated couples; professionals (especially at lunch)
Lunch:	Monday–Friday, 11 A.M.–2:30 P.M.
Dinner:	Monday–Thursday, 5:30–11 P.M.; Friday and Saturday, 5:30–11:30 P.M.; Sunday, 5–10 P.M.

Atmosphere/setting: Open kitchen with wood-burning oven and rotisserie highlighted by a blue Spanish tile backdrop produces a warm, inviting interior. Rustic decor: brick walls; wooden floors, beams, and chairs; track lighting and columns. Sophisticated blue velvet drapes enhance the room along with white linen-covered tables spaced for privacy; elegant bar; decorative colorful and shapely antique bottles.

House specialties: House specialties: Antipasti assortment, displayed near entrance (includes sweet peas with prosciutto, Tuscan beans, roasted summer squash, Prusciutto di Parma, frittata, Sardinian pecorino, Reggiano Parmigiano, and roasted red peppers); zucchini blossoms filled with fontina cheese, delicately fried, over fresh tomato purée (summer season). Rotisserie special of the day (e.g., lamb); bistecca alla fiorentina (grilled rib-eye steak, seared with herb oil); cacciucco

(continued)

(Tuscan fish stew); succulent scampi al forno con caponata (prawns wrapped in pancetta, wood-roasted, with spicy tomato purée and vegetable caponata); roasted vegetables; ravioli filled with asparagus (changes occasionally); wood-roasted whole fish (e.g. salmon with green lentils, fried sage, and roasted garlic); a five-star tender Provimi veal chop (pounded flat) grilled, in a magnificent sauce with sautéed wild mushrooms, mashed potatoes. Signature dessert is cioccolato fondente con gelato cappuccino—flourless chocolate cake with a warm mousse center and cappuccino ice cream; crostata di frutti di bosco congelato di ricotta (fresh blueberry and plum tart with ricotta ice cream).

Other recommendations: Risotto del Giorno (chef's special cavnoroli rice of the day); coscia di agnello al giarrosto (leg of lamb seasoned with fresh herbs, slowly cooked on the rotisserie, thinly sliced, and served with potatoes); duck breast with chanterelle mushroom and farro, ancient Tuscan grain (whole emmer wheat); osso buco (veal shank); vegetali al forno (assorted thinly-sliced seasonal vegetables with extra virgin olive oil, baked in a wood-burning oven). Desserts: A most unusual gelato Parmigiano, drizzled with 35-year aged balsamic vinegar, served with walnut crostini and grapes; pane cotta con salsa di caramello; semifreddo alla nocciola.

Summary & comments: Chicagoan Tony Priolo, the new executive chef, worked at Spago Chicago and Coco Pazzo Cafe before taking the culinary reins here. He prepares creative, hearty Tuscan-style dishes; specialties change every day. The pastry chef, Tanya Hemphill, bakes bread and luscious, simple, flavorful desserts such as budino al sapore di limone (lemon pudding with berry compote) and blueberry and plum crostata (tart). This restaurant, which translates to "crazy chef," and CoCo Pazzo Cafe (636 North St. Clair; (312) 664-2777) are restaurateur Pino Luongo's only Chicago entries of his successful group of New York–based dining establishments.

Honors/awards: *Mobil Travel Guide* Award; AAA four diamonds, DiRoNA Award.

CORNER BAKERY

	Bakery Cafe
	★★★½
	Inexpensive/Moderate
	Quality 90 Value B

Zone 4   The Loop
516 North Clark Street
(312) 644-8100

Zone 4   The Loop
Santa Fe Building,
224 South Michigan Avenue (at Jackson Boulevard)
(312) 431-7600

Reservations:	Not accepted
When to go:	Any time; busiest at peak breakfast and lunch hours
Entree range:	Loaves, $1.50–6; sandwiches and soups, $1.95–5.25
Payment:	All major credit cards
Service rating:	★★★★ (since self-serve, pertains to clerks)
Friendliness rating:	★★★★½
Parking:	Street or nearby garages or lots
Bar:	None
Wine selection:	None
Dress:	Casual
Disabled access:	Yes; call first
Customers:	Varied, professionals (before and after work and for lunch)
Open:	Monday–Friday, 6:30 A.M.–9 P.M.; Saturday and Sunday, 7:30 A.M.–9 P.M.; call individual locations for hours since some vary

Atmosphere/setting: The original Clark Street location is a small, cozy shop with several tables near windows; hearth bakery; great aromas. The Santa Fe Building is historic, and the 80-seat bakery is about the largest of the ten locations; the sidewalk cafe on Michigan Avenue is open in the summer. Other locations are slightly different, but the basic concept is the same.

House specialties: A variety of about 25 breads baked fresh daily, including baguettes, country loaves, and specialty breads such as kalamata olive, chocolate-cherry, multi-grains, and ryes. Lunch items: focaccia and various sandwiches such as chicken pesto with tomato and arugula on a baguette, or tuna salad with sweet red onion and sprouts on an olive baguette; roasted vegetable salad; Oriental pasta salad; rope pasta salad with butternut squash, goat cheese, and spinach tossed in sherry vinaigrette with rosemary.

(continued)

Other recommendations: Raisin-nut bread; kugelhopf (seasonal); mushroom pizza (oyster, shiitake, and white cap mushrooms with mozzarella and Asiago cheeses); cheese bread; tomato flatbread (thin, crackerlike); variety of muffins (good blueberry); bars (try lemon and apricot); cookies (pecan chocolate chip); mini Bundt cakes; hot chocolate; juices; cappuccino.

Summary & comments: This bakery concept, originated by Lettuce Entertain You Enterprises and chef Jean Joho in 1991, produces some of the finest hearth-cooked, European-style breads and rolls anywhere; therefore, their sandwiches are excellent. An assortment of about 25 freshly baked loaves are available daily. The number of locations is growing: bakeries are now in the Water Tower Place, Union Station, Oak Brook, Old Orchard, and Schaumburg, and adjacent to some Maggiano's Little Italy restaurants. The success of this place proves that people have been starving for great bread and baked items.

Courtwright's

Zone 8   Southern Suburbs
8989 Archer Avenue, Willow Springs
(708) 839-8000

Creative American
★★★★½
Moderate/Expensive
Quality 96   Value B

Reservations:	Necessary Saturday; recommended for large groups
When to go:	Any time
Entree range:	Lunch, $5.95–10.95; dinner, $14.95–24.95
Payment:	AMEX, D, DC, MC, VISA
Service rating:	★★★★★
Friendliness rating:	★★★★★
Parking:	Lot
Bar:	Full service
Wine selection:	More than 500 offerings; 40 by the glass, from $4.50; $18 a bottle; strong on verticals (3 or more vintages of the same wine)
Dress:	Chic casual, business or dressy
Disabled access:	Yes
Customers:	Professionals, romantic couples, locals
Lunch:	Monday–Friday, 11:30 A.M.–2:30 P.M., Saturday, 11:30 A.M.–2 P.M.
Dinner:	Monday–Thursday, 4:30–10 P.M.; Friday and Saturday, 4:30–11 P.M.; Sunday, 4–9 P.M.

Atmosphere/setting: Beautiful indoor/outdoor architecture with large windows overlooking a garden sculpted into the woodland hillside. A winding staircase bordered by flowers leads to the charming gazebo outside. Inside, a five-sided curved ceiling, globe chandelier and sconces, white linens, and spectacular floral arrangements. Painted tile inserts in the lounge fireplace symbolically represent the three generations of management here, and the animal carvings in the dining room's fireplace represent William, Rebecca, and their children.

House specialties: Appetizers: the popular lobster purse (medallions of Australian lobster, roasted red peppers, sweet peas, and baby leeks wrapped in crisp phyllo with sauce américaine; spring vegetable terrine (charcoal-grilled portobello, baby artichokes, and asparagus); special soup one night was roasted garlic, garnished with croutons and slivers of bell peppers and carrots; house salad (organic mesclun and seasonal vegetables with herb Balsamic vinaigrette). Entrees: medallions of lobster with sautéed Gulf shrimp and freshwater prawn;

(continued)

medallions of pork tenderloin marinated in lemongrass and truffle oil, sautéed and dressed in a sweet-tart, sun-dried mango wine sauce; rock Cornish hen stuffed with mushroom game mousse served with wild rice pilaf and sun-dried cherries, vegetables, and Riesling reduction; rack of New Zealand lamb (encrusted in fresh herbs, seared, and oven-roasted with potato galette); char-grilled 10-oz. prime filet mignon (served with sautéed portobello mushroom and pinot noir reduction). Chef's degustation five-course menu, $44.95 a person.

Desserts are prepared on the premises and change regularly: rich Chocolate Fantasy, a trio of white, dark, and milk chocolate mousse with caramelized orange rum sauce. A lighter creation is Rainbow Fruit Mousse, a stunning tricolored wedge of layered raspberry, mango, and kiwi mousses with three fruit purees: black-berry, gooseberry, and raspberry; berries are arranged on the plate and a delicate pastry decorates the top. Homemade ice creams; tropical fruit sorbets in champagne with edible flowers; raspberry pecan tart with passion fruit ice cream.

Other recommendations: Warm Brie and poached pear salad (served with honey-ginger dressing and toasted pistachios). Entrees: sautéed jumbo shrimp and sea scallops on capellini with oyster mushrooms, baby artichoke halves, arugula, and a lemon pesto sauce; vegetarian bouquet (quiche of sautéed shiitake, baby leeks, roasted peppers, asparagus, and Asiago cheese); grilled fillet of fresh Atlantic salmon, ginger couscous, asparagus, and lemon-tarragon beurre blanc. White chocolate mousse cake; espresso crème anglaise; cheeses served with walnuts and grapes.

Entertainment & amenities: Occasional special events, such as wine-tasting dinners and fund-raisers with other southwest suburban chefs cooking along with the chef here.

Summary & comments: There's a family legacy at Courtwright's that goes back more than four decades in the dining business, beginning in 1956, when Ken Courtwright, Sr., and his bride, Sally, opened Ken's in Chicago's Beverly area. After expanding, the Courtwright hallmark became known for caring, friendly service as well as for good food. The business grew to include several more restau-rants, including Courtwright's in March 1995. William Courtwright, the second son, and his wife, Rebecca, created this beautiful place and now manage it. Three of their four children assist. The creative American cuisine here attests to great cooking skills and shows a sensitivity to combining compatible flavors and ingredi-ents. This is definitely a destination fine-dining place that is perfect for special occa-sions or any time you'd like to have an aesthetic, educational culinary experience.

Honors/awards: Good press, including *Fox Valley Villages 60504.*

CROFTON ON WELLS

Zone 3   Near North
535 North Wells
(312) 755-1790

New American
★★★½
Moderate
Quality 91   Value B

Reservations:	Recommended; often necessary three weeks in advance for weekends
When to go:	Weeknights
Entree range:	$16–35
Payment:	All major credit cards
Service rating:	★★★½
Friendliness rating:	★★★
Parking:	Valet, lunch and dinner, $6
Bar:	Full
Wine selection:	Fairly extensive international list, from $6–12
Dress:	Casual
Disabled access:	Yes
Customers:	Mixed, all ages; mostly professionals and locals; Crofton fans
Lunch:	Monday–Friday, 11:30 A.M.–2:30 P.M.
Dinner:	Monday–Thursday, 5–10 P.M.; Friday and Saturday, 5–11 P.M.

Atmosphere/setting: Contemporary intimate space with classical accents and tones of river stone, beige, and silver was designed by chef-owner Crofton. Sophisticated, serene, and rather austere with unadorned light gray walls (no paintings). Attractive bar surrounded by glass votives. Curvaceous gilt mirror on back wall; sheer drapes artistically divide the dining room from the kitchen area.

House specialties: Soup: sweet corn garbure (cabbage, chicken stock, bacon) with cilantro pesto; appetizer crabcake of jumbo lump crabmeat, bound by shrimp mousse, with sweet red peppers, chives, served with piquant Creole mustard sauce (a must). Entrées: sublime roast Atlantic salmon, roasted baby cauliflower, sweet pea emulsion, white truffle oil; succulent pan-roasted diver scallops with a Mediterranean touch of ratatouille, saffron-mussel sauce, basil oil. Made-to-order desserts: indulge in the warm macaronnade of extra bittersweet chocolate, a soufflé-like cake with a runny center, with raspberries and crème fraîche; crème brulée, "Jean Banchet," a tribute to the master chef, with candied orange zest and Grand Marnier.

(continued)

Other recommendations: Appetizer timbale of grilled vegetables and goat cheese, grilled wild scallion broth; sauté of wild mushrooms, bacon, cracked peppercorn cream in fried leek basket. Entree: herb-roasted poussin (French, young chicken), champagne grapes, vegetable couscous, verjus reduction. Dessert: warm feuilleté of peach and raspberry, caramel sauce, Poire William cream.

Entertainment & amenities: Special menus and celebrations.

Summary & comments: Crofton's background in classical French cuisine is evident in her American seasonal cooking, which she finds more creative since she can experiment with a broad range of ingredients. She had experience at Le Francais with Jean Banchet, at Montparnasses in Naperville with owner Jean-Paul Eskenazi, a Parisian, and then worked at the former Cassis. This is her first restaurant, and her signature is imprinted here from the interior to the food. The moderate prices belie the labor intensity of this exciting cuisine.

Honors/awards: 3 stars from both *Chicago Sun-Times* and *Chicago Tribune*; 4 gavels, *Chicago Lawyer.*

Cucina Roma

	Italian Bistro
	★★★½
Zone 8 Southern Suburbs	Inexpensive/Moderate
1163 East Ogden Avenue at Iroquois Center, Naperville	
(630) 355-4444	Quality 89 Value B

Reservations:	Accepted up to about half-capacity
When to go:	Avoid peak time, 6:30–8:30 P.M.
Entree range:	$9.50–18.95
Payment:	Major credit cards
Service rating:	★★★
Friendliness rating:	★★★½
Parking:	Shopping mall lot
Bar:	Full service; extensive martini list
Wine selection:	Italian; from $16 a bottle and $5 a glass
Dress:	Casual
Disabled access:	Yes
Customers:	Diverse; families, young professionals, and seniors
Dinner:	Monday–Thursday, 4–9:30 P.M.; Friday, 4–11 P.M.; Saturday, 4–11 P.M.; Sunday, 4–9 P.M.

Atmosphere/setting: A bit of nature enlivens the split-level space as hand-painted grapevines climb the creamy-hued walls and woodwork. Each of the four nonsmoking dining rooms is intimate yet allows space for privacy.

House specialties: Polenta con funghi (baked polenta with mushroom sauce); marinated sweet roasted peppers; antipasto alla Roma; escarole, white bean, and sausage soup (called "our specialty"—it's worth the trip here); veal osso buco (braised shank); farfalle Stefano; whitefish Milano. Chocolate blackout cake; fat-free cheesecake; frutti de bosco.

Other recommendations: Grilled portobello; stuffed artichoke; chicken and sausage pot pie; veal marsala; veal chop classico; bread pudding served with gelato; Italian lemon ice.

Entertainment & amenities: Outdoor cafe; cigar parlor; executive dining room.

Summary & comments: An impressive, lengthy menu features several categories, including the "Cucina Lite." Most entrees are grilled with bold flavors and seasoned with garlic and herbs. The chef uses vegetables liberally, which balances meals and adds texture and flavor. Cucina Roma opened in Naperville in 1997, fashioned after its successful sibling in Westmont. The caring management, fine food, and pleasant atmosphere make it one of the best Italian bistros in the suburbs.

Cuisines

Zone 4   The Loop
Renaissance Chicago Hotel,
  One West Wacker Drive
(312) 795-3330

Reservations:	Requested and suggested
When to go:	Weekdays
Entree range:	$8.95–29; one item at $32.95
Payment:	VISA, MC, AMEX, D, DC, CB, JCB
Service rating:	★★★★½
Friendliness rating:	★★★★★
Parking:	Valet
Bar:	Full service
Wine selection:	Extensive. Over 220 bottles with focus on French, Italian, and Californian; many nice vertical cabernet sauvignon tasting possibilities; 8-page list and 1-page wines-by-the-glass list.
Dress:	Tastefully casual (no shorts or T-shirts); dressier on Friday and Saturday evenings
Disabled access:	Yes
Customers:	Hotel guests, locals, theatergoers
Lunch:	Monday–Friday, 11:30 A.M.–2 P.M.
Dinner:	Daily, 5–9 P.M.

Atmosphere/setting: The decor is not the airy and light Mediterranean style popular in some places—this is more opulent: plush, romantic, elegant with comfortable banquettes; wood and marble; open kitchen with wood-burning oven.

House specialties: Starters of four cheese ravioli, pesto cream; braised artichokes and wild mushrooms; shaved truffles. Entrees: horseradish-crusted salmon; Mediterranean mixed grill (quail, venison, lamb). Desserts: Granny Smith apple pie, cinnamon ice cream, warm chocolate zuccotto with white chocolate ice cream, seasonal fruit crostata, pyramid (white and dark chocolate mousse).

Other recommendations: Robust, grilled small pizza with dried tomato and fontina; appetizer of crabmeat and shiitake mushrooms in phyllo; grilled swordfish (ordered with accompaniments from red snapper—ragout of artichokes, leeks, tomato, and muscat wine); chocolate and wild berry pizza; ethereal tiramisu with braided cherries.

Summary & comments: Start with the nine-page wine list here, then look at the one-page menu for dishes to match your bottle selection. The menu leans

(continued)

156

toward Italian with many French, some American, and a few Middle Eastern choices. There's a Mediterranean influence, and overall the cooking has bold flavors from herbs, sun-dried items, and olives. There's an element of surprise (e.g., a salad of field greens with quail eggs and prosciutto cracklings) and a comfort zone with standards like minestrone. A refreshing complimentary fruit plate arrives at the end of the meal—a very thoughtful touch. The value here is excellent considering the food, wine, and hospitality.

   Honors/awards: *Wine Spectator* Award of Excellence, 1992–1998.

Cy's Crab House

Zone 1   North Side
3819 North Ashland Avenue
(773) 883-8900

Seafood/Persian	
★★★	
Inexpensive/Moderate	
Quality 84	Value B

Reservations:	Recommended for 5 or more
When to go:	Monday–Thursday
Entree range:	$6–22 and market price
Payment:	VISA, MC, AMEX
Service rating:	★★★½
Friendliness rating:	★★★★½
Parking:	Owns 2 adjacent lots
Bar:	Full service
Wine selection:	American; several by the glass, $3–5
Dress:	Casual
Disabled access:	Yes, including rest rooms
Customers:	Locals, diverse, professionals, couples, families
Lunch/Dinner:	Sunday–Thursday, 11:30 A.M.–11 P.M.; Friday and Saturday, 11:30 A.M.–midnight

Atmosphere/setting: Simple contemporary decor; semiformal, spacious, two-level main dining room; Recently remodeled outdoor/indoor casual cafe with patio. New raw bar with specials for $9.95.

House specialties: Prawns stuffed with crabmeat; Cy's crab cake; joojeh kebab (charcoal-broiled, marinated chicken); prime dry-aged steaks.

Other recommendations: Mussels steamed with garlic; oysters on the half shell; garlic blue crab claw; Key lime pie; turtle cheesecake. Cy's Crab platter with Alaskan, Dungeness, king, and snow crabs.

Entertainment & amenities: Eating all the oysters you can for $9.95 at the raw bar from 4 P.M. until closing.

Summary & comments: Daily ordering ensures that about ten different fish are offered in addition to the shellfish during the week; occasionally the restaurant runs out of a particular fish item—a good sign of turnover. One page of Cy's menu features Persian specialties, including vegetarian dishes and many kebabs—some with mahi mahi, shrimp, and scallops; combination platters include "crabs and slabs" (barbecue baby-back ribs and snow crab legs). Besides this six-year-old restaurant, Cy Sadaka owns King Crab, an affordable, casual seafood restaurant at 1816 North Halsted Street ((312) 280-8990); his newest restaurant is Cy's Steak & Chop House at 4138 North Lincoln Avenue ((773) 404-5800).

Cyrano's Bistrot & Wine Bar

Zone 3   Near North
546 North Wells Street
(312) 467-0546

French Bistro	
★★★½	
Inexpensive/Moderate	
Quality 90 Value B	

Reservations:	Accepted
When to go:	Any time
Entree range:	$10.95–15.95
Payment:	Major credit cards
Service rating:	★★★★
Friendliness rating:	★★★★
Parking:	Valet, $6
Bar:	Full service
Wine selection:	Country French selections; fairly priced; some by the glass
Dress:	Casual
Disabled access:	Yes
Customers:	Young professionals, couples, families
Open:	Sunday–Thursday, 11:30 A.M.–10 P.M.; Friday and Saturday, 11:30 A.M.–11 P.M.

Atmosphere/setting: Mustard-yellow walls, burgundy banquettes, wooden beams, mirrors, and a sidewalk cafe with riotous fresh flowers (during fine weather) give the feeling of a cozy cafe in France.

House specialties: Rotisserie duck maison; bouillabaisse; Bergerac-style braised pork and beef tips; Simone's simply steamed artichoke with sauce tartare; house-cured salmon gravlax with cucumber rémoulade; steamed mussels marinière in wine cream; sweet onion and mushroom tart with petite salade; salad of red leaf lettuce, frisée, Belgian endive, blue cheese, and walnuts in garlic vinaigrette; Cyrano's salade maison; warm apple tart with rosemary ice cream.

Other recommendations: Grilled steak; coq au vin bordelaise; cassoulet from Toulouse with duck, lamb, sausage, and white beans; ostrich country pâté; les fromages plate (at least four imported cheeses); chocolate bread pudding.

Summary & comments: Cyrano's, one of Chicago's newest French bistrots, is the husband-and-wife operation of chef Didier Durand, a native of Bergerac, France, and his wife, Jamie Pellar, who directs the front of the house and the wine cellar. Durand prepares variations on the classical French cuisine of his roots, an approach that's proving successful. This is a nonsmoking environment. Many love "Le Grand Lunch Express," a four-course meal on an oversized tray for $10.96.

Honors/awards: Sherman Kaplan's Top 13 Restaurants of 1996.

Del Rio

Zone 11   Northern Suburbs
228 Green Bay Road, Highwood
(847) 432-4608

Italian
★★★
Inexpensive/Moderate

Quality 83   Value B

Reservations:	Recommended for 6 or more
When to go:	5–6 P.M.
Entree range:	$10.95–24
Payment:	All major credit cards
Service rating:	★★★½
Friendliness rating:	★★★★
Parking:	Lot
Bar:	Full service
Wine selection:	Extensive, international; one of the largest selections in the Midwest
Dress:	Moderately casual to dressy
Disabled access:	Yes
Customers:	Diverse, including loyal locals
Dinner:	Monday–Thursday, 5–10 P.M.; Friday and Saturday, 5–11 P.M.

Atmosphere/setting: Home-style "family restaurant look"; linen tablecloths; dimly lit and cozy; nice bar.

House specialties: Veal Del Rio and other veal dishes; homemade gnocchi; ravioli al forno; tortelacci with spinach and chees filling;low-fat healthy chicken items; polenta; risotto with red sauce. Desserts: tiramisu; custard grussini.

Other recommendations: Steak; fresh fish (e.g., salmon modenese); and pasta items (ask server for recommendations). Desserts: cannoli; pane cotta.

Entertainment & amenities: Reviewing the grand wine list.

Summary & comments: This is one of the oldest Italian family-owned restaurants in Highwood—having just celebrated the big 75th anniversary—a major milestone in this competitive restaurant field! Family pride in overseeing the operation keeps it running smoothly. Cooking is solid, with the predictable standards, and you can be blown away by the scope and quality of the wines.

The Dining Room

Zone 3 Near North	New French
The Ritz-Carlton Hotel,	★★★★★
160 East Pearson Street	Moderate/Expensive
(312) 266-1000, ext. 4223	Quality 97 Value C

Reservations:	Required for weekends and holidays; call one week ahead for Sunday and holidays, and mid-week for weekends
When to go:	Weekends are busiest; business depends on conventions in the hotel and Chicago events
Entree range:	$30–36
Payment:	VISA, MC, AMEX, DC, CB
Service rating:	★★★★★
Friendliness rating:	★★★★★
Parking:	3 hours free with validation at restaurant; car parked by valet at hotel entrance
Bar:	Full service; 2 bars in hotel
Wine selection:	Extensive 50-page list with about 500 selections; more than 20,000 bottles in temperature-controlled cellars; from $30–2,200 per bottle; mostly French Burgundy and Bordeaux with a fair number of American wines
Dress:	Jacket required, tie optional; brunch, casual—no cutoffs or tank tops
Disabled access:	Yes, entrance and rest room
Customers:	Many hotel guests and locals; not touristy; families and couples, honeymooners and anniversary celebrators
Brunch:	Sunday, 2 seatings for buffet brunch at 10:30 A.M. and 1 P.M. Seasonal menus.
Dinner:	Monday–Saturday, 6–11 P.M.; Sunday, 6–10 P.M.

Atmosphere/setting: Luxurious Edwardian-style two-level room with carved French pine, beveled mirrors, crystal, and Louis XV chairs at tables in the central area. Quiet, cozy niches; large tables for families; intimate banquettes in raised tier for couples. Sunday brunch served on outdoor terrace.

House specialties: Maine lobster with couscous and stuffed zucchini blossom filled with seafood mousseline, with shellfish-chive jus; applewood home-smoked salmon with traditional garnishes; Beluga caviar parfait with corn cake;

(continued)

chilled terrine of artichokes, baby spinach, and oven-dried tomatoes, and French green bean salad; veal chop with spring morel mushrooms and asparagus–Italian parsley salad; four to five items change daily; always five meat entrees and five seasonal fish; verbal special of the day.

Other recommendations: Shrimp cake with an assortment of Kingsfield green beans and honey-thyme vinaigrette; Colorado rack of lamb glazed with thyme and honey, artichoke hearts, and lamb shank and braised fennel gratin; sautéed swordfish with portobello mushroom and tomato Provençale, in a mustard–red wine vinaigrette; six-course vegetarian degustation menu, $50; set pre-theater menu from 6–7 P.M.; six-course degustation menu, $60.

Entertainment & amenities: Pianist (classical, contemporary, and requests) during dining hours.

Summary & comments: Voted by readers of several magazines to be the best hotel dining room in Chicago, and every visit here proves why. Top-flight, progressive French cuisine, opulent atmosphere, and professionally friendly— never intimidating—service. This is a stellar dining experience at one of the finest hotels anywhere. Sarah Stegner became the chef of the Dining Room in 1991 and has won numerous awards since. Her inspirational cooking is predominantly light, incorporating low-fat alternative cuisine dishes and featuring an abundance of vegetables, herbs, and strong flavors, while stressing simplicity in presentation.

Honors/awards: Chef Sarah Stegner won *New York's* James Beard Award for upcoming chefs; *Gourmet* magazine, "Best Restaurant in Chicago," 1996; *Bon Appetit* magazine, "One of the Top 13 Hotel Dining Rooms in the United States," 1996; wine list received the *Wine Spectator* Grand Award for 14 years in succession.

Don Juan

Zone 1   North Side
6730 North Northwest Highway
(733) 775-6438

Mexican	
★★★½	
Inexpensive	
Quality 93	Value B

Reservations:	Recommended for 5 or more; not accepted on Friday and Saturday
When to go:	Monday–Thursday; Sunday is good for families
Entree range:	$6.95–13.25 on menu; up to $21 on special menu
Payment:	All major credit cards
Service rating:	★★★
Friendliness rating:	★★★★
Parking:	Free lot or street
Bar:	Full service; all Mexican beers
Wine selection:	Spanish, Chilean, and some Mexican wines
Dress:	Very casual
Disabled access:	Yes
Customers:	Families, couples, 20-somethings; mostly local
Lunch/Dinner:	Monday–Thursday, 11 A.M.–10 P.M.; Friday and Saturday, 11 A.M.–11 P.M.; Sunday, noon–9 P.M.

Atmosphere/setting: Mexican feeling in split-level dining room with many artifacts and colorful touches. Can be noisy.

House specialties: Seafood dishes on daily special menu; game such as grilled venison chop, barley risotto with wild mushrooms, and dried blueberry pasilla sauce. From the regular menu, traditional items such as classic steak tacos, burrito Don Juan, and enchiladas suizas.

Other recommendations: Nachos de marisco with crabmeat and shrimp; stuffed jalapeños; duck tamales; fajitas with chicken, steak, pork, or shrimp—a combo or vegetarian. Flan, good sorbets and ice creams, and plum-almond tart.

Entertainment & amenities: Variety (except in the summer), including flamenco guitar and a harpist.

Summary & comments: Named for the legendary promiscuous lover, Don Juan has a flirtatious menu appeal with a creative departure from the carbon-copy Mexican fare. Allow yourself to be seduced by the chef's creative specials. On busy nights, the restaurant's noise level can be annoying. Private party room available for up to 30 people.

Honors/awards: *Chicago* magazine's Best Fajita.

DON ROTH'S IN WHEELING

	American
	★★★
	Moderate
	Quality 84 Value C

Zone 10   Northwest Suburbs
61 North Milwaukee Avenue, Wheeling
(847) 537-5800

Reservations:	Recommended
When to go:	Any time
Entree range:	$15.95–27.95
Payment:	VISA, MC, AMEX, D, DC, CB
Service rating:	★★★
Friendliness rating:	★★★★
Parking:	Lot
Bar:	Full service
Wine selection:	Limited—mostly American and French
Dress:	Smart casual
Disabled access:	Yes
Customers:	Families, suburban locals, professionals
Lunch:	Monday–Friday, 11:30 A.M.–2:30 P.M.
Dinner:	Monday–Thursday, 5:30–9:30 P.M.; Friday, 5–10:30 P.M.; Saturday, 5–11 P.M.; Sunday, 4–8:30 P.M.

Atmosphere/setting: Memorabilia dating back to 1920, when owner Don Roth's father Otto started and ran the famed former Blackhawk Restaurant downtown, a popular, big-band supper club; Don Roth operated it for decades afterward. Lovely outdoor garden.

House specialties: Roast prime ribs of beef (three cuts); Boston scrod; the legendary Spinning Salad Bowl and special dressing with blue cheese, egg, and shrimp (included with entree).

Other recommendations: Sirloin strip steak; specials such as broiled Lake Superior whitefish and chicken Blackhawk.

Entertainment & amenities: Tapes of WGN broadcasts from the former Blackhawk Restaurant.

Summary & comments: Owner Don Roth is a veritable encyclopedia of history from the big-band supper club era, and he has wisely displayed his memorabilia collection. Together with prime rib and his famous Spinning Salad Bowl (dressing now sold), he transformed his restaurant from costly big-band entertainment to entertaining customers tableside, where "food is the show." Seniors especially enjoy browsing at this Wheeling location. The menu is simple, the cooking good, and the service consistently accommodating.

Honors/awards: Don Roth has received many awards over the years.

Don's Fishmarket and Tavern

	Seafood
	★★★★
Zone 11 Northern Suburbs	Inexpensive/Expensive
9335 Skokie Boulevard, Skokie	Quality 93 Value B
(847) 677-3424	

Reservations:	Accepted
When to go:	Any time
Entree range:	*Fishmarket,* $15.95–40; *Tavern,* $8–12
Payment:	VISA, MC, DC, CB
Service rating:	★★★½
Friendliness rating:	★★★★
Parking:	Lot
Bar:	Full service, extensive beer list
Wine selection:	Award-winning California wines; nice glass selections; fairly priced; tavern more limited, but good varietal list by glass and bottle
Dress:	Casual, both places
Disabled access:	Yes, both places
Customers:	Diverse, both places; some moviegoers (theaters across the road); local North Shore and city; travelers
Lunch:	*Fishmarket:* Monday–Friday, 11:30 A.M.–2:30 P.M. *Tavern:* Monday–Saturday, 11:30 A.M.–4 P.M.
Dinner:	*Fishmarket:* Monday–Thursday, 5–10 P.M.; Friday and Saturday, 5–11 P.M.; Sunday, 4–9 P.M. *Tavern:* Monday–Saturday, 5–11 P.M.; Sunday, 4–9 P.M.

Atmosphere/setting: The Fishmarket has a comfortable and sophisticated ambience with a homey atmosphere and slight nautical decor. The Tavern is more casual and rustic; overall it's cozy and dimly lit.

House specialties: *Fishmarket:* baby octopus marinated with olive oil, lemon, and spices, and mesquite grilled with sautéed spinach and tomato; fresh Caribbean red snapper, mesquite grilled and topped with sun-dried tomato and pesto beurre blanc; Don's platter (combo of grilled swordfish, pan-blackened catfish, and broiled Lake Superior whitefish over spinach). *Tavern:* New England clam chowder; peel-n-eat shrimp; Snug Harbor mussels (steamed in garlic, butter, and sherry broth); blackened tuna salad; lobster pasta (with linguini); eggplant Parmigiano.

(continued)

Other recommendations: *Fishmarket:* sautéed fresh Florida diver scallops; steaks and chops (12-ounce New York strip, 20-ounce porterhouse, lamb rack). *Tavern:* fish and chips, ocean perch, tempura shrimp, jambalaya, fajitas.

Summary & comments: Don's Fishmarket has been a dependable, comfortable North Shore seafood restaurant for over 20 years. Daily menus list origins of the freshline seafood and the day's features. Chef Domingo Shavaz offers a mix of low-fat preparations with vinaigrettes, as well as some with butter and cream sauces. The restaurant plans seasonal seafood promotions, such as a summer "Thrill of the Grill," a Crabfest and a Lobsterfest, and an Autumn Oktoberfest. The Tavern features special bargain deals at special times on certain days (e.g., shrimp and oysters, 40 cents each, Tuesday, 2–11 P.M.).

Earth

Zone 3 Near North	Healthy Cuisine
738 North Wells Street	★★★½
(312) 335-5475	Moderate/Expensive
	Quality 90 Value C

Reservations:	Dinner only, strongly recommended
When to go:	Anytime; weeknights usually less busy
Entree range:	$14.95–18.95
Payment:	AMEX, D, DC, MC, VISA
Service rating:	★★★½
Friendliness rating:	★★★★
Parking:	Valet at dinnertime, $6
Bar:	Several good organic beers; one organic vodka
Wine selection:	Carefully selected list of domestic and imported eco-friendly wines; several from insecticide-free vineyards. Almost all available by the glass $4.95–7.95; bottles $22–60
Dress:	Casual
Disabled access:	Yes, but one step in front; staff will assist. Ramp in back; call first
Customers:	Sophisticated; mostly professionals of all ages, especially 35–50; also the health-and environment-conscious
Lunch:	Monday–Saturday, 11:30 A.M.–2:30 P.M.
Dinner:	Tuesday–Thursday, 5:30 A.M.–9 P.M.; Friday and Saturday, 5:30 A.M.–10 P.M.

Atmosphere/setting: Pristine storefront interior is bright and elegant in its simplicity. Attractive lighting; an artistic row of glass block vases with seasonal flowers accent white walls. The restaurant was constructed from natural materials and non-toxic substances. Wooden tables and bar. Beautiful hickory floor the result of an environmental project to use wood that usually is made into sawdust.

House specialties: Creative soups of the day, such as corn and sweet potato soup with chiles and cilantro; the signature mussels steamed in fresh apple cider, plump and flavorful. Great salads: spring shoot salad with mesclun greens and pink peppercorn yogurt dressing; Earth salad with house honey-mustard dressing. Entrees: Vegetable strudel with or without shrimp; roasted monkfish with Indian pesto fettuccine and curry sauce; sea bass fillet topped with Swiss chard; slightly sweet-spicy jungle curry with tofu, colorful vegetables and brown rice (chef does

(continued)

creative things with tofu here). From the substantial dessert menu, a delicious semisweet and milk chocolate mousse; individual lemon tart with fresh fruit; rosemary-scented crème brûlée; fresh fruit sorbets in exotic flavors such as guanabana and passionfruit (dairy-free, fat-free, no refined sugar).

Other recommendations: Sautéed sea scallops with jicama and endive in citrus sauce; naturally smoked salmon with fresh herbed goat cheese and chive oil. Entrée: marinated seitan (wheat protein) changes with season, such as with lotus root, soba noodles, vegetables, and eggplant caviar in seaweed broth (vegan, indicated by "V"). Dessert: Ginger, coconut, and lemongrass tapioca pudding in a phyllo cup.

Entertainment & amenities: Special events to increase environmental awareness, such as Harvest Moon festival in October, which promotes Midwestern organic produce.

Summary & comments: Earth is a profound name for a restaurant, and this River North place lives up to the high expectations of the environment- and health-conscious. Owner Barry Bursak, who is committed to the environmental cause, has made his restaurant as pure as possible while offering exciting cuisine in a fine dining atmosphere. The flavorful, clean fare here is prepared by classically-trained Chef Charles Warshawsky, who elevates low-fat, healthful cooking from the commonplace to an upscale gastronomic landscape. He creatively blends together Asian, French, and Mexican ingredients that result in robust, flavor-packed, seasonal dishes that have gained him a following. This is not a vegetarian restaurant, but there are many vegetarian items, and those that are vegan are indicated by a "V."

Honors/awards: Three-star review in *Chicago Tribune*; "Hot Spot" feature in *Chicago Sun-Times*; named one of the "best new restaurants of the year" by *Chicago* magazine; one of six healthful restaurants in the United States, *Bon Appetit* (September, 1998); and featured on the Television Food Network.

El Dinamico Dallas

Zone 1   North Side
1545 West Howard Street
(773) 465-3320

Caribbean	
★★½	
Inexpensive	
Quality 79	Value B

Reservations:	Accepted but not necessary
When to go:	Any time
Entree range:	$3.95–16; dinner buffet weekend evenings, $9.95
Payment:	Major credit cards
Service rating:	★★½
Friendliness rating:	★★★★
Parking:	Street
Bar:	None
Wine selection:	BYOB; corkage fee is only 50 cents per glass
Dress:	Casual
Disabled access:	Yes
Customers:	Locals, ethnics, students
Open:	Monday, Wednesday–Saturday, noon–9 P.M.; Sunday, 5–9 P.M.

Atmosphere/setting: Down-home, colorful, plant-filled storefront reminiscent of the Caribbean. Very casual.

House specialties: Spicy jerk pork or chicken; curried chicken; chilindron de chivo (goat meat stewed in beer and wine); lambi (conch in Creole tomato-wine sauce). Desserts made by co-owner Armonize Dallas include sweet potato pie, carrot cake, and chocolate caramel cake. Homemade tropical juices, such as papaya, orange banana, or passion fruit.

Other recommendations: Curried goat; black bean soup; Armonize tamales; fried plantains and congri (rice and beans); banana bread. The dinner buffet includes many hot and cold items, some of them changing; some standards are curried chicken, spaghetti with ground turkey, rum pound cake, and fruit punch.

Summary & comments: This long-lived Caribbean cafe is owned by the energetic husband-and-wife team, chef Erick and Armonize Dallas. It offers a slice of Caribbean island culture and well-prepared Jamaican, Cuban, and Haitian dishes that reflect the owners' heritage. The service is friendly and relaxed, and the menu is just as laid back; some items require translations and descriptions, so feel free to ask. Homemade bread comes with dinner, and banana bread can be ordered as dessert. Bring your own wine, or try their delightful array of tropical juices. They also make shakes. Catering is available.

El Tipico

Mexican
★★½
Inexpensive
Quality 79　　Value B

Zone 1　　North Side
1836 West Foster Avenue
(773) 878-0839

Zone 11　　Northern Suburbs
3341 Dempster Avenue, Skokie
(847) 676-4070

Reservations:	Recommended for weekends
When to go:	Weekdays
Entree range:	$5–13
Payment:	All major credit cards
Service rating:	★★★
Friendliness rating:	★★★★
Parking:	Yes
Bar:	Full service; Mexican beers and margaritas
Wine selection:	Limited; mostly American
Dress:	Casual
Disabled access:	Yes
Customers:	Mixed, young professionals, families, professionals
Lunch/Dinner:	Sunday–Thursday, 11 A.M.–midnight; Friday and Saturday, 11–2 A.M.

Atmosphere/setting:　Intimate, charming, colorful, with some authentic artifacts; quiet overall. Nonsmoking dining rooms. Outdoor garden.

House specialties:　Appetizer combo: shrimp fajitas (also chicken and beef), steak tacos, pollo en mole, burrito ranchero; steak a la pequeña. Huge portions.

Other recommendations:　Traditional Mexican dishes (e.g., enchiladas) and good flan.

Entertainment & amenities:　Occasional weekend trio.

Summary & comments:　Very comfortable and pleasant neighborhood restaurant serving good, fresh, south-of-the-border fare and huge portions at reasonable prices. Attractive setting and caring management, plus the good value aspect, make it a place for repeat visits.

Elaine's

Zone 3 Near North	New American
448 East Ontario Street	★★★½
(312) 337-6700	Inexpensive/Moderate
	Quality 89 Value B

Reservations:	Accepted for parties of 5 or more
When to go:	Any time
Entree range:	$12.25–24.95
Payment:	Major credit cards
Service rating:	★★★★½
Friendliness rating:	★★★★½
Parking:	Discounted; validated in same building; enter 441 East Erie
Bar:	Martini bar is featured behind the neighborhood horseshoe bar with 10 seats. Wine and beer.
Wine selection:	Recently expanded to about 110; international, mostly domestic West Coast choices plus French, Italian, Spanish. Large selection of 45 by the glass, $4.75–20; bottles, $19–76; ½ bottles including Champagnes
Dress:	Casual
Disabled access:	Yes
Customers:	Mix of professionals, tourists, locals, suburbanites
Brunch:	Sunday, 8 A.M.–2 P.M.
Lunch:	Monday–Saturday, 11 A.M.–2 P.M.
Dinner:	Monday–Saturday, 5–10 P.M.

Atmosphere/setting: The atrium has seating for those desiring quick meals. Lovely, spacious, 95-seat dining room with painted columns, sky-blue ceiling and cinnamon-and-teal-hued walls holding vintage French posters and large canvases. Dining room overlooks the sidewalk cafe. Accents of antique armoires, bentwood chairs, and bistro-style paper-topped white tablecloths. Cozy area to west of entrance, decorated with wine racks, serves as alternative space to have an espresso, sample wines, and enjoy dessert. Private dining room, decorated with whimsical works by local artists, accommodates 45.

House specialties: Lunch/dinner: medley of three grains salad with Moroccan couscous; cheese-filled ravioli and recently, wild mushroom ravioli in sage brown butter. Dinner: Soup of the day, such as roast butternut squash, apple and fresh rosemary; salad of forelle pears, watercress, Stilton cheese, Balsamic

(continued)

vinaigrette. Fish of the day; pan-seared salmon, lemon caper sauce; baked pork tenderloin with couli of roast red peppers; bistro steak with red wine shallot sauce, roast potatoes, fresh vegetables. Desserts: Key lime pie; chocolate chip angel food cake; crisps filled with fresh seasonal fruit; strawberry and blueberry short-cake; plum tart.

Other recommendations: Pasta with shrimp, artichoke hearts, black olives, anchovies, fresh tomato, and garlic; Colorado lamb chops with wild mushrooms and fresh asparagus. Desserts: turtle cheesecake; angel food cake with chocolate chips; apple pie.

Entertainment & amenities: Espresso bar; pastry shop; sidewalk cafe where you can see Navy Pier and its Ferris wheel and fireworks.

Summary & comments: This is the reincarnation of the former five-year-old Ina's Kitchen & Elaine's Patio, a smaller location known for great breakfasts. The restaurant moved here in spring 1997 as Elaine and Ina's, and recently co-owner Elaine Farrell bought out her partner Ina Pinkney, and changed the name. Everything is baked here except the bread. Elaine, a graduate of The School of the Arts Institute in Chicago, always had a passion for cooking although her experience has been in architecture and interior design. She helped design the place to evoke a feeling of a bistro in a small Provençal town. Her goal is that locals enjoy Elaine's as their neighborhood restaurant. From decor to the food and wine, everything is finely tuned.

Eli's, the Place for Steak

Zone 3   Near North
215 East Chicago Avenue
(312) 642-1393

Steak
★★★½
Moderate/Expensive
Quality 88   Value C

Reservations:	Accepted
When to go:	Early or late for both lunch and dinner
Entree range:	$17.50–32
Payment:	All major credit cards
Service rating:	★★★½
Friendliness rating:	★★★★
Parking:	$5 with validation at garage next door
Bar:	Full service
Wine selection:	Mostly American, with some French and Italian selections, ranging from $16–260 (the highest for Roederer Cristal Champagne) per bottle; most in the $20–42 range.
Dress:	Casual
Disabled access:	Yes
Customers:	Mixed, professionals (especially at lunch), tourists, locals
Lunch:	Monday–Friday, 11 A.M.–3 P.M.
Dinner:	Sunday–Thursday, 5–10:30 P.M.; Friday and Saturday, 5–11 P.M.

Atmosphere/setting: Photo gallery of celebrities who have dined here with the late founder Eli Shulman and his son Mark, now the owner; comfortable carpeted dining room with white tablecloths, candle lamps, and paintings; a charming enclosed sidewalk cafe with half curtains on doors that open in the summer.

House specialties: Complimentary iced relishes, chopped liver, and breads; Eli's special New York sirloin steak, seasoned with crushed black peppercorns and served with onion, red-and-green-pepper relish, and a choice of cottage or steak fries or a baked potato; Eli's house salad (lettuce, tomatoes, beets, croutons) with good creamy garlic dressing; Eli's Famous Garbage Salad (garden vegetables served over mixed salad greens tossed in Eli's dressing)

Other recommendations: Soup of the day: good creamy tomato-based seafood chowder. Eli's famous potato pancakes, served with applesauce and sour cream; Eli's chicken and matzo ball soup; Eli's Caesar salad; calf's liver Eli, sautéed

(continued)

173

with onions, green peppers, and mushrooms. Eli's cheesecake (usually about a dozen varieties of this famous item on the dessert tray; try key lime, cappuccino hazelnut, mint chocolate chip, toffee top, peanut butter blast, or praline). If you're not fond of cheesecake, Eli's bakery also makes carrot cake, apple tart, and "Midnight sensation" chocolate cake.

Summary & comments: You'll never forget where you are dining, since Eli's name is reinforced throughout the menu. In addition, when I asked our waiter to recommend several items for dinner, he repeated three times, "Eli's is the place for steak." We got the message. Naturally, we ordered the special New York sirloin steak with crushed black peppercorns, and it was delicious and properly prepared to a medium-rare, as ordered. I also enjoyed salmon fillet pesto, and they cook fish well here, too. Although Eli's is expensive, at least you get relishes, chopped liver, delicious bread, and potato included in the entree price here, unlike some steak houses.

Emilio's Tapas Chicago

	Spanish/Tapas/Paella
Zone 1 North Side	★★★★
444 West Fullerton Avenue	Moderate
(773) 327-5100	
	Quality 91 Value C

Reservations:	Accepted Monday–Thursday and Saturday
When to go:	Weekdays
Entree range:	$13–14; tapas, $2–12
Payment:	VISA, MC, AMEX, DC
Service rating:	★★★½
Friendliness rating:	★★★★
Parking:	Valet; nearby garages
Bar:	Full service
Wine selection:	Mostly Spanish, including sangría; good range of types and prices, from $15 a bottle
Dress:	Casual
Disabled access:	Yes
Customers:	Diverse
Lunch/Dinner:	Sunday–Thursday, 11:30 A.M.–10 P.M.; Friday and Saturday, 11:30 A.M.–11 P.M.

Atmosphere/setting: Colorful ceramic decor complements the setting, which has the feel of Andalucia, the Spanish province from which Emilio hails.

House specialties: Paella de mariscos (seafood); patatas con aïoli tortilla española (a Spanish omelette with onions and potatoes); salpiçon de Burgos (marinated shrimp, scallops, and monkfish with tri-colored peppers, leeks, olive oil, and sherry vinaigrette); gambas a la plancha (grilled shrimp brochette served in garlic butter); pincho de pollo al mojo picon (grilled, marinated chicken brochette with cumin mayonnaise); datiles con bacon (dates wrapped in bacon, roasted red pepper–butter sauce).

Other recommendations: Empanada de cordero con curri (puff pastry filled with lamb, chorizo, and curry, served with tomato–basil sauce); mejillones al ajillo (black mussels served in a garlic sauce).

Entertainment & amenities: Flamenco on occasion.

Summary & comments: Known as the King of Tapas, Emilio Gervilla brought the Spanish tapas concept to Chicago more than a decade ago. Since then he's expanded to several more, mostly in the western suburbs. Emilio is from Granada, knows his cuisine well, and is a hands-on restaurateur. This place offers an authentic, delicious trip to Spain.

EMPEROR'S CHOICE

Zone 5 South Loop	Chinese
2238 South Wentworth Avenue,	★★★½
Chinatown	Inexpensive/Moderate
(312) 225-8800	Quality 88 Value B

Reservations:	Recommended on weekends
When to go:	Weekdays are less busy
Entree range:	Lunch, $5.95–9.95; dinner, $6.95–19.95
Payment:	VISA, MC, AMEX, D
Service rating:	★★★★
Friendliness rating:	★★★★
Parking:	Validated parking in Chinatown lot
Bar:	Full service
Wine selection:	Limited; several by the glass
Dress:	Casual
Disabled access:	Yes
Customers:	Family, locals, tourists
Lunch:	Monday–Friday, 11:30 A.M.–3 P.M.
Lunch/Dinner:	Monday–Saturday, 11:30–1 A.M.; Sunday, 11:45 A.M.–midnight; kitchen closes half an hour before dining room

Atmosphere/setting: Intimate storefront with tablecloths and walls decorated with framed prints of the most famous emperors of the ten dynasties. The focal point of this cozy restaurant is a robe worn by a Ching dynasty emperor.

House specialties: Seafood dishes such as Maine lobster baked with ginger and onion; pea pod sprouts with crabmeat sauce; Empress's beef (marinated tenderloin); sole two ways.

Other recommendations: Scallops and shrimp with walnuts; shrimp and chicken in bird's nest; pot stickers; Emperor's egg rolls; Peking duck (with one-day notice).

Summary & comments: One of the best restaurants in Chinatown and one of the most creative for seafood dishes. Quality ingredients, careful cooking, and attentive service have made this place popular for years, and it continues to get great reviews from critics. The food is served on beautiful china in a regal fashion, and happily, the prices are not royal. This is one of the best values for excellent Chinese cuisine.

Entre Nous

	French
Zone 4 The Loop	★★★★½
Fairmont Hotel,	Moderate/Expensive
200 North Columbus Drive	
(312) 565-7997	Quality 90 Value C

Reservations:	Recommended
When to go:	Early evenings
Entree range:	Dinner, $19–34
Payment:	All major credit cards
Service rating:	★★★★½
Friendliness rating:	★★★★★
Parking:	Hotel garage, validated; valet, $12
Bar:	Full service
Wine selection:	Award-winning, international, world-class collection; lovely wine library in the dining room
Dress:	Moderately upscale
Disabled access:	Yes
Customers:	Mostly locals, a few tourists
Dinner:	Tuesday–Saturday, 5:30–10:30 P.M.

Atmosphere/setting: Elegant, plush, and sophisticated. Large table with flowers and display of some dishes is the central focus of dining room, and one wall is a wine library.

House specialties: Specialties change daily. Dinner appetizer: pan-fried Chesapeake crab cakes (with sautéed arugula and lobster sauce). Dinner entrees: pot-au-feu of grouper and prawns with root vegetables and basil; roast rack of Sonoma lamb with mustard-herb crust and rosemary lentils. Weekly table d'hôte four-course dinner menu, $29; $44 with wine.

Other recommendations: Lobster bisque; applewood smoked chicken breast with caraway cabbage and fire-roasted chestnuts. Dessert tray holds several light, layered pastries; almond cheesecake; chocolate raspberry torte.

Entertainment & amenities: Ask about dinner-jazz package in Entre Nous.

Summary & comments: Entre Nous (between us) is an intimate French phrase and charming name for this romantic hotel dining room. The creative cuisine has many innovative touches (marrow melted over herbed tenderloin, for example). The service is gracious and accommodating and, overall, dining here is distinctive.

Honors/awards: Wine collection has received the Award of Excellence from *Wine Spectator* for three consecutive years; four stars from *Mobil Travel Guide*; DiRoNA Award.

ERWIN

Zone 1   North Side
2925 North Halsted Street
(773) 528-7200

New American/Midwestern
★★★★
Inexpensive/Moderate

Quality 94   Value B

Reservations:	Accepted
When to go:	Any time; early dinner is usually less busy
Entree range:	$7.95 (hamburger), $12.95–16.95
Payment:	AMEX, C, DC, MC, VISA
Service rating:	★★★★½
Friendliness rating:	★★★★½
Parking:	Valet
Bar:	Full service, including microbrewery beers
Wine selection:	International; 75% American, 25% mixed; several by the glass
Dress:	Casual and chic; business
Disabled access:	Completely
Customers:	Professionals, couples, families, locals
Brunch:	Sunday, 10:30 A.M.–2:30 P.M.
Dinner:	Tuesday–Thursday, 5:30–10 P.M.; Friday and Saturday, 5:30–11 P.M.; Sunday, 5–9:30 P.M.

Atmosphere/setting: Inviting, casual bistro. Whimsical border mural of city rooftops.

House specialties: Smoked trout in thin herbed pancake with salmon caviar; vegetable tart; tomato salad; whitefish; sautéed calf's liver; wood-grilled flank steak; caramel pot de crème; chocolate–sour cherry torte; seasonal fruit pie.

Other recommendations: Gazpacho with wood-grilled shrimp; seared rare tuna with salad, vegetables, and fried wontons; wood-grilled salmon or hamburger; vegetarian dish of roasted stuffed sweet pepper; pecan-maple tart à la mode; seasonal fruit sorbets.

Entertainment & amenities: Seasonal cooking classes; off-premises catering; private parties on Monday for dinner and daily for lunch.

Summary & comments: Owners chef Erwin and his wife, Cathy Drechsler, are seasoned restaurateurs; details matter. Chef Drechsler's cooking techniques have a French foundation, but the end result is American with assertive flavors. Erwin's menu is efficient; each dish is listed by its main ingredient. The savvy staff is educated in theoretical and practical topics of food, wine, and service.

Honors/awards: *Wine Spectator* Award of Excellence; *Wine Enthusiast* award for creativity and excellence; *Bon Appetit* Best New Restaurant 1994; chef Erwin is a member of Chef 2,000 (top 2,000 chefs in North America).

EVEREST

French	
★★★★★	
Expensive	

Zone 4   The Loop
440 South LaSalle Street (One Financial
    Place, 40th Floor)
(312) 663-8920

Quality 98   Value C

Reservations:	Required
When to go:	Varies; call before you go
Entree range:	À la carte, $26.50–32.50; pre-theater menu, $44; evening tasting menu, $79
Payment:	All major credit cards, plus JCB
Service rating:	★★★★★
Friendliness rating:	★★★★½
Parking:	Complimentary valet in building garage
Bar:	Full service
Wine selection:	Extensive award-winning list with 1,000 international wines, mostly French, Alsatian, and American; $39-plus per bottle; 10–12 selections by the glass
Dress:	Jacket and tie suggested
Disabled access:	Wheelchair accessible; call ahead for special accommodations
Customers:	Upscale; professionals, couples
Dinner:	Tuesday–Thursday, 5:30–9:30 P.M.; Friday and Saturday, 5:30–10 P.M.; Sunday and Monday, closed

Atmosphere / setting: Softly lit, romantic, simple elegance; flowers and candlelight; 75-seat dining room separated into an atrium level for a private atmosphere and a spectacular western view of Chicago; tuxedo-clad waiters. Six private dining rooms for parties of eight or more are open every day for breakfast, lunch, and dinner (reservations must be made in advance for these rooms).

House specialties: Smoked salmon served with warm oatmeal blinis (cold appetizer); creamless navy bean soup and confit of rabbit; terrine of pheasant, partridge, and squab marbled with wild herbs and vegetables; Maine lobster roasted with Alsace Gewurtztraminer and ginger.

Other recommendations: Ballotine of wild Atlantic salmon and marinated cabbage, Alsace-style; double lamb consommé, mini–goat cheese ravioli; New York State foie gras; saddle of Millbrook venison, wild huckleberries, Alsace Wassertriwella; ballotine of skate stuffed with mushrooms and wrapped around

(continued)

non-sour Alsatian sauerkraut in a light Riesling juniper berry sauce. Pre-theater dinner menu that changes monthly with seatings at 5:30 P.M., $44; degustation menu, $79 per person.

Entertainment & amenities: The spectacular western view of Chicago.

Summary & comments: Mount Everest was climbed first by Sir Edmund Hillary, and chef Jean Joho has succeeded in making his Everest the pinnacle of French gastronomy in Chicago—in fact it's one of the country's premier restaurants. In partnership with Lettuce Entertain You Enterprises, Joho is a protégé of Paul Haeberlin of the acclaimed L'Auberge de L'Ill in Alsace, France. He began training at 13 as an apprentice. His education continued in French, Italian, and Swiss kitchens, and at age 23, he became sous-chef of a Michelin two-star restaurant with the command of a staff of 35. His French cuisine is masterful, with much use of his beloved Alsatian homeland's ingredients; each dish is a work of art to behold. Dining here is truly tops for food, service, and view of the city.

Honors/awards: Four-star reviews from the *Chicago Tribune,* the *Chicago Sun-Times, Chicago* magazine; featured in *Playboy* and *Esquire;* winner of Ivy Award and Gault Millau honors; chef-owner Jean Joho won the James Beard Award for Best Chef in Midwest and *Food and Wine* magazine's Top Chef of the Year Award; he's been inducted into *Nation's Restaurant News'* Fine Dining Hall of Fame and received the *Wine Spectator* Award of Excellence, 1992, 1997–98. Reba Mandari Culinary Award of Excellence, 1998.

Filippo's

Italian
★★★
Inexpensive/Moderate

Quality 82   Value C

Zone 1   North Side
2211 North Clybourn Avenue
(773) 528-2211

Reservations:	Recommended
When to go:	Any time
Entree range:	$6.95–16.95
Payment:	VISA, AMEX, MC
Service rating:	★★★½
Friendliness rating:	★★★★
Parking:	Street, theater lot; may have a valet soon
Bar:	Full service, including grappa selection
Wine selection:	Italian, 30-plus types; $16–55 a bottle; several by the glass
Dress:	Casual to dressy
Disabled access:	Yes
Customers:	Professionals, dates, families
Lunch:	Planning to serve lunch soon
Dinner:	Monday–Thursday, 5–11 P.M.; Friday and Saturday, 5 P.M.–midnight; Sunday, 5–10 P.M.

Atmosphere/setting: Intimate storefront with gold-hued walls and old-world Italian touches, such as pictures of cherubs and an antique copper cappuccino machine. Tables are covered with mix-and-match tablecloths handmade by one owner's mother.

House specialties: Homemade ravioli annarella (ricotta and spinach in cream sauce with Parmigiano); daily fish (swordfish steak with Mediterranean sauce of lemon, olive oil, basil, rosemary, and garlic); veal scaloppine in sage sauce with mushroom and mozzarella. Desserts: flourless chocolate espresso cake, chocolate hazelnut torte, zuccotto.

Other recommendations: Calamari fritti; antipasto vegetariano (assorted grilled veggies); fettuccine Giorgione (light tomato sauce, sautéed chicken breast, broccoli, and blue cheese).

Summary & comments: The owners take great pride in their homey place. The atmosphere is warm and inviting—customers are personally greeted at each table. The menu includes the chef's refined interpretations of dishes his mother cooked for everyday meals.

Flat Top Grill

American Stir-Fry	
★★★	
Inexpensive	
Quality 85	Value B

Zone 3   Near North
319 West North Avenue
(312) 787-7676

Zone 11   Northern Suburbs
707 Church Street, Evanston
(847) 570-0100

Zone 2   North Central/O'Hare
1000 West Washington
(312) 829-4800

Reservations:	Not accepted
When to go:	Earlier in the week
Entree range:	$9.95 for dinner; $6.95 for lunch; $4.95 for children (11 years old and under) on weekends, free Monday–Thursday evenings
Payment:	All major credit cards
Service rating:	★★★½ (partly self-serve)
Friendliness rating:	★★★★½
Parking:	*Chicago:* car valet, $6; bicycle and rollerblade valet, $2.50; *Evanston:* car valet, $4; city garage
Bar:	Full service; Asian beers; signature drinks like Tricky Vicky Punch and Singapore Slings
Wine selection:	A small selection of American, including Kendall Jackson chardonnay and Buena Vista sauvignon blanc; from $3.95–5.95 a glass and $15–29 a bottle; reserve list available.
Dress:	Casual
Disabled access:	Yes
Customers:	Urban professionals, locals, theatergoers, students
Lunch:	*Chicago:* Saturday and Sunday, 11:30 A.M.–3 P.M.; *Evanston:* Daily, 11:30 A.M.–3 P.M.
Dinner:	*Chicago:* Sunday–Thursday, 5–10 P.M.; Friday and Saturday, 5–11 P.M.; *Evanston:* Monday–Thursday, 5–9:30 P.M.; Friday and Saturday, 5–10:30 P.M.; Sunday, 4–9 P.M.

Atmosphere/setting: A casual, bustling atmosphere with an open kitchen featuring the flat-top grill in the front window. Overwhelming blackboard menus hang on the walls. There are both raised and lowered mahogany wood tables and

(continued)

182

chairs and cushioned booths; wood-paneled ceiling; soft lighting; and loud rock/pop music in the background.

House specialties: Flat Top Grill Sauce is a citrus- and soy-based sauce that mixes well with the other sauces and combinations of vegetables and meats; David's recipe (two ladles of Flat Top Grill Sauce, one ladle of oyster sauce, one ladle of ginger water, one ladle of plum sauce, fresh garlic to taste, raw egg (optional) as a binder, one ladle of red chili paste) is great with seafood, salad, noodles, mu shoo, chicken, or rice on the side; fresh fruit sundae with orange-ginger sauce drizzled over peach ice cream and fresh raspberries and black raspberries (or whatever fruits are in season), topped with a sprig of mint; chocolate storm, a rich chocolate brownie with French vanilla ice cream; mango juice; and mocha java coffee.

Other recommendations: Mu shoo (stir-fry variation); vegetable broth (stir-fry variation); salad (stir-fry variation); organic mixed greens with cucumber dressing; and cinnamon apple crisp.

Summary & comments: This create-your-own stir-fry restaurant has the comforts of a full-service restaurant. Customers create their own stir-fry meals by choosing from a food line that offers a bountiful selection of more than 70 fresh organic vegetables, spices, rice, noodles, meats, poultry, and seafoods complemented with a choice of 20 Asian sauces. Customers simply drop off their filled bowls at the end of the line and relax while it is cooked on the restaurant's custom flat-top grill and returned promptly to their tables. Guests are not limited to stir-fry. They can also create soup, salad, and moo shoo with a little help from the chefs. If you are overwhelmed by all the stir-fry ingredients offered, the large blackboard menu and helpful servers offer suggestions about what combinations of sauces and ingredients make a great stir-fry meal.

More than one-third of the stir-fry selections showcase organically grown, locally distributed vegetables, including organically grown bok choy, mushrooms, broccoli, corn, and red onions. While chicken and beef remain a staple, the fresh food bar offers a daily rotation of meats and seafood, including shrimp, squid, turkey, lamb, and pork. The Flat Top Grill recently began offering monthly exotic meats (such as buffalo, ostrich, and alligator). This is the only restaurant of its type that we know of offering these upscale ingredients. Carryout available during business hours.

foodlife

American
★★★
Inexpensive

Quality 82   Value C

Zone 3   Near North
835 North Michigan Avenue,
   Water Tower Place
(312) 335-3663

Reservations:	Parties of 6 or more only
When to go:	Avoid lunchtime and rush hour
Entree range:	$6.95–9.95
Payment:	All major credit cards
Service rating:	★★★ (largely self-serve)
Friendliness rating:	★★
Parking:	Water Tower underground garage
Bar:	Wine, beer, and sangría only
Wine selection:	Wine by the glass only
Dress:	Casual
Disabled access:	Yes
Customers:	Professionals, shoppers, tourists, families, couples
Open:	*Juice, espresso, and Corner Bakery:* daily, 7:30 A.M.–9 P.M.; Sunday, 7:45 A.M.–9 P.M.; *all other kiosks:* Monday–Thursday, 11 A.M.–9 P.M.; Friday and Saturday, 11 A.M.–10 P.M.; Sunday, 11 A.M.–9 P.M.

Atmosphere/setting: Attractive food court that resembles an outdoor cafe with trees. Environment-friendly atmosphere. Credo is "Be kind; eat true; it's now." Large variety of food stations; all food is displayed in an appealing manner.

House specialties: Thirteen food stations: juice bar, grains, burgers, Mexican, greens, pizza, pasta, hot stuffs (stuffed potatoes), rotisserie chicken, stir-fry heaven, desserts, sacred grounds (espresso, candy, cakes, cookies), and Corner Bakery. Mediterranean rice dishes; "enlightened" Caesar; pot stickers; homemade pies and cookies.

Other recommendations: Cold and hot bean salads; health burgers; salsa bar; stir-frys with Pan-Asian influences; yogurt-fruit shakes and power drinks.

Summary & comments: This food court concept is one of the most innovative by Rich Melman of Lettuce Entertain You Enterprises. He explains, "We have a social life, a business life, a family life, and a love life. Now there is an environment dedicated to your food life. It's about choices." Whatever your craving, you can eat healthfully, indulge, or compromise a bit in between. Customers are given a sensor card which tracks purchases at each station. You give the card to the cashier before you exit, and the total cost is tallied. A new adjacent foodlife market offers freshly prepared foods for carryout. Call (312) 335-3663.

184

Francesco's Hole in the Wall

	Italian
	★★★
Zone 11 Northern Suburbs	Inexpensive/Moderate
254 Skokie Boulevard, Northbrook	
(847) 272-0155	Quality 83 Value B

Reservations:	Not accepted
When to go:	Early, just after 5 P.M.
Entree range:	$12 average
Payment:	Cash only
Service rating:	★★★½
Friendliness rating:	★★★★
Parking:	Lot
Bar:	Limited; liquor provided on request
Wine selection:	Fairly extensive; all Italian; several by the glass
Dress:	Casual
Disabled access:	No
Customers:	Diverse, from locals to celebrities
Lunch:	Monday, Wednesday–Friday, 11:30 A.M.–2:15 P.M.
Dinner:	Monday, Wednesday, and Thursday, 5–9:15 P.M.;
	Saturday, 5–10:15 P.M.; Sunday, 4–8:45 P.M.

Atmosphere/setting: Rural Italian; unfinished wooden floor; blackboard menu. Nonsmoking. Small and intimate, but larger than the original.

House specialties: Chicken and veal Vesuvio; fettuccine with shrimp, scallops, broccoli, tomato, and Asiago; porcini ravioli; osso buco; risotto pichi-pachi (Italian rice with sautéed spinach and tomato sauce). The special house salad is like a tossed antipasto with greens, pepperoni, cheese, and roasted peppers.

Other recommendations: Spidini (homemade bread rolled around mozzarella and tomato); thin pizza; bruschetta; lemon-roasted chicken, broccoli, and red peppers. Unusual dessert: chocolate cannoli with chocolate ricotta, studded with tiny chocolate chips.

Summary & comments: This small restaurant's comical name dates to pre-expansion, when a full house meant 21! The daily menu is written on the board, but certain specialties are frequently available. This is a casual, whimsical place with no pretense. Limos are often seen in the parking lot, a testimonial to the good food here. The well-heeled and celebrities mingle here with average diners. The owner opened an Italian bistro next door, and named it just that— Next Door, (847) 272-1491.

Froggy's French Café

New French

★★★

Moderate

Quality 84   Value B

Zone 11   Northern Suburbs
306 Green Bay Road, Highwood
(847) 433-7080

Reservations:	Accepted for 6 or more
When to go:	Monday–Wednesday, early and late
Entree range:	$11.95–18.95
Payment:	All major cards except AMEX
Service rating:	★★★★
Friendliness rating:	★★★★½
Parking:	Street, lot at library
Bar:	Yes
Wine selection:	About 100 selections; changes every 45 days; $13.95–150 a bottle; 3–4 selections by the glass, $4–5
Dress:	Chic casual
Disabled access:	Entrance, yes; rest rooms, no
Customers:	Locals, professionals, tourists, families, couples
Lunch:	Monday–Friday, 11:30 A.M.–2 P.M.
Dinner:	Monday–Thursday, 5–10 P.M.; Friday and Saturday, 5–11 P.M.

Atmosphere/setting: Casual and comfortable; low-key and a bit old-fashioned in decor. Frog theme is depicted in charming ways. Outdoor seating.

House specialties: Salads (e.g., Belgian endive salad, sweet onion confit); lobster with vanilla sauce; cassoulet of duck or tripe; broiled salmon in Provençal sauce; baked red snapper or striped bass with herbs. Menu changes every 90 days. Pastries: meringue with espresso; cappuccino mousse; custard with orange blossom caramel; during the Christmas season, bûche de Noël.

Other recommendations: Ostrich with raspberry vinaigrette; venison in pastry shell; a special of roast pheasant with chestnut puree and port wine sauce; rack of lamb; desserts (e.g., lemon mousse in pastry shell).

Entertainment/amenities: The Gourmet Frog, the owner's pastry shop three doors away; classes, including private lessons, offered.

Summary & comments: Chef Thierry Lefeuvre has consistently produced appealing French food at modest prices. He wanted to prove that French cuisine need not include costly ingredients and a high price tag, and he considers cost one of the challenges of cooking. With his keen marketing and kitchen skills, he's proven that dining in a French restaurant can be affordable.

FRONTERA GRILL

Zone 4   The Loop
445 North Clark Street
(312) 661-1434

Mexican
★★★★
Inexpensive
Quality 93   Value B

Reservations:	For parties of 5–10
When to go:	Tuesday, Wednesday, or Thursday; early or late
Entree range:	$8–17
Payment:	All major credit cards
Service rating:	★★★½
Friendliness rating:	★★½
Parking:	Valet, $7; public lots; street.
Bar:	Full service
Wine selection:	Quite extensive; very international
Dress:	Casual
Disabled access:	Yes
Customers:	Mixed, locals and travelers, professionals, couples
Lunch:	Tuesday–Friday, 11:30 A.M.–2:30 P.M Saturday, 10:30 A.M.–2:30 P.M..
Dinner:	Tuesday–Thursday, 5:20–10 P.M.; Friday and Saturday, 5–11 P.M.

Atmosphere/setting: Casual and rustic; attractive Mexican art and touches; sidewalk cafe.

House specialties: Menu changes every two weeks. Examples include: tacos al carbón (beef, poultry, or fish grilled over a wood fire, with roasted pepper raja, salsas, other accompaniments, and homemade tortillas); wood-grilled fish and meats such as pork tenderloin marinated in red chili–apricot mole sauce, and black tiger shrimp in green pumpkin seed mole with roasted chayote and zucchini.

Other recommendations: Tortilla soup; jicama salad; pollo en crema poblana. Various types of chiles are used in sauces that range from mild and earthy to hot and spicy. Good desserts, such as special ice cream and cooked plantains.

Summary & comments: The menu offers a great variety of some rarely known dishes from regional Mexican cuisine. Owners Rick Bayless (chef) and wife Deanne (manager) lived in Mexico and co-authored a cookbook, *Authentic Mexican,* which was published about the time this restaurant opened several years ago. Both the book and restaurant received good reviews. Reports indicate that service could be more accommodating.

Honors/awards: *London Herald* and *New York Times* reviews. Recognized as the best-researched Mexican restaurant offering regional dishes.

GABRIEL'S RESTAURANT

French/Italian

★★★★

Moderate/Expensive

Quality 93   Value C

Zone 11   Northern Suburbs
310 Greenbay Road, Highwood
(847) 433-0031

Reservations:	Recommended
When to go:	Busiest on weekends but also full during week
Entree range:	$17–29; 4-course degustation menu, $40
Payment:	All major credit cards
Service rating:	★★★★½
Friendliness rating:	★★★★½
Parking:	Street and behind restaurant
Bar:	Full service; also separate bar from dining area
Wine selection:	180 French, Italian, and Californian; $26–225 a bottle; $6 and up a glass
Dress:	Upscale casual, from chic shorts to business suits
Disabled access:	Yes
Customers:	Varied; couples, families, professionals, locals
Dinner:	Tuesday–Saturday, 5–10 P.M.

Atmosphere/setting: European bistro with mahogany trim; beautiful open kitchen with the chef-owner and several sous chefs in white toques; well-lit, alive, and active. When bustling, it can be noisy.

House specialties: Pastas such as the flavor-intense fettuccine with artichokes, sun-dried tomatoes, and crespelle with spinach and cheese; roasted capon with prosciutto and mushrooms; papillote of bass (beautifully served with the top of the paper wrap peeled off, showing the bass and potatoes with green herbs around); tender veal saltimbocca.

Other recommendations: Risotto (e.g., with corn, spinach, Gorgonzola); roasted saddle of rabbit with rosemary sauce. Desserts like roasted pear with mascarpone cream and warm apple tart with caramel ice cream.

Summary & comments: Gabriel Viti was executive chef at Carlos' in nearby Highland Park after working with some of the best European chefs in France, Switzerland, and Italy. In May 1993, he opened his own place and designed it to be relaxed and comfortable, offering both Italian and French cooking at moderate prices. He avoids the luxury high-priced items, but uses his classic techniques on quality ingredients and produces some wonderful food, all served with style. Try the degustation meal, a surprise menu from the chef, which includes an appetizer, pasta, entree, and dessert.

188

Gateway Bar & Grill

Zone 1 North Side	Eclectic
7545 North Clark Street	★★★
(773) 262-5767	Inexpensive/Moderate
	Quality 85 Value B

Reservations:	Accepted 5 or more only
When to go:	Weekdays; late Wednesday–Saturday for music
Entree range:	$7.95–16.95
Payment:	All major credit cards
Service rating:	★★★½
Friendliness rating:	★★★★½
Parking:	Ample free lots nearby
Bar:	Full service
Wine selection:	Primarily American; inexpensive to moderate
Dress:	Casual, no jacket required
Disabled access:	Yes
Customers:	Regulars, jazz and blues enthusiasts, fish and BBQ lovers
Dinner:	Tuesday–Thursday, 3:30–10:30 P.M.; Friday and Saturday, 3:30 P.M.–12:30 A.M.; Sunday, 3:30–9:30 P.M.

Atmosphere/setting: Contemporary supper club; lovely wall mural in lounge of Lake Shore Drive and waterfront. Airy, bright decor in dining rooms.

House specialties: Shrimp de Jonghe; oysters Rockefeller; tilapia broiled Grecian-style; grilled salmon with smoked apple broth; Grecian-style broiled Lake Superior whitefish; Cajun vegetarian penne; BBQ ribs; Grand Marnier custard crème brûlée; black bottom pie.

Other recommendations: Wood-grilled octopus; catfish with Thai shrimp gumbo; fajitas; London broil; barbecued pulled pork; Key lime pie.

Entertainment & amenities: Live jazz, blues, and easy-listening music in lounge: Wednesday–Saturday, starting at 9 P.M. Wednesday is open mic night, with New Orleans food (music starts earlier). Occasional music on Sundays.

Summary & comments: Formerly My Place For?, it changed its name to Gateway Bar & Grill because of the large Gateway Plaza Shopping Center development in the area (indicating the gateway from Evanston to Chicago). Changes include redecorating, menu refocusing, and hiring a new executive chef, Nick Furlan, who has added some new dishes. Ownership, headed by Steve Dorizas, is the same. The management wisely adjusts the menu for current dining needs.

Geja's Cafe

Zone 1   North Side
340 West Armitage Avenue
(773) 281-9101

Fondue	
★★★½	
Expensive	
Quality 90	Value B

Reservations:	Accepted Sunday–Thursday; on Friday and Saturday first seating at 5 P.M.
When to go:	Weeknights, early in evening
Entree range:	$75 dinner for 2 includes appetizer, wine, entree, and dessert
Payment:	Major credit cards
Service rating:	★★★★
Friendliness rating:	★★★★½
Parking:	Valet, $6
Bar:	Full service
Wine selection:	250 international selections; 30 by the glass
Dress:	Upscale casual to formal
Disabled access:	Stairs; no access
Customers:	Couples, professionals, yuppie, all ages
Dinner:	Monday–Thursday, 5–10:30 P.M.; Friday, 5 P.M.–midnight; Saturday, 5 P.M.–12:30 A.M.; Sunday, 4:30–10 P.M.

Atmosphere/setting: Intimate and charming, with secluded booths and tables; wine bottle decor; dimly lit and romantic. Recently refurbished.

House specialties: Classic cheese fondue; seafood, chicken, steak, and combo fondues; chocolate fondue served with fruit and cake.

Other recommendations: Sausage and cheese platter with salad.

Entertainment & amenities: Nightly flamenco and classical guitarist.

Summary & comments: Walk down a few steps into a romantic oasis in Lincoln Park and enter a sensual culinary experience that was created over three decades ago by visionary and wine lover John Davis. Fondue is a communal way of dining, and it's alive and thriving at Geja's. Order à la carte or the complete dinners. For a taste of Switzerland, try the classic cheese fondue made with Gruyère and kirschwasser, served with bread and crisp apple wedges for dipping. Flaming chocolate fondue is flambéed with orange liqueur and served with fruit and pound cake for dipping.

Honors/awards: Voted Most Romantic Restaurant many times by *Chicago* magazine and other publications.

190

Gibson's Steakhouse

Zone 3   Near North
1028 North Rush Street
(312) 266-8999

	Steak
	★★★★½
	Moderate/Expensive
	Quality 94 Value C

Reservations:	Recommended
When to go:	Crowded most evenings; go early
Entree range:	$20–25; colossal surf and turf, $85
Payment:	All major credit cards
Service rating:	★★★★½
Friendliness rating:	★★★★½
Parking:	Valet, $7
Bar:	Full service; the signature drink is the Gibson (large martini)
Wine selection:	International; mostly Californian and French
Dress:	Business, dressy—tuxedos are not unusual
Disabled access:	Yes
Customers:	Diverse, masculine group spanning various backgrounds; mostly locals ages 20–60; lots of local and international celebs
Dinner:	Monday–Saturday, 3 P.M.–midnight; Sunday, 4 P.M.–midnight; bar remains open every day, noon–12:30 A.M.

Atmosphere/setting: 1940s clubby wooden art deco; looks old (but not worn) with antiques and dated photos; comfortable.

House specialties: Steaks are prime aged. Bone-in sirloin (also known as Kansas City strip); Chicago cut (huge rib-eye steak with fat trimmed); snow and stone crab claws appetizer.

Other recommendations: Lobster tail; planked whitefish; chargrilled swordfish; ¼-lb. baked potatoes, carrot cake.

Entertainment & amenities: Live piano every evening; lively bar.

Summary & comments: Recognized by steak aficionados as one of the city's top place for prime cuts, with prices to match. All the quality steakhouses are expensive, so this one is competitive with the herd. Food is elegantly served by polite waiters in attractive, comfortable surroundings.

Golden Ox

Zone 1   North Side
1578 North Clybourn Avenue
(312) 664-0780

German/American
★★★★
Moderate

Quality 90   Value C

Reservations:	Recommended
When to go:	Any time
Entree range:	$11.50–25
Payment:	All major credit cards
Service rating:	★★★
Friendliness rating:	★★★½
Parking:	Free valet
Bar:	Full service
Wine selection:	Substantial international list; French, Spanish, German, domestics
Dress:	Casual to formal
Disabled access:	Yes
Customers:	Diverse, locals, travelers, couples, professionals
Lunch/Dinner:	Monday–Saturday, 11 A.M.–11 P.M.; Sunday, 3–9 P.M.

Atmosphere/setting: Magnificent and very comfortable. Intricate decoration with shiny brown shellacked walls, paintings, murals depicting classics (the Ziegfield and Brunhilde story), cuckoo clocks, ornate beer steins. Looks like an ancient castle or museum. Carpeted; red ceiling with black beams; fireplace; brown leather chairs; gold tablecloths with white covers; dirndl-clad waitresses.

House specialties: Bavarian-style bratwurst; smoked Thuringer; potato pancakes; Wiener schnitzel; sauerbraten; paprika rahm schnitzel; crisp half roasted duckling; fresh seafood (e.g., imported Dover sole, broiled walleyed pike). Entrees are served with choice of spaetzle, potato, or butter noodles

Other recommendations: Hasenpfeffer (in season—imported rabbit, marinated and stewed); sausage plate; fresh chopped chicken liver; oyster à la Golden Ox; kalte kartoffel (cold potato) suppe; tortes.

Entertainment & amenities: Zither player on Saturday evenings; strolling musician on Friday evenings. Browsing through the spectacularly decorated rooms.

Summary & comments: Pricier than most German restaurants, but Golden Ox has a fuller traditional German menu—well-prepared—and an exquisite atmosphere. It is the best German restaurant I know of. Quality has been maintained over the years, but service can be slow and occasionally uninformed in the wine area. Overall, friendly and accommodating.

Honors/awards: *Food Industry News* award for Best German Restaurant.

192

GREEN DOLPHIN STREET

Zone 1 North Side	Contemporary/Eclectic
2200 North Ashland Avenue	★★★
(773) 395-0066	Moderate/Expensive
	Quality 91 Value C

Reservations:	Accepted
When to go:	After 7 P.M. to hear jazz right after dinner
Entree range:	$16.50–27
Payment:	AMEX, VISA, DC, MC, D
Service rating:	★★★★
Friendliness rating:	★★★★
Parking:	Valet/lot
Bar:	Complete with bar menu of snacks, sandwiches, and pizza
Wine selection:	Large international list; leading with the United States and France; some selections from Italy, Australia, Germany, and Austria. About 17 by the glass. $5.50–12; bottles start around $28 and reach to $120; many in the $30s.
Dress:	Chic casual; business; in jazz club, from casual to dressy evening attire
Disabled access:	Yes
Customers:	Locals, suburbanites; professionals who enjoy jazz
Dinner:	Daily, 5:30–10 P.M.

Atmosphere/setting: What was once an eyesore junkyard and auto glass repair shop has become a lovely, large jazz club with a spectacular outdoor garden on the river. Outdoor garden is beautiful with tables and umbrellas and flowers, and a landing dock for boats down the stairs at the river's edge. Contemporary dining room is simply decorated and comfortable, and dimly lit in the evening. Jazz club with bar and stage is spacious and more functional than decorated. Central bar opens onto a glass-enclosed room overlooking the garden.

House specialties: The menu changes daily, but some signatures follow. Appetizers: tuna tartare with wasabi caviar and Thai chili coconut sauce; tempura soft chell crab, spicy cabbage salad and cherry ginger reduction, decorated with green shiso oil (summer); seared day boat scallops with summer vegetable melange and fresh herb emulsion (the best scallops I ever met!). Fantastic salad of baby arugula, watercress, grilled figs, red grapes, summer melon, Smithfield ham, and aged goat cheese; endive frisee, Stilton, toasted walnuts, and apple vinaigrette;

(continued)

chilled tomato soup with garlic croutons, tomato basil pesto, and fresh mozzarella (summer); roasted onion, leek, and potato soup. Entrees: Grilled applewood, smoked beef tenderloin with potato-mushroom pavé and port wine reduction; a stellar sautéed white bass with roasted fingerling potatoes, Maine crab, snap peas, and tomato relish; a most creative and delicious grilled duck breast over Himalayan red rice, Chinese broccoli rapini, grilled peaches, and spiced pecan jus. Desserts by pastry chef Kim Myers: served on a 12-inch plate, a choclate mousse and praline torte with brandy-soaked cherries, with tuille. Unusual chevre cheesecake with fresh peppered strawberries, basil syrup; chef's selection of sorbets and ice creams.

Other recommendations: Appetizers: Asparagus and morel mushroom risotto; seafood stew steamed in tomato crazy water with sage and thyme croutons; carrot chowder. Entrees: Grilled ancho-crusted pork loin chop with jicama chayote salad, tortilla flan, and "mole" broth; sautéed salmon with grilled portobello mushrooms, parsley, potato mash, mushroom sauce, and dill oil; herbed potato gnocchi with portobello mushrooms, pea shoots, and white truffle oil. Desserts: Rum-soaked bananas in phyllo with black sesame seeds and mango; coconut almond chocolate tart with chocolate ice cream; selection of European cheeses.

Entertainment & amenities: Jazz club Sunday, Monday (8 P.M. showtime); Tuesday–Thursday (8:30 P.M. showtime); Friday, Saturday (9:30 P.M. showtime). Can usually hear music from dining room. Stunning outdoor garden patio on the river with a dock; some guests come by boat.

Summary & comments: This is one restaurant where diners can arrive by land or water. Most of them drive and park in the large adjacent lot, some bike, and others take their boats, which they can leave at the dock. When dining outdoors in the lovely garden, stroll over to the landing stairway and look down along the river's edge. Rick Gresh was promoted to executive chef in June 1999, after serving as chef de cuisine for one year. His credentials include working at New York City's Waldorf-Astoria Hotel, Trio in Evanston, Illinois, and the Celebrity Cafe in the former Hotel Nikko. He incorporates diverse ingredients and flavors in his creative dishes on a menu that touches different parts of the globe. French, Italian, and Asian cuisines predominate along with Mexican influences. These merge with regional ingredients for a tantalizing contemporary American cuisine that has become lighter and more consistent in style. Be sure to call first about the time of the jazz performance.

Honors/awards: Much good press.

THE GREENERY

Zone 10   Northwest Suburbs
117 North Avenue, Barrington
(847) 381-9000

New American
★★★½
Moderate/Expensive

Quality 88   Value C

Reservations:	Recommended
When to go:	Any time
Entree range:	$16–24
Payment:	All major credit cards
Service rating:	★★★★
Friendliness rating:	★★★★★
Parking:	Street
Bar:	Full service, including award-winning beer list
Wine selection:	Extensive, award-winning all-American list
Dress:	Casual but elegant
Disabled access:	Has 3 front stairs, but staff will help those in wheelchairs
Customers:	Diverse
Dinner:	Monday–Thursday, 5:30–9 P.M.; Friday and Saturday, 5:30–10 P.M.

Atmosphere/setting: Casually elegant. Housed in a wing of an 1850 schoolhouse. White linen-covered tables, fresh flowers.

House specialties: Seasonal menu; jumbo Gulf shrimp and grilled sausage; sauté of wild mushrooms; Maryland blue crab cakes with three-citrus sauce; barbecue pork tenderloin; sweet corn puree; blue cheese with potatoes; pesto-marinated Chilean sea bass with angel hair; blackened beef tenderloin with Cajun crab enchiladas and lobster. Apple pie with caramel.

Other recommendations: Grilled Missouri pheasant with leeks, roasted red peppers, and jalapeños; roasted South Carolina quail stuffed with caramelized garlic and mashed potatoes; hickory-grilled breast of turkey with sage-mustard marinade; southern Florida spicy chicken and sweet potato salad. Banana cream pie.

Entertainment & amenities: Jazz music.

Summary & comments: The menu here takes the diner on a regional tour of America with many state foods featured, including Wisconsin goat cheese and Missouri pheasant, and a sprinkling of Creole and other New Orleans touches. The added pleasure of dining at the Greenery is the charming historical building and peaceful setting. It's worth a drive from the city—unless there's a snowstorm.

Honors/awards: *Wine Spectator* Award of Excellence since 1988; three stars by the *Chicago Tribune*; four stars by *North Shore* magazine.

Hans' Bavarian Lodge

Zone 10 Northwest Suburbs	German/American
931 North Milwaukee Avenue, Wheeling	★★★
(847) 537-4141	Inexpensive/Moderate
	Quality 80 Value B

Reservations:	Recommended
When to go:	Weekdays
Entree range:	Lunch, $6.25–9.25; dinner, $13.95–18.95
Payment:	All major credit cards
Service rating:	★★★
Friendliness rating:	★★★½
Parking:	Lot
Bar:	Full service
Wine selection:	Limited German, Californian; by the glass (from $3) or bottle (from $13.95)
Dress:	Casual
Disabled access:	Yes, including rest rooms
Customers:	Locals; busloads come for Oktoberfest
Lunch/Dinner:	Tuesday–Thursday, 11:30 A.M.–11 P.M.; Friday and Saturday, noon–9 P.M.; Sunday, noon–4 P.M.

Atmosphere/setting: Warm family atmosphere. Large old world decor; quaint stained-glass windows.

House specialties: Sauerbraten; beef roulade; veal creations (e.g., Wiener Schnitzel; mushroom schnitzel, natur schnitzel Berghoff); German pizza.

Other recommendations: Roast duck; chicken schnitzel; filet mignon; combinations; American items (e.g., crab cakes and stuffed mushrooms).

Entertainment & amenities: Friday, zither and piano player; Saturday and Sunday, strolling accordionist.

Summary & comments: This suburban restaurant is owned by a member of the famous Berghoff restaurant family and is hugely successful. They sure know how to throw a big Oktoberfest that continues for weeks, all under heated tents with many bands. People come in from all over the Midwest for it. The beer garden features beers from around the world while in season.

Honors/awards: Rated Number One German Restaurant by *North Shore* magazine.

HARRY CARAY'S

Zone 4   The Loop
33 West Kinzie Avenue
(773) 465-9269

American/Italian
★★★½
Moderate/Expensive
Quality 86   Value C

Reservations:	Lunch, recommended; dinner, recommended for 8 or more
When to go:	Any time
Entree range:	Lunch, $8.95–39.95; pastas average $9.95; steaks average $28.95
Payment:	Major credit cards
Service rating:	★★★★
Friendliness rating:	★★★★
Parking:	Valet
Bar:	Full service; bar is 60 feet, 6 inches long, which is the same distance from home plate to the pitcher's mound; American and imported beers, featuring Bud beers, of course; a caricature of Harry on the menu states, "I'm a Cub fan, I'm a Bud man!"
Wine selection:	Extensive Italian and American, as well as several champagnes. Table wines start at an affordable $13 per bottle with many in the $20s–30s; several by the glass
Dress:	Casual; you'll see a good share of Cubs wear
Disabled access:	Yes, including rest rooms
Customers:	Diverse, locals, baseball fans, couples
Lunch:	Monday–Saturday, 11:30 A.M.–3 P.M., appetizers and sandwiches served in the bar daily
Dinner:	Monday–Thursday, 5–10:30 P.M.; Friday and Saturday, 5–11 P.M.; Sunday, 4–10 P.M.

Atmosphere/setting: Located in a historic red-brick building. Pictures, memorabilia of the late, great sportscaster; active bar/lounge; comfortable—usually busy—dining room. Private rooms upstairs.

House specialties: Chef Abraham's calamari; steamed mussels, red or white sauce; chicken Vesuvio with terrific potatoes (can be ordered with all white meat for $3 extra); grilled New York sirloin steak (16 ounces) with peppercorns or Vesuvio style.

(continued)

Other recommendations: Harry's Italian salad; cheese ravioli with marinara sauce; grilled fresh fish (marinated tuna, lightly crumbed, seasoned with rosemary, shines); trio of double lamb chops oreganato. Desserts include a great carrot cake and small ice cream profiteroles with hot fudge and crème anglaise.

Entertainment & amenities: Browsing through the Harry Caray memorabilia. Gift shop with line of Harrywear and souvenirs.

Summary & comments: You can't miss the Chicago restaurant because Harry Caray's favorite exclamation, "Holy Cow!," is emblazoned on an outside wall. Named for the late Cubs' announcer, Harry Caray's is a splendid dining experience from the masterful opening pitch all the way through. Unlike many celebrity sports-figure places, this one takes the restaurant business seriously. Harry Caray loved Italian fare, so it's on the menu, from salads to pastas and chicken Vesuvio (really a Chicago invention—not Italian). All the fish is fresh and grilled or otherwise cooked to perfection. Fresh herbs season much of the food. Weekend lunch-goers might try the sandwich cart. Good Italian desserts and wines. Harry Caray's dream was fulfilled when his widow, Dutchie, son Skip, and grandson Chip, together with managing partner Grant DePorter, opened Harry Caray's Rosemont, 10233 West Higgins Road adjacent to the Hawthorn Suites Hotel, (847) 699-1200. It was fashioned after the original Chicago location, complete with memorabilia. Harry's historic menu, created by Harry's close personal friend and the restaurant's Corporate Executive Chef Abraham Aguirre, is prepared at this location by Executive chef Hans Ladwein.

(continued)

Hatsuhana

Zone 3   Near North
160 East Ontario Street
(312) 280-8808

Japanese
★★½
Inexpensive/Moderate

Quality 76   Value C

Reservations:	Recommended
When to go:	Early for lunch and before 7 P.M. for dinner
Entree range:	$11–18; Hatsuhana special, complete dinner, $30
Payment:	All major credit cards except DC
Service rating:	★★★
Friendliness rating:	★★★
Parking:	Public lot nearby
Bar:	Wine and Japanese beer
Wine selection:	Mostly Japanese; cold sake, some hot; limited Californian
Dress:	Casual, business
Disabled access:	Yes, including rest rooms
Customers:	Locals, mostly Americans
Lunch:	Monday–Friday, 11:45 A.M.–2 P.M.
Dinner:	Monday–Friday, 5:30–10 P.M.; Saturday, 5–10 P.M.

Atmosphere/setting: Designed to be a classic Japanese sushi bar with tables off to the side for those who prefer not to sit at the sushi bar. Simple, contemporary look. Often busy at lunch and certain dinner times.

House specialties: American combination sushi and chef's choice sushi. This is the best reason for coming here. Picture menus assist in ordering.

Other recommendations: Tempura and teriyaki dinners, which include soup, rice, and dessert. Some items available à la carte.

Entertainment & amenities: Sitting at the sushi bar to watch the chefs' skilled hands quickly cut fish fillets into sashimi. Order as you eat for more inter-action and fun.

Summary & comments: Long-standing Gold Coast place with a loyal following as well as some newcomers and tourists. Pricey compared to neighborhood sushi houses, but quality and variety are usually very good. Sushi bar items are the highlight; some Japanese dishes are inconsistent, as is the service.

Heaven on Seven

Zone 4   The Loop
111 North Wabash Avenue
(312) 263-6443

Cajun/Creole	
★★★½	
Inexpensive	
Quality 86	Value B

Reservations:	Not accepted
When to go:	Breakfast, 7 A.M.; lunch, 11:30 A.M.; before the lines or after lunchtime
Entree range:	$3.50–9.95
Payment:	Cash only
Service rating:	★★★½
Friendliness rating:	★★★★
Parking:	Garage
Bar:	None
Wine selection:	Some Californian, Chilean, French, and Italian; $15–75 by the bottle, $4.50–6.50 by the glass
Dress:	Casual
Disabled access:	Yes
Customers:	Diverse; professionals, shoppers
Breakfast/Lunch:	Monday–Friday, 8:30 A.M.–4:30 P.M.; Saturday, 10 A.M.–3 P.M.
Dinner:	Every third Friday of the month, 5:30–9:30 P.M.; and Fat Tuesday with live New Orleans jazz

Atmosphere/setting: Upbeat; wooden floor, red plantation plants, big hot-sauce collection, New Orleans art.

House specialties: Southern fried chicken salad; soft-shell poboys; pasta shrimp angry, pasta shrimp voodoo; crayfish tamales; jambalaya; Louisiana soul.

Other recommendations: Crab cakes; chicken-fried steak; rabbit with mushroom étouffée.

Summary & comments: Funky place on the seventh floor of the Garland building in the Loop, which began as the Garland Restaurant and Coffee Shop. The Bannos family–owned place still serves regular breakfast, but has made its reputation on the great Creole and Cajun fare (including the Creole and Cajun breakfast), every bit as delicious as in Louisiana. Long lines at lunch move quickly. Those who love food with a burn will have a field day trying the various hot sauces on the table. After a meal here, you'll think you've gone to Cajun heaven. A new location at 600 North Michigan Avenue, (312) 280-7774, serves lunch and dinner.

Honors/awards: Recommended by *Newsweek, National Geographic,* and local publications.

HOME BAKERY

Zone 2   North Central/O'Hare
2931 North Milwaukee Avenue
(773) 252-3708

	Polish/European
	★★½
	Inexpensive
Quality 77	Value B

Reservations:	Recommended
When to go:	Any time
Entree range:	$5–10
Payment:	VISA, MC, D
Service rating:	★★½
Friendliness rating:	★★★½
Parking:	Street; can be somewhat difficult
Bar:	Beer, wine, vodka, cognac, and limited mixed drinks
Wine selection:	About 10 selections; $12–15 a bottle; $3 by the glass
Dress:	Casual; dressier on the weekend
Disabled access:	Yes
Customers:	International; couples, professionals, families, locals, out-of-towners
Open:	Monday–Saturday, 8 A.M.–9 P.M.; Sunday, 9 A.M.–9 P.M.

Atmosphere/setting: Space includes shop, deli, bakery, and 100-seat restaurant. Semiromantic, medium lighting; gallery of paintings on the wall.

House specialties: Soups: chicken noodle, white borscht. Roast duck with rice, peppers, and mushrooms; Wiener Schnitzel; beef Stroganoff; Polish hunter's stew (bigos); Hungarian goulash; pierogi (dumplings stuffed with choice of cheese, potato, meat, blueberry, or strawberry filling).

Other recommendations: Polish plate; Swiss steak; large, crispy potato pancakes (some of the best); chicken Kiev; variety of herring; barley sausage. Soups of the day, such as tomato soup and potato soup on Wednesday. Polish pastries and torte.

Summary & comments: Food is simple, honest, well seasoned, and very home-style. Menu is varied enough for a variety of tastes. Breakfast items include omelets, waffles, and cereal. Lunch includes sandwiches and an à la carte special. Dinner can be à la carte or, for $1 more, complete with potato, rice or dumplings, vegetables, choice of Polish salad, soup, and dessert. This is one of the few places in the city where you can have a full dinner for about $5—amazing.

Hong Min Restaurant

Zone 5   South Loop
221 West Cermak Road, Chinatown
(312) 842-5026

Zone 8   Southern Suburbs
8048 West 111th Street, Palos Hills
(708) 599-8488

Chinese/Dim Sum
★★★
Inexpensive/Moderate

Quality 85   Value B

Reservations:	Only accepted for 6 or more
When to go:	Weekdays; weekends 11 A.M.–3 P.M. and 6–8 P.M. are busiest
Entree range:	$6.95–19.95 (1 item $21)
Payment:	*Chicago:* VISA, MC; *Palos Hills:* MC, AMEX
Service rating:	★★
Friendliness rating:	★★½
Parking:	*Chicago:* 2-hour free parking at community lot on Cermak and Wentworth with validation; *Palos Hills:* 60-car lot
Bar:	*Chicago:* BYOB; *Palos Hills:* full service
Wine selection:	*Chicago:* international; *Palos Hills:* mostly domestic
Dress:	Casual
Disabled access:	*Chicago:* no; *Palos Hills:* yes
Customers:	Locals, ethnics, professionals, tourists
Lunch/Dinner:	*Chicago:* Daily, 10–2 A.M.; *Palos Hills:* Daily, 11:30 A.M.–10 P.M.

Atmosphere/setting: *Chicago:* casual storefront with booths and tables. *Palos Hills:* casual, American, booths and tables.

House specialties: Seafood (e.g., fish with black bean sauce; steamed sole; butterfly scallops); dim sum; special hot pot dishes.

Other recommendations: Special menu with over 75 special Chinese dishes (e.g., bird's nest soup; duck of West Lake with barbecue pork and vegetables; kung pao chicken with roasted peanuts and hot sauce).

Summary & comments: Chef-owner William Tam created a very ambitious menu, including some items the Chinese love, such as duck feet with black mushrooms, and some mundane chop suey and egg foo yong items. Virtually every category holds some culinary treats.

House of Blues

	American/Southern
	★★★½
Zone 3 Near North	Inexpensive/Moderate
329 North Dearborn Street	
(312) 527-2583	Quality 90 Value B

Reservations:	Recommended
When to go:	Any time; Sunday gospel brunch (if you want hand-clapping, joyful, uplifting participating entertainment with your buffet brunch); Music Hall: whenever there is a concert you want to attend
Entree range:	$8.50–12.95
Payment:	All major credit cards
Service rating:	★★★½
Friendliness rating:	★★★½
Parking:	Valet
Bar:	Full service, including imported and domestic beers at both Foundation Room and restaurants
Wine selection:	*House of Blues restaurant:* mostly domestic, some international; several selections by the glass; *Foundation Room:* international list
Dress:	Casual
Disabled access:	Yes
Customers:	Varied from tourists to all types of locals, especially those who enjoy blues, country, jazz, and other featured music and southern fare
Open:	Daily, 11:30–1 or 1:30 A.M. (depending on entertainment); Sunday gospel brunch, seatings at 9:30 a.m., noon, and 2:30 P.M.

Atmosphere/setting: Spectacular, with every inch painted and somehow covered with art. House of Blues supposedly has the largest Delta folk art collection anywhere, and it's evident here in the halls and on the walls and ceiling. Even the bathrooms are worth seeing. Three dining rooms, including the Chicago Room (dedicated to this city's blues legends) and the Delta Room (dedicated to Delta blues greats), are alive with ceiling panels of bas-relief portraits of blues icons. With the feeling of a southern "juke joint," the restaurant also showcases a B.B. Blues Bar and stage.

(continued)

House specialties: Appetizers: Mississippi cat bites (tender farm-raised cat-fish, lightly floured, fried, and served with slightly spicy Cajun tartar sauce); shrimp rémoulade, with capers, chopped egg, and black olives; New Orleans–style chicken and sausage gumbo. Entrees: étouffée (fresh crawfish and gulf shrimp with rich, medium-spiced sauce, with rice); jambalaya ("The Big Easy" shrimp, tender chicken, smokehouse ham, and Andouille sausage tossed in Creole sauce, Cajun rice).

Other recommendations: Crawfish cheesecake appetizer; Memphis barbe-cue chicken; mesquite-grilled veggie sandwich; sides of cornbread with maple butter and turnip greens; pecan tasty (a tart made of homemade cream cheese pas-try crust with Southern roasted pecans, sugar cane, and caramel filling) with ice cream. Gospel brunch (with eggs, sausage, jambalaya, bread pudding), so popular there are now three seatings.

Summary & comments: This largest of the House of Blues locations is one of those places that must be seen and experienced to be believed. It defies description, since there is so much soul, care, and money invested in this music sanctuary—you'll be transported when you step inside. Founder Isaac Tigrett said this HOB opening (November 1996) was the most important one he'll ever do, since Chicago is the living home of the blues. This multimedia restaurant accom-modates over 300 in its three dining areas, and the menu offers good Southern specialties by executive chef Samuel McCord, who had the same post at HOB in New Orleans. "Help Ever—Hurt Never" is one of the mottos here, typifying the HOB mission statement that celebrates the diversity and brotherhood of world culture and promotes racial and spiritual harmony through love, peace, truth, righteousness, and nonviolence. Just getting that message makes everyone feel accepted and respected.

(continued)

Hubbard Street Grill

Zone 4 The Loop	New American
351 West Hubbard Street	★★★
(312) 222-0770	Inexpensive/Moderate
	Quality 81 Value C

Reservations: Recommended
When to go: Any time
Entree range: Lunch, $6.95–15.95; dinner, $7.95–24.95
Payment: VISA, MC, AMEX, D, DC
Service rating: ★★★½
Friendliness rating: ★★★★
Parking: Valet for dinner
Bar: Full service
Wine selection: 100 American; up to $35 a bottle; 9 by the glass,
                       $3.95–4.95
Dress: Chic casual
Disabled access: Yes
Customers: Mixed locals, couples
Lunch/Dinner: Monday–Thursday, 11:30 A.M.–10 P.M.; Friday,
                       11:30 A.M.–11 P.M.
Dinner: Saturday, 5–11 P.M.

Atmosphere/setting: Large loft space decorated in muted greens; recently remodeled banquet room. Open kitchen; chic and casual interior; art gallery.

House specialties: Dill-cured king salmon with Dijon glaze. Mixed grill with salmon fillet, shrimp skewer (the best of the trio), and skirt steak (slightly dry); award-winning barbecue ribs; grilled ahi tuna steak (was properly cooked); grilled Gulf shrimp with angel hair; herb-roasted half chicken. All entrees come with generous sides, such as roasted garlic-Romano mashed potatoes; wilted spinach with olive oil and lemon; and steamed broccoli.

Other recommendations: Boneless grilled chicken breast with goat cheese–pesto filling; Caesar salad; superb Grillroom salad; grilled calamari appetizer; Ketchapeño, the chef's creation—a ketchup-jalapeño blend.

Entertainment & amenities: Pianist Wednesday–Saturday evenings.

Summary & comments: This sophisticated but casual modern American grill opened in spring 1994; David Schy, who bought out his partner and is now chef-owner, is offering all his favorite dishes. Portions are large, so many appetizers can be shared. Cooking is hearty but light, using naturally reduced sauces and lively salsas. A couple of items were bland, such as the red chile–black bean couscous. The menu has something for just about any taste. Service is attentive, knowledgeable, and cordial.

Hudson Club

Zone 1   North Side
504 North Wells
(312) 467-1947

New American/Continental
★★★★½
Moderate

Quality 95   Value B

Reservations:	Yes
When to go:	Well after dark, to see the interior in the night light and to experience the evening energy.
Entree range:	$12.95–24.95
Payment:	All major credit cards
Service rating:	★★★★½
Friendliness rating:	★★★★★
Parking:	Valet, $7
Bar:	Impressive long bar. Aggressive, user-friendly wine program; extensive beer list, with three beer flights. Scheduled wine and beer tastings.
Wine selection:	Extraordinary! 24 flights (tastings of four wines related to each other by grape varietal, geographic region or style) and an amazing 175-plus selections by the glass. Cards with the list of wines in each flight are given to the customer, a helpful educational tool.
Dress:	Chic casual to business and dressy
Disabled access:	Complete
Customers:	Sophisticated food and wine lovers and the hip but uninitiated eager to learn about wine in an unpretentious atmosphere; mostly professionals; Gen-X-ers; all ages. Locals and travelers.
Dinner:	Monday–Thursday, 5:30–10 P.M.; Friday and Saturday, 5:30–11 P.M.

Atmosphere/setting: Sleek, sensuous, spacious, resembling a luxury liner and a jet airliner merged with a swank 1940s supper club with an elongated bar. Hudson Club was based on the aerodynamic flourishes of the Hudson Hornet automobile.

House specialties: Menu is printed weekly. Cold appetizers of house-smoked salmon with beets, waffle chips, parsley oil, crème fraîche, and sturgeon caviar; Hudson Club Caesar salad with paprika croutons and asiago cheese; pear salad, watercress, frisée, Maytag blue cheese, shallot vinaigrette, and port wine syrup;

(continued)

206

caviar flight (selection of Carolyn Collins' American caviar); lobster martini (a delicious gimmicky arrangement of the shellfish on mashed potatoes with green peas and red wine butter in a martini glass); chef's cheese flight. Entrees: wood-roasted bluenose grouper, potatoes, spinach, cucumber, and vegetable-basil vinaigrette; roasted vegetable strudel; grilled pork tenderloin, glazed Brussels sprouts, spaetzle, roasted red peppers and mustard vinaigrette. Desserts (changing menu): pastry chef Mandy Franklin's dessert flight (seven miniature desserts); chocolate hazelnut café (chocolate cake with coffee cream, hazelnut ganache layers and Kahlua coffee ice cream; ginger orange crêpes (fresh pineapple and mango in ginger crêpes with orange crème fraiche sauce); homemade ice creams (e.g. lemon grass, pistachio) and creative sorbets (e.g. lemon chile, strawberry daiquiri).

Other recommendations: Corn flake–crusted shrimp, fennel-celery root slaw, sherry-honey glaze; tuna tartare, olive tapenade, saffron garlic oil, orange supremes, herb salad. Entrees: poppyseed-coated halibut, French beans, leeks, lemon beurre blanc; wood-roasted chicken, Boursin cheese potatoes, French green beans, sun-dried tomato rosemary sauce. Desserts: summer fruits and berries in almond basket with two sauces (in season); chocolate lava cake with liquid cherry truffle center.

Entertainment & amenities: Live jazz Wednesday evenings. Monthly wine tastings, $20, by Curt Burns, The Wine Guy. Trying wine or beer flights; taking off on a fantasy flight while being swept away by the interior design.

Summary & comments: Hudson Club is sophisticated yet casual and never snobbish about its extraordinary bar and educational wine and beer program. Key players here are Howard Natinsky and Steve Soble, Chicagoans with a vision who hung up their business suits, changed careers, and opened a classy neighborhood pool hall, Corner Pocket. Now their company, Spare Time, Inc., owns several properties, including Trocadero Bistro & Bar in Lincoln Park, and Hudson Club is their first restaurant. They brought in a professional team, including managing partner Larry Dwyer (from an advertising career); wine expert Curt Burns, whose card says "wine guy," indicating his down-to-earth style; new executive chef Lisa Schmidt, and pastry chef Mandy Franklin. In spring 1999, the menu was revamped to serve classics reminiscent of a 1940s supper club.

Honors / awards: *Chicago* magazine, "Best New Restaurants," May, 1997, and other features.

Indian Garden

Zone 8   Southern Suburbs
6020 South Cass Avenue, Westmont
(630) 769-9662

Indian	
★★★★	
Inexpensive/Moderate	
Quality 94	Value C

Reservations:	Accepted
When to go:	Dinner is less busy
Entree range:	Lunch buffet, $7.95; menu, $7.95–27.95
Payment:	All major credit cards
Service rating:	★★★
Friendliness rating:	★★★★
Parking:	Free parking lot
Bar:	Full service; Indian beers; 20 single-malt Scotches
Wine selection:	International, especially American, French and Italian; from $16 a bottle and $4 a glass
Dress:	Casual
Disabled access:	Yes
Customers:	Professionals, groups for Indian banquets
Lunch:	Monday–Friday, 11:30 A.M.–2:30 P.M; Saturday and Sunday, noon–3 P.M.
Dinner:	Sunday–Thursday, 5–9:45 P.M.; Friday and Saturday, 5–10:30 P.M.

Atmosphere/setting: Lovely, elegant interior, including Indian statues in the entryway; saltwater fish tank with exotic blue fish, and white coral. Monsoon Bar; Rainbow Dining Room.

House specialties: Fritters and tandoori preparations; tandoori pesh kash (vegetable samosa, onion kulcha, khurmi naan). Entrees: Lamb dum biryani (Basmati rice and lamb with saffron); tandoori shrimp; reshmi kebab (boneless chicken marinated in sour cream); baigan bharta (roasted eggplant, mashed and marinated in blend of mugblai spices). Desserts: Indian unchurned ice cream; lassi (churned yogurt drink served sweet, salted or masala) and mango lassi.

Other recommendations: Mulligatawny soup. Entrees: Sag paneer (spiced spinach cooked with cubes of cottage cheese); murg Badami (chicken cubes cooked in a rich almond-flavored sauce).

Summary & comments: Now in the lovely west-suburban location of the former Indian Summer, Indian Garden continues to produce dishes that are lighter than the usual Indian cooking. For those who have a fear of hot Indian food, spicing is moderate and can be turned up on request.

Iron Mike's Grille

Zone 3   Near North
100 East Chestnut
(312) 587-8989

Classic American Bistro
★★★½
Moderate/Expensive
Quality 90   Value C

Reservations:	Required on weekends
When to go:	Avoid peak meal times unless you have a reservation
Entree range:	$9.89–28.89
Payment:	VISA, MC, DC, D
Service rating:	★★★★½
Friendliness rating:	★★★★½
Parking:	Valet, $6
Bar:	Full service
Wine selection:	International, with largest selection from California and Northwest America; a good selection of French and Italian; a couple of Australian selections
Dress:	Upscale, dressy
Disabled access:	Yes
Customers:	Football fans, Italian food lovers, professionals, couples, tourists
Open:	Monday–Thursday, 7 A.M.–11 P.M. (bar open until 2 a.m.); Friday and Saturday, 7 a.m.–midnight; Sunday, 7 A.M.–10 P.M.

Atmosphere/setting: Located in the charming Tremont Hotel, the main floor includes a traditional, mahogany bar with split-level seating and a handsome dining room with golden globe ceiling fixtures, gold-and-green-striped drapes, white tablecloths, and glass-enclosed displays of the omnipresent sports memorabilia. Upstairs you'll find the cigar parlor in a denlike, couch-filled setting, and a dining room with leather-upholstered booths, beamed ceilings, and a fireplace.

House specialties: Ditka's favorite—pork chops with grilled pancetta and honey–green peppercorn sauce; "Black and blue" tuna putannesca (richly flavored with olives and red peppers); "duck cigar," a crêpe filled with braised duck (shredded to resemble tobacco!) and caramelized onions, served (believe it or not) on a wooden cigar box; Grabowski sausage cassoulet (grilled pheasant and duck sausage with white beans); Grille (house) salad with sherry vinaigrette.

(continued)

Other recommendations: Breakfast: "The Midwesterner" (Ditka's famous French toast or pancakes with maple syrup and cinnamon whipped cream, bacon or sausage, juice, and morning beverage), "The Training Meal" (beef filet, eggs, potatoes, juice, bread, and beverage), and several other options, including "Hall of Fame Omelette." Lunch is similar to dinner, with lighter items. Fridge Burger is available for both lunch and dinner. Angel hair with pesto and oven-dried tomatoes; linguini with shrimp, calamari, scallops, mussels, and spicy sauce; crispy cayenne-crusted oysters with balsamic-jalapeño mayonnaise (a touch of New Orleans, reflecting Ditka's former job as coach for the Saints); Superbowl salad (a huge football player's size) of mixed greens, arugula, French beans, red peppers, walnuts, avocado, smoked bacon, artichoke chips, kalamata olives, and Parmesan.

Summary & comments: Over 2,000 people, including many VIPs, attended the grand opening in 1997, making big news everywhere. Da Coach himself, Mike Ditka, was there to greet wellwishers, as were the Carlucci brothers, Joe and Charlie, who are partners with Ditka in this venture. Located in the beautiful Tremont Hotel, site of the former Crickets and then Cafe Gordon, this refurbished space has been handsomely appointed to exude a masculine ambience. The menu features Ditka's favorites, including the famous pork chops (among the best!), as well as Carlucci's Italian specialties and some New Orleans items. The prices end in numbers reflecting important years for Da Coach, such as side dish prices of $3.20–4.20, symbolizing Super Bowl XX, when he coached the Bears to the national championship.

(continued)

Jack's

Zone 1   North Side
3201 North Halsted
(773) 244-9191

New American
★★★½
Moderate
Quality 90   Value B

Reservations:	Accepted
When to go:	Mondays and Wednesdays less busy
Entree range:	$13.95–18.95
Payment:	Major credit cards
Service rating:	★★★★
Friendliness rating:	★★★★½
Parking:	Valet, $6.
Bar:	Full
Wine selection:	Emphasis on American, with mostly west coast domestic; some international, especially French and Italian, intelligent selection; affordable, from $19-58; some half bottles; glasses from $4.75-6.50, about 14 selections available.
Dress:	Casual
Disabled access:	Yes
Customers:	Mixed, all ages; mostly professionals; those seeking flavorful food and moderate prices
Brunch:	Sunday, 10:30 A.M.–2 P.M.
Dinner:	Monday–Thursday, 5:30–10:30 P.M.; Friday and Saturday, 5–11:30 P.M.; Sunday 5–10:30 P.M.

Atmosphere/setting: Rehabbed corner storefront with large windows, attractive bar in left corner of L-shaped space; banquettes and tables spaced comfortably. Unusual modern American lighting with beams and an antique silver ceiling. Chef-owner's brother Michael designed the interior. Comfortable and cozy.

House specialties: Starters of quesadillas with chipotle shrimp and roasted poblano peppers, sweet onions, pepper Jack and goat cheese, tomato avocado salsa; grilled calamari over black linguini in spicy tomato basil sauce; grilled portobello mushroom over mixed greens, toasted goat cheese in sun-dried tomato vinaigrette; specials such as homemade mozzarella, assorted tomatoes, mixed greens with balsamic vinaigrette. Main courses: perfectly grilled Norwegian salmon with mango mustard glaze, sundried tomato mushroom risotto cake and ratatouille (chef replaced it with grilled cedar plank salmon with fresh horseradish and caper crust); the very "in" seared ahi tuna with coriander crust over bok

(continued)

211

choy with wasabi mashed potatoes and stir-fried vegetables, sweet sake ginger lime sauce; lemon pepper linguini with scallops, shrimp, mussels, and clams, spicy tomato sauce (generous portion). Desserts: Jack's chocolate kahlua cake with coffee ice cream (lusty); New Orleans-style bread pudding with Jack Daniel's caramel sauce.

Other recommendations: Starter of seafood ravioli with basil-lemon cream sauce. Specials such as sautéed soft shell crab with apple cole slaw and jalapeño tartar (in season). Main courses: pesto grilled chicken over pasta with roasted vegetables and blackened tomato sauce; couscous jambalaya (vegetarian). Desserts: chocolate raspberry terrine with raspberry sauce, coffee ice cream; Door County cherry pie with slivered almonds and vanilla ice cream.

Entertainment & amenities: Special menus, such as one that celebrates the solstice, June 20–July 4.

Summary & comments: Jack's is a hidden gem that is well worth the trip, even from a distant location. Jack Jones, the eponym here, renders cooking so outstanding for the modest cost that even with taxi fare from downtown factored in, the bill will be less than most tabs at comparable downtown restaurants. The steady clientele come here for the robustly flavored yet simple bistro fare that Jones calls an American blend because he incorporates global elements. Some creations are not what you'd expect at a typical bistro. There is a healthy dose of Italian in his cooking, since the chef was greatly influenced by his Italian grandma who cooked well. He has a special talent for packing a big flavor punch into each dish, which causes diners to exclaim, "Is this good!" Friendly service and a savvy wine list are bonuses. After graduating culinary school in 1987, Jones worked in several fine restaurants before opening his first bistro, Daniel J's (Daniel is his middle name), in 1993, sold after he opened Jack's. Now his fans come here to satisfy their cravings for his cooking. At presstime he was about to open Atlantique, a contemporary seafood restaurant at 5101 North Clark Street (773) 275-9191.

Honors/awards: Media coverage, including the dailies and the *Chicago Reader*, named one of the 20 best new restaurants in the city by *Chicago* magazine.

Jilly's Cafe

Zone 11 Northern Suburbs	New American
2614 Green Bay Road, Evanston	★★★½
(847) 869-7636	Inexpensive/Moderate
	Quality 85 Value B

Reservations:	Recommended
When to go:	Any time
Entree range:	$9–15
Payment:	VISA, MC, AMEX, DC
Service rating:	★★★★
Friendliness rating:	★★★★½
Parking:	Street
Bar:	Wine and beer
Wine selection:	International; $15–72; many by the glass, $3.50–6
Dress:	Casual to elegant
Disabled access:	Yes
Customers:	North Shore clientele; professionals, couples
Brunch:	Sunday, 10:30 A.M.–2 P.M.
Lunch:	Tuesday–Friday, 11:30 A.M.–2 P.M.
Dinner:	Tuesday–Thursday, 5–9 P.M.; Friday and Saturday, 5–10 P.M.; Sunday, 5–8 P.M.

Atmosphere/setting: Charming, intimate setting—resembles cozy French country inn with white stucco and dark wood walls. Nonsmoking restaurant.

House specialties: Escargot with Gorgonzola cream and grilled polenta; daily focaccia; fresh fish, such as oven-roasted Chilean sea bass with sesame-seed crust and stir-fry angel hair pasta in ginger tomato broth. Nicely balanced small menu with pastas, seafood, fowl, game, beef, and veal, such as the creative scaloppine with Maytag blue cheese. Pastries are handmade. Trio of desserts: strawberry crème brûlée (flavors change); ice cream and lemon sherbet with raspberry sauce; chocolate apricot cake with chocolate sauce.

Other recommendations: Special appetizer: toasted cheese ravioli with tomato sauce; vegetarian entree: eggplant Napoleon with sweet potato haystack and vegetable coulis; special lamb chops and mashed potato topped with mashed sweet potato; apricot-almond tart.

Summary & comments: A little gem in Evanston that's worth seeking out. The atmosphere is charming, and the service reflects the tastes of the attentive European owner, Eric, and his wife, Diane, who is the pastry chef. Many of the staff are French; service is attentive and friendly. Generally full-flavored, healthful cooking. Entrees come with soup or house salad and sorbet intermezzo. A great value.

Honors/awards: Two stars from *Mobil*.

Joe's B-Bop Cafe

Zone 3   Near North
1 Navy Pier, 600 E. Grand Ave.
(312) 595-5299 (JAZZ)

BBQ and Southern
★★★½
Inexpensive/Moderate

Quality 90   Value B

Reservations:	Only parties of 6 or more
When to go:	Lunch if walking around the pier during the day; evenings for music and dinner; Sunday jazz brunch if your desire is a buffet.
Entree range:	$10.95–17.95 or market price of fish; Sunday brunch buffet $16.95; kids ages 5–12 $5.95; kids under age 5 free
Payment:	AMEX, D, DC, MC, VISA
Service rating:	★★★★½
Friendliness rating:	★★★★½
Parking:	Lot on Navy Pier; valet weekends at Pier entrance
Bar:	Full; good selection of beers. At Sunday brunch, Joe's Fabulous Bloody Mary Bar with selection of 100 spices, condiments, garnishes to accompany three blends of mix from mild and medium to "watch out!"
Wine selection:	Limited, six American selections, all available by the glass; affordable, $5–6.25; bottles $20–26
Dress:	Casual and very casual
Disabled access:	Yes
Customers:	Mix of locals and tourists, families and singles, people of all ages who enjoy jazz
Brunch:	Sundays from Labor Day until Memorial Day, 10:30 A.M. –2:30 P.M.
Lunch/Dinner:	*Summer,* Monday-Saturday 11 A.M.–11 P.M.; Sunday, 10:30 A.M.–10 P.M. *Regular fall, winter, spring,* Monday-Saturday 11 A.M.–9 P.M.; Sunday 10:30 A.M.–9 P.M.

Atmosphere/setting: Casual, energetic, fun. Focus of the spacious 190-seat dining room is a monumental, 135-foot-long colorful mural, History of Jazz, on a serpentine wall above the perimeter banquette seats; photos of jazz greats share wall space with a faux radio tower with the call letters, "WBBQ-Ham Radio;"

(continued)

wood-topped tables; lively red, black, and mustard-hued linoleum-like floor; band-stand on far end in front of windows opens out onto the patio on the pier and the lake beyond; 60-seat glass-enclosed area of dining room for private parties.

House specialties: Appetizers: Crunchy sweet potato chips with a dynamite honey-mustard dip; jalapeño poppers (red ones that are not fiery); cheese-filled, crunchy, homemade salsa with a kick; smoked chicken quesadillas with salsa. Main courses: Be-Bop BBQ™ combos: King Oliver (baby-back ribs and half a Yardbird chicken™); Duke Ellington (ribs and brisket, formerly pulled pork). Pulled pork bun (Memphis-style with mustard slaw on top, with Carolina-style hot five sauce on the side); jambalaya, a robust mix of smoked chicken, Cajun andouille sausage, and bayou rice with a tomato sauce; mild-flavored crawfish étoufée (a good rendition of the New Orleans classic rice dish). Fats' corn-bread™. "Last licks": Sumpin' choclit (recommended—luscious enough to satisfy any chocolate lover's craving); fudgey layered cake with a rich sauce.

Other recommendations: Appetizers of New Orleans–style popcorn shrimp with cilantro; barbecued rib tips and buffalo wings. Shrimp & sausage filé gumbo; Big Band Salad (over a dozen players including pulled chicken, corn, beans, three lettuces); southwest chicken salad in a 13-inch, deep-fried tortilla bowl; spinach salad with warm bacon dressing. Main courses: Separate BBQ items (include each of the above, ribs, chicken, and brisket, plus rib tips and center cut boneless pork chops). Veggie Jive sandwich. Accompanists, such as smoky beans & things (fla-vorful melange of three types of beans, pulled pork, and bacon) and red beans and rice. Homemade fruit cobbler, with or without ice cream; Eli's cheesecake.

Entertainment & amenities: Live jazz nightly; weeknights usually 6 P.M.–9:30 P.M., until 10:30 P.M. in summer; weekends 7 P.M.–11 P.M.(call for infor-mation); no cover charge. Gift shop sells jazz memorabilia and Joe's Be-Bop sauces. Outdoor patio with 115 seats, depending on weather.

Summary & comments: This Navy Pier restaurant is an energetic mix of good BBQ and southern-style items and groovy, live jazz. The place swings, espe-cially later in the evening. Wayne Segal, who operated Jazz Showcase founded over 50 years ago by his father, Joe, and the Chicago Restaurant Corp. teamed up to open this place in spring 1997. The chef who gets credit for the spicy Southern cooking is Michael Gilreath, and the pitmaster is Irving Vance, who turns out some satisfying, soulful Memphis Tennessee BBQ using a dry rub.

Honors/awards: *Chicago* magazine featured the Bloody Mary bar Septem-ber 1997; *N-Digo* featured the brunch, March 1998; *Chicago Tribune,* Tempo sec-tion, June 3, 1997; *Chicago Defender,* September 10, 1997; *Daily Herald,* "Pick of the Week" July 4, 1997; *Chicago Reader,* positive review, December 19, 1997.

Julio's Latin Cafe

Zone 10   Northwest Suburbs
99 South Rand Road, Lake Zurich
(847) 438-3484

Caribbean	
★★★	
Moderate	
Quality 83	Value C

Reservations:	Recommended
When to go:	Any time
Entree range:	$11.95–18.95
Payment:	VISA, MC, AMEX, D, DC
Service rating:	★★★★
Friendliness rating:	★★★★
Parking:	Free lot
Bar:	Small bar; several types of margaritas
Wine selection:	American, Chilean, Argentinean, Spanish, and Californian
Dress:	Casual
Disabled access:	Yes
Customers:	Locals
Lunch:	Monday–Friday, 11:30 A.M.–2:30 P.M.
Dinner:	Monday–Thursday, 5–9 P.M.; Friday and Saturday, 5–10 P.M.; Sunday, 4–8:30 P.M.

Atmosphere/setting: Casual fine dining; cozy with South American touches.

House specialties: Pollo Caribe (skinless, boneless chicken sautéed, garnished with shrimp, and served with mango sauce); paella (seafood, chicken, and sausage over Spanish saffron rice); parrillada gaucho (grilled New York strip steak with chicken and turkey sausage, roasted bell peppers, and fried bananas).

Other recommendations: Ceviche; shrimp avocado salad; Caribbean Cornish hen (semi-boneless with sweet-sour tamarind sauce).

Entertainment & amenities: Live entertainment on weekends, 7:30–10:30 P.M. Classical and jazz guitarist from Brazil; Spanish and English singers. Mexican guitarist, Saturday, 5:30–8:30 P.M; Sunday, piano player.

Summary & comments: This intimate spot has carved a niche for itself in the northwest suburban area. Discriminating diners enjoy the food and the friendly service anytime, and the bonus of live jazz on weekends doubles the pleasure. Recently expanded.

Karyn's Fresh Corner

Zone 1   North Side
3351 Lincoln Avenue
(773) 296-6990

Vegetarian/Natural	
★★★	
Inexpensive	
Quality 84	Value C

Reservations:	Accepted
When to go:	Any time
Entree range:	$5.25–11
Payment:	All major credit cards
Service rating:	★★½
Friendliness rating:	★★★½
Parking:	Street
Bar:	None; BYOB
Wine selection:	None
Dress:	Casual
Disabled access:	Yes
Customers:	Locals, psychics, musicians, professionals, families
Open:	Monday–Friday, 11:30 A.M.–9 P.M.; Saturday and Sunday, 10 A.M.–9 P.M.

Atmosphere/setting: Spacious, with a garden motif; ledges decorated with fresh flowers, sprouts, wheat grass, and herbs; attractive place mats on tables; ozonated and oxygenated air; and an open kitchen.

House specialties: Gazpacho; vegan Caesar salad; veggie burger in a pita; taco roll; wheatgrass juice; raw apple pie (raw apples, bananas, dates, cashew-and-almond butter, tahini, honey, cinnamon, and vanilla in a dehydrated pie shell).

Other recommendations: Raw zucchini "pasta" with pesto; Sicilian pizza (raw, cured eggplant, fresh or sun-dried tomatoes, heavy garlic, select mushrooms on a creamy pesto sauce); banana delight (fresh bananas with a vibrant protein seed mixture, topped with a cashew sauce); and paradise pies of mango, blueberry, or the best fruit in season.

Entertainment & amenities: Nutrition classes and a detox program. Outdoor cafe and retail shop. Toys for kids. Dog biscuits and water for canines.

Summary & comments: Proprietor and nutritional counselor Karyn Calabrese advocates eating organic and uncooked foods and juices; all her dishes are vegan and most are not cooked. She believes these uncooked foods, known as raw living foods, leave all the vitamins, minerals, and enzymes available for the body's total use, thus helping the body to fend off sickness and the aging process. When Calabrese has to dehydrate some foods, nothing is heated over 105° Fahrenheit. For those who do enjoy a hot meal, Calabrese now offers some international cooked foods such as Spanish rice and meatless hot dogs.

Katsu Japanese Restaurant

Zone 1   North Side
2651 West Peterson Avenue
(773) 784-3383

Japanese	
★★★½	
Inexpensive/Moderate	
Quality 90	Value B

Reservations:	Recommended
When to go:	Early weekday evenings
Entree range:	$10–20
Payment:	VISA, MC, AMEX, DC, D
Service rating:	★★★★
Friendliness rating:	★★★★★
Parking:	Abundant on street; city lot nearby
Bar:	Full service
Wine selection:	Small; Californian and Japanese
Dress:	Casual
Disabled access:	Yes
Customers:	Japanese, locals, sushi lovers
Dinner:	Daily, 5–11 P.M.

Atmosphere/setting: Newly remodeled with a contemporary Japanese decor. Sushi bar and dining room with benches and tables.

House specialties: Katsumaki (avocado, crab stick, cucumber, and fresh tuna); sushi; authentic Japanese ramen noodles.

Other recommendations: Tempura; combination box; beef roll; grilled squid; gomae (steamed spinach with delicate sesame sauce); maki sushi (popeye roll, spinach roll, and salmon roll); combination dinners.

Summary & comments: A charming, quiet, little Japanese jewel in an inconspicuous northwest neighborhood. Japanese businessmen who work and live in the suburbs come here weekly or more often for their sushi and home-style food fix, and they entertain clients here as well. Prices are right and encourage repeat visits. Some dishes served are only found in Japanese homes, not in restaurants. Husband-and-wife team excels in service and graciousness. Kampai! (Bottoms up!)

Honors/awards: Highest rating by Sherman Kaplan, dining critic at WBBM (CBS) Radio.

Kiki's Bistro

Zone 3 Near North	French Bistro
900 North Franklin Street	★★★★
(312) 335-5454	Inexpensive/Moderate
	Quality 94 Value C

Reservations:	Recommended for lunch and dinner
When to go:	Any time
Entree range:	Lunch, $8.50–12; dinner, $13–22
Payment:	All major credit cards
Service rating:	★★★★
Friendliness rating:	★★★★
Parking:	Free valet
Bar:	Full service; bar/lounge separate from dining room
Wine selection:	20 French and 15 American (Californian) white wines, over 30 reds, $20–60; 8 champagnes, $35–100; 12 by the glass, $4.50
Dress:	Informal; no athletic wear
Disabled access:	Yes, entrance and rest rooms
Customers:	International, celebrities (Prince Albert), professionals, families, couples
Lunch:	Monday–Friday, 11:30 A.M.–2 P.M.
Dinner:	Monday–Thursday, 5–9:45 P.M.; Friday and Saturday, 5–10:45 P.M.; Sunday, closed

Atmosphere/setting: Resembles a French inn; lovely cottage-style woodwork and rustic decor; romantic and intimate. Noise level can be high with a full house.

House specialties: Duck pâté with pistachio; Roquefort terrine with frisée and green apple salad, port wine reduction; tarte de Provençe (ratatouille and goat cheese in a light pastry). Sautéed breast of duck on wild rice with corn sauce and red pepper; daily fish (bouillabaisse a la Marseillaise; honey-glazed wild striped bass; pan-roasted Atlantic flounder with crispy polenta; or grilled Alaskan halibut with artichoke broth). One lunch special was fine: flounder on a bed of spinach with an unusual cranberry sauce. Steak au poivre with cognac cream sauce. Chef's new creations include non-French Oriental lobster salad; wasabi caviar; ragoût of assorted mushrooms with escargots in phyllo, shallot port wine sauce; roast guinea hen with wild rice, Swiss chard, and vegetables with natural jus and figs; and cassoulet Toulousain with duck confit, lamb, and garlic sausage. Desserts:

(continued)

chocolate terrine in a crust and another rich chocolate creation topped with glazed sliced bananas with several sauces.

Other recommendations: Onion soup gratinée; poulet roti (roast chicken marinated in olive oil, herbs de Provençe, and garlic in natural jus, with mashed potatoes); steak pommes frites; soup, pasta, and pizza du jour; seared quail with red cabbage and mixed greens; crème brûlée; croustade de poire (pear in pastry with caramel sauce); crème caramel; sautéed bing cherries with goat cheese ice cream.

Summary & comments: Many of the French bistro standards—steak pommes frites, onion soup gratinée, and poulet roti—are standouts, prepared expertly by new chef Jose Calzada. Owner Georges Cousances (Kiki) is an experienced restaurateur who makes certain the place runs smoothly. Service, food, wine, and charming atmosphere combine to make this a quintessential bistro without the claustrophobic closeness of many others.

Kinzie Street Chophouse

Zone 4   The Loop
400 North Wells Street, Chicago
(312) 822-0191

	Steak
	★★★★
	Moderate
	Quality 91 Value B

Reservations:	Suggested
When to go:	4:30–6 P.M.
Entree range:	$8.95–27.95
Payment:	All major credit cards
Service rating:	★★★★½
Friendliness rating:	★★★★½
Parking:	Free lot
Bar:	Full service
Wine selection:	Italian, Spanish, Australian, Californian, and French; reserve lists; ports; several by the glass, $4.95–5.95
Dress:	Casual, business
Disabled access:	Yes
Customers:	Suburbanites to locals, professionals, executives, operagoers
Lunch/Dinner:	Monday–Saturday, 11 A.M.–10 P.M.; Sunday, 4–10 P.M.

Atmosphere/setting: Dimly lit and welcoming with a masculine look: dark brown wild-grain oak paneling and oak floor; cozy banquettes; many private tables well spaced.

House specialties: Sesame-crusted yellowfin tuna; Australian lobster tail (mammoth!); 20-oz. porterhouse; daily specials: live Maine lobsters.

Other recommendations: Garlic shrimp scampi; wild mushroom and goat cheese tart; cheddar-stuffed jalapeños; black bean soup; filet mignon; double-cut domestic lamb chops; surf and turf; crispy onions; baked scallion smashed potatoes (with pieces of skins); asparagus, hot with hollandaise.

Summary & comments: Excellent-quality steaks and seafood in generous portions. A fine, dependable place for a business meal. Attentive, savvy, good-humored staff take great pride in their work. Well-rehearsed waiters roll over a cart and show the plastic-wrapped raw products to assist you in ordering. Service is professional but never intimidating.

Kitty O'Shea's

Zone 5   South Loop
Chicago Hilton and Towers,
    720 South Michigan Avenue
(312) 922-4400

Irish Pub	
★★★	
Inexpensive	
Quality 81	Value B

Reservations:	No
When to go:	Evenings, later for music
Entree range:	$7.25–12.75
Payment:	All major credit cards
Service rating:	★★★
Friendliness rating:	★★★½
Parking:	Street and valet
Bar:	Full service, including Guinness, Harp, and various Irish items and local microbrews
Wine selection:	American
Dress:	Casual
Disabled access:	Yes
Customers:	Locals, convention attendees
Open:	Daily, 11–1:30 A.M.

Atmosphere/setting: Dimly lit, Dublin-style pub with authentic antiques, including the beer taps.

House specialties: Potato and leek soup; Irish lamb stew; shepherd's pie; Blarney Burger Deluxe with Irish cheese and O'Shea's fries; Biddy Mulligan's fish and chips.

Other recommendations: Dublin wings; Kitty's corned beef and cabbage; Brannigan's bread pudding.

Entertainment & amenities: Monday–Saturday, 9 P.M.–1 A.M., live performances of traditional Irish folk music

Summary & comments: You can't get more Irish than Kitty O'Shea's. Not only is much of the interior imported from Ireland, so is the old sod staff. Guinness and Harp are drawn from antique beer taps (try the layered black and tan), the food is simple pub fare, and the spirited entertainment (some big names) completes the picture. Customers seem to love the lively musical groups here. It's hand-clapping fun!

Klay Oven

Zone 4   The Loop
414 North Orleans Street
(312) 527-3999

Indian
★★★★
Moderate
Quality 94   Value B

Reservations:	Highly recommended
When to go:	Anytime; week nights tend to be less busy, but usually can get reservations for weekends
Entree range:	$6.95–24.95
Payment:	AMEX, VISA, MC, DC
Service rating:	★★★★½
Friendliness rating:	★★★★½
Parking:	Street and garage nearby
Bar:	Full service; Indian beer and a large single-malt Scotch collection
Wine selection:	Extensive: American, French, and Italian, with several nice choices by the glass. Pricing is fair.
Dress:	Moderately casual to upscale
Disabled access:	Yes
Customers:	International; professionals, especially at lunch
Lunch:	Monday–Friday, 11:30 A.M.–2:30 P.M.; Saturday and Sunday, noon–3 P.M. (buffet)
Dinner:	Sunday–Thursday, 5:30–10 P.M.; Friday and Saturday, 5:30–10:30 P.M.

Atmosphere/setting: Upscale casual with lots of light wood, white table-cloths, elegantly folded napkins, lovely screen-like wall coverings, and beautiful art. The space is divided nicely into intimate alcoves, some of which are perfect for private parties.

House specialties: Appetizers: Matar aloo samosa (triangular pastry stuffed with mixture of peas and potatoes flavored with ginger, coriander leaves, and dried mango powder) and keema samosa (lamb in pastry), served with spicy coriander and sweet tamarind-banana chutneys. Murg pakora (boneless chicken pieces coated in seasoned chickpea flour and deep-fried). Baingan ka salad (cooked eggplant with tomatoes and onions, rolled in chef's dressing). Murg makhani (curry of clay oven chicken sautéed in butter with coriander, onions, and tomato sauce); two types of raita (yogurt sauce). From the tandoori (the namesake clay oven): tiger prawns marinated in spiced yogurt; tandoori lobster (seasoned yogurt-marinated lobster tail); Klay Oven Mixed Grill (combination of

(continued)

boneless lamb, boneless chicken, and prawn, each marinated differently); lemon-marinated rack of lamb; murgh malai tikka (marinated boneless chicken breast cubes) and machali ke tikke (marinated mahi mahi fillets), served with mild yogurt-cucumber and spicy mint chutneys. Side items include: great breads, such as paratha (whole wheat) and piaza kulcha (flatbread with onion filling), and a favorite rice dish, vegetable biryani. A great finale is ras malai, an exquisite dessert pudding of milk, honey, and pistachio. Masala, the steamed cardamom tea, is settling after a spicy meal and can be a dessert unto itself.

Other recommendations: Appetizer: Reshmi kabab (chicken spiced with cumin, cloves, and cinnamon); tamatar shorba (spicy classical soup). Main courses from the karahi (Indian wok): Bhuna gosht (boneless lamb cooked with onions, ginger, and fresh coriander leaves); chooza tikka masala (boneless chicken breast cubes marinated in yogurt and lemon juice, roasted in the tandoori and sauteed with fresh tomatoes, green chili, ginger, and onions); palak paneer (house-made cheese cubes cooked with spinach, tomatoes, onions, and green chili), and baingan piaz masala (tandoori-roasted eggplant, sautéed in fresh tomatoes, onions, green chili, ginger root, and fresh coriander leaves); dum ki gobhi (cauliflower and potatoes, steamed with onions and spices), and new items such as crab masala, lamb karhai, and paneer rasmissa (vegetarian dish of homemade cheese cubes, onions, tomatoes, and butter in masala-seasoned sauce). Gajjar halvah (sweetened finely shredded carrot-almond dessert).

Summary & comments: Klay Oven elevates Indian cuisine to a fine dining experience, from the refined, freshly cooked food to the non-smoking environment, serene setting, and professional service. The centuries-old clay oven (tandoor) and the Indian wok (karahi) are virtually greaseless cooking methods. The nan bread takes 30 seconds to cook while the shrimp takes only 4 seconds. Prem Khosla, owner since 1995, is a seasoned restaurateur. He has made some changes, including removing some partitions to open up the dining space and adding some new menu items. The menu is well designed and educational, giving descriptions of dishes and special ingredients. The quality of the food and the polite service are excellent.

Honors/awards: *Chicago* magazine's "Critic's Choice Top 25 Restaurants;" *Food Industry News*, Silver Platter Award of Excellence, 1996–97; Zagat Survey Award of Excellent 1997, 1998, 1999

Korea Garden

	Korean
Zone 8 Southern Suburbs	★★★½
204 North Cass Avenue, Westmont	Inexpensive/Moderate
(630) 852-1900	
	Quality 88 Value B

Reservations:	Accepted only for 6 or more
When to go:	Any time
Entree range:	$8.95–15.95
Payment:	All major credit cards
Service rating:	★★★★
Friendliness rating:	★★★★½
Parking:	Street; free city lot across the street on Cass
Bar:	No mixed drinks, only liquor on the rocks and beer
Wine selection:	Very small; some by the glass
Dress:	Casual
Disabled Access:	Yes
Customers:	Mixed; about half Korean, half American
Lunch/Dinner:	Monday–Saturday, 11:30 A.M.–10 P.M. (discount lunch menu only available Monday–Friday, 11:30 A.M.–3 P.M.); Sunday, 2–10 P.M.

Atmosphere/setting: Clean, modern decor; serene music. Some tables have an authentic Korean wood charcoal grill (and a vent hood). Comfortable chairs.

House specialties: Goomandoo (pan-fried Korean dumplings); kim chi; bindaetok (Korean pancake made with mung bean flour with pork and vegetables); chapchae (a mixture of mushrooms, clear noodles, vegetables, and beef in a sweet, mild sauce); bulgogi (thin slices of marinated beef grilled at the table, served with the nontraditional moderately spicy miso sauce, doenjang, and lettuce leaves); saewoo gui (shrimp and marinated vegetables); bi-bim-bop (stir-fried vegetables, bulgogi, and fried egg and rice); marinated calamari (listed as calamary) with mushrooms and vegetables; salmon charbroiled.

Other recommendations: Roasted seaweed; gahlbi (pork with rind marinated in hot sauce); Spanish mackerel; yellow corvina (light-fleshed Asian fish).

Summary & comments: Korea Garden touts its cuisine as "truly authentic Korean, no MSG . . . using corn oil and sesame oil." It offers a large amount of seafood for a Korean restaurant. You can grill your own meats and vegetables. Complimentary orange slices and hot corn tea are served at the end of the meal. One of the better Chicago-area restaurants for a fine Korean dining experience. Ingredients are fresh, sauces are richly flavored, and the management is attentive.

Kuni's

Zone 11   Northern Suburbs
511 Main Street, Evanston
(847) 328-2004

★★★★½
Inexpensive/Moderate

Quality 96   Value C

Reservations:	Accepted only for 6 or more
When to go:	Any time
Entree range:	$10–18.50 and up
Payment:	VISA, MC, AMEX
Service rating:	★★★★
Friendliness rating:	★★★★
Parking:	Street
Bar:	Wine and beer, including Japanese beers
Wine selection:	Limited; more Japanese sake than American
Dress:	Casual
Disabled access:	No
Customers:	Locals, Northwestern students, sushi devotees
Lunch:	Monday, Wednesday–Saturday, 11:30 A.M.–1:45 P.M.
Dinner:	Monday, Wednesday–Sunday, 5–9:45 P.M.

Atmosphere/setting: Simple, clean decor. Lovely sushi bar with great fish display.

House specialties: Sushi and sashimi: pristinely fresh, top-quality, expertly sliced, and a great variety; try chef's favorites. Sunomono (sashimi salads): oyster, crab, and mixed; maki sushi of several types, such as tekkamaki (tuna and rice in seaweed wrap, sliced); omakase maki (tuna and avocado rolled inside-out with black seaweed center, rice outside); and spider maki (soft-shell crab and shredded mushrooms). À la carte items: excellent age dashi tofu (fried, with delicate sauce); oshitashi (steamed spinach and Japanese-style sauce); gyoza (fried/steamed meat dumplings); tairagai no butteryaki (scallops broiled in butter).

Other recommendations: Cooked food: tempura (shrimp and vegetables); soft-shell crab in season; chicken teriyaki; fish teriyaki; and sukiyaki (sliced beef and vegetables). Kuni's special includes tempura, sushi, or sashimi; a teriyaki dish; gomae; sunomono; bean soup, salads, steamed rice, and green tea.

Summary & comments: By far in a class by itself when it comes to top-flight sushi and sashimi. Owner-chef Yuji Kunii is a master sushi expert. Our last waitress was extraordinarily well informed, patient, and efficient. International celebrities and other sushi enthusiasts stop here to indulge. Some connoisseurs say there are few other sushi bars as fine as this in the entire country!

L'Olive Cafe

Zone 1   North Side
1629 North Halsted Street
(312) 573-1515

French/Moroccan
★★★★
Inexpensive

Quality 92   Value A

Reservations:	Recommended for 5 or more
When to go:	Any time; late night for jazz on weekends
Entree range:	$12–19
Payment:	VISA, MC, DC, D
Service rating:	★★★★
Friendliness rating:	★★★★½
Parking:	Street and valet, $6
Bar:	Full service
Wine selection:	International, with about a dozen selections of French, Italian, Moroccan, New Zealand, Chilean, and Californian wines. Prices by the glass range from $3.75–$8. Bottles range from $24–45.
Dress:	Casual
Disabled access:	Elevator; call to make arrangement for wheel-chair; bathrooms are accessible
Customers:	Local, international, Moroccan, French (especially chefs), politicians; all ages; couples; families
Dinner:	Daily, 5–11:30 P.M.; late-night jazz bar with late dinner served 11:30 P.M. until 2 A.M.

Atmosphere/setting: L'Olive moved about two-and-a-half miles south to larger, upscale digs in this lovely two-level space on Halsted St. Still intimate but not as homey as the former diner, this more elaborate dining room is several steps down from the sidewalk and has a welcoming bar area. Chairs and Moroccan banquettes are comfortable; pumpkin-colored tablecloths are capped with glass tops. Beautiful tiles from Morocco add the perfect authentic touch to the bar and form a wall border near the ceiling, and multi-hued curtains make a colorful splash. Paintings and photos of Morocco and a fountain add visual appeal. A rounded tile archway leads to a stairway up to a private upstairs room with seating for 60.

House specialties: Appetizer: The well-named Humus Nervana is a must with goat cheese and roasted peppers (named the best humus in Chicago by *Chicago Tribune*, 1998); Bastilla (traditional flaky pigeon pie), here with chicken, almonds, and rose water; vegetarian version bursts with flavor from preserved

(continued)

lemons, olives, summer squash, goat cheese, and spinach; can request without cheese. Merguez (spicy lamb sausage); warm fig salad tossed with walnuts, ginger, and a sweet honey-spiced dressing. Several versions of the national dish, couscous (steamed semolina grains): vegetarian with raisins, cinnamon, sweet potato, and almonds; a dramatic black couscous au calamare with chickpeas, corn, and spinach; royale (lamb, chicken, merguez, and shrimp); and couscous seafood (calamare, shrimp, and scallops); these are enhanced by spicy harissa sauce. Tagines (oven-braised dishes cooked in conical clay pots), deliciously moist with lamb or chicken (on menu), with saffron, dried fruits, or preserved lemons and olives; specials might be seafood, poultry, or meat. Signature dish is braised lamb tagine, with saffron, apricots, and raisins.

Other recommendations: Moroccan olives; harira (hearty bean soup redolent of cinnamon and ginger); zaalouk (roasted eggplant and roasted tomato with preserved lemon); sautéed jumbo shrimp with mild harissa; braised, chilled spinach with olive oil, lemon, and chickpeas; sautéed fresh sardines stuffed with lemon, garlic, and cilantro; shen salad with orange, dates, cinnamon, orange water, and roasted almonds. Desserts: new at this location is Mediterranean plate, a nice sampling of several pastries with a variety of tastes and textures, including semolina cake; walnuts in phyllo (similar to baklava), a cashew roll, and shredded wheat cake with pistachios and dates. A seasonal item is berries in an orange-water sauce. On occasion, a warm, flaky apple tart with caramel sauce might appear. Try the Moroccan mint tea.

Summary & comments: L'Olive (pronounced "low leave" in French) is aptly named, since the olive is a key Mediterranean ingredient and paramount to Morocco, the North African homeland of chef/owner Mohamed Ben Mchabcheb. He introduced Moroccan cuisine to Chicago in 1988, and food-lovers soon became fans of this aromatic and sweet-spicy cuisine that is not hot. His French cuisine training and passion for his native cuisine show in his exquisite versions of bastilla, couscous, and tagines. The authentic Moroccan and French/Moroccan cuisine that he produces here is exciting. With the many appetizers offered, it's fun to share several as openers. Daily specials provide a forum for the chef's creativity. The chef does catering, private parties, and carryout. Definitely worth going out of your way for a meal here. Excellent value for this exotic food.

Honors/awards: Rated among top ten restaurants in Chicago by WBBM; three stars from *Chicago Tribune.* Positive reviews by the *Chicago Sun-Times* and *Gayote* publication.

(continued)

La Bocca della Verità

Zone 1   North Side
4618 North Lincoln Avenue
(773) 784-6222

Italian	
★★★	
Inexpensive/Moderate	
Quality 84	Value B

Reservations:	Required
When to go:	Weekdays less busy
Entree range:	Pastas, $9.75–12.95; segundis, $12.75–19.95
Payment:	VISA, MC, AMEX, D
Service rating:	★★★★
Friendliness rating:	★★★★½
Parking:	Street
Bar:	Full service, including about 10 beers
Wine selection:	Fairly extensive; almost all Italian, a few French champagnes; about 12 by the glass, $4.25; bottles, $13–190
Dress:	Casual
Disabled access:	Yes
Customers:	Diverse, locals, students; all ages
Dinner:	Daily, 5–11 P.M.

Atmosphere/setting: Cozy and loaded with European charm. Smoking and nonsmoking dining areas; new 50-seat party room.

House specialties: Menu changes every week. Antipasto misto; calamari affogati (marinara sauce, white wine); risotto asparagi with cream sauce; whole sea bass baked in salt (old recipe); whole sea bass prepared with fresh thyme, rosemary, olives, and white wine; whole Dover sole sautéed, then baked; pollo campagnola (chicken breast, roasted potatoes); grilled baby Mediterranean octopus.

Other recommendations: Shrimp and baby artichokes; carpaccio; insalata della casa; gnocchi al pomodoro (potato dumplings, tomato sauce, basil, Parmigiano); ravioli Anatra (ravioli filled with duck breast, sage, and shallot filling). Desserts are made in-house, including tiramisu and covilio (espresso gelato, amaretto cookie, Strega liqueur).

Summary & comments: The restaurant's name means "the mouth of the truth," and the owner, Cesare, has put up a whimsical mask with a moving mouth at the doorway. This comical practice stems from the old custom in an Italian city of having a hole in a building's wall where people could denounce infidels and other trespassers. If people weren't truthful, their hands would be "bitten" when in the hole. Altogether, this place is delightful and homey; our waitress was caring and attentive. The place has grown a bit more sophisticated in the past two years. A hidden Italian gem.

229

La Crêperie

Zone 1   North Side
2845 North Clark Street
(773) 528-9050

French Cafe
★★½
Inexpensive/Moderate

Quality 80   Value A

Reservations:	Only for 6 or more; not accepted on holidays
When to go:	Any time; Thursday evenings for the music
Entree range:	$6.25–15
Payment:	All major credit cards
Service rating:	★★★½
Friendliness rating:	★★★★½
Parking:	Street or public garage across the street
Bar:	Full service, including French waters and ciders
Wine selection:	Mostly French; $15–29 a bottle; $3.25–5 a glass
Dress:	Casual
Disabled access:	Yes
Customers:	Some foreigners, especially French; families, locals, professionals, celebrities
Lunch:	Tuesday–Friday, 11:30 A.M.–3:30 P.M.
Brunch:	Saturday and Sunday, 11 A.M.–4 P.M.
Dinner:	Tuesday–Saturday, 5–11 P.M.; Sunday, 5–9 P.M.

Atmosphere/setting: A romantic, homey setting with a "lived in" look. In the evening the garden cafe is magical, lit with lanterns and tiny lights—it transports you to a French country garden.

House specialties: Crêpes Bretonnes (large buckwheat crêpes folded into squares) are the house specialty, including coq au vin, boeuf bourguignonne, and seafood and sauce crêpes. Also pâté, salade maison, onion soup gratinée. Dessert crêpes: chocolate crêpe and Grand Marnier crêpe.

Other recommendations: Spinach creme crêpe; chicken and mushroom crêpe; orange roughy; and bananas Sara. Brunch: egg crêpe; cream cheese and chive omelet; and crêpe Florentine.

Entertainment & amenities: A strolling accordionist, Thursdays 8–11 P.M.

Summary & comments: La Crêperie features buckwheat crêpes like those from Brittany, the homeland of chef-owner Germain Roignant. La Crêperie celebrated its 25th anniversary in 1997 and still makes all the crêpes by hand. The dinner that includes a cup of soup du jour or salade maison, one entree crêpe, and one dessert crêpe costs just $14—a bargain. A seafood entree crêpe dinner is only $15. La Crêperie's prepackaged crêpes are sold in supermarkets.

La Strada

	Italian
Zone 4 The Loop	★★★★
155 North Michigan Avenue at	Moderate/Expensive
Randolph Street	
(312) 565-2200	Quality 90 Value C

Reservations:	Accepted; especially for lunch
When to go:	Any time; can be busy at lunch
Entree range:	Lunch, $10–15; dinner, $20–30
Payment:	All major credit cards
Service rating:	★★★★½
Friendliness rating:	★★★★½
Parking:	Lunch, street or garage; dinner, valet
Bar:	Full line of all spirits, grappas, cognacs, ports, beers, and cordials
Wine selection:	Over 200 selections from Italy, France, Spain, and California; several nice choices by the glass
Dress:	Business, semiformal; no shorts
Disabled access:	Glass elevator, rest rooms accessible
Customers:	Diverse, professionals, travelerss, and celebrities (mayor, other politicians)
Lunch:	Monday–Friday, 11:30 A.M.–4 P.M.
Dinner:	Monday–Thursday, 4–10 P.M.; Friday, 4–11 P.M.; Saturday, 5–11 P.M.; Sunday, closed

Atmosphere/setting: Crystal chandeliers, elegant tabletops, large booths and spacious tables for privacy; Renaissance frescoes; recently renovated.

House specialties: Wild mushroom torte (layers of mushrooms with fontina cheese crêpes, tomato sauce); penne con vodka (tube pasta, with tomato and meat ragu, flavored vodka). La Strada House Salad (fresh Boston lettuces, artichoke hearts, hearts of palm, tomatoes, Belgian endive, creamy Dijon dressing. Prime provimi veal chops with thick polenta fries, shredded sweet potato fries, and roasted three onion butter; potato crusted salmon; artichoke and gaeta olive crusted lamb rack with assorted creative vegetables; young organic greens, roasted baby leeks, pickled cucumber, egg, crisp prosciutto, garlic crostini, herbed vinaigrette; breaded potato crusted crisp shrimp scampi, sage butter sauce. Dolci: La Strada Tiramisu Cake; torte Midici (flourless chocolate cake, warm Chambord raspberry compote, melted white chocolate); fruit lasagna (seasonal fruit compote layered with phyllo and Frangelico whipped cream).

(continued)

La Strada *(continued)*

Other recommendations: Ravioli del giorno; carpaccio della Strada. Vegetarian prix fixe luncheon. Stuffed calimari, rich breaded herbs, shrimp and gaeta olives, sauce meunièr; homemade fettuccini with shelled Maine lobster, tomato confit, basil relish, chive-infused olive oil (was a bit bland with a thick sauce); Dover sole meunièr or grilled; whole fish of day, oven-roasted with clams, mussels, and shrimp, carved tableside. Dolci: zabaglione (serves two; delicate sweet marsala froth, sugar and egg yolks, whipped tableside; served over fresh berries); floating island surprise.

Entertainment & amenities: Every night, cocktail lounge; Thursday through Saturday nights, live piano entertainment.

Summary & comments: This downtown Michigan Avenue restaurant always exudes a special feeling of fine dining, and it's one of the few places to find classical Italian regional cuisine with an emphasis on the Northern area. The menu was changed considerably in 1998 by new Executive Chef Marc Rosen (Remi Ristorante and Russian Tea Room, New York City; Palm Aire Resort and Spa, Pompano Beach, Florida). His colorful food is served in sumptuously comfortable, private surroundings with attentive service that borders on lavish. It comes as no surprise that this is one of Mayor Richard Daley's favorite places, and that it has cultivated its followers over 18-plus years in business. The restaurant's adjacent casual eatery is J. Randolph's Bar & Grill (phone (312) 565-2203), serving breakfast, lunch, and dinner; it features historical Chicago photos, sports memorabilia, and televised sporting events. The owners' new location is Cafe La Strada in the Hotel Moraine, Highwood, Illinois (847) 433-0065.

Honors/awards: *Travel Holiday* awards program for 12 years; *DiRoNA* founding member; *Chicago Sun-Times*, three stars.

LAWRY'S THE PRIME RIB

Zone 3   Near North
100 East Ontario Street
(312) 787-5000

Prime Rib
★★★★
Moderate
Quality 90   Value B

Reservations:	Highly recommended
When to go:	Weekday lunch or dinner usually less crowded
Entree range:	Lunch, $5.95–10.95; dinner, $18.95–25.95
Payment:	All major credit cards
Service rating:	★★★★
Friendliness rating:	★★★★
Parking:	Valet during dinner, $6
Bar:	Full service
Wine selection:	Very good; mostly American, some French; featured wines; several by the glass
Dress:	Lunch, business; dinner, casual to dressy
Disabled access:	No
Customers:	Professionals, conventioneers, families, couples
Lunch:	Monday–Friday, 11:30 A.M.–2 P.M.
Dinner:	Monday–Thursday, 5–10:30 P.M.; Friday and Saturday, 5 P.M.–11:30 P.M; Sunday, 3–9:30 P.M.

Atmosphere/setting: Housed in the stately century-old McCormick family mansion on the Gold Coast, with stunning winding staircases, splendid woodwork, and fireplaces. From the 1890s, when it was a setting for receptions for foreign dignitaries, the mansion changed hands several times until Richard N. Frank, CEO of Lawry's, bought and renovated it and opened the doors to become the second Lawry's in 1974. The original Lawry's The Prime Rib opened in 1938 in Beverly Hills, California.

House specialties: This is the reason for coming here: roast prime ribs of beef, available in four cuts: California (smaller), English (thinner slices), Lawry (traditional, generous), and Chicago (extra-thick with rib bone). Original spinning bowl salad; Yorkshire pudding; mashed potatoes and whipped cream horseradish come with prime rib; à la carte Lawry's baked potato is almost a meal itself—share it.

Other recommendations: Dinner fish special, such as grilled marlin with roast tomato vinaigrette or grilled ahi tuna served with ginger soy sauce; à la carte creamed spinach. Lunch: prime rib of beef; turkey, pastrami, and corned beef sandwiches; Lawry's Cobb salad; English trifle.

(continued)

Summary & comments: The name says it all—prime rib is the menu here. The tradition of over 50 years is a magical formula that works because of the restaurant's commitment to the finest prime, dry-aged beef and other quality ingredients prepared to perfection. The general consensus is that Lawry's can't be beat on prime rib. Wine list includes Lawry's private selection and two featured wines. Attention to detail and service is impressive, and the elegance of the mansion setting gilds the lily. They've broadened their menu with fish specials; the quick "ale and sandwich bar" offers an affordable, casual lunch in a majestic mansion—a rare treat. Since Jackie Shen was appointed executive chef (formerly of Jackie's), diners can continue to enjoy her signature dessert: chocolate bag filled with white chocolate mousse, strawberries, and kiwi, with raspberry sauce.

Honors/awards: *North Shore* magazine, "Best Prime Rib."

Le Colonial

Zone 1 North Side	French/Vietnamese
937 North Rush Street	★★★½
(312) 255-0088	Moderate
	Quality 88 Value C

Reservations:	Recommended
When to go:	Avoid peak meal times unless you have a reservation
Entree range:	$12.50–19
Payment:	VISA, MC, AMEX, DC
Service rating:	★★★★
Friendliness rating:	★★★★
Parking:	Valet, $7
Bar:	Full service
Wine selection:	French and American wines, including dessert wines, ranging from $18–225; four each of red and white, as well as two champagnes and several ports, available by the glass, $5–16
Dress:	Business casual
Disabled access:	Yes, also rest rooms
Customers:	Chic professionals; couples, especially weekends
Lunch:	Monday–Saturday, noon–2:30 P.M.
Dinner:	Monday–Friday, 5–11 P.M.; Saturday, 5 P.M.–midnight; Sunday, 5–10 P.M.

Atmosphere / setting: The interior design by Greg Jordan, who was inspired by the film *Indochine,* offers patrons a choice of two atmospheres: the bar and tranquil dining room downstairs with rattan chairs and louvered shutters; and the romantic lounge upstairs with overstuffed sofas and chairs, and a terrace (weather permitting). The decor transports diners to the 1920s era of French-colonial Southeast Asia. Potted palms, fans whirring overhead, and rattan furniture sustain the Pacific tone set by Le Colonial's exotic, fresh cuisine.

House specialties: Chao tom (grilled shrimp wrapped around sugarcane with angel hair noodles); steamed dumplings with chicken and mushrooms; spicy beef salad with lemongrass and basil; crisp-seared whole red snapper with a spicy sour sauce; sautéed jumbo shrimp with eggplant in curried coconut sauce; banana tapioca pudding; tropical fruit sorbets.

Other recommendations: Pho (hearty oxtail soup with rice noodles, beef, and herbs); spring rolls made with shrimp, pork, and mushrooms; oven-roasted

(continued)

235

chicken with lemongrass and lime dipping sauce; ginger-marinated roast duck with tamarind dipping sauce; grilled eggplant in a spicy basil lime sauce; stir-fried rice with lemongrass, shrimp, and toasted sesame seeds.

Summary & comments: You can't miss Le Colonial from Rush Street, since the dove gray vintage townhouse with its lovely balcony, ceiling fans, columns, and cast-iron railing are clearly from another era and place. When you enter downtown Chicago's first French-Vietnamese fine dining restaurant, you get lost in an Asian time warp from the early 20th century, when the French-colonial period was at its peak in Vietnam. Ceiling fans stir the banana trees and palms. Taking the stairway to the lounge gives a wonderful view of the attractive main floor dining room. Photos of life in Saigon during the 1920s dot the walls. Le Colonial is owned by Jean Goutal and Rick Wahlstedt, who are partners in Le Colonial in Manhattan; there is a third location in Los Angeles owned by the other two New York partners.

LE FRANÇAIS

	American Brasserie
Zone 10 Northwest Suburbs	★★★★★
269 South Milwaukee Avenue, Wheeling	Very Expensive
(847) 541-7471	Quality 99 Value C

Reservations:	Required
When to go:	Anytime, but weeknights might sometimes be less busy
Entree range:	$27–30.50; 4-course dinner (by 6 P.M.), $35
Payment:	AMEX, D, MC, VISA
Service rating:	★★★★★
Friendliness rating:	★★★★★
Parking:	Free valet in lot
Bar:	Full service
Wine selection:	The wine cellar will grow larger soon. About 125 bottles, 100 of which are French; the balance is American. Evenly split between whites and reds; 16 sparkling wines; 11 by the glass: $7-14, champagne, whites, reds, sauternes.
Dress:	Jacket required, tie preferred
Disabled access:	Yes
Customers:	International visitors and locals; couples, professionals, celebrators; connoisseurs
Dinner:	Monday–Thursday, 5:30–9:30 P.M.; Friday and Saturday, 5:30 and 9:30 P.M.

Atmosphere/setting: Exquisite with the same country-style wooden ceiling beams and wainscoting. The renovation lightened the interior and mixes classicism and modernism, as designed by environmental artist Vicky Tesmer. Fabric wall coverings are soothing hues of sages, golds and ecrus, echoed by carpets with touches of metallic. A new 10-foot-by-4-foot window, framed by copper pots, allows guests to view the chefs in the spectacular kitchen; and when it's time to clean the kitchen at the end of service, a blind comes down for privacy. Room is comfortable, quiet, romantic, elegant, and full of flowers. Beautiful Villeroy & Boch china and delicate, angular U.Y. Deorenne silver tableware is used. Non-smoking dining room. Private dining capacity for 20.

House specialties: Preludes: Charlotte of Peekytoe crab, with roasted heirloom tomatoes, celery root salad, gazpacho coulis and light curry sauce (most creative, with Spanish and Indian influences); foie gras cold and hot: a slice of the

(continued)

cold goose liver on mesclun salad; the hot piece was pan-seared, delicious in sauternes sauce with tiny figs—great with a glass of Sauternes, and one of the richest dishes! Less rich are seafood terrine with aïoli, tomato vinaigrette and micro greens; and trilogy of salmon: marinated, tartare, and smoked. Banchet's patés are the best, such as symphony of duck liver paté with truffles and ballotine of pistachios, foie gras, and rillette. Salade of watercress, Belgian endive, and Roquefort cheese with walnut vinaigrette and chopped nuts. Entrees: trio of lamb: mustard-crusted rack, cumin-dusted loin and braised shoulder with natural jus—perfectly cooked and exciting flavors. Pan-seared cod with brandade, pommes Maxim's, and mussel juice emulsion; a daily special of roasted grouper fillet with sautéed spinach and julienne of mixed vegetables in a pastry basket, with celery and olive oil emulsion. Desserts: Lemon sabayon tart with raspberry sorbet and coulis; Tahitian vanilla crème brûlée with fresh berries; oven-roasted Granny Smith apple, topped with nut streusel and orange sorbet, caramel sauce.

Other recommendations: Preludes: duck consommé "Paul Bocuse" style; warm lobster salad gourmande with truffle oil vinaigrette; farm-raised escargots with scallops Provençale. Entrees: tournedos of beef "Rossini Style" with black truffle sauce; wild mushroom and goat cheese–stuffed Amish capon with salsify, haricots verts, and rosemary-chicken jus. Desserts: warm flourless chocolate cake, Piedmont hazelnut ice cream and rum sauce; assortment of homemade sorbets in a sugar nest.

Summary & comments: Internationally acclaimed Master Chef Jean Banchet has reclaimed Le Francais after a decade's hiatus. Both the refurbished restaurant and the Banchet's cooking are more "au courant" in style, since tastes have changed in the past ten years. Some of the old favorites are still there, but most of the items are lighter and derive flavor from reductions, fresh herbs, and spices, instead of the classic French haute cuisine's reliance on cream and butter.

Given Banchet's rigorous classical training at the best restaurants in France, and the fact that his techniques and skills are rated as perfection, he continues to work with classic ingredients, cooking methods, and presentations; however, the outcome is simpler and reflects his personal interest in healthful dining. Banchet made 34-year-old David Sanders his chef de cuisine/partner. The service here is tops, with the cheerful staff showing attentiveness but never hovering, offering knowledge without arrogance, and balancing just enough commentary without imposing.

Honors/awards: More than fit on this page. Some are AAA five diamonds; five stars, *Mobil Travel Guide*; *Wine Spectator* Grand Award last several years; listed in *Tradition Et Qualité* and *Relais Et Chateaux* guides.

Le Titi de Paris

Zone 10 Northwest Suburbs	New French
1015 West Dundee Road,	★★★★½
Arlington Heights	Moderate/Expensive
(847) 506-0222	Quality 97 Value C

Reservations:	Required on weekends
When to go:	Weeknights
Entree range:	$19.75–28
Payment:	All major credit cards
Service rating:	★★★★★
Friendliness rating:	★★★★½
Parking:	Free lot
Bar:	None
Wine selection:	Over 700, French, American; $18 and up; 7 by the glass, from $5
Dress:	Jacket preferred; dressy
Disabled access:	Yes, entrance and rest rooms
Customers:	Mostly couples, some families; professionals (lunch), celebrators
Lunch:	Tuesday–Friday, 11:30 A.M.–2:30 P.M.
Dinner:	Tuesday–Thursday, 5:30–9:30 P.M.; Friday, 5:30–10 P.M.; Saturday, 5–10:30 P.M.

Atmosphere/setting: Gracious, romantic, comfortable elegance—filled with flowers. A high level of service without stuffiness.

House specialties: Sampler of hot and cold foie gras on toasted brioche; terrine of vegetable mousse; lobster bisque; assortment of pâtés. Norwegian salmon; roasted rack of lamb and confit of duck; daily specials. Napoleon; chocolate symphony; pyramid of pear with chocolate, Kahlúa mousse; opera pastry.

Other recommendations: Nut-crusted wild striped bass; panache of quail filled with spinach mousse, sweetbreads and veal loin; nouveau seafood cassoulet. Fresh fruit tart; manjari (bittersweet chocolate and passion fruit); circus fantasy.

Entertainment & amenities: Maître d' plays guitar and sings; wine and regional dinners. Bastille Day celebration.

Summary & comments: Owner-chef Pierre Pollin is one of the finest French chefs in the area and certainly one of the most easygoing, which may be why his employees stay a long time. He offers the traditional regional dishes of bouillabaisse and cassoulet Tuesday–Friday, January–March. This place has never been pretentious—just warm and inviting.

Honors/awards: DiRoNA Award, 1994.

Le Vichyssoise

Zone 10   Northwest Suburbs
220 West Route 120, Lakemoor
(815) 385-8221

French
★★★★½
Moderate

Quality 95   Value B

Reservations:	Suggested
When to go:	Wednesday or Thursday evenings, early Friday or Saturday evenings
Entree range:	$14.95–29.95
Payment:	VISA, MC, DC
Service rating:	★★★★½
Friendliness rating:	★★★★½
Parking:	Lot
Bar:	Full service
Wine selection:	100 French and American, $18–132; 15 by the glass, $4–8
Dress:	Moderately casual, neat
Disabled access:	Yes
Customers:	Young and old, couples, professionals
Dinner:	Wednesday and Thursday, 5:30–9 P.M.; Friday and Saturday, 5:30–10 P.M.; Sunday, 4:30 P.M.–9 P.M.

Atmosphere/setting: Authentic French country inn style with lovely table settings and a display of oil paintings for sale. Comfortable and cozy.

House specialties: Seafood and desserts are the chef's forte. House salad included with entree. Start with the vichyssoise (hot or cold). Other soups: shiitake mushroom and asparagus, morel, or crayfish. House pâtés: duck, quail, rillette. Escargots and mushroom gâteau; warm salmon crêpes and salmon caviar; Dover sole with vermouth sauce; roast duck in sherry wine-vinegar sauce; veal loin medallions; salmon en croûte in champagne sauce.

Other recommendations: Warm terrine of pike, salmon, and crayfish; French green beans, morels, mesclun, goat cheese, and walnut oil dressing; roasted rack of lamb with tarragon sauce; tournedos bordelaise; lobster à la nage. Three-course Country Bistro Menu, $21.50 (not served on Saturday).

Summary & comments: The first taste of chef Bernard Cretier's creations justifies the 50-mile trip northwest of Chicago. Cretier says, "I am free-spirited and didn't want a partner; I found this place—the price was right, the location was not. I hoped Chicagoans would make the trip." They did, and they've been making the pilgrimage since he and his partner and wife, Priscilla, opened in Lakemoor in 1976. The menu is seasonal with creative daily specials.

Louisiana Kitchen

Zone 1 North Side	Cajun/Creole
2666 North Halsted Street	★★★½
(773) 529-1666	Inexpensive/Moderate
	Quality 91 Value B

Reservations:	Parties of 6 or more
When to go:	Weekend evenings for the liveliest atmosphere; Sunday brunch for a great jazz experience
Entree range:	$9.95–17.95
Payment:	All major credit cards
Service rating:	★★★
Friendliness rating:	★★★★½
Parking:	Valet, $4
Bar:	Full, with good selection of beers; specialty drinks
Wine selection:	About two dozen international selections and several domestics from California; gently priced from $20–35/bottle, and from $4–6/glass for the dozen so offered
Dress:	Casual; very casual in garden
Disabled access:	Yes
Customers:	Mixed, all ages; jazz lovers; aficionados of Louisiana cuisine
Brunch:	Saturday, 11 A.M.–3 P.M.; Sunday jazz brunch (served, not buffet), 11 A.M.–3 P.M.
Lunch/Dinner:	Saturday, 3 P.M.–midnight; Sunday, 3–10 P.M.
Dinner:	Tuesday and Wednesday, 5–10 p.m.; Thursday, 5–11 P.M.; Friday, 5 P.M.–midnight

Atmosphere/setting: Interior is intimate with white tablecloths and blue-cushioned chairs; casual mood with wooden floors and lower half wall and enlarged portrait photos of jazz greats. Lively and electric; music loud but not offensively so. Lovely outdoor garden reminiscent of Bayou country with brick patio floor, wrought iron fence and gate, and a large central tree illuminated by tiny lights.

House specialties: Appetizers: fried alligator, crispy bite-size nuggets, delicious with Creole honey mustard sauce (some of the best, per New Orleans customers); Louisiana's seafood gumbo (thick, slightly spicy). Entrees under "Lagniappe" (a little something extra): Sautéed shrimp and blackened catfish Acadienne, with garlic, tomatoes, green onions, herbs, and white wine; catfish seasoned

(continued)

241

with Mama Bazzell's cajun seasoning, with seasoned rice and blackened vegetables. Desserts: Louisiana bread pudding, warm and sweet with butter-rum sauce; bourbon pecan torte (pie-like); mocha hazelnut truffle (dense cake cut into wedges).

Other recommendations: Appetizers: Blackened shrimp with house seasoning mix; fried oysters and lobster (tail). French Quarter specialties: Louisiana jambalaya, a robustly flavored rice combination with chicken and smoked sausage (shrimp option too). Desserts: Mississippi mud pie with chocolate sauce; variety of cheesecakes.

Entertainment & amenities: Live jazz for Sunday brunch, which is served. Fine quality taped jazz other times. Mardi Gras celebration.

Summary & comments: A fourth-generation French Creole/Cajun cook, owner John Moultrie grew up in Chicago and learned his culinary secrets from his grandmother, who told him stories about her parents' Florida restaurant, Bazzell's, which opened in 1910. Moultrie's first solo venture was the popular Jazz Oasis in River North, and then Bazell's French Quarter Bistro in Old Town, which he closed and plans to relocate. Louisiana Kitchen is the only city restaurant I know of specializing in authentic Louisiana fare in a relaxed, fine dining, jazz-oriented setting.

Honors/awards: 1998 Silver Platter Award.

Lulu's

<table>
<tr><td></td><td>Pan-Asian</td></tr>
<tr><td>Zone 11   Northern Suburbs</td><td>★★★</td></tr>
<tr><td>626 Davis Street, Evanston</td><td>Inexpensive</td></tr>
<tr><td>(847) 869-4343</td><td></td></tr>
<tr><td></td><td>Quality 85   Value B</td></tr>
</table>

Reservations:	Not accepted
When to go:	Afternoon
Entree range:	$5.75–6.95
Payment:	VISA, MC, AMEX
Service rating:	★★★
Friendliness rating:	★★½
Parking:	Street, city lot
Bar:	Limited selection of beer and wine
Wine selection:	Limited, mostly white wines; several by the glass
Dress:	Very casual; T-shirts okay because that's what the staff wears
Disabled access:	Yes
Customers:	Locals, Northwestern University students, Chicago food lovers
Lunch/Dinner:	Monday–Thursday, 11:30 A.M.–10 P.M.; Friday and Saturday, 11:30 A.M.–11 P.M.; Sunday, 11:30 A.M.–9 P.M.

Atmosphere/setting: Bright; open kitchen; nonsmoking restaurant.

House specialties: Japanese, Chinese, and Vietnamese noodles served in styles from soups to salads to stir-fry; many vegetarian versions. From "Small Eats" section of menu: dim sum; vegetable spring rolls; gyoza filled with pork and scallions; blue mussels in spicy chile–garlic broth; crispy fried sesame ball with mochi rice around sweet bean paste. From "Big Eats" section: Japanese udon noodle soup with chicken, mushrooms, and bamboo shoots; spicy barbecue pork and thin Chinese egg noodles stir-fried.

Other recommendations: Charcoal-grilled steak salad with mixed greens and fresh vegetables; jumbo shrimp and mixed veggies with Thai panang coconut curry and rice.

Summary & comments: Chef Daniel Kelch opened this casual spot in Evanston with his wife and partner, Laura Van Dorf. The dishes are alive with flavor and are served in a no-frills environment for very reasonable prices. It was an instant success, and the people keep returning. They've opened their second location in Hyde Park, another university community.

Lutnia Continental Cafe

Zone 2 North Central/O'Hare	Polish
5532 West Belmont Avenue	★★★½
(773) 282-5335	Inexpensive/Moderate
	Quality 87 Value C

Reservations:	Recommended
When to go:	Any time
Entree range:	$8.95–20
Payment:	Major credit cards
Service rating:	★★★★
Friendliness rating:	★★★★
Parking:	City garage
Bar:	Full service, including Polish vodka
Wine selection:	International, including Hungarian
Dress:	Casual and dressy, depending on occasion
Disabled access:	Yes
Customers:	Local, some Europeans, professionals, couples
Lunch/Dinner:	Saturday and Sunday, 1–11 P.M.
Dinner:	Tuesday–Friday, 5–11 P.M.

Atmosphere/setting: Elegant and romantic: candelabras, red carpet, and musical instruments and paintings on walls; white tablecloths with fresh roses and candles; some intimate tables; white baby grand piano

House specialties: Duck breast flambé in orange sauce; stroganoff tenderloin flambé served in pastry shell; stuffed boneless quail with cranberry sauce. Besides flambéed dishes, there is tableside service of certain salads, such as Caesar (for two). Traditional Polish dishes all get high marks: potato pancakes, pierogi (stuffed dumplings), and bigos (hunter's stew).

Other recommendations: Mushrooms stuffed with escargots and scallops; white borscht (tart, with sour cream and sausage); cucumber salad; spinach salad. Homemade apple cake and flambéed blintzes; Polish old-fashioned coffee with honey liqueur.

Entertainment & amenities: Live piano on weekend nights playing romantic music, such as Chopin.

Summary & comments: Gracious Polish couple, Chris and Evana Ruban, are owners; the recipes served here are Chris's. Dinner includes an appetizer, bread, soup, and a vegetable. The upscale food is very good, served on fine china by an attentive staff with European flair.

Honors/awards: *North Shore* magazine, Best Eastern European Restaurant.

244

Maggiano's Little Italy

Italian
★★★
Moderate

Quality 81   Value C

Zone 4   The Loop
516 North Clark Street
(312) 644-7700

Zone 8   Southern Suburbs
Route 83 at 22nd Street
Oak Brook Center, Oak Brook
(708) 368-0300

Zone 11   Northern Suburbs
175 Old Orchard, Skokie
(847) 933-9555

Reservations:	*Chicago and Skokie:* accepted; *Oak Brook:* for 6 or more
When to go:	Any time; weekends busiest
Entree range:	*Chicago:* $8.50–26.95; *Oak Brook:* $12–22; *Skokie:* $10–25
Payment:	Major credit cards
Service rating:	★★★
Friendliness rating:	★★★½
Parking:	*Chicago:* valet $4; *Oak Brook:* mall lot, valet $3.50; *Skokie:* mall lot
Bar:	Full service
Wine selection:	Italian; small by-the-glass selection
Dress:	Casual
Disabled access:	Yes; call first
Customers:	Mixed
Lunch:	*Chicago:* Monday–Saturday, 11:30 A.M.–2 P.M.
Dinner:	*Chicago:* Monday–Thursday, 5–10 P.M.; Friday, 5–11 P.M.; Saturday, 2–11 P.M.; Sunday, noon–10 P.M.
Lunch/Dinner:	*Oak Brook:* Monday–Thursday, 11:15 A.M.–10 P.M.; Friday and Saturday, 11:15 A.M.–11 P.M.; Sunday, noon–9 P.M. *Skokie:* Monday–Thursday, 11:15 A.M.–10 P.M.; Friday and Saturday, 11:15 A.M.–11 P.M.; Sunday, noon–10 P.M.

Atmosphere/setting: Re-creation of a New York City prewar "Little Italy" dinner house; simple decor in large dining room. The three locations are similar in style.

(continued)

245

MAGGIANO'S LITTLE ITALY *(continued)*

House specialties: Grand portions of classic Italian-style pasta, chicken, veal, and steaks; country-style rigatoni; whole roast chicken with rosemary and garlic.

Other recommendations: *Chicago:* garlic shrimp with shells; apple crostada. *Oak Brook:* angel hair al'arrabbiata; escarole with white beans and sausage. *Skokie:* roasted shells with vegetables; Maggiano salmon; chicken Parmesan; tiramisu.

Entertainment & amenities: Each has an outdoor cafe for summer dining with a full menu available.

Summary & comments: The Maggiano's Little Italy concept of traditional Italian cuisine with generous portions was so successful that the restaurant expanded to several other locations, including Schaumburg (phone (847) 240-5600). Downtown, you enter the restaurant through the Corner Bakery, which provides the great variety of breads and some of the desserts served. The 190-seat restaurant has old-Italian charm and hearty food, and it encourages sharing by offering half- or small orders of many items. Family dinners are served for parties of eight or more. In the Chicago location, the salmon oreganato was under-cooked, but everything else was perfectly prepared and robustly seasoned. Call other locations for specifics. Menus are basically the same with the exception of several specialties. Private party facilities can handle large groups.

Mama Desta's Red Sea Ethiopian Restaurant

Ethiopian	
★★★	
Inexpensive	
Quality 86	Value B

Zone 1   North Side
3216 North Clark Street
(773) 935-7561

Reservations:	Recommended for 4 or more
When to go:	Weekdays after 7 P.M.
Entree range:	$6–8.50
Payment:	Major credit cards
Service rating:	★★★★
Friendliness rating:	★★★★
Parking:	Public lots nearby
Bar:	Full service
Wine selection:	Mixed; mostly African and American
Dress:	Casual
Disabled access:	Yes
Customers:	Diverse, local, international, usually the 20–30-something age group
Lunch:	Friday–Sunday, 11:30 A.M.–3 P.M.
Dinner:	Monday–Thursday, 3–11 P.M.; Friday–Sunday, 3 P.M.–midnight

Atmosphere/setting: Two cozy, candlelit rooms. Diners can sit at tables and in booths in one room or at mesobes (large woven baskets that serve as tables; no chairs) in another room. The decor is simple but tasteful: white tablecloths, red carnations, and candles.

House specialties: Yemisir wat (spiced green lentils, pureed until very smooth); doro wat (chicken simmered with garlic and onions in spicy berbere sauce, including coriander, cumin, garlic, and cardamom); zizil wat (beef simmered in mildly spiced berbere sauce); yasa tibs (sautéed boneless catfish with onions, green peppers, spices, and herbs). Dessert: Red Sea cream (pudding of sweet and sour creams, brown sugar, raspberry puree, with crème de cacao).

Other recommendations: Yebeg tibs (lamb cubes sautéed with peppers, onions, spices, berbere sauce); Tej (sweet Ethiopian wine).

Summary & comments: The saucy dishes are hearty, wholesome, and colorful, and are served family style on classic injera, a tart sourdough pancakelike bread made from teff (milletlike grain). The injera is placed on a large metal platter. To eat Ethiopian style, pick up one type of food with a piece of torn bread and eat together. Ethiopians do not use knives and forks. Injera is both a plate and spoon.

Honors/awards: *Chicago Tribune,* three stars.

Mandar Inn

Zone 5 South Loop	Chinese
2249 South Wentworth Avenue, Chinatown	★★★½
	Inexpensive/Moderate
(312) 842-4014	Quality 88 Value C

Reservations:	Accepted; recommended for weekends
When to go:	Any time
Entree range:	$6.50–28
Payment:	VISA, MC, AMEX, DC
Service rating:	★★★★
Friendliness rating:	★★★★★
Parking:	Community Chinatown lot offers 2 hours free with restaurant validation
Bar:	Full service
Wine selection:	Mostly Californian, some French (including Wan Fu), Asian; inexpensive; 8 by the glass
Dress:	Casual, some dressy
Disabled access:	No
Customers:	Locals, some families, suburbanites, tourists, mix of Asian and non-Asian patrons
Open:	Sunday–Thursday, 11:30 A.M.–9:30 P.M.; Friday and Saturday, 11:30 A.M.–10:30 P.M.

Atmosphere/setting: Decorated in shades of rose and maroon with comfortable green banquettes. Attractive 95-seat space; artistic touches.

House specialties: Flaming appetizers (for two), including shrimp toast, egg roll, ribs, and barbecue pork; kwoh-te (freshly made pot stickers); empress chicken; Szechuan green beans (great texture and flavor); Szechuan eggplant; lobster and scallops volcano (seafood with pea pods and mushrooms in wine and oyster sauce, dramatically served on a sizzling hot platter).

Other recommendations: Orange chicken; moo shi pork; Peking duck (one day's advance notice; compared to most other places and downtown prices, it's a bargain); beef in a nest.

Summary & comments: You can get more than Mandarin cuisine at this respected Chinatown restaurant, which has been in this location for over 13 years. Szechuan, Hunan, and Cantonese cuisines are also offered on the extensive menu. If you're dining with a group, consider the fixed-price Mandar dinners listed for parties of two to eight. Owner Sharolyn Jay develops the recipes and oversees the operation, and her daughter assists with the front of the house. Their graciousness prevails, and customers feel very welcome.

Honors/awards: Three stars from *Mobil Travel Guide*.

248

Mangia Italiano Ristorante

Zone 2 North Central/O'Hare	Italian
4920 West Irving Park Road	★★★★
(773) 205-4354	Inexpensive
	Quality 94 Value B

Reservations:	Accepted and suggested, especially weekends and for large groups
When to go:	For conversation, Monday through Thursday and Friday, Saturday, 5-8 P.M. are quieter. Friday and Saturday evenings after 8 for the additional live musical bonus
Entree range:	$9.96–16.95 or market price for fish of the day
Payment:	VISA, MC, AMEX
Service rating:	★★★★
Friendliness rating:	★★★★★
Parking:	Street; nearby city lot free 24 hours
Bar:	Full service, fully stocked
Wine selection:	Balanced two dozen selection of Italian, Spanish, and Chilean wines. Several by the glass, including Chianti, Merlot, Cabernet Sauvignon, and two each Pinot Grigios and Chardonnays.
Dress:	Chic casual; some dressy; business
Disabled access:	Complete
Customers:	Mostly locals; mix of all ages, professionals; couples, groups of friends and families
Lunch:	Monday–Friday, 11:30 AM–2:30 P.M.
Dinner:	Monday–Thursday, 5–10 P.M.; Friday and Saturday, 5–11 P.M.

Atmosphere/setting: Cheerful interior with white walls and wood borders; clean, contemporary look; spacious with half walls dividing window alcoves near entryway. Soft lighting and tables covered with green and white cloths, well spaced for privacy. Photos of family and friends in antique gold and silver frames on back wall add a cozy touch to the comfortable room.

House specialties: Antipasti: scungili alla Veneziana (tender conch in piquant tomato sauce); antipasti della casa (marinated peppers, imported cheeses); calamari fritti with sauce of choice; bruschetta (Italian bread topped with fresh mozzarella, tomatoes, garlic). Pastas: colorful and delicious fettuccine alla Carolina (green pasta with spinach, red peppers, and pine nut sauce); linguine del giorno (chef's creation).

(continued)

Entrees: grilled salmon with tomato vinaigrette and fresh vegetables; pollo offered five ways, including scarpara (chicken breast and Italian sausage with green peppers) and Mangia Italiano (chicken breast with mushrooms, artichokes, two scampi, in white wine sauce). Risotto del giorno, gnocchi del giorno (stuffed with prosciutto or ricotta or spinach), and pesce del giorno. Desserts: Homemade tiramisu (no rum or liqueur); zupa Inglesa (sponge cake soaked in rum, layered with custard, chocolate mousse, topped with meringue); cannoli.

Other recommendations: Antipasti: mussels in piquant marinara sauce; special of grilled portobello mushroom with special garlic and white wine sauce; house salad (comes with entrees); zuppa del giorno. Pasta: tortellini alla Baronese (stuffed pasta in cream sauce with peas and pine nuts). Entrees: special calamari ripini (squid stuffed with shrimp and breadcrumbs, in lemon butter sauce); filetto di Manzo con funghi (prime beef filet in savory Madeira sauce); special of grilled swordfish with vegetables. Dessert: fresh fruits (summer); zabaglione; occasional Italian cheesecake.

Entertainment & amenities: Live music Friday and Saturday evenings starting at 8 p.m. Folk guitarist Nelson Sosa, from Chile, performs the rhythmic music of Latin America on Fridays 8 P.M.–I A.M. Eric Mueller, keyboardist, performs a variety of music on Saturday night, starting at 8 p.m.Occasionally, guitarist and vocalist, Ossie Arciniega, sings songs from his homeland, Peru, as well as Mexico, Argentina, Chile, and Spain. Private parties from 50–140 can be booked on Sundays.

Summary & comments: This family-run neighborhood restaurant in Portage Park, an area lean on fine dining, is a shining gem. Considering the fine quality of cooking, cheerful and accommodating service, and weekend live music for the low prices, Mangia Italiano is a terrific bargain. It's a personal favorite because of those factors and I especially enjoy the fact that a single diner is made to feel comfortable in the friendly environment.

Maple Tree Inn

Zone 8   Southern Suburbs
13301 South Western Avenue
(708) 388-3461

Cajun/Creole
★★★½
Inexpensive/Moderate
Quality 88   Value B

Reservations:	Required for 7 or more
When to go:	Any time; usually busier on weekends
Entree range:	$10–19
Payment:	VISA, MC, D
Service rating:	★★★
Friendliness rating:	★★★½
Parking:	Street
Bar:	Full service, including Southern Comfort, New Orleans punch, and Dixie Jazz Light; 27 beers on draft, all craft-brewed; reasonably priced
Wine selection:	International; by the glass or bottle; affordable
Dress:	Casual
Disabled access:	Yes
Customers:	Mixed
Dinner:	Tuesday–Thursday, 5–9 P.M.; Friday and Saturday, 5–10 P.M.

Atmosphere/setting: This second location resembles an old New Orleans building with a covered outdoor verandah. Three dining rooms (a full-length alligator and large flying frog hang from the ceiling of one room); two bars; a fun atmosphere.

House specialties: Alligator and oyster gumbo; hickory-buttered barbecued shrimp; Dixie stuffed pork chop; Creole jambalaya; pork chop with sun-dried sweet cherries and bourbon glaze; chocolate mud mousse in a pastry shell.

Other recommendations: Seafood okra gumbo; oyster assortment (Bienville, Rockefeller, deviled); jumbo blackened scallops; New Orleans boiled dinners (crawfish, shrimp, or blue crab); crawfish A-2-Fay; Miz Ruby's shrimp Creole (available occasionally); bread puddin' with Rebel Yell bourbon sauce.

Summary & comments: You don't find many places with alligator both on the menu and hanging from the ceiling. Maple Tree Inn has settled in its new location with a fun atmosphere; it has been serving Cajun/Creole cuisine in this general area for many years. The whimsical menu is one of the most complete of its type. The former location was like a big house with a lovely outdoor patio under a maple tree—thus the restaurant name. Maple Tree Inn has lost its real tree, but it has become the tree of Cajun/Creole life in this area and is one of the best restaurants on the South Side.

Mei-Shung Chinese Restaurant

	Chinese/Taiwanese
	★★★½
	Inexpensive
Zone 1 North Side	
5511 North Broadway	Quality 87 Value B
(773) 728-5778	

Reservations:	Suggested on weekend evenings
When to go:	Any time; weekdays less busy
Entree range:	Lunch, $6.95–10.95; dinner, $6.95–14.95
Payment:	VISA, MC, AMEX, DC
Service rating:	★★★★
Friendliness rating:	★★★★★
Parking:	Street and church lot
Bar:	BYOB
Wine selection:	BYOB
Dress:	Casual
Disabled access:	Yes
Customers:	Diverse; locals, ethnics
Lunch/Dinner:	Tuesday–Saturday, 11:30 A.M.–11 P.M.; Sunday, noon–9:30 P.M.

Atmosphere/setting: Elegantly decorated storefront; lovely plants and flowers add warmth and color. Comfortable, white tablecloth atmosphere.

House specialties: Taiwanese menu: Mei-Shung scallops; prawn with spiced salt; pineapple with shrimp; steamed bean curd roll (ugly but very good); delicious chicken shreds salad; sliced chicken with sweet basil. Regular menu: pot stickers; three in a nest (chicken, shrimp, and scallops with vegetables); two color shrimp. Complimentary chocolate fortune cookies and jasmine tea.

Other recommendations: Taiwanese menu: dry-cooked string beans; red-cooked beef noodles; stir-fried crab. Regular menu: moo shu pork; Mongolian chicken; pressed duck; Peking duck (order 24 hours in advance; one of the best prices for this specialty at $19.95).

Summary & comments: A Chinese jewel on the mid–North Side, Mei-Shung has an ambitious menu of mostly Mandarin, but also Hunan, Szechuan, and Cantonese cuisine and an entire Taiwanese menu. Everything is expertly prepared and nicely served. Many creative items are not seen elsewhere. Staff and couple who own the restaurant are delightful and maintain fine quality here.

Honors/awards: Voted one of the 15 best restaurants in Chicago by *Chicago* magazine.

Meson Sabika's Tapas Bar Restaurant

Spanish/Tapas
★★★★
Moderate

Zone 8   Southern Suburbs
1025 Aurora Avenue, Naperville
(630) 983-3000

Quality 93   Value C

Reservations:	Accepted; after 6 P.M. Friday and Saturday, limited to 6 or more
When to go:	Weekdays
Entree range:	$9.95–13.95; tapas, $2–12
Payment:	Major credit cards
Service rating:	★★★½
Friendliness rating:	★★★★
Parking:	Lot
Bar:	Full service; the spirits are Spanish
Wine selection:	Largely Spanish; from $15 a bottle; about 13 by the glass, $3.50–5; 2 sangrias; many sherries
Dress:	Casual to formal
Disabled access:	Yes
Customers:	Diverse
Brunch:	Sunday, 11 A.M.–2 P.M.
Lunch/Dinner:	Monday–Thursday, 11:30 A.M.–10 P.M.; Friday, 11:30 A.M.–11 P.M.
Dinner:	Saturday, 5–11 P.M.; Sunday, 4–10 P.M.

Atmosphere/setting: In the elegant 1847 Willoway Manor mansion, with six dining rooms, extended patio, and outside bar. Murals, hand-painted Spanish ceramics, mosaics, and lace curtains create a distinct authentic flair.

House specialties: Patatas con aïoli (cold potato salad); ostras a la pimienta (grilled fresh oysters); sautéed escargot paella a la Valenciana; sofrito de vieras con pasta (sautéed chopped tomato with scallops and pasta); flan de cafe; caramelized bread pudding.

Other recommendations: Thin roast veal slices, sun-dried tomatoes with raspberry vinaigrette; gambas al ajillo (grilled shrimp); daily special of imported white asparagus spears with a yellow tomato relish (in season); cazuela (earthenware stew pot) de pulpo (marinated octopus); citrus rice pudding.

Entertainment & amenities: Flamenco guitarist and dancer Friday evening.

Summary & comments: Formerly Emilio's Meson sabika, the new owners have opened another Meson Sabika in Northfield (310 Happ Road; (847) 784-9300). The food and service have improved over the years.

MIA FRANCESCA

	Italian
	★★★
	Inexpensive/Moderate
	Quality 82 Value B

Zone 1   North Side
3311 North Clark Street
(773) 281-3310

Reservations:	First-come, first-served basis
When to go:	5–5:15 P.M. or after 9 P.M.
Entree range:	$7–14
Payment:	AMEX, VISA, MC
Service rating:	★★★
Friendliness rating:	★★★
Parking:	Valet
Bar:	Full service
Wine selection:	Fairly extensive; all Italian; good by the glass
Dress:	Casual, chic
Disabled access:	Yes, including rest rooms
Customers:	Yuppies, young local couples, groups
Dinner:	Sunday–Thursday, 5–10:30 P.M.; Friday and Saturday, 5–11 P.M.

Atmosphere/setting: Simple interior; ceiling fans; paper-covered white tablecloths. It's well lit and noisy—the opposite of romantic. Outdoor garden.

House specialties: Pollo a la Romano; mussels and spicy pomodoro. Menu changes daily; robust thin-crust pizzas are made in individual serving sizes.

Other recommendations: Lusty al dente pastas such as spicy penne alla verdure (sautéed wild mushrooms, cherry tomatoes, vegetables, garlic); fish dishes such as salmon and calamari (both sautéed with roasted peppers, capers, lemon, garlic).

Summary & comments: Very popular with young professionals who enjoy noisy, crowded places. Although not for everyone, this place serves excellent food with full flavors, and the prices are reasonable for the quality. Chef-owner Scott Harris created a magical blend of robust Italian cooking, generous portions, affordable prices, and a handwritten (photocopied) daily menu at Mia Francesca on Clark Street in Chicago, and then he repeated the concept at two suburban locations: La Sorella di Francesca (18 West Jefferson Street, Naperville, (630) 961-2706), and Francesca's North (Northbrook Shopping Plaza, 1145 Church, Northbrook, (847) 559-0260).

Honors/awards: Voted Best Italian Restaurant by the *Chicago Sun-Times*.

Mirabell Restaurant

Zone 2   North Central/O'Hare
3454 West Addison Avenue
(773) 463-1962

German/American
★★★½
Inexpensive/Moderate

Quality 88   Value B

Reservations:	Required Friday and Saturday
When to go:	Weekdays
Entree range:	$9.95–17.95
Payment:	All major credit cards
Service rating:	★★★★
Friendliness rating:	★★★★½
Parking:	K–Mart lot across the street is free
Bar:	Full service; schnapps and imported beers
Wine selection:	Fairly extensive; mostly German, several by the glass; affordable
Dress:	Casual
Disabled access:	Yes, including rest rooms
Customers:	Local and suburban
Lunch:	Monday–Saturday, 11:30 A.M.–2:30 P.M.
Dinner:	Monday–Thursday, 5–10 P.M.; Friday and Saturday, 5–11 P.M.

Atmosphere/setting: Charming German motif. Nonsmoking room behind the bar has spectacular murals; garden room has display of Hummel figurines (now a banquet room).

House specialties: Wiener schnitzel, any type; Kalbsteak Mirabell (sautéed veal); wiener roastbraten (New York sirloin steak); old-world classics (e.g., sauerbraten; Bavarian-style braised beef, dumplings).

Other recommendations: Veal fricassee; steaks (pepper steak, New York sirloin tips); Hungarian chicken paprikash; seafood platter; goulash soup; Hungarian goulash. Most entrees come with spaetzle or noodles and a vegetable.

Summary & comments: This establishment, tucked away in a neighborhood, has an old-world exterior with a colorful garden. Anita and chef Werner Heil, the owners, are attentive and caring, and their pride and joy in their work shows. They offer a large selection of ethnic specialties and several American selections. Prices here are in between the bargain Berghoff and the top-shelf Golden Ox. Mirabell seems to be even better today (their rating has gone up), although little has changed on the menu, including the reasonable prices.

Honors/awards: Only German restaurant listed in *Ochsner Pocket Guide to Finest Restaurants in the World.*

The Mity Nice Grill

Zone 3   Near North
835 North Michigan Avenue,
    Water Tower Place, Mezzanine
(312) 335-4745

American
★★★½
Inexpensive/Moderate

Quality 86   Value C

Reservations:	Strongly recommended
When to go:	Any time
Entree range:	Lunch, $11–13; dinner, $13–18
Payment:	All major credit cards
Service rating:	★★★½
Friendliness rating:	★★★★½
Parking:	Water Tower underground garage (discount after 5 P.M.)
Bar:	Full service
Wine selection:	Good selection; several by the glass
Dress:	Casual
Disabled access:	Yes
Customers:	Professionals, couples, families, shoppers, tourists
Lunch/Dinner:	Monday–Saturday, 11 A.M.–10 P.M.; Sunday, 11 A.M.–9 P.M.

Atmosphere/setting: Casual, neighborhood-style spot downtown. Classic bar for people-watching; comfortable 180-seat restaurant, simply decorated. A 1940s-style decor with a 1990s grill.

House specialties: Grilled flatbreads, roasted crisp with a variety of toppings (especially featured at lunch); ginger chicken potstickers; turkey steak; an herb- and a garlic-roasted chicken; garlic-crusted Lake Superior whitefish, and daily specials, such as Saturday's aged prime rib, horseradish potatoes, and jus; abundant salads, including namesake chopped salad. Sweets: great homemade crumble-topped apple pie; fat-free frozen yogurt shakes.

Other recommendations: "Minute Chicken Terri D.," a loyal customer's favorite dish named for her; vegetarian chili; grilled steaks; simple pastas, such as angel hair, vegetable marinara; weekly specials based on seafood, etc., in season; Mity Nice hamburger, with deluxe version.

Summary & comments: Rich Melman, founder of Lettuce Entertain You Enterprises, says, "Today, more than ever, we need to be nice to each other. That's why I decided to call it 'Mity Nice Grill.'" It's a great concept for a restaurant in our increasingly stressful world. The staff is mity nice here, and so is the food, prepared by new chef Rose Ludwig. The menu is available at the bar as well, and includes reminders for your health and to be nice.

Mon Ami Gabi

Zone 1 North Side	French Bistro
2300 North Lincoln Park West	★★★½
(773) 348-8886	Moderate
	Quality 92 Value C

Reservations: Recommended
When to go: Early weeknights; late weekends
Entree range: Appetizers, $3.50–7.95; entrees, $14.95–25.95
Payment: All major credit cards
Service rating: ★★★½
Friendliness rating: ★★★
Parking: Valet, $6
Bar: Full service; cocktail lounge for customers
Wine selection: 50 selections, French and American; affordable
                        $10–35 a bottle; 8 by the glass, $4.95–8
Dress: Casual
Disabled access: Yes; call ahead for special accommodations
Customers: Casual crowd, locals, media, city people; low-key
                        after opera and art gallery crowd
Dinner: Monday–Thursday, 5:30–10 P.M.; Friday, 5:30–
                        10:30 P.M., Saturday, 5–10:30 P.M.; Sunday, 5–9 P.M.

Atmosphere/setting: Continental flair and unique style in an elegant, renovated old hotel with high ceilings and French doors. Feels like a bistro on the
West Bank of Paris; chic; intimate outdoor garden; seats 120.

House specialties: Onion soup, crock-baked with croutons and Gruyère;
steak frites; herb-roasted Amish chicken with pearl onions, mushrooms, and cafe
frites; sautéed Hawaiian black bass with potato puree and roasted tomato-saffron
jus; sautéed red snapper with roasted root vegetables and lemon-herb jus.

Other recommendations: Seafood risotto with mussels, shrimp, scallops;
potato–goat cheese salad with watercress and balsamic vinaigrette

Entertainment & amenities: Taking in the stately architecture and charming atmosphere, including the Lincoln Park Conservatory across the street.

Summary & comments: The grand architecture, classic Gallic bistro cuisine,
and very competent service here combine to make this restaurant a lovely French
bistro experience. The cooking is directed by Lettuce Entertain You Enterprises
managing partner Gabino Sotelino, who hired Kenneth Harris as executive chef.

Honors/awards: Gold Cup Award.

Mongolian Barbeque

Zone 1   North Side
3330 North Clark
(773) 325-2300

Zone 8   Southern Suburbs
221 South Washington, Naperville
(630) 428-0300

Asian Grill	
★★★	
Inexpensive	
Quality 85	Value B

Reservations:	Recommended for parties of 6 or more
When to go:	Avoid the peak hours between 7:30 and 9 P.M.
Entree range:	Lunch, $6.95; one-bowl stir-fry with one trip to soup and salad bar, $8.95; all-you-can-conquer Mongolian feast, $9.95 (lunch) or $11.95 (dinner). Children ages 12 and under, $4.95
Payment:	AMEX, D, MC, VISA
Service rating:	★★★½ (largely self-serve)
Friendliness rating:	★★★★½
Parking:	*North Side:* Public lot or street; *Naperville:* street and nearby free municipal lot
Bar:	Full service, including 6 taps, microbrewed and international beers
Wine selection:	Mostly American, some Italian; several by the glass, $3.95 and up
Dress:	Very casual
Disabled access:	Yes
Customers:	*North Side:* largely young professionals; *Naperville:* locals, families, older couples, young couples on dates
Open:	*North Side:* Monday–Thursday, 11:30 A.M.–10 P.M.; Friday and Saturday, 11:30 A.M.–11 P.M.; Sunday, noon–10 P.M. *Naperville:* Monday–Thursday, 11 A.M.–10:30 P.M.; Friday and Saturday, 11 A.M.–11:30 P.M.; Sunday, noon–10 P.M. Carry-out available.

Atmosphere/setting: The spacious Naperville interior has contemporary and upbeat decor, but diners get a peek at the Mongolian culture and lifestyle of the past; there is a huge mural of a Mongolian village and a large *yurt,* a replica of a traditional Mongolian mud home, suspended over the six-foot grill. The North

(continued)

258

Side location is smaller and seems more crowded but is basically similar. Not a relaxed or romantic setting.

House specialties: Diners create their own stir-fry dishes by selecting from a variety of fresh meats, seafoods, vegetables, sauces, spices, and oils. They then take their creations to the grill where the cooks prepare the stir-fry. The restaurant's advice is to use only one meat at a time, at least two ladles of sauce, and one ladle of oil. Be careful not to overdo it with the spices. Reeses peanut-butter pie; Oreo cream pie (special).

Other recommendations: Cream of broccoli soup (daily special); salad from salad bar with garlic or blue cheese dressings. Snickers bar pie; caramel-apple cobbler.

Entertainment & amenities: Watching the grillers; hearing them clang the bell when they get a tip in the bowl.

Summary & comments: Mongolian Barbeque is very popular with the young crowd who like noise, entertainment, action, and interactive dining, especially because it's affordable. It's a fun date. Favorite recipes from customers might appear on the recipe cards displayed at the beginning of the ingredient bar. Those with big appetites can return to the salad and ingredient bars as many times as they wish. The service here is friendly and accommodating. The ingredients are fresh, the variety will please most people, and the sauces and oils are well defined and flavorful. The company's press-release description, "eatertainment in an atmosphere of controlled chaos," is apt.

Montparnasse

Zone 8 Southern Suburbs	New French
200 East 5th Avenue, Naperville	★★★★½
(630) 961-8203	Moderate/Expensive
	Quality 95 Value C

Reservations:	Required for dinner
When to go:	Weeknights
Entree range:	Lunch, $8–15; dinner, $27–33
Payment:	All major credit cards
Service rating:	★★★★½
Friendliness rating:	★★★★½
Parking:	Free lot
Bar:	Full service bar
Wine selection:	Over 200 French and Californian selections, $18–100 a bottle; 8 by the glass, $3.50–7
Dress:	Nice casual; chic; some dressy
Disabled access:	Yes, entrance and rest rooms
Customers:	Mixed, couples, professionals, local; French food lovers
Lunch:	Monday–Friday, 11:30 A.M.–2 P.M.
Dinner:	Monday–Saturday, 6–9:30 P.M.; Sunday, closed

Atmosphere/setting: Not the usual fine-dining French restaurant look. The interesting two-level space is a rehabilitated factory boiler room with brick walls; quiet, soft lighting and casual elegance.

House specialties: Appetizers: crab cake, mustard beurre blanc; grilled squab salad, quail egg, sauce Perigueux; Montparnasse smoked salmon, Beluga caviar, crème fraîche. Entrees: (daily and seasonal) rabbit roulade with shrimp, tarragon vinaigrette, and mango; assiete de gibiers (venison and pheasant), natural fowl jus; fresh fish of the day, such as sautéed John Dory (in season) with preserved lemon and basil butter; pan-roasted Atlantic salmon with artichokes and woodland mushrooms; Wisconsin range pheasant, garlic potato, black peppercorn sauce. Desserts: Crème brûlée, Jean Banchet; lemon custard tart with berries; handmade ice creams and sorbets; warm macaronade of chocolate with crème fraîche and raspberries; mango and cashew tart.

Other recommendations: Appetizers (daily and seasonal selection): grilled foie gras, roasted pineapple, vanilla sauce; cassolette of wild mushrooms and fried leeks. Burgundian escargots with tomato, garlic butter; French onion soup gratinée. Entrees: roasted rack of lamb and tenderloin, sauce Perigueux; saddle of

(continued)

venison on foie gras, sauce Grand Veneur. Desserts: hot apple tart, cinnamon ice cream and caramel sauce; hazelnut cream puffs with chocolate ice cream.

Summary & comments: Jean-Paul Eskenazi, an alum of Le Français, was a pioneer in opening this fine dining French restaurant in Naperville in October 1989. Since then, the area has greatly increased in population and in numbers of restaurants. The cuisine here has received praise and garnered a steady clientele since opening. New chef de cuisine, Kei Uchikawa, who was the personal chef for the consul general of Japan and most recently assistant to the executive chef at Le Francais, continues the style here in preparing creative, contemporary French cooking. The menu changed about 60 percent since he's taken over. There are about seven daily specials, including appetizers and entrees. Four desserts are also listed. The carte de maison is a thoughtful mix of tempting items from soup (French onion gratinée) to nuts (brioche bread pudding, dried fruits, and walnuts). The personable Eskenazi, a former captain at Le Français under Jean Banchet, utilized his expansive knowledge to plan Montparnasse, and he organized a terrific wine list with great variety. In October 1995, he turned the upstairs level into Fifth Avenue Bistro, with a more casual menu and relaxed prices; that menu is available downstairs for lunch. This growing Naperville suburban area needed a fine-dining French establishment. No surprise that it's been a great success, but it would be in most locations. This is one of the best restaurants in the southwestern suburbs.

Honors/awards: Excellent reviews in local newspapers, including top five stars in Sun Publications and Copley Newspapers; DiRoNA Award 1993.

Morton's of Chicago

Zone 3   Near North
1050 North State Street
(312) 266-4820

Zone 8   Southern Suburbs
One Westbrook Corporate Center
22nd Street and Wolf Road, Westchester
(708) 562-7000

Zone 2   North Central/O'Hare
9525 West Bryn Mawr Avenue, Rosemont
(847) 678-5155

Zone 10   Northwest Suburbs
1470 McConnor Parkway, Schaumburg
(847) 413-8771

Steak	
★★★★	
Expensive	
Quality 93	Value C

Reservations:	Suggested
When to go:	Any time
Entree range:	$17–30
Payment:	All major credit cards
Service rating:	★★★★½
Friendliness rating:	★★★★½
Parking:	Free *(Rosemont and Westchester)*; call other places for details
Bar:	Full service; 40 varieties of martinis
Wine selection:	Extensive; several selections by the glass
Dress:	Jacket preferred, tie optional (but flexible)
Disabled access:	Yes, for all locations
Customers:	Diverse, local, professionals, couples, travelers; downtown location also gets celebrities
Lunch:	*Westchester:* Monday–Saturday, 11:30 A.M.–2:30 P.M.
Dinner:	Monday–Saturday, 5:30–11 P.M.; Sunday, 5–10 P.M.

Atmosphere/setting: Comfortable, well appointed. Suburban places are quieter and more intimate; downtown is bigger and more crowded.

House specialties: 24-oz. porterhouse steak, also available as a 3-lb. double; whole baked Maine lobsters; special-fed, farm-raised salmon; black bean soup; steamed asparagus with hollandaise.

(continued)

Other recommendations: Sicilian veal chop; domestic rib lamb chops; fresh Cockenoe oysters on the half shell to start; Caesar salad; sautéed fresh spinach and mushrooms; baked Idaho potato; Godiva hot chocolate cake; soufflé for two—chocolate, Grand Marnier, or lemon.

Entertainment & amenities: Watching the "show and tell" performance by the waiters with the display cart of huge cuts of steaks, chops, live lobsters, and other raw ingredients.

Summary & comments: Many steak connoisseurs stake their claim in Morton's as their favorite place for porterhouse or certain other cuts. The management is a stickler for quality, and the kitchen prepares the meat properly to order. The diner pays dearly for this high quality. The $29 steak gets only a garnish; everything must be ordered à la carte, as is the case in many steak restaurants. Clockwork service makes everything move along at a great pace. Needs are anticipated by the professional servers. The downtown place is the most bustling and noisiest of the three locations. The three suburban siblings with similar menus cover the territory fairly well.

MOSSANT

Zone 4   The Loop
255 North Wabash Avenue
adjacent to Hotel Monaco, Chicago
(312) 236-9300

French Bistro
★★★★
Moderate

Quality 94   Value C

Reservations:	Recommended
When to go:	Anytime
Entree range:	$14.95–248.95
Payment:	All major cards
Service rating:	★★★★½
Friendliness rating:	★★★★★
Parking:	Valet, $7
Bar:	Full service with menu; open one hour later than dining room service
Wine selection:	Lengthy eight-page list with over 85 French and American selections. About 14 by the glass.
Dress:	Chic casual; business; dressy
Disabled access:	Yes
Customers:	Mixed, locals, travelers, professionals, couples
Breakfast:	Monday–Friday, 7–10 A.M.
Brunch:	Saturday and Sunday, 8 A.M.–2 P.M.
Lunch:	Monday–Friday, 11:30 A.M.–2:30 P.M
Dinner:	Sunday–Thursday 5–10 P.M.; Friday and Saturday, 5–11 P.M.

Atmosphere/setting: Dramatic exterior facade painted red, traditionally decorated. Entryway has decorative molded plaster ceiling, fancy ironwork, and a golden glass chandelier. Cozy bar with hearth oven. Main dining room, several steps below the bar, opens into a high-ceilinged room made stunning with large vintage French popsters and hat-themed portraits reflecting the Mossant name. Rich mahogany trim, deep red leather booths lit with wall sconces, high wainscoting, antique sideboards, and cherrywood floor. Open cook line provides patrons a look at the staff in action as freshly baked breads and pastries emerge.

House specialties: Hors d'oeuvres: Tomato tartar with French green beans, hazelnuts, frisée; potato crusted shrimp with salt cod purée, pepper oil; foie gras hot and cold, sweet pea emulsion, baby watercress, and shallot rings. Salad of seven lettuces, aged Balsamic vinaigrette, red currant tomatoes. Entrees: Rare tuna stuffed with asparagus, northern beans, preserved lemon rings, herb broth; lamb

(continued)

chops stuffed with pistou, guinea, spinach, and bacon ragout, lamb jus. Desserts: Tarte tatin; profiteroles with white chocolate, roasted pistachio ice cream, bittersweet chocolate sauce; crème brûlée with madeleine cookies.

Other recommendations: Hors d'oeuvres: Mossant's daily soup; spiced smoked salmon with terrine of blue cheese, candied walnuts, brioche, and red wine syrup, with caper, cucumber, and lemon relish. Entrees: Snapper baked in a saffron fennel broth, candied oven-dried tomato, potato and saffron sauce; duck roasted on-the-bone with cabbage, fingerling potatoes, and pineapple glaze. Desserts: Fromages; sorbet du jour; mousse aux chocalats; coupe poire Belle Helene.

Summary & comments: The lively taste of Paris meets the fun of Chicago, per a motto on one of the menus at Mossant, and many who have dined here agree. With a whimsical logo of a red glove tipping a red derby-style chapeau, Mossant immediately offers some Parisian personality: exciting and warm, and sophisticated yet down-to-earth. The hat is a nod to the famous French milliner namesake, and coincidentally, a Chicago hat factory once was housed on the site. Adjacent to the newly renovated building, now the Hotel Monaco, Mossant is located to the south of the Chicago River, on North Wabash at Wacker. The restaurant's street entrance is distinguished by its red facade with traditional moldings and leaded glass and golden ochre transoms. The interior is stunning and energetic, although it's possible to have a private conversation over dinner. The waitstaff is dressed in bistro vests and aprons to underscore the 19th Century Parisian theme.

Chef Steven Chiappetti took over the kitchen in early 2000 and created a simplified menu based on key ingredients. His philosophy is to highlight the natural flavors in a dish without overpowering those ingredients. Trained in classic and contemporary French cuisine, Chiappetti brings fine expertise and energy to Mossant as its third chef. Private party facilities for up to 200.

Honors/awards: In 1996, Chef Steven Chiappetti won the national competition required to earn him the privilege of being the only American chef eligible to compete for the prestigious Bocuse d'Or, an international "chef cook-off" held annually in Lyons, France. He ranked in the top ten of his peers, the best chefs from around the world.

265

MRS. PARK'S TAVERN

	Creative American
Zone 3 Near North	★★★½
198 East Delaware Place	Inexpensive/Moderate
(312) 280-8882	Quality 89 Value C

Reservations:	Recommended
When to go:	Any time, but weekends are busier
Entree range:	$13–28.50
Payment:	All major credit cards
Service rating:	★★★★
Friendliness rating:	★★★½
Parking:	Valet, $7
Bar:	Full service
Wine selection:	Extensive, international; about 250 full-bottle wines, starting at $18; 15–18 half-bottles, starting at $7; several by the glass, starting at $5.25
Dress:	Casual
Disabled access:	Yes
Customers:	Gold Coast residents, tourists, and celebrities, including Julia Roberts and Dennis Rodman
Breakfast:	Every day, 6:30–10:30 A.M.
Lunch/Dinner:	Every day, 11:30–2 A.M.

Atmosphere/setting: Unique, fascinating interior; the tavern's flag motif is enhanced with a full-wall American flag mural, a monumental folk-art American flag sculpture suspended in one of the dining rooms, a star-studded back bar, and a bounty of whimsical American folk art that makes for interesting browsing when customers take a break from eating.

House specialties: Spice-glazed crab cakes; barbecued chicken and jack cheese dumplings; Phil's Gold Coast chips with goat cheese fondue; tuna won ton, deep fried; pastrami salmon on rye bagel; ditali with tomato, basil, and parmesan; roasted chile-rubbed half chicken; chili-oil whipped potatoes; mushroom hash; Mrs. Park's crème brûlée.

Other recommendations: Duck liver pâté; spinach salad with ratatouille and goat cheese parfait; Grace Ann's cheddar cheese meat loaf. Warm java pudding; peanut-butter crunch; tempting house-made ice creams and sorbets.

Summary & comments: The mix of informal ambience, appealing American bistro menu, and professional service at moderate prices make Mrs. Park's Tavern ideal for casual dining. The restaurant's savvy wine list and well-informed servers allow diners to match appropriate wines with their orders.

266

Mykonos

Zone 11   Northern Suburbs
8660 Golf Road, Niles
(847) 296-6777

Greek	
★★★½	
Inexpensive/Moderate	
Quality 92	Value B

Reservations:	Recommended for 4 or more
When to go:	Weekdays; avoid weekend evenings
Entree range:	$6–15
Payment:	Major credit cards except DC
Service rating:	★★★★½
Friendliness rating:	★★★★½
Parking:	Valet in own lot
Bar:	Full service
Wine selection:	Mostly Greek, with about 24 selections; several ordinary Californian
Dress:	Casual
Disabled access:	Yes, including rest rooms
Customers:	Diverse; Greek Americans
Lunch/Dinner:	Monday–Thursday, 11 A.M.–11 P.M.; Friday and Saturday, 11 A.M.–midnight; Sunday, 11 A.M.–10 P.M.

Atmosphere/setting: Decorated in blue and white; charming interior resembles a cafe on the picturesque "white" island it's named for. Also a beautiful outdoor cafe.

House specialties: Broiled Florida red snapper, Greek-style with lemon juice and oregano (filleted by server on request); shrimp saganaki ala Mykonos (baked with tomato sauce, onions, peppers, and feta); tender spring lamb with artichokes in egg-lemon sauce; individual giouvetsi à la Mykonos (baked lamb with pasta and cheese); chicken breast à la Dimitri (sautéed in white wine, lemon, and spices); avgolemono soup; baby octopus vinaigrette. Baklava, rice pudding, and crema caramele.

Other recommendations: Homemade loukaniko (Greek sausage with orange peel); souvlaki (shish kebab of marinated pork tenderloin); broiled lamb chops; house-made gyros with yogurt sauce; light, custardy galaktoboureko and nougatina desserts.

Summary & comments: This suburban restaurant is far more serene than the lively spots in Greektown. Owner-chef Dimitri has a penchant for preparations of fresh fish and his never-fail treatment for tender baby octopus. He cares about all the details, so his restaurant is well managed. Dining here is always uplifting.

267

N. N. SMOKEHOUSE

Zone 1   North Side
1465–1467 West Irving Park Road
(773) TNT-4700

Barbecue/Filipino
★★★
Inexpensive/Moderate

Quality 82   Value B

Reservations:	Required for 10 or more
When to go:	Any time; busy during mealtimes
Entree range:	$5.85–14.95
Payment:	VISA, MC, DC, D
Service rating:	★★★½
Friendliness rating:	★★★★½
Parking:	Street, lot in back
Bar:	BYOB
Wine selection:	None
Dress:	Casual
Disabled access:	Yes
Customers:	Professionals, locals, suburbanites
Lunch/Dinner:	Tuesday–Thursday, 11:30 A.M.–10 P.M.; Friday, 11 A.M.–11 P.M.; Saturday, noon–11 P.M.; Sunday, noon–9 P.M.

Atmosphere/setting: Comfortable, very casual place with hand-painted mural. Blues background music and black-and-white photos of blues musicians.

House specialties: Award-winning, tender barbecue-smoked ribs; pulled Memphis pork; barbecue half-chicken dinner; house platter from the smoker (beef brisket, ribs, pulled pork, and turkey); pancit noodles (Filipino), either vegetarian or meat.

Other recommendations: Spicy seafood jambalaya; famous Mediterranean Salad (grilled breast of chicken on romaine with feta, chopped tomatoes, and Dijon dressing); Mississippi catfish sandwich (steaks); Mother Mildred's velvety sweet potato pie; pecan pie.

Summary & comments: The barbecue sauce is a 100-plus-year-old recipe, according to owner Larry Tucker, who runs this bustling restaurant and a great catering business with his wife, Nida. His father lived for several years in the Philippines, Nida's homeland—thus the Filipino touches. Tucker is expanding N. N. Smokehouse and renovated the space next door. He recently installed a new kitchen. Several VIPs frequent this place for their barbecue fix.

Honors/awards: Won Illinois State Fair Number One Pork Ribs, August 1997.

Nhu Hoa Cafe

Zone 1   North Side
1020 West Argyle
(773) 878-0618

Vietnamese/Laotian	
★★★½	
Inexpensive/Moderate	
Quality 89 Value B	

Reservations:	Recommended
When to go:	Wednesday and Thursday are less busy
Entree range:	$6.95–18.95
Payment:	All major credit cards
Service rating:	★★½
Friendliness rating:	★★★
Parking:	Street or lot 3 blocks away
Bar:	Limited selection of mixed drinks and beers
Wine selection:	Very small, domestic; from $2.75 a glass and $14 a bottle
Dress:	Casual
Disabled access:	Yes
Customers:	Ethnically diverse; locals, professionals, families
Lunch/Dinner:	Daily, 11:30 A.M.–10 P.M.

Atmosphere/setting: Two lion statues at the front door are believed to protect guests who enter.

House specialties: Banh xeo (Vietnamese pancakes with bean sprouts, pork, shrimp); banh cuon cha lua (steamed rice paper rolled with ground pork); com ga xao xa ot (steamed rice with spicy chicken); goi cuon (shrimp, pork, and vegetables rolled in rice paper); tom cuon chien (Vietnamese shrimp rolls); goi tom thit (a mixed vegetable salad with shrimp and pork); ca kho to (catfish simmered in a clay pot); ga xao xa ot (stir-fried chicken with lemongrass); keng som kung (Laotian tangy soup with shrimp, tomatoes, mushrooms, and lemongrass); Laotian garlic shrimp stir-fried with cucumber and broccoli; hot and sour shrimp stir-fried with ginger, garlic, onions, peppers, and steamed broccoli; vit tay cam (stewed roast duck and quail egg); tamarind duck (boneless roast duck stir-fried with mixed vegetables).

Other recommendations: Pho tai (beef with rice noodle soup); bun thit heo nuong cha gio (rice noodles with grilled pork and egg roll); com bi suon cha (steamed rice with grilled pork chops, minced pork pie, and egg); mi xao tom (crispy fried or soft egg noodles with shrimp and vegetables); hu tieu xao tom thit (pan-fried rice noodles with shrimp and barbecue pork); cha gio (egg rolls); sup mang cua (crab meat asparagus soup); ca hong chien nuoc mam toi ot (crispy,

(continued)

fried whole red snapper); bo xao xa ot (stir-fried beef with lemongrass); satay (choice of chicken, beef, or pork marinated in Laotian herbs served with peanut sauce and cucumber salad); papaya salad; spicy seafood stir-fried with bamboo shoot, red and green peppers, and peanuts in a red curry sauce; som varn (stir-fried tomatoes, onions, cucumbers, red and green peppers, and pineapple in a delicious sweet-and-sour sauce); Laos noodles (stir-fried noodles with shrimp, chicken, egg, green onions, and bean sprouts topped with ground peanuts and chilies); Laos special fried rice with onions, tomatoes, bean sprouts, and cucumber topped with egg, served with your choice of beef, chicken, pork, shrimp, squid, mussels, or mixed seafood; and vegetable rainbow (stir-fried assorted vegetables in a light brown sauce).

Entertainment & amenities: One dining room is equipped with a video projector that plays Vietnamese music videos and concerts.

Summary & comments: The lengthy menu has over 206 items, with a nice variety of Vietnamese and Laotian dishes. Something for everyone. The owner is reputedly planning to open a Cambodian/Laotian/Vietnamese restaurant, called Indochine.

Honors/awards: Positive reviews from local newspapers, including the *Chicago Tribune* and the *Chicago Sun-Times*.

Nick's Fishmarket

	Seafood
	★★★★½
	Moderate/Expensive
	Quality 95 Value D

Zone 4   The Loop
One First National Plaza, Monroe Street
   at Dearborn Street
(312) 621-0200

Zone 2   North Central/O'Hare
10275 West Higgins Road, O'Hare International Center, Rosemont
(708) 298-8200

Reservations:	Recommended
When to go:	Weekdays
Entree range:	Lunch $14–25; Dinner $18–47 (Maine lobster top price)
Payment:	All major credit cards
Service rating:	★★★★½
Friendliness rating:	★★★★½
Parking:	Valet, validated self-parking in First National garage *(Downtown)*; Lot *(Rosemont)*
Bar:	Full service
Wine selection:	Extensive (over 100) international; French, Italian, domestic, $20–200 a bottle; about 18 choices by the glass, $4.95 and up
Dress:	Jacket suggested; collared shirt or sweater required
Disabled access:	Yes
Customers:	Largely professionals, couples
Lunch:	*Downtown:* Monday–Friday, 11:30 A.M.–3 P.M.
Dinner:	*Downtown:* Monday–Thursday, 5:30–11 P.M.; Friday and Saturday, 5:30 P.M.–midnight; *Rosemont:* Sunday–Thursday, 6–10 P.M.; Friday and Saturday, 6–11 P.M.

Atmosphere/setting: Downtown, the new location across the plaza from the original space overlooks the Marc Chagall mosaic and the lively fountain. Ambience of a 1930s oceanliner with art deco–inspired carpeting, window treatments, furnishings, and art with a contemporary touch. New entryway from sidewalk leads to Nick's Bar & Grill with scaled down prices, a chic bar, and 90 seats. The escalator takes diners down to the plaza level to the new comfortable fine dining room with 150 seats and tuxedoed waiters. Rosemont has lovely aquari-

(continued)

ums and plush, comfortable club-like setting; tuxedoed waiters; private room seats 35. Lavish interior exudes posh and pizazz.

House specialties: Appetizers such as seared black and blue ahi, with baby bok choy; jumbo lump crabcake with spinach sauté, pineapple rémoulade and sweet soy wasabi; outstanding seafood crêpes topped with lobster and vermouth sauce. Entrees: Chef's favorite Dover sole, boned tableside with an exquisite caviar vermouth sauce; grilled or sautéed Hawaiian or other fresh fish, such as the uliehu (Hawaiian bluenose snapper) special with carved potato "mushrooms," snowpea pods, and carrots; linguini with black trumpet mushrooms, rosemary cream; peanut-crusted breast of capon with pocket of roasted artichoke mousseline; New York strip steak with mushroom sauté, light peppercorn sauce. Classic house salad (à la carte) topped with tiny shrimp. Desserts: Towers of Chicago (a construction of a quartet of mousses with raspberry sauce); excellent tart Key lime pie.

Other recommendations: Lobster bisque with lobster ravioli and sherry finish; cold appetizers of smoked salmon Napoleon with Roquefort and caper Bavarian, and roasted chicken and goat cheese terrine with sun-dried tomato couscous. Entrees: Alaskan halibut, fennel salad, caviar chardonnay sauce, and marinated shrimp; roasted Maine lobster clam bake; Holland turbot fillet, chanterelle and asparagus sauté, mustard and summer truffles (in season); California abalone specials if you can afford them (chef's cost is $64/pound!). Desserts: chocolate gateau; white chocolate crème brûlée.

Entertainment & amenities: Live music at both locations; call for specifics.

Summary & comments: Top-quality seafood place with pristinely fresh catches, many from Hawaiian waters. Well-known owner/founder Nick Nicholas owns several restaurants in Boca Raton, Florida; Washington D.C.; Philadelphia; and Las Vegas besides here, and he brings seafood in fresh to Chicago. He has a savvy staff with a penchant for serving seafood properly. Service is proficient and gracious, geared to expense-account business clientele. Steer toward the simpler preparations, such as roasted Maine lobster rather than the Thermidor with the classic but rich Mornay sauce. New chef André Halston has created a revised menu with some exciting dishes accented by unusual accompaniments (e.g. spinach and eggplant cake with dates and mint jus for rack of lamb), while keeping the signature items and longtime favorites.

Honors/awards: DiRoNA 1994-1997; Mobil 4-Star AAA Award 1977-1997; _Gourmet Magazine_, Top 20 Restaurants in Chicago—Readers' Poll 1996, 1997; _Wine Spectator_, Award of Excellence, 1997.

North Pond Cafe

<table>
<tr><td>Zone 1   Northside</td><td>New American Organic
★★★★
Moderate

Quality 92   Value B</td></tr>
<tr><td>2610 North Cannon Drive
(773) 477-5845</td><td></td></tr>
</table>

Reservations:	Highly recommended
When to go:	Depends on whether you prefer lunch in daylight by the pond, especially outdoors, or indoors for dinner
Entree range:	$16–24; 3-course prix fixe, $21
Payment:	AMEX,DC,MC.VISA
Service rating:	★★★★
Friendliness rating:	★★★★
Parking:	Street
Bar:	Full; Outdoor liquor license as of summer 1999
Wine selection:	Domestic, selected to be appropriate with Midwestern cuisine; about 75 selections, $25–180; more than 20 by the glass, from $6–9.
Dress:	Business; casual
Disabled access:	Yes
Customers:	Mixed; all ages; families with children; couples; singles; mostly locals
Brunch:	Sunday, 11 A.M.–2:30 P.M.
Dinner:	Tuesday–Sunday, 5:30–10 P.M.

Atmosphere/setting: Lovely setting in a beautiful part of Lincoln Park on North Pond; idyllic; removed from the traffic and city noise. Interior pond mural around ceiling reprises the beautiful exterior pondscape. Attractive posters of Midwestern activities. In 1999, added a modified pier that extends from the restaurant onto the pond, so diners may get a better view of the city before and/or after dinner.

House specialties: Menu is constantly changing. Appetizers such as excellent house-cured salmon with fingerling potatoes, lemon "gem" dressing; Lou Polley's summer squash soup with crab succotash; grilled calamari, spicy orange tomato jam, and arugula pizza (thin-crusted and flavorful). Entrees: roasted halibut and salmon fish cakes, bacon, and orange mash potatoes; grilled yellow tail snapper with sprouted beans and four-grain risotto with rock shrimp accents; pepita toasted Amish chicken with tortilla stuffing, cauliflower, mole sauce. Daily specials, including at lunch, such as omelet with white Cheddar cheese and salad

(continued)

on the side. Desserts: Selection of three cheeses from Indiana, Wisconsin, and Massachusetts, served with crouton and fresh fruit. Pies of all kinds, such as blueberry, sweet potato, and blueberry rhubarb with crumbled topping.

Other recommendations: Cornmeal-crusted oysters with oyster mushrooms, arugula, and corn, Tabasco butter sauce; dandelion greens, cauliflower, and goat cheese pasty. Entrees: Vegetarian menu, a three-course menu selected daily; sumac berry crusted turkey breast with saffron potatoes, natural jus, tarragon butter; lobster pot pie; sassafras grilled duck breast with Smithfield ham and oyster gumbo. Desserts: sorbets, such as Champagne rose petal, lemon, and raspberry merlot.

Entertainment & amenities: Viewing the North Pond with ducks and surrounding nature. Selection of pies in the retail shop.

Summary & comments: Chef-owner Mary Ellen Diaz, formerly of Printer's Row, has been inspired by the turn-of-the-century Arts and Crafts movement, which reasserted the link between art and function and emphasized an appreciation for nature. She cooks with organic ingredients, which underscore her philosophy that life's essence is in the natural connections of the environment. The location in a former warming shed, situated on the pond, seems perfectly suited to Diaz's style.

Honors/awards: Lots of media praise since opening spring of 1998; *Chicago Sun-Times* feature, and three-star review April 17, 1998s.

OCEANIQUE

Zone 11   Northern Suburbs
505 Main Street, Evanston
(847) 864-3435

French/American
★★★½
Moderate/Expensive

Quality 88   Value C

Reservations:	Recommended for weekdays, required for Saturday
When to go:	Avoid weekends; 6:30–8:30 P.M.
Entree range:	$13.95–28.95
Payment:	All major credit cards
Service rating:	★★★½
Friendliness rating:	★★★★
Parking:	Valet and metered street
Bar:	Full service, including Bombay martinis
Wine selection:	Award-winning wine and reserve wine lists; 500 whites and reds, about 100 reserves; 10 by the glass, $5.75–12; bottles, $24–900; reserve bottles, $85–900
Dress:	Dressy casual, no jacket or tie required
Disabled access:	Yes, entrance and rest room
Customers:	North Shore locals, couples, professors from Northwestern University
Dinner:	Monday–Thursday, 5:30–9:30 P.M.; Friday and Saturday, 5:30–10:30 P.M.

Atmosphere/setting: Spanish-style building; quaint French decor, tile floor from the 1900s, white tablecloths, mahogany chairs. Two separate dining rooms.

House specialties: Roasted beet salad served warm with grilled scallops and tarragon; bouillabaisse Oceanique with salmon, bass, shrimp, squid, mussels, clams, and aïoli; summer squash, mushrooms, tomatoes, basil, garlic, and cream; skate sauté. Seasonal fish changes daily. Pastries, ice cream, sorbets.

Other recommendations: Chilled Maine lobster; farfalle pasta tossed with grilled eggplant; sautéed Lake Superior whitefish; roast Australian rack of lamb; pan-roasted sirloin of beef.

Summary & comments: The name says it for this chef-owned restaurant—French seafood. Local ingredients are used, and there are many Italian, Spanish, and Asian influences in the cooking. New rest rooms and air-conditioning system; 99 percent smoke-free; smokers must make reservations and specify that they're smokers. Chef Mark Grosz is a Jean Banchet disciple and demonstrates his fine training and talent here.

Honors/awards: *Wine Spectator* Award of Excellence, 1994–96.

Olive Branch

Zone 3 Near North	Lebanese/Vegetarian
615 North Wells Street	★★★
(312) 587-0721	Inexpensive
	Quality 85 Value B

Reservations:	Recommended for weekends
When to go:	Any time
Entree range:	$5.50–12.95
Payment:	All major credit cards
Service rating:	★★½
Friendliness rating:	★★★★
Parking:	2 hours free; lot on Erie and Wells
Bar:	Full service
Wine selection:	Recently expanded to be international; still limited: Domestic, especially Californian; French, Italian, Chilean, Australian selections $18–22 a bottle; only 4 by the glass, $3.50–3.75
Dress:	Casual
Disabled access:	Yes, including rest rooms
Customers:	95% local, some Middle Eastern, professionals
Lunch/Dinner:	Monday–Thursday, 11 A.M.–10 P.M.; Friday, 11 A.M.–9 P.M.; and Saturday 12 P.M.-10 P.M.; Sunday, closed.

Atmosphere/setting: Beautiful Assyrian and Lebanese murals depicting ancient life, including design circa 800 B.C.; main dining area has been reduced to a single, enlarged room; white tablecloths covered with paper.

House specialties: Dolmeh (stuffed grape leaves with meat or vegetables); kibbeh (fried cracked wheat and meat mixture); tabbouleh (cracked wheat salad); baba gannoujh (eggplant-tahini dip); Branch platter: shawerma (gyros), kifta kebab, lamb kebab, and chicken.

Other recommendations: Vegetarian entrees, including a combo plate; couscous (meat or vegetarian).

Summary & comments: This downtown gem is still one of the best Middle Eastern restaurants around for its charming atmosphere, array of skillfully prepared dishes, and friendly staff. Originally Ishtar Inn, the new owner renamed it again recently. The last visit revealed that lamb kebabs were slightly tough and the service had some rough edges. The cuisine is very meat-and-vegetable oriented—no fish. All the dishes sampled were robustly well flavored and fresh; entrees come with salad, rice, and pita bread. The bargain prices are unheard of downtown—a real find!

ONE sixtyblUE

		New American
Zone 2	North Central/O'Hare	★★★★
160 North Loomis		Moderate/Expensive
(312) 850-0303		
		Quality 92 Value C

Reservations:	Yes
When to go:	Any time
Entree range:	$20–29
Payment:	VISA, MC, AMEX, D, DC
Service rating:	★★★★½
Friendliness rating:	★★★★½
Parking:	Valet, $6
Bar:	Full
Wine selection:	International, wine organized by varietals on list; about 100 selections, from $200 up; several by the glass
Dress:	Casual
Disabled access:	Yes, except no ramps; several steps
Customers:	Mixed; mostly sophisticated professionals; including Michael Jordan who frequents this place
Dinner:	Sunday–Thursday, 5–10 P.M.; Friday and Saturday, 5–11 P.M.

Atmosphere/setting: Cohesive amalgam of contemporary materials; incredibly spacious with wonderful lighting; linear shapes; curved, brushed stainless steel lighting fixtures and paper-covered shades over chocolate brown light boxes; zinc-topped bar. Adam Tihany, one of the most recognized name in restaurant design, is the designer of one sixtyblue.

House specialties: "Two begin:" wood-roasted kataifi-wrapped asparagus with parma ham, red bell pepper coulis, and sweet lemon pulp; mixed wild mushroom sauté with mascarpone polenta, fresh herbs, and mushroom juices. "Four dinner": low roasted lemon verbena salmon with warmed spinach, potato brandade, and summer truffle; roast loin of monkfish with overnight tomato, chanterelles, and a shellfish, crème fraîche nage; macadamia nut–crusted sturgeon with a salad of braised onion, watercress, and a fresh crab emulsion vinaigrette. Desserts: chocolate soufflé; almond-based spongecake.

Other recommendations: "Two begin": Peeky toe crab sandwich with roasted tomato vinaigrette and basil oil; salad of baby greens and fresh herbs turned in a hazelnut vinaigrette. "Four dinner": pan-seared sea scallops with melted leeks,

(continued)

grilled oyster mushrooms, and a sauce of orange and rosemary; prime-aged del-
monico steak with portobello mushroom, shipped yukon gold potato, and a light
sauce of balsamic vinegar and ginger.

Summary & comments: For a top-dollar restaurant in a burgeoning real
estate area, one sixtyblue offers a wonderfully generous amount of per-diner
space, which, coupled with the lustrous lighting on white walls, gives a sense of
freedom and ease. The Michael Jordan mystique is so closely coupled with one
sixtyblue that it has been the subject of controversy related to his former namesake restaurant (soon to reopen as Sammy Sosa's). People come here mainly for
the wonderful food prepared by talented chef Patrick Robertson (from well
known restaurants in New York, France, and Italy), not necessarily to see Jordan,
but the fact that he frequents this place makes it more exciting.

P. S. Banqkok

Thai
★★★
Inexpensive
Quality 84   Value A

Reservations:	Recommended on weekends
When to go:	Any time, but especially Sunday brunch
Entree range:	$5.95–9.95; market price for some dishes
Payment:	VISA, MC, AMEX, D, DC
Service rating:	★★★½
Friendliness rating:	★★★½
Parking:	Street
Bar:	Beer and wine only
Wine selection:	Fairly extensive list of 30 types
Dress:	Casual
Disabled access:	Yes, except no ramps; several steps
Customers:	Locals, couples, some families, ethnics
Brunch:	Sunday, 11:30 A.M.–4 P.M.
Lunch/Dinner:	Tuesday–Thursday, 11:30 A.M.–10 P.M.; Friday and Saturday, 11:30 A.M.–11:30 P.M.; Sunday, 5–10 P.M.

Atmosphere/setting: Large, ornately decorated room filled with plants, Thai antiques, art, and other artifacts. A large Thai musical instrument, a *lanat*, is displayed on the windowsill, and there is an unobtrusive Buddhist shrine. The Thai garden party room has a waterfall, pond, and private bar.

House specialties: Banana blossom salad (with shrimp, chicken, peanuts, roasted garlic, and coconut); steamed fish with fresh Thai herbs; stuffed Pacific langoustine.

Other recommendations: Love Me Tender duck over crispy rice noodles with Thai sauce; lotus blossom curry with seafood; Thai-style chicken cashew. From the special menu: buttercup squash–curry patty (appetizer); Siamese red curry noodle; house-made Thai cantaloupe cake.

Summary & comments: The authentic menu lists 115 items plus many specials, and it is as ambitious and elaborate as the cooking. Pay attention to dishes listing hot chilies or having "fiery" in the title; they may be incendiary, although some are described as mild. The restaurant honors requests for substitutions. If you are a die-hard Thai-food fan, go to the Sunday brunch, which features more than 100 vegetarian, seafood, and meat dishes. Service is courteous and efficient. Catering, takeout, and delivery are available.

Palm Restaurant

Zone 4   The Loop
Swissôtel Chicago,
   323 East Wacker Drive
(312) 616-1000

Reservations:	Recommended
When to go:	Any time, but can be busy at peak lunch and dinner hours
Entree range:	Lunch, $8–14; dinner, $18–36
Payment:	VISA, MC, AMEX, DC
Service rating:	★★★★½
Friendliness rating:	★★★★½
Parking:	Valet ($5), street, and nearby lot
Bar:	Full service; handsome bar area
Wine selection:	Fairly extensive with 92 by the bottle ($21–210) and another 12 by the glass; mostly American with several French and Italian and a couple of Australian selections
Dress:	Casual to dressy
Disabled access:	Yes
Customers:	Diverse; locals, tourists, celebrities
Lunch/Dinner:	Daily, 11:30 A.M.–11 P.M.

Atmosphere/setting: The new, spacious setting at the Swissôtel offers several dining areas with comfortable tables and booths, some with views of the city lakefront. The rooms are beautifully decorated in forest green and dark wood with white tablecloths. The highlight is the Palm's traditional "Wall of Fame," featuring caricatures of about 250 VIPs and Chicago's movers and shakers (many of them are personally signed). Take advantage of great views of Navy Pier from the second level, including the rest rooms. Outdoor patio dining with a lake view is available in summer.

House specialties: Jumbo Nova Scotia lobsters, three pounds and more; a variety of steaks: prime-aged New York Sirloin, filet mignon, porterhouse, and prime rib; Gigi salad (shrimp, lettuce, tomato, green beans, radicchio, chopped egg, and bacon); good selection of sides, such as creamed and leaf spinach, hash browns, and cottage fries. One lunch special is a lobster club, a towering layered bun sandwich of lobster salad with bacon, tomato, red onion, lettuce, and fries. Chef Paul Principato's creativity is expressed in daily specials, such as spicy lobster fra diablo (cooked with garlic, crushed red pepper, plum tomatoes, white wine, and basil,

(continued)

served over linguine) and crab cakes (jumbo lump crab, celery, onion, and pimento). Excellent desserts include Key lime pie and rich chocolate pecan pie.

Other recommendations: Linguini with red or white clam sauce; pasta of the day; veal in different styles, including Milanese, Marsala, and Piccata; Caesar and other salads. Daily lunch specials might be grilled amberjack and asparagus Ferrara, named after a waiter (served with fresh tomato, marinara sauce, and melted Gruyère) and grilled or steamed vegetable platter. They are best-known for New York cheesecake (which, unfortunately, was once served still slightly frozen); another good dessert is the deep dish apple cobbler.

Entertainment & amenities: Reading the "Wall of Fame."

Summary & comments: The luxury Swissôtel Chicago became the new site of the Palm in the fall of 1996, after a 14-month hiatus. Formerly at the Mayfair Regent Hotel for 15 years, the restaurant was forced to move when the hotel was sold and the building converted into a residential property. With a more beautiful setting overlooking the lakefront and almost double the space on two levels, the new Palm retained its menu and veteran staff. Known for its spirited service, this restaurant is also fun and entertaining because of the caricatures on the walls and characters at the tables. John Ganzi and Pio Bozzi started their Palm Restaurant in 1926 in an Italian neighborhood on Second Avenue in New York City. Wally Ganzi, Jr., and Bruce Bozzi, third-generation owners, expanded the original Palm and, in the early 1970s, began opening Palms in other cities, beginning with Washington, D.C. The menu is standard across the United States. Today other locations include Los Angeles, Houston, Atlanta, Boston, and Mexico City. The Palm's secret for success seems to be consistency in its nonfussy, quality food with professional service in an upbeat, comfortable setting.

Pampanga Restaurant

	Filipino
	★★½
	Inexpensive
	Quality 77 Value B

Zone 1   North Side
6407 North Caldwell Avenue
(773) 763-1781

Reservations:	Recommended
When to go:	4–7 P.M.
Entree range:	$5.95–9.95
Payment:	VISA, MC
Service rating:	★★★
Friendliness rating:	★★★★
Parking:	Street in front; parking also in back of restaurant
Bar:	BYOB
Wine selection:	BYOB
Dress:	Casual
Disabled access:	Yes
Customers:	Mixed; locals, Filipinos, couples, professionals
Lunch/Dinner:	Monday, 3–8:30 P.M.; Wednesday–Sunday, 11:30 A.M.–8:30 P.M.

Atmosphere/setting: Colorful, tropical decor. Charming artifacts from the Philippines, including wood carvings and paintings; intimate.

House specialties: Lumpia frito (traditional egg roll); lumpianitas (bite-size spring rolls); ukoy (fritters of shredded vegetables topped with shrimp); pancit bihon guisado (rice noodles stir-fried with vegetables and with—or without—pork, fish ball, sausage, and shrimp); Pampanga's fried rice; tocino (Pampanga's homemade, cured, sliced pork).

Other recommendations: Pork or chicken adobo; beef or goat kalderetang. Wonderful dessert (not on menu) is a coconut rice-flour cake baked in a banana leaf. Calamansi (Filipino lemonade—very refreshing); Filipino tea is oolong, brewed with toasted rice.

Summary & comments: Pampanga is a province near Manila in the near-north section of the Philippine Islands. The owner started this restaurant in 1977, and it's evident there's a lot of family caring and a loyal clientele. Although Tagalog is the national language, Filipinos speak Spanish since the islands were under Spanish rule for about 500 years. There's Spanish influence in the cuisine, but many items are distinctively Filipino, utilizing tropical fruits and vegetables, seafood, and pork. One of the few places serving Filipino food.

Pane Caldo

Zone 3   Near North
72 East Walton Street
(312) 649-0055

Northern Italian
★★★½
Inexpensive/Moderate

Quality 89   Value D

Reservations:	Highly recommended
When to go:	At lunch or early dinner, between 5–6 P.M.
Entree range:	Pastas, $9.50–16.50; meat, chicken, and fish dishes, $13.50–19.95
Payment:	VISA, MC, AMEX
Service rating:	★★★★
Friendliness rating:	★★★★
Parking:	Reduced-rate parking next door
Bar:	Full service, with about 16 grappas and several sambuca selections
Wine selection:	Fairly extensive (about 67; 8 by the glass), mostly Italian with several Californian and several French champagnes; small riserva list
Dress:	Casual
Disabled access:	Yes
Customers:	Diverse, professionals, couples, Gold Coast shoppers and tourists
Lunch:	Daily, 11:30 A.M.–2:30 P.M., when lunch menu (sandwiches, salads, pizza, pasta) and regular dinner menu are available
Dinner:	Sunday–Thursday, 5–10:30 P.M.; Friday and Saturday, 5–11:30 P.M.

Atmosphere/setting: Intimate trattoria-style setting. Sophisticated, soft lighting; burnt gold walls, decorated with original paintings; attractive floral arrangements. Dining room seats 78; bar seats 10; cozy private room seats 20; new private party room seats 100.

House specialties: Tortelloni di zucchini al Parmigiano (homemade, stuffed with acorn squash in light Parmesan cheese sauce); ravioli stuffed with lobster in creamy saffron sauce. Antipasti: grilled, marinated calamari with scampi in aromatic olive oil; the unusual mille foglie di pollo (layers of chicken, prosciutto, spinach, and mozzarella in wine mushroom sauce).

Other recommendations: Antipasti: duck and chicken dumplings, "Polpettine di anatra e pollo" with onion confit marmalade; porcini mushroom risotto.

(continued)

Great grilled double lamb chops with garlic, rosemary, and mustard sauce. Roasted veal chop stuffed with Gorgonzola cheese (a special). Daily "Progressive Sampling" menu, $45 per person, and a vegetarian version, $39 per person, minimum 2 people. Also daily specials, including antipasti, fish, pasta, risotto, and other secondi.

Entertainment & amenities: On-premise bakery that supplies delicious "warm bread," as the restaurant's name suggests.

Summary & comments: Pane Caldo, "warm bread," is an appropriate name since there's an on-premise bakery that makes warm bread for diners—delicious focaccia and rosemary bread, as examples—with the complimentary olive tapenade and cheecha (dried pomodoro dip: tomato-parsley-balsamic vinaigrette) at the start. Additional bonuses include an intermezzo apple-Armagnac sorbetto and chocolate truffles and sweets at the finish. Menu changes monthly and includes many unusual items, such as the mille foglie di pollo mentioned. Chef Maurice Bonhomme produces at least six vegetarian menu items using organic ingredients. The patissiere offers a "Dolci" menu with more than a dozen temptations, including homemade sorbettos, Tarte D'Opera (chocolate cake with hazelnut-coffee mousse, raspberry sauce), and warm almond tart with fresh pears in a vanilla-rhubarb sauce. Owner Antoine Cedicci, who started Pane Caldo in 1992, also owns La Borsa, 375 North Morgan Street.

Honors/awards: Voted best salmon in Chicago by *New York Times* in 1993; voted most authentic Italian cuisine by *Chicago* magazine in 1994.

Papagus Greek Taverna

	Greek
	★★★★
	Moderate
	Quality 90 Value C

Zone 3   Near North
Embassy Suites Hotel,
   620 North State Street
(312) 642-8450
Zone 6   South Central/Midway
270 Oakbrook Center, Oakbrook
(630) 472-9800

Reservations:	Recommended
When to go:	Any time for mezedes (little plates); lunch or dinner
Entree range:	$7–25
Payment:	Major credit cards
Service rating:	★★★★
Friendliness rating:	★★★½
Parking:	Valet, $7 for 3 hours; validated parking in Embassy Suites underground lot (Monday–Friday); free mall lot at Oakbrook
Bar:	Full service
Wine selection:	Expansive; mostly Greek
Dress:	Casual to dressy
Disabled access:	Yes
Customers:	Mixed; locals, travelers, professionals
Lunch/Dinner:	Monday–Thursday, 11:30 A.M.–10 P.M.; Friday, 11:30 A.M.–midnight; Saturday, noon–midnight; Sunday, noon–10 P.M.

Atmosphere/setting: Comfortable, rustic old-world-style taverna.

House specialties: Mezedes (appetizers) are the centerpiece here: taramosalata (cod or lobster roe salad); spanikopita (spinach pie); saganaki (flambéed cheese); grilled garlic-marinated shrimp. Main courses: Greek roast chicken; spicy lamb and beef meatballs; braised lamb with orzo.

Other recommendations: Roasted eggplant spread; marinated char-grilled octopus; olive bread salad; char-grilled skewer of swordfish.

Summary & comments: Some of the best light renditions of traditional Greek cuisine, served in a colorful, rustic setting. Chef uses a creative license on many items. This may not be in Greektown, but it has brought a good taste of Greece to the downtown area. Even the earlier skeptics have conceded that this place knows its stuff. Greek family-style feast is available.

Honors/awards: *Chicago Tribune,* "the best Greek restaurant in Chicago."

Pappagallo's

Zone 11   Northern Suburbs
246 Greenbay Road, Highwood
(847) 432-6663

Italian/American	
★★★	
Inexpensive/Moderate	
Quality 84	Value B

Reservations:	Recommended
When to go:	During the week
Entree range:	$9.95–20.95
Payment:	All major credit cards
Service rating:	★★★½
Friendliness rating:	★★★½
Parking:	Lot
Bar:	Full service
Wine selection:	Extensive
Dress:	Casual
Disabled access:	Yes
Customers:	Locals, professionals, couples
Lunch:	Daily, 11 A.M.–3 P.M.
Dinner:	Monday–Thursday, 4–10 P.M.; Friday and Saturday, 4–11 P.M.; Sunday, 4–8:30 P.M.

Atmosphere/setting: Bright and cozy; green and white tablecloths; canopied front porch for al fresco summer dining.

House specialties: Mama Lena's tortellacci (with three cheeses and spinach—great al forno); award-winning artichoke fritters; veal Pappagallo (scaloppine sautéed with lemon, butter, artichokes, and asparagus); grilled Norwegian salmon; grilled calamari; steak al forno; grilled swordfish; pollo Maria (a "heart smart" item of angel hair pasta with grilled chicken). Chocolate dream dessert; camparama dessert (almond cookie with amaretto, hazelnut whipped cream, and a chocolate shell).

Other recommendations: Bruschetta alla Pappagallo; fried calamari; grilled baby lamb chops; linguine alla Pappagallo (sautéed shrimp and scallops with sun-dried tomatoes, Italian mushrooms tossed with pesto, and black and white linguine); spicy chicken Vesuvio; grilled eggplant topped with marinara sauce ("heart smart"). Spumoni; tiramisu.

Summary & comments: Formerly Bertucci's, the family name. The restaurant, ten years old in 2000, has otherwise remained the same—known for its steak and seafood with Italian specialties. They now offer home catering, according to manager Bruce Bertucci, who is usually around to greet guests.

Park Avenue Cafe

	New American
Zone 3 Near North	★★★★
199 East Walton Place	Moderate/Expensive
(312) 944-4414	
	Quality 94 Value C

Reservations:	Recommended
When to go:	Avoid peak meal times unless you have a reservation
Entree range:	$18–29; tasting menu, $52
Payment:	AMEX, VISA, MC, D, DC
Service rating:	★★★★½
Friendliness rating:	★★★★½
Parking:	Valet
Bar:	Full service with full list of single malts and cognacs
Wine selection:	Ambitious list, mostly American; some French and Italian; $18–392 per bottle; extensive list of ports.
Dress:	Casual; no T-shirts or cutoffs
Disabled access:	Yes
Customers:	Locals, travelers, professionals, couples, singles; families, especially at brunch
Brunch:	Sunday, 10:30 A.M.–2 P.M., $30; children, $11.
Dinner:	Monday–Saturday, 5–11 P.M.; Sunday, 5–10 P.M.

Atmosphere/setting: Country contemporary design with wood floors, open kitchen, and bake shop; several interconnected dining areas are separated by niches decorated with American folk sculpture, some of it whimsical; tubs of floral and wheat arrangements; warm lighting from forest green shades suspended over seating.

House specialties: Menu changes daily according to freshest possible seasonal ingredients. One signature is Chef David Burke's trademarked Smoked Pastrami Salmon, an appetizer of thin slices of the peppered fish complemented by a corn blini. Entrees: slow-roasted honey-glazed duck that melts in the mouth and might include cranberry in the glaze and a wild rice pancake on the side; oven-roasted pork with shellfish "paella;" lemon roasted chicken with prawns and linguini; Burke's trademarked Swordfish Chop (a fillet of swordfish cleverly molded around a chop bone) offered as a special. For dessert, try the restaurant's classics, including The Chocolate Cube, a unique firm chocolate shell that hides chocolate

(continued)

mousse surrounding more white mousse. Another whimsical dessert is The Park Avenue Park Bench, a sculptured replica made of dark chocolate and a luscious praline mousse, a dark chocolate lamp pole with a flourless chocolate cake base, and a white chocolate truffle globe.

Other recommendations: Appetizers such as chestnut bisque with duck confit; country salad with walnuts, and goat cheese fondue. Entrees with creative twists such as seared duck with bleu cheese–stuffed pear and caramelized endive; miso-glazed sea bass with shrimp tortellini. Desserts range from fanciful, such as poached pear financier with white wine ice cream and pumpkin crème brûlée to basic American favorites like warm blueberry cobbler with ice cream.

Summary & comments: This fine dining restaurant on the second level of the DoubleTree Guest Suites Chicago opened here in 1995, and its contemporary American cuisine quickly received high praise. New Chef de Cuisine Jason Handelman, who was executive sous chef, took over the kitchen in 1998 and added some new items. The wonders he works with American cuisine, combining excellence and whimsy, would make any American diner feel patriotic. Pastry chef Delfina Perez Najera also has a magic touch, both in her creation of edible sculptures and in producing traditional full-flavored desserts. Just downstairs from the restaurant, at street level, is Mrs. Park's Tavern (see profile), a more casual, less expensive cafe. Both restaurants hold frequent wine promotions to showcase their varied, extensive lists. Park Avenue Cafe introduced the first American dim sum brunch, with more than 50 tasting portions of the restaurant's specialties along with Asian items, served traditionally from rolling carts.

Honors/awards: AAA, four diamonds; *Chicago Tribune*, three stars.

Pars Cove

Zone 1   North Side
435 West Diversey Parkway
(773) 549-1515

Persian	
★★★½	
Inexpensive	
Quality 89	Value B

Reservations:	Recommended
When to go:	Any time
Entree range:	$5.95–11.95
Payment:	All major credit cards
Service rating:	★★★½
Friendliness rating:	★★★★½
Parking:	Limited parking behind restaurant; street and nearby garage
Bar:	Full service
Wine selection:	International; several by the glass
Dress:	Varied; can range from casual to formal
Disabled access:	No, but willing to help; 4 steps down
Customers:	Diverse; professionals, ethnic, couples
Open:	Daily, 11 A.M.–11 P.M.; Friday, Saturday, customers can stay until midnight.

Atmosphere/setting: The decor is attractive and cozy, especially the front non-smoking room. The restaurant features nice Persian decorative touches and plants in window alcoves by the stairs. It's dimly lit; romantic.

House specialties: Chicken fessenjan, (chicken breast simmered with pomegranate and walnut sauce); charbroiled kebabs of lamb, beef, or filet mignon; seasonal fresh fish, including salmon, whitefish, swordfish, trout, and red snapper. Vegetarian specialties such as veggie Mediterranean (in split pea–tomato-lime sauce) and veggie fessenjan.

Other recommendations: Appetizers, including baba gannoujh, hommus, dolmeh, tabbouleh, and herb yogurt served with Persian bread. Lentil soup; Pars salad (tomato, cucumber, and onion with lemon dressing). Zolobia, a fried Persian dessert with yogurt and honey.

Summary & comments: This place has had a following since the owner had his first restaurant in a different location. The fish and seafood have always been its strength, but chicken, meat, and vegetarian items are equally savory and somewhat exotic. Persian cooking uses lots of herbs, citrus marinades, and pomegranate juice, so sauces tend to be fragrant and slightly sweet-tart. Most entrees come with fluffy Persian rice pilaf. Portions are generous, and service is gracious.

Honors/awards: *Chicago Tribune* and *Chicago* magazine, four stars.

THE PARTHENON

	Greek
Zone 4 The Loop	★★★★½
314 South Halsted Street, Greektown	Inexpensive/Moderate
(312) 726-2407	
	Quality 95 Value B

Reservations:	Recommended
When to go:	Weekdays usually less busy
Entree range:	$6–10
Payment:	Major credit cards
Service rating:	★★★★½
Friendliness rating:	★★★★★
Parking:	Free valet
Bar:	Full service, with cocktails like "Grecian Mud-slide" and "Trojan Horse"
Wine selection:	Extensive, mostly Greek; house wines available by the glass, carafe, and bottle
Dress:	Casual
Disabled access:	Wheelchair access, rest rooms
Customers:	Greek American, diverse Americans
Lunch/Dinner:	Sunday–Friday, 11–1 A.M.; Saturday, 11–2 A.M.

Atmosphere/setting: Barbecuing lamb on a spit and gyros in the window; enter through the original bar area. New chic, contemporary bar and lounge with tables was recently added in the space next door. Several cozy dining rooms, some with lovely murals; lively Greek setting with waiters' shouts of "Opa!" as they flambé saganaki with brandy. Everyone seems to have an enjoyable time here, but it's quiet enough to have a private conversation over a meal.

House specialties: Flaming saganaki (kasseri used instead of the saltier kefalotiri) and succulent homemade gyros—both introduced to Chicago here. Great assortment of mezedes (substantial appetizers) such as spinach-feta pies, mini–chicken breast shish kebabs, braised octopus, tzatziki, and homemade sausage; a special assortment platter with about 11 items and pita for two or more, $10.95 per person. Entrees: meatballs à la Smyrna (Tuesdays and Wednesdays); Greek-style broiled whole red snapper or sea bass, filleted tableside if desired; top-quality lamb prepared in various ways: rotisserie-roasted, extra thick prime chops, broiled to order, and fork-tender with artichokes avgolemono; and (more unusual) tigania (pork tenderloin chunks marinated in wine sauce). Succulent Athenian broiled chicken and a new item, chicken breast spanaki (skinless breast

(continued)

290

stuffed with spinach and feta and served with rice pilaf). Desserts: Galakto-bourika (phyllo filled with custard, baked in syrup); creme caramele.

Other recommendations: Kotopitakia (chicken and vegetable phyllo pie); dolmades (herbed rice- or meat-stuffed vine leaves); broiled octopus; vegetarian moussaka (layered eggplant and potato dish); family-style vegetarian dinner ($14.50 per person for two or more, also available with meat); lamb sweetbreads; shrimp flambée; Aegean platter (panfried scallops, codfish, baby squid, and smelt, with skordalia—garlic potato dip). Daily specials: sautéed feta in tomato sauce and salad with chicken (Monday); fricasse of lamb and romaine in egg-lemon sauce. Desserts: crispy walnut-rich baklava; homemade yogurt with walnuts; rice pudding and assorted traditional cookies.

Summary & comments: The Parthenon is the oldest restaurant in Greektown, having celebrated its 30th anniversary in July 1998 (the former first Greektown restaurant has closed). Of all the Greek restaurants in the Chicago area, this reliable establishment, appropriately named for the majestic structure on the acropolis of Athens, has remained tops for the most comprehensive menu, consistent quality of food, and gracious service. The name carries a deep responsibility for excellence, and the Liakouras family never takes that lightly. Chris Liakouras, who started this second restaurant in Greektown in 1968 with his brother Bill, now runs it with his daughter, Joanna, and son, Pete. Joanna is now a partner, along with chef Sotiris Stasinos, and her father, who remains the main partner. John, one of the managers, has been an anchor for many years, and much of the staff is loyal and stable. Here, new dishes are always being added to the ambitious menu, which is in English and Greek, and there are daily dinner specials. The family-style dinner is large and complete ($13.50). Many items are à la carte, "so ordering is more flexible," according to Chris. Most of the mezedes on the menu are offered in two portion sizes. This basic concept is ideally suited to the Greeks' cultural sense of *filoxenia* (hospitality) and the centuries-old tradition of getting together with friends to eat several little dishes, drink wine, and talk. You couldn't find a better place than here. Everyone has fun. Returning to the Parthenon after just one visit is like coming home. *Kaly orczi!* (Good appetite!)

Honors/awards: Much continuing great press over the years, including *Chicago* magazine, the *Chicago Tribune,* the *Chicago Sun-Times,* and various television and radio stations.

PASTEUR

Zone 1   North Side
5525 North Broadway
(773) 878-1061

Vietnamese	
★★★★	
Inexpensive/Moderate	
Quality 92	Value B

Reservations:	Required on weekends
When to go:	Early dinner
Entree range:	$8.95–13.50; market price
Payment:	All major credit cards
Service rating:	★★★
Friendliness rating:	★★★
Parking:	Street; church lot across street
Bar:	Full service
Wine selection:	Limited; affordable; bottles, $18–69; by the glass, $4–5.50
Dress:	Casual
Disabled access:	Yes
Customers:	Mixed
Lunch/Dinner:	Wednesday–Sunday, noon–10 P.M.; Friday and Saturday, noon–11 P.M.
Dinner:	Monday and Tuesday, 4–10 P.M.

Atmosphere/setting: Spectacular split-level interior; large palm trees, ceiling fans. Beautiful private dining room upstairs; charming, cozy bar area; added another private room next door. Sidewalk cafe.

House specialties: Appetizers: Goi cuon (spring roll of shrimp, vegetables, noodles); banh tom co ngu (traditional Hanoi dish of shrimp, yams, and bananas, lightly fried); pho (Hanoi soup specialty: aromatic beef broth over rice noodles and beef strips). Entrees: Tom sa-te (sautéed jumbo shrimp); ga kho gung (clay pot chicken); scallop kao me (with sesame seeds, grilled). Mango mousse cake.

Other recommendations: Appetizers: bo tai chanh (spicy charbroiled beef 1strips); chao tom (shrimp paste wrapped around fresh sugarcane, grilled). Entrées: bo cuon la lot (grilled beef rolls stuffed with chicken and shrimp); bo luc lac (sautéed marinated beef chunks); ca-ry ga (Saigon specialty of delicate curry broth with chicken slices).

Summary & comments: Pasteur has been reborn in a new location, and is a truly upscale Vietnamese fine-dining establishment at affordable prices. Ingredients mingle well in various specialties here, and there is a profusion of fresh herbs. It's more fun to dine with three or four for a better sampling. Pasteur also offers full-blown services for banquets, catering, carryout, and delivery. Definitely destination dining.

Pazzo's Cucina Italiana

		New Italian	
Zone 2	North Central/O'Hare	★★½	
8725 West Higgins Road		Inexpensive/Moderate	
(773) 714-0077			
		Quality 79	Value C
Zone 8	Southern Suburbs		

Three Westbrook Corporate Center,
  22nd and Wolf Road, Westchester
(708) 531-1112 or (708) 531-TOGO

Reservations:	Accepted
When to go:	Off-peak times
Entree range:	Most items around $10
Payment:	VISA, MC, AMEX, DC
Service rating:	★★★
Friendliness rating:	★★★★★
Parking:	Building lots, street, free garage
Bar:	Full service
Wine selection:	Extensive; bottles of Pazzo's chianti placed on tables (using the honor system), $3.75 a glass
Dress:	Casual
Disabled access:	Yes
Customers:	Professionals, locals, families
Lunch/Dinner:	Monday–Thursday, 11 A.M.–10 P.M.; Friday, 11 A.M.–11 P.M.; Saturday, 4:30–11 P.M.

Atmosphere/setting: Contemporary, casual, and spacious with an open kitchen. Private rooms are available at each location for parties.

House specialties: Brick-oven pizza selection; Pazzo's Caesar with mixed greens, herb croutons, shaved Parmigiano, and Pazzo's creamy Caesar dressing; insalatina di gamberetti (marinated shrimp on butter lettuce, radicchio, cucumbers, with lemon caper dressing); polenta cup filled with basil pesto and ragout of vegetables, black olives, and spicy tomato sauce. Fresh pastas: zebra panzottini (striped semolina pasta filled with ricotta and spinach in pepper cream sauce); mushroom-filled tortelloni with prosciutto, mushrooms, and tomatoes in a Parmesan cream sauce; pollo rigatoni (square rigatoni with chicken, roasted peppers, black olives, and spinach in a white cream sauce). Veal chop Milanese, breaded, sautéed, and baked with garlic mashed potatoes; Pazzo's strip steak; Pollo Della Casa (panfried breast, seasoned in homemade breadcrumbs, with lemon, capers, and mushrooms). Dolci: chocolate raspberry cake; homemade tiramisu; gelato.

(continued)

Pazzo's Cucina Italiana   *(continued)*

Other recommendations: Oriental lime chicken salad with mixed greens, peanuts, sesame seeds, and crispy noodles in a mustard vinaigrette; Mediterranean salad of romaine lettuce, cucumbers, bell peppers, tomatoes, and onions, tossed with kalamata olives, oils, and feta.

Summary & comments: Fun and delicious Italian cuisine, colorful presentations, generous portions, low prices, and friendly staff—these are the key buzz words that spell success for this California-based chain. The first Chicago location debuted in 1993 under the former name, Milano's Italian Kitchen. The name change for only the Chicago restaurants occurred in 1994; the eight other locations around the country will keep the Milano's name. It's not surprising that this place wins over first-time customers. Diners get a bonus at the new Westchester location—live entertainment by singing servers.

Honors/awards: *Chicago Sun-Times'* "Top Three Caesar Salads in the City" award.

PEGASUS RESTAURANT
AND TAVERNA

Zone 4   The Loop
130 South Halsted Street, Greektown
(312) 226-3377

Greek	
★★★	
Inexpensive/Moderate	
Quality 83	Value C

Reservations:	Recommended
When to go:	Weekdays; Friday and Saturday are busy
Entree range:	$5.75–19.75
Payment:	Major credit cards
Service rating:	★★★★
Friendliness rating:	★★★★
Parking:	Valet
Bar:	Full service
Wine selection:	Mostly Greek (about 98 percent)
Dress:	Casual
Disabled access:	Yes, including rest rooms
Customers:	Diverse; internationals, tourists, and locals
Lunch/Dinner:	Monday–Thursday, 11 A.M.–midnight; Friday, 11–1 A.M.; Saturday, noon–1 A.M.; Sunday, noon–midnight

Atmosphere/setting: Bright with Mediterranean colors and murals of Mykonos. Summer roof garden. Dramatic view of the Chicago skyline from rooftop.

House specialties: Shrimp Alexander; broiled lamb chops; whole red snapper; Athenian-style chicken; beef tash kebab (in wine-tomato sauce); briami (cooked fresh vegetables); traditional Greek dishes such as pastitsio (baked macaroni and meat with béchamel).

Other recommendations: Grilled marinated baby octopus; Alexander's salad; swordfish kebab. Special walnut-raisin cake; creamy rice pudding.

Entertainment & amenities: Lovely roof garden.

Summary & comments: The menu is a blend of authentic and original home-style dishes from several regions, prepared in a light, healthy way. A mezedes (small course) menu was created for the roof garden, which is especially pleasant on a warm summer evening.

PRAIRIE

Zone 5   South Loop
500 South Dearborn Street
(312) 663-1143

Midwestern	
★★★★½	
Moderate/Expensive	
Quality 95	Value C

Reservations:	Recommended
When to go:	Monday is the slowest, but any time is fine
Entree range:	Lunch, $9.75–18.25; dinner à la carte, $16–27
Payment:	All major credit cards
Service rating:	★★★★
Friendliness rating:	★★★★½
Parking:	Valet ($5 day, $8 evening)
Bar:	Full service
Wine selection:	Mostly Californian; some from Oregon and Washington; 7 available in smaller bottles; about 11 available by-the-glass.
Dress:	Summer, casual to formal; winter, business and dressy (suits and ties optional)
Disabled access:	Yes, including rest rooms
Customers:	Professionals, theatergoers, couples, Bears football fans on Sunday morning, some foreign and domestic tourists
Breakfast:	Monday–Friday, 6:30–10 A.M.; Saturday and Sunday, 7–10 A.M.
Brunch:	Saturday and Sunday, 11 A.M.–2 P.M.
Lunch:	Monday–Friday, 11:30 A.M.–2 P.M.; Saturday, 11 A.M.–2 P.M.
Dinner:	Monday–Saturday, 5–10 P.M.; Sunday, 5–9 P.M.

Atmosphere/setting: Striking split-level space with tall windows and honey-colored oak cathedral ceiling. The interior is patently a Frank Lloyd Wright design—a fine example of the Prairie School of Architecture. Attractive display case, open kitchen, and comfortable lounge area.

House specialties: Midwestern duck, local corn, Illinois and Wisconsin cheeses, and other heartland products are prepared in seasonal ways (e.g., Wisconsin Cheddar and dark ale soup; appetizer: sauté of wild mushrooms in a crispy sweet potato basket with sour cream and corn puree—beautiful presentation); farm-raised coho salmon, poached with leeks, pea cakes, and sun-dried tomato jus, topped with daikon sprouts; Wisconsin honey-coated duck breast, stuffed pear

(continued)

in Frangelico berry sauce; sweet onion crusted pork (boneless chop with roasted corn vegetable slaw); black bean and cilantro-encrusted whitefish with cucumber onion relish, carrot jus; warm strawberry-rhubarb tart with apple-cinnamon ice cream (in spring).

Other recommendations: Prairie duck breast (spice-rubbed with white Cheddar rice and honey malt demi). Entrees: Dried mushroom filet of beef, herb-crusted tart with wild mushrooms, mascarpone cheese; domestic lamb rack, stuffed with apple sausage, Yukon potato leek salad, and BBQ chili oil; breast of chicken, stuffed with asparagus and endive wrapped in prosciutto with plum fig compote.

Summary & comments: New Executive Chef André Bienvenu succeeds original Chef Stephen Langlois, who opened this restaurant after avidly combing old heartland cookbooks and unearthing authentic recipes from farm cooks, then imaginatively incorporating seasonal ingredients into his stunningly visual creations. Bienvenu carries on that tradition with his own twist, such as adding a flavorful crust of herbs, onion, or dried fruit to meats, fish, and a mushroom tart. The only restaurant here devoted exclusively to Midwestern cuisine.

Honors/awards: DiRoNA Award, 1996–97.

The Primavera Ristorante

	Italian
Zone 4 The Loop	★★★½
Fairmont Hotel,	Inexpensive/Moderate
200 North Columbus Drive	
(312) 565-6655	Quality 88 Value C

Reservations:	Required
When to go:	Any time
Entree range:	$11–22; cover charge $1.50 a person
Payment:	All major credit cards except DC
Service rating:	★★★
Friendliness rating:	★★★★
Parking:	Valet
Bar:	Full service; the Primavera Bar is well known for its signature drink of a yard or half-yard of beer served tableside; it also features a microbrewed beer each month and a wall-size television screen
Wine selection:	Mostly Italian, Californian, French; nice choices by the glass
Dress:	Semicasual; dressier when people are celebrating
Disabled access:	Yes
Customers:	Families and celebrators; couples; tourists, professionals, conventioneers, celebrities, music lovers
Breakfast:	Monday–Sunday, 6–11:30 A.M.
Lunch:	Monday–Sunday, 11:30 A.M.–2 P.M.
Dinner:	Monday–Friday, 5:30–10:30 P.M.; Saturday, 5:30–11 P.M.; Sunday, 5:30–10 P.M.

Atmosphere/setting: The ambience of an Italian country trattoria is enhanced with a glorious floral display, cozy banquettes, and wall-size frescoes. Female servers wear colorful peasant dresses and male servers wear red bandannas and black coats, giving a theatrical flair.

House specialties: Appetizers: antipasto della casa (chef's selection of assorted specialties); prosciutto, mozzarella, pomodori secchi (prosciutto di Parma, fresh mozzarella, sun-dried tomatoes, dates); calamari fritti con limone (fried squid with lemon); insalata romana (Italian Caesar salad). Entrees: rigatoni con pollo e basilico (rigatoni tossed with grilled breast of chicken, mushrooms, Gorgonzola); ravioli ai quattro formaggi con funghi (four-cheese and shiitake ravioli baked with tomato and basil cream sauce); linguine ai frutti di mare (linguine, shrimp, scallops, calamari, clams, and mussels); lasagna di spinaci e vegetali (spinach lasagna with fresh seasonal

(continued)

vegetables, Asiago, mascarpone, and ricotta); Branzino dell adriatico (sautéed striped bass with fresh clams, mussels, and calamari on angel hair). Desserts: chocolate mousse cake is the complimentary birthday cake; award-winning tiramisu; cannoli alla Primavera (filled with white and dark chocolate mousse); and caffe di amaretto (cappuccino, amaretto, and fresh whipped cream).

Other recommendations: Appetizers: polenta con vegetali e salsa di funghi (soft polenta, grilled vegetables, wild mushroom sauce, and goat cheese); fresh seafood risotto; seasonal vegetable risotto; porcini mushroom risotto; spaghetti con funghi e gamberi (with wild mushrooms and shrimp); petti di pollo Vesuvio (sautéed breast of chicken); scaloppine di vitello della casa (veal scaloppine sautéed with shiitake mushrooms and fresh baby artichokes); castolette di agnello alla grigalia (roast rack of lamb). Desserts: amaretto crème brûlée; torta di ricotta (ricotta, roasted pine nut, and citron tart); torta di cioccolato al zabaione (rich chocolate mousse cake); and espresso affogato (espresso, vanilla gelato, and sambuca).

Entertainment & amenities: Every evening for dinner, the "Primavera Singers" perform favorite songs from operas, operettas, and musical comedies in between taking orders and delivering meals. Some of their resumes boast leading roles in productions by the Chicago Lyric Opera, New York City Opera, Chicago Symphony Orchestra, and San Francisco's Opera Merola Program.

Summary & comments: Music and dining are two of life's greatest pleasures, and they come together beautifully at Primavera Ristorante. Diners can pick up a playbill here to read about the performers, who are also the servers. The waitsstaff is very cheerful, and it's evident they love their jobs as performers, too. Chef Giovanni De Nigris enhances his cooking with his commitment to freshness, simplicity, taste, consistency, and presentation. In fact, he often visits with the guests and will go out of his way to prepare a dish per a guest's request.

There might be an occasional lag in the service, but Primavera can be forgiven minor flaws considering the dual roles of the servers. Dinner at Primavera is one of the best ways to celebrate a birthday, anniversary, or any day you want a musical lift. For a birthday, all the singers gather around, serve the cake with a candle, and sing the Happy Birthday song (lyrics by Eric Barnes, copyrighted) to the Hallelujah chorus—spectacular!

Honors/awards: Silver Platter Award, 1995 and 1996. *Food Industry News* magazine honored Chef Giovanni De Nigris as one of its 1995 Top Five Italian Chefs and honored the Primavera Ristorante with its Top Five Italian Restaurants awards in Chicago.

Printer's Row

Zone 5   South Loop
550 South Dearborn Street
(312) 461-0780

New American
★★★★
Moderate
Quality 95   Value B

Reservations:	Recommended
When to go:	Any time; weekdays usually less busy
Entree range:	Lunch, $8.50–12.95; dinner, $13.95–21.95
Payment:	VISA, MC, AMEX, D
Service rating:	★★★★½
Friendliness rating:	★★★★
Parking:	Street or lots nearby
Bar:	Full service
Wine selection:	Big American list; many by the glass, bottle, or half-bottle
Dress:	Casual
Disabled access:	Yes
Customers:	Locals, professionals, travelers, suburbanites
Lunch:	Monday–Friday, 11:30 A.M.–2:30 P.M.
Dinner:	Monday–Thursday, 5–10 P.M.; Friday and Saturday, 5–11 P.M.

Atmosphere/setting: In the historic Printers Row area, this establishment is both sophisticated and comfortable. Great private party location.

House specialties: Grilled duck breast; weekly menu features a shellfish or wild and farm-raised fish and a venison item (e.g., venison chop with a sun-dried blueberry–grappa sauce). Tuna seared with Chinese molasses, cucumber, and chile vinaigrette is an example of the Asian influence here. Vegetable paella, mildly spicy with saffron rice, satisfies any Spanish cravings.

Other recommendations: Grilled salmon with prosciutto-pasta cake; roasted custom-cut pork chop; various ice creams; coffee crème brûlée (flavors change); pear tart with lemon ice cream.

Summary & comments: Chef-owner Michael Foley opened this restaurant more than 20 years ago when the Printers Row area was not yet renovated. This pioneer soon received recognition for his innovative American cooking, which is committed to healthful preparations based on fresh, local products and is influenced by his travels. Menus change weekly and focus on servicing daily diners through à la carte items. This remains one of Chicago's best dining experiences. Can accommodate private functions from 15 to 120.

Honors/awards: *Travel Holiday* magazine Good Dining Award, 1992–94; *Wine Spectator*'s Award of Excellence, 1988–93; DiRoNA Award, 1993.

The Pump Room

Zone 3 Near North
Omni Ambassador East Hotel,
 1301 North State Parkway
(312) 266-0360

French/American
★★★★
Expensive
Quality 93   Value C

Reservations:	Recommended
When to go:	Friday or Saturday evenings for the full experience with music; weeknights for a quiet dinner
Entree range:	Breakfast, $7.95–14; lunch, $10.50–16; dinner, $21–34
Payment:	All major credit cards
Service rating:	★★★★
Friendliness rating:	★★★★½
Parking:	Valet, $11; nearby self-park garage
Bar:	Full service; a list of cognacs, sherries, single-malt scotches, and ports is available for after-dinner sipping; new special menu
Wine selection:	International list of about 120 selections; several fine selections available by the glass
Dress:	Days, business, no jeans or tennis shoes; evenings, dressy; gentlemen required to wear jackets after 4 P.M. Casual wear is discouraged at all times.
Disabled access:	No
Customers:	Professionals, mostly 30-plus, many celebrities, stylish couples and singles
Breakfast:	Daily, 7–10 A.M.
Brunch:	Sunday, 11 A.M.–2:30 P.M.; set price
Lunch:	Monday–Saturday, 11:30 A.M.–2:30 P.M.
Dinner:	Monday–Thursday, 6–10 P.M.; Friday and Saturday, 5–midnight; Sunday, 5–10 P.M.
Byfield's Lobby Bar:	Light menu Sunday–Thursday 11 A.M.–midnight; Friday and Saturday, 11 A.M.–1 A.M.

Atmosphere/setting: This legendary place reopened in 1998 after a seven-month, $2 million restoration. It returned to its original colors of blue and gold, and now tables are graced with Bernardaud Limoges china and the original flatware pattern. The formal, elegant, split-level dining room still features Booth One and the intimate Green Booth. Sparkling split-level dining room is lavishly appointed with stunning crystal chandeliers, lush floral arrangements, and sheer

(continued)

ceiling drapes. This atmosphere and the restaurant's six-decade history still cast a spell. Bar at entryway in upper level seats 80; private dining suites available.

House specialties: Chef Martial Noguier's signature items include crunchy Maryland crab cakes with Savoy cabbage cole slaw and basil oil; veal sweetbreads with foie gras, served a variety of ways with different vinaigrettes, such as black truffle or sherry; and vichyssoise (cold potato-leek soup) with Osetra caviar. Entrees: Excellent American red snapper with saffron pearl pasta, crawfish, and lobster sauce; roasted Muscovy duck breast with couscous, dried apricots, and carrot sauce; perfectly seasoned and cooked-to-order Colorado rack of lamb with riso pasta, ratatouille, and roasted garlic sauce; dry-aged New York sirloin steak with potato gratin, French beans, and roasted shallot sauce. Desserts (changing list) are delicious and beautiful: The Pump Room Baked Alaska; The Pump Room Vacherin with raspberry sauce; hot chocolate cake with orange Grand Marnier; mixed berry salad "surprise;" and sometimes, porcupine with chocolate meringue—great presentation!

Other recommendations: Appetizer: Smoked salmon terrine with cucumber salad, Tobiko caviar; Entrees: Norwegian salmon with ratatouille "crust" (I had it with asparagus "crust") and roasted bell pepper sauce; roasted Amish chicken breast with baby artichokes and chicken jus. Desserts: Selection of fine cheeses; hazelnut chocolate bar with Tahitian vanilla sauce; crème brûlée "Black and White" (custard with chocolate mousse layer and caramelized crust); fruit tart with fig puree.

Entertainment & amenities: Live entertainment in lounge with dancing.

Summary & comments: "Booth One" is a legend made famous by this Chicago landmark, a premier celebrity gathering place since October 1, 1938. The Pump Room was named after the famous watering place in Bath, England. Allow time to have an aperitif in the lounge, then browse through the "who's who in entertainment" photo exhibit before dining. New owners hired Executive Chef Martial Noguier, a talented Parisian who worked with top chefs in France. He revamped the menu, now French-inspired American, and he offers a Pre-Theatre Menu ($29), The Pump Room Tasting Menus (four-course, $48 pp; five-course, $56 pp); vegetable tasting (four-course, $38 pp). I expect The Pump Room to get even better now that the restaurant appointed Arthur Greenan as general manager, who brings extraordinary credentials, including Chicago's Spiaggia and Manhattan's Four Seasons. This is truly a special place for business meals, celebrity sightings, and romantic dinners. Phil Collins got turned away because of no jacket, so entitled his 1987 album, "No Jacket Required."

Honors/awards: AAA four diamonds; *Chicago Tribune*, Best Brunch; Chef Martial Noguier prepared a five-course degustation dinner to members of the James Beard Foundation at the Beard House in New York in September, 1999.

R. J. Grunts

Zone 1   North Side
2056 Lincoln Park West
(773) 929-5363

American
★★★
Inexpensive
Quality 82   Value A

Reservations:	Accepted
When to go:	Any time a craving hits
Entree range:	$7.95–15.95
Payment:	Major credit cards
Service rating:	★★★
Friendliness rating:	★★★½
Parking:	Street
Bar:	Full service; imported, domestic, on-tap brews
Wine selection:	Mostly lower-priced domestic; very limited; 6 by the glass or half-carafe; 2 by the bottle
Dress:	Blue-jean casual
Disabled access:	Yes; call first
Customers:	Mixed; families, singles, couples, all ages
Brunch:	Sunday, 10 A.M.–2:30 P.M.
Open:	Monday–Thursday, 11:30 A.M.–9 P.M.; Friday and Saturday, 11:30 A.M.–10:30 P.M.; Sunday, 3–10 P.M.

Atmosphere / setting: Casual; stucco walls showcase original comical art, including a tribute to the waitresses. Centerpiece salad bar provides colorful decor.

House specialties: Signature salad bar with 40-plus items, including prepared salads and fresh fruit; oversized cheeseburgers or other options, including the turkey burger; award-winning vegetarian chili and steak Terry Yaki-Witch (sandwich); baby-back ribs; R. J.'s chop stake (as spelled on menu).

Other recommendations: Vegetarian items in every menu category except "Flashbacks," and even that might have a veggie quiche of the day.

Summary & comments: This first Lettuce Entertain You creation is still alive and well and basically unchanged after 27 years. This place recognizes the importance of choices and offers a varied menu. In recent years, it expanded the menu with vegetarian offerings in each category. This funky place launched the original salad bar in 1971; most entrees include the salad bar—a real deal. Odd placement of some salad bar items (such as chocolate mousse next to chopped chicken liver) results in occasional surprises in the mouth. Even the beverages—fresh-squeezed juices, herbal teas, giant malts and shakes, and espresso—follow the motto of catering to our variable tastes.

Red Tomato

	Italian
Zone 1 North Side	★★★
3417 North Southport Avenue	Inexpensive
(773) 472-5300	
	Quality 84 Value B

Reservations:	Accepted Friday and Saturday, but limited
When to go:	Early evenings any day
Entree range:	$8.95–15
Payment:	All major credit cards
Service rating:	★★★
Friendliness rating:	★★★★
Parking:	Street
Bar:	Full service
Wine selection:	Extensive, mostly Italian; $20–125; several by the glass, $3.50–4.50
Dress:	Casual
Disabled access:	Yes, including rest rooms
Customers:	Locals, professionals, couples
Lunch/Dinner:	Monday–Thursday, 11 A.M.–9:30 P.M.; Friday and Saturday, 11:30 A.M.–10:30 P.M.; Sunday, 1–9 P.M.

Atmosphere/setting: Colorful exterior; near El tracks in a Northwest Side neighborhood. Two sections—one is casual and the other is semiformal; also an outdoor dining section.

House specialties: Scaloppini al Red Tomato (medallions of veal over fresh tomato sauce topped with buffalo mozzarella); lasagnas; pizza ochri; pizzette Red Tomato (artichoke, tomato, capers, onion, and pepper).

Other recommendations: Fresh fish specialties (e.g., salmone al vapore—fillet steamed and served over Chianti sauce); involtini di melenzane (grilled eggplant rolled with spinach and ricotta, topped with Bel Paese cheese and roasted peppers); beef and veal items.

Summary & comments: The chef-owner Joe Divenere is dedicated to creating dishes and adding his mark to regional recipes. Meet him and you'll witness how much he loves his work. The restaurant grew out of the original pizza place next door, and the pizzette is quite good. This is one Italian place without a pasta emphasis; it's refreshing to see many alternatives. It can be bustling on weekends.

REZA'S

Zone 1   North Side
5255 North Clark Street
(773) 561-1898

Zone 3   Near North
432 West Ontario Street
(312) 664-4500

Persian/Vegetarian
★★★½
Inexpensive/Moderate
Quality 89   Value C

Reservations: Recommended Thursday, Friday, and weekends
When to go: Avoid end of week and weekends
Entree range: $6.95–14.95
Payment: VISA, MC, AMEX, DC, D
Service rating: ★★★½
Friendliness rating: ★★★★½
Parking: Valet (downtown); free lot (Clark Street)
Bar: Full service
Wine selection: Extensive; fairly priced; several by the glass
Dress: Moderately casual
Disabled access: Yes, including rest rooms; elevators
Customers: Diverse; more local at Clark Street; more profes-
                        sionals downtown
Lunch/Dinner: Daily, 11 A.M.–midnight

Atmosphere/setting: Clark Street location is modern Persian; spacious, casual, attractive. Ontario location is site of a former working brewery, with the vats visible; attractive, spacious room with exposed brick walls and wood trim.

House specialties: Vegetarian samplers and seafood dishes Persian-style; eggplant steak appetizer (thick eggplant slice broiled in robust herbed sauce of onion, garlic, and tomatoes); grilled mushrooms (trio of skewered charbroiled mushrooms with tart marinade that tastes of lemon juice); Reza's salad (mixed lettuce with radish, tomato, black olives, feta, green pepper, and croutons); kebabs: lamb and chicken combo with grilled vegetables and Persian dill rice; shrimp and filet with veggies.

Other recommendations: Variety of appetizers such as dolmeh felfel (stuffed green pepper), baba gannoujh, tabbouleh, hummus; Reza's special chicken (two strips of marinated boneless breast, with grilled veggies and Persian dill rice); duck breast with sweet and sour pomegranate sauce and walnuts; marinated charbroiled quail.

Summary & comments: The original Reza's has expanded several times and does a brisk business. The huge, newer place on the west side of downtown is in the former Sieben's Brewery, and is a great place for casual business lunches. Both are large and bustling, with a regular following.

RiVA

Zone 3   Near North
700 East Grand Avenue, Navy Pier
(312) 644-7482

Seafood/Steak/Pasta
★★★½
Moderate/Expensive

Quality 90   Value C

Reservations:	Recommended
When to go:	Avoid peak meal times unless you have a reservation
Entree range:	Lunch, average $14; dinner, $10.95–24.95
Payment:	Major credit cards
Service rating:	★★★½
Friendliness rating:	★★★½
Parking:	Sheltered valet parking, $7
Bar:	Full service
Wine selection:	Lengthy international list that leans toward Californian and Italian; reserve list; a good selection of wines by the glass
Dress:	Casual to dressy
Disabled access:	Yes, elevator available
Customers:	Tourists, locals, celebrities, politicians (including Bill and Hillary Clinton)
Brunch:	Sunday, 11:30 A.M.–3 P.M.
Lunch:	Monday–Saturday, 11 A.M.–3 P.M.
Dinner:	Monday–Saturday, 5–11 P.M.; Sunday, 3–9 P.M.

Atmosphere/setting: Beautiful restaurant with expansive windows offering a premier view of Navy Pier, Monroe Harbor, and Chicago's downtown skyline. Spacious main dining room with exposed brick walls, mahogany trim, brass chandeliers and ceiling fans, and a lobster tank in the center; colorful decor; 40-foot-long display kitchen with upper-wall mural depicting Navy Pier's history; welcoming bar area; three private dining rooms.

House specialties: Appetizers: Crab cakes with jalapeño tartar sauce and radicchio slaw; Vegetarian Heaven (grilled vegetables, roasted garlic, baked goat cheese, chile sun-dried tomato salsa); baby spinach salad with oranges, toasted pecans, gorgonzola, and citrus champagne vinaigrette. Entrees: fillet mignon of tuna, marinated, grilled, over horseradish mashed potatoes, roasted shallot sauce; BBQ Pacific salmon over black bean and corn salad with chipotle-cilantro vinaigrette; Tasmanian Devil "rack of lamb." Desserts (changing list): Death By Chocolate (chocolate in several forms, in a thick layer of dense, flourless cake with

(continued)

mousse, topped with ganache); Zuccata (thin band of sponge cake layered with white chocolate and chocolate mocha mousse, hazelnuts, and chocolate chips, topped with chocolate truffle ganache.

Other recommendations: Appetizers: From the steam pot, black mussels and New Zealand Greenlip mussels; lobster corn bisque soup; portobello mushroom Napoleon. Entrees: Swordfish "Monte Cristo" (steak grilled, topped with asparagus, crab, and hollandaise); Lake Erie whitefish Barcelona (baked on a plank under a horseradish crust, with roasted potatoes and spicy coleslaw); mesquite grill items, such as Hawaiian striped marlin, Alaskan Troll King salmon and Dover sole from Holland (locations listed for each fish); Alaskan King crab legs. Desserts: Black and White Scallop (dark and white chocolate scallop shell filled with vanilla and chocolate ice cream topped with chocolate sauce and wafers); mango crème brûlée; occasionally, atomic cake (three layers of banana, vanilla chiffon, and chocolate chiffon cakes with fruit and custards, whipped cream filling); daily homemade ice cream selections. Yes, there's tiramisu, too.

Summary & comments: President and Mrs. Clinton were here, and there's a photo to prove it. The city's politicians and other dignitaries have visited, as well, and there has been a steady flow of locals and tourists since the grand opening in 1995. Riva is Italian for "shoreline," and restaurateur Phil Stefani's newest place is aptly named since it has one of the most breathtaking views of Chicago's Lake Michigan shore. While some have reported uncaring service here, my experiences have been favorable. Experienced Chef Charles Weber knows his cooking well and took over the kitchen here recently after experience at many fine restaurants. Definitely a destination restaurant. Riva Cafe, on the first floor downstairs, is more informal and serves light fare; it opens onto an outdoor dining area in warm weather.

Rodiys

	Greek
	★★★
	Moderate
	Quality 89 Value B

Zone 4   The Loop
222 South Halsted Street, Greektown
(312) 454-0800

Reservations:	Recommended
When to go:	Weekdays; avoid busy weekends
Entree range:	$6.95–15.50; market price
Payment:	VISA, MC, AMEX
Service rating:	★★★★½
Friendliness rating:	★★★★½
Parking:	Lot across the street
Bar:	Full service
Wine selection:	Mostly Greek (about 16; 3 by the glass); 3 American
Dress:	Casual
Disabled access:	Wheelchair access, including rest rooms
Customers:	Diverse; some Greeks, mostly Americans
Lunch/Dinner:	Sunday–Friday, 11–1 A.M.; Saturday, 11–2 A.M.

Atmosphere/setting: Attractive two-room space balances classical and modern impressions; open feeling from high ceilings and mirrors in the south room. Relaxed.

House specialties: Rodiys special platter mixes hot spinach-cheese pie with cold items (e.g., taramasalata, cheeses, octopus salad); broiled octopus appetizer; broiled fresh red snapper. Lamb dishes such as unusual village-style cutlets (minichops pan-fried and then flambéed with green peppers, onions, garlic, and tomato); braised lamb in tomato sauce; roast lamb; broiled lamb chops.

Other recommendations: Whole fried squid; horta (boiled dandelions); large dolmades with beef and rice; broiled whitefish. Rice pudding; nougatina.

Summary & comments: The slightly spicier, home-style traditional cooking here gives this 24-plus-year-old place its large Greek following, especially after church on Sunday. Half of the menu is in Greek, which testifies to the clientele. This place and the Parthenon tend to be where most local Greeks like to dine.

Rosebud Cafe

Zone 5   South Loop
1500 West Taylor Street
(312) 942-1117

<table>
<tr><td>Italian</td></tr>
<tr><td>★★★</td></tr>
<tr><td>Inexpensive/Moderate</td></tr>
<tr><td>Quality 83   Value C</td></tr>
</table>

Reservations:	Highly recommended
When to go:	Before 7 P.M. and after 9 P.M.
Entree range:	Pastas, $10.95–15.95; chicken, $14.95; veal, $29.95
Payment:	All major credit cards
Service rating:	★★½
Friendliness rating:	★★★
Parking:	Lot, valet (4$)
Bar:	Full service
Wine selection:	Extensive; international; some outstanding Italian choices
Dress:	Upscale casual; no jacket required
Disabled access:	Yes, including rest rooms
Customers:	Locals, internationals, tourists
Lunch:	Monday–Friday, 11 A.M.–3 P.M.
Dinner:	Monday–Thursday, 5–10:30 P.M.; Friday and Saturday, 5–11:30 P.M.; Sunday, 4–10 P.M.

Atmosphere/setting: Loud, crowded, very "in Chicago." New second floor where 120 can be seated for private dining.

House specialties: Calamari and mussels in either light red wine or white wine broth; chicken Vesuvio; pappardelle (square noodles) marinara; baked cavatelli; special pasta such as tortiglioni arrabbiata (spirals in spicy red sauce).

Other recommendations: Roasted red peppers; veal Parmigiana; lemon ice; cannoli.

Summary & comments: This Taylor Street mecca of fine, traditional Italian cooking is a true trattoria; service is friendly and knowledgeable, the portions are too generous, and the place is often packed. Waits are common even with reservations. It has been widely recognized by the press, and it has maintained a steady customer flow for over 25 years, which is admirable. Not a place to go for a quiet business dinner or romantic evening. Offshoots of this restaurant are on Rush Street and other locations, and newest additions to the family are La Rosetta (70 West Madison) and Rosebud in Naperville.

RUSSIAN TEA TIME

Zone 4   The Loop
77 East Adams Street
(312) 360-0000

<table>
<tr><td>Russian</td></tr>
<tr><td>★★★★</td></tr>
<tr><td>Moderate</td></tr>
<tr><td>Quality 93   Value C</td></tr>
</table>

Reservations:	Highly recommended
When to go:	Quieter from 2 to 5 P.M.
Entree range:	$10–26
Payment:	Major credit cards
Service rating:	★★★★
Friendliness rating:	★★★★½
Parking:	Lots nearby
Bar:	Full service, including Russian vodkas and caviar
Wine selection:	Two dozen selections; mainly French, Italian, California, and Washington wines; several by the glass
Dress:	Casual to moderately upscale and dressy
Disabled access:	Yes; menus available in braille
Customers:	Diverse, Russian-American, symphony and opera crowd, talk-show hosts and guests from television and radio stations nearby
Lunch/Dinner:	Monday, 11 A.M.–9 P.M.; Tuesday–Thursday, 11 A.M.–11 P.M.; Friday and Saturday, 11 A.M.–midnight; Sunday, 11 A.M.–9 P.M.

Atmosphere/setting: Cozy, old-world atmosphere with a great deal of woodwork, Russian urns, pots, and tablecloths; well-spaced booths and tables; dessert display case.

House specialties: Blini with top-quality Russian caviar; borscht; goriachaya zakuska (appetizer platter for two-plus including chicken dumplings, stuffed cabbage, and beets); wild game (e.g., stuffed quails with pomegranate sauce); vegetarian dishes (e.g., jumbo stuffed mushrooms with spinach, onion, and cheese); hot farmer's cheese blintzes.

Other recommendations: Elaborate kulebiaka (meat pie) filled with ground beef, cabbage, and onions; blinchiki (crêpes—the beef stroganoff are great; also salmon and cheese); roast pheasant "Erevan" with Armenian brandy, walnut, and pomegranate sauce, and brandied prunes; Tashkent carrot salad (named for hometown of owners; à la carte or comes with entrees); chicken croquettes; hearty

(continued)

homemade apricot-plum strudel is the thick-crusted Russian version; Russian tea (blend of three, including black currant).

Summary & comments: The only serious Russian restaurant in town (the Russian Palace opened nearby), this exquisite cafe received rave reviews within the first several months of opening in fall 1993. The Chicago Symphony bought the building the cafe was originally in, and the conductor, former conductor, symphonygoers, and operagoers all dine here, before or after events. The cafe also expanded its vegetarian options recently; the *Chicago Sun-Times* has named Russian Tea Time as one of the city's Top 10 vegetarian-friendly spots. Owner Vadim Muchnik is the gracious host and kisses ladies' hands, while his mother, Klara, heads the kitchen. The ambitious menu is about as long as Tolstoy's *War and Peace,* and the menu describes customs and a bit of historical background of dishes and their famous namesakes. This is a fine ethnic experience. Catering available.

Honors/awards: *Vegetarian Journal* voted it among the ten best restaurants in North America.

Ruth's Chris Steakhouse

Zone 4   The Loop
431 North Dearborn Street
(312) 321-2725

Steak	
★★★★	
Moderate/Expensive	
Quality 93 Value B	

Reservations:	Recommended
When to go:	Avoid peak times, 6–8 P.M. weekends
Entree range:	$10–27
Payment:	All major credit cards
Service rating:	★★★½
Friendliness rating:	★★★★
Parking:	Valet, $7
Bar:	Full service
Wine selection:	International, especially American, French, and Italian; heavy California bent; several by the glass
Dress:	Casual to dressy
Disabled access:	Yes
Customers:	Very local, have a following
Lunch/Dinner:	Monday–Friday, 11:30 A.M.–11 P.M.; Saturday, 4:30–11 P.M.; Sunday, closed

Atmosphere/setting: Clubby; plaid carpet; lots of sports memorabilia.

House specialties: All prime cuts here: New York strip steak, 16–18 ounces; 20-ounce T-bone; petite filet of beef tenderloin, 8-ounce; provimi veal chop. Veal sweetbreads; barbecued shrimp Orleans; three classic sauces offered with entrees and sides.

Other recommendations: Fish of the day; live Maine lobster; porterhouse for two; Prince Edward's mashed potatoes with garlic; turtle soup served with sherry; gumbo Louisiane; bread pudding with Jack Daniel's whiskey sauce; pecan pie.

Summary & comments: This New Orleans franchise spot arrived on the Chicago dining scene several years ago and is most successful. It was the #1 Ruth's Chris Steakhouse worldwide in 1996 for the greatest number of steaks sold. The menu pays tribute to its roots with several New Orleans touches. Steaks sizzle appealingly because they get a coating of butter. Juices are sealed into steaks on the hottest 1,800° F grill. One of a fast-growing chain with a good reputation.

Sai Cafe

Zone 1   North Side
2010 North Sheffield
(773) 472-8080

Japanese	
★★★½	
Inexpensive/Moderate	
Quality 91	Value B

Reservations:	Now accepts parties of 25–30
When to go:	Anytime; weeknights sometimes less busy
Entree range:	$10.95–23.95
Payment:	AMEX, MC, VISA
Service rating:	★★★½
Friendliness rating:	★★★★½
Parking:	Valet
Bar:	Full; Oriental beers (Sapporo, Kirin); specialty wines (Kinsen plum wine; Ozeki hot sake; variety of cold sakes, including a house cold sake)
Wine selection:	Limited, with 6 selections from California, France, and Italy.
Dress:	Casual
Disabled access:	Yes
Customers:	Mixed ethnic and American; all ages; Japanese sushi lovers
Lunch:	Monday–Saturday. 11 A.M.–4:30 P.M.; Sunday, 11 A.M.–3:30 P.M.
Dinner:	Monday–Thursday 4:30-11 P.M.; Friday and Saturday, 4:30–midnight; Sunday 3:30–10.P.M.

Atmosphere/setting: Cheerful, light wood; several rooms. Recent expansion added 50 more seats. Attractive sushi bar where diners can order anything from the menu while watching the sushi chefs prepare the colorful specialty served on wooden boards. Cozy, nonsmoking back dining room, with tables rather close together, is decorated with sake aging drums and other artifacts.

House specialties: Pan-fried scallops with a flavorful house sauce; Gyo-za (Japanese pan-fried dumplings, 6 pieces); kani-su (Alaskan King crab with cucumber marinated in vinegar sauce). Main courses: À la carte sushi, selected from a list of about 32; I loved the maguro (tuna), hamachi (yellow tail), and namasake (fresh salmon, as opposed to smoked), all attractively arranged on a wooden board with the pickled ginger slices and wasabi and dipping sauce; maki-mono, from 23 choices—California maki (avocado, crab stick, flying fish egg, and cucumber) and

(continued)

soft shell crab maki, also known as spider roll (deep-fried soft shell crab wrapped with avocado, cucumber, mayonnaise, flying fish egg) were two of the best. Ethereal vegetable tempura (nice variety of vegetables with a lacy coating, fried crisp, served with a flavorful dipping sauce; shrimp and combo available). Some entrees come with soup and rice, others with soup only. Complimentary dessert of orange segments in orange shell baskets; red bean or green tea ice cream.

Other recommendations: Appetizers: ikura oroshi (salmon roe with sliced cucumber; sashimi (variety of raw fish); goma-ae (boiled spinach with sesame-flavored sauce, a tad bitter once). Main courses: "Chef Special Hand-rolled" including regular or spicy scallop rolls. Cooked dishes include sukiyaki (sliced beef, bean curd, mushroom, napa, yam noodles, green onion cooked in broth) and teriyaki (charcoal broiled chicken, beef, or fish with teriyaki sauce). Dessert: regular ice cream; mango.

Entertainment & amenities: Watching the sushi chefs perform their magic and turning out the beautiful orders of sushi and maki (hand rolls).

Summary & comments: From the first call, I realized this restaurant had a friendly and helpful attitude, and it carries through from owner James Bel, who is usually on hand to greet guests and oversee his operation. Our waitress was always smiling and accommodating, and the service was well paced. This hospitality plus the top-quality fish and seafood and the attractive presentations encourage diners to return—and is why this spot is usually crowded.

Honors/awards: Media features and reviews, including *Chicago* magazine.

THE SALOON

Zone 3   Near North
200 East Chestnut Street
(312) 280-5454

Steak
★★★½
Moderate/Expensive

Quality 89   Value C

Reservations:	Accepted
When to go:	Before 8 P.M.
Entree range:	$9.95–26.95
Payment:	All major credit cards
Service rating:	★★★★
Friendliness rating:	★★★★
Parking:	Doorman parks cars; no valet
Bar:	Full service
Wine selection:	Extensive; large Meritage and Californian list
Dress:	Casual to jacket-and-tie dressy
Disabled access:	Yes
Customers:	Professionals, theatergoers, tourists
Lunch/Dinner:	Daily, 11:30 A.M.–11 P.M.

Atmosphere/setting: Enter through the handsome bar with a two-tone wood floor. Dining room has a warm, comfortable atmosphere; tiny candle lamps give soft lighting.

House specialties: Smoked 16-ounce pork chop; 48-ounce porterhouse steak; 18-ounce Kansas bone-in strip; 14-ounce filet mignon; surf and turf; potato-crusted fish of the day (e.g., walleyed pike); beefsteak tomato and onion with blue cheese; crispy calamari.

Other recommendations: Appetizer sampler plate (cheddar cheese–stuffed jalapeños, house smoked barbecue chicken skewers, and blackened scallops); buffalo mozzarella salad; shrimp cocktail; wood-grilled lobster tail; tuna tartare; baked jumbo asparagus; garbage salad. Desserts: banana steak, fresh fruit cobbler, Key lime tart, and crème brûlée.

Summary & comments: The Saloon was opened on the Gold Coast in 1991 by the Restaurant Development Group, which also owns Kinzie Street Chophouse. The two places have some similarities but more differences. A signature item here is the potato-crusted fish; the concept is great and usually works well, although one time the walleyed pike lacked seasoning and its crust was slightly greasy—the only minor flaw. To his credit, our well-schooled waiter noticed that the steak we ordered as medium-rare arrived more medium, and he whisked it back for another. Order several items and share, if possible. Save room for dessert.

¡Salpicón!, A Taste of Mexico

	Mexican
	★★★½
Zone 3 Near North	Inexpensive/Moderate
1252 North Wells	Quality 85 Value C
(312) 988-7811	

Reservations:	Recommended
When to go:	Dinner; less crowded weekdays
Entree range:	$12.95–22.95
Payment:	All major credit cards
Service rating:	★★★★½
Friendliness rating:	★★★★½
Parking:	Street or nearby garages
Bar:	Full service; super- and ultra-premium tequilas; tequila flights (1 ounce of 4); ¡Salpicón! Margarita; Mexican and microbrew beers
Wine selection:	Extensive; several by the glass, $6–13.50; bottles, $21–295; reserve list
Dress:	Casual
Disabled access:	Yes
Customers:	Locals, professionals, theater and opera crowd
Brunch:	Sunday, 11 A.M.–2:30 P.M.
Dinner:	Wednesday–Monday, 5 P.M.; set-price early menu before 6:30 P.M.

Atmosphere/setting: Brightly painted storefront; colorful art by renowned Mexican artist Alejandro Romero. Recently expanded to include a dining area behind the bar.

House specialties: Jalapeños rellenos de queso capeados (jalapeños stuffed with Chihuahua cheese, dipped in a light egg batter, sautéed); Chiapas-style tamale with chicken and a sweet-seasoned pork picadillo with a classic mole poblano; ensalada de espinaca con queso de cabra (fresh spinach salad with goat cheese, toasted sesame seeds, and caramelized red onions in a spicy chipotle-honey dressing); codornices en salsa de chile ancho con miel (garlic-marinated and grilled Manchester Farm quail served in a sauce of ancho chiles, garlic, caramelized onions, and honey with cilantro, potato, and queso anejo cakes); flan de caramelo (classic egg custard with a rich caramel sauce); arroz con leche (traditional rice pudding); pastel tres leches (light orange-flavored cake soaked in a trio of milks, served with fresh fruit sauce).

(continued)

Other recommendations: Tostaditas de Tinga (crispy small tortillas mounded with shredded pork and chorizo in a roasted tomato-chipotle sauce); jaibas al mojo de ajo (summer special: Chesapeake Bay soft-shell crabs sautéed); and cinnamon crêpes stuffed with mango and fresh raspberries under a house-made goat's milk caramel (special).

Summary & comments: Salpicón translates as a "splash," and owners Vincent and Priscila Satkoff truly bring a splash of Mexico to Chicago with their Old Town restaurant. Mexican-born chef Priscilla Satkoff's expert culinary skills and passion for food were inspired and developed by her grandmother and mother, who were gourmet cooks but didn't know it. Only high-quality seafood and meats are used, and plate presentations are just as festive as the restaurant interior. All salsas and sauces are prepared fresh daily and everything is homemade, including tortillas (here usually a smaller size) and totopos (chips). The service staff is exceptionally friendly and well informed.

Honors / awards: *Wine Spectator* Award of Excellence, 1996; three stars from both the *Chicago Tribune* and the *Chicago Sun-Times. Chicago* magazine named it one of the top ten new restaurants of 1995.

SANTORINI

	Greek
	★★★
	Inexpensive/Moderate
	Quality 89 Value C

Zone 4   The Loop
800 West Adams Street, Greektown
(312) 829-8820

Reservations:	Recommended
When to go:	Weekdays
Entree range:	$8–16
Payment:	Major credit cards except DC
Service rating:	★★★★
Friendliness rating:	★★★★
Parking:	Free valet
Bar:	Full service
Wine selection:	International: Greek, American, French, Italian
Dress:	Varies from casual to formal
Disabled access:	Yes, including rest rooms
Customers:	Diverse; about one-third Greeks
Lunch/Dinner:	Sunday–Thursday, 11 A.M.–midnight; Friday and Saturday, 11–1 A.M.

Atmosphere/setting: Cozy with fireplace in room's center. Lovely authentic interior decorated with plates and baskets; art depicts the hilly island of Santorini.

House specialties: Seafood is the showcase: charcoal-grilled octopus; shrimp à la Santorini; charcoal-grilled swordfish steak with Santorini sauce; bacalao and garlic sauce; broiled red snapper fillet (unique here, instead of whole fish); shrimp Tourkolimano (butterflied jumbos baked in tomato and feta sauce); baked fish à sla spetsiota; Santorini salad; sokolatina (semisweet chocolate mousse cake) with "Santorini" written over each slice.

Other recommendations: Appetizer spreads such as eggplant, fish roe, and spicy feta; tzatziki (cucumber-yogurt dip); chicken à la Santorini; lamb scharas (thin slices charcoal grilled and prepared the original Greek way); seafood platter (shellfish and fish); homemade yogurt with honey and nuts; nougatina (rich crème and nut cake).

Summary & comments: This fairly recent addition to Greektown is upscale and refined, and probably the most expensive. Many inexpensive items are on the menu, but there is an absence of the traditional dishes, which tend to be less costly. Daily specials are creative and enticing; some are repeated several times weekly, such as the lamb stamnas (crêpe filled with lamb, vegetables, cheeses, and pine nuts). Service is attentive and knowledgeable.

Seasons Restaurant

	American
Zone 3 Near North	★★★★★
Four Seasons Hotel,	Moderate/Expensive
120 East Delaware Place	
(312) 280-8800, ext. 2134	Quality 99 Value C

Reservations:	Recommended
When to go:	Any time
Entree range:	$22–34
Payment:	VISA, MC, AMEX, DC, D
Service rating:	★★★★★
Friendliness rating:	★★★★★
Parking:	Valet at the hotel entrance or self-parking on Rush or Walton streets with covered access to hotel's seventh-floor lobby; parking is discounted with validation
Bar:	Full service
Wine selection:	320 selections of domestic and imported wines including California sparkling wines and French champagnes; many fine selections by the glass
Dress:	Jacket required for men; upscale casual; dressy
Disabled access:	Yes
Customers:	Travelers, professionals, locals
Breakfast:	*Seasons Restaurant:* Monday–Saturday, 6:30–10:30 A.M.; Sunday, 6:30–10 A.M. *Seasons Cafe:* Sunday–Thursday, 8–11:30 A.M.; Friday and Saturday, 8 A.M.–12:30 P.M.
Brunch:	Sunday, 10:30 A.M.–1:30 P.M.
Lunch:	Monday–Saturday, 11:30 A.M.–1:30 P.M.
Dinner:	Daily, 6–10 P.M.

Atmosphere/setting: Opulent carpeted dining room with drapes, crystal sconces, and white tablecloths; lovely floral arrangements; elegant; artwork on walls; nice view from tables near windows. The adjacent cafe is also swank with a more casual approach.

House specialties: Menu changes each season. Some examples: grilled portobello mushroom with foie gras and balsamic syrup; organic field greens, raspberry vinaigrette, and goat cheese crouton; naturally farmed veal chop, pickled corn relish, and arugula whipped potatoes. Specials such as pan-seared Gulf snapper with

(continued)

basil oil; vegetable-potato Napoleon; and Japanese buckwheat noodles. Desserts such as warm fig and blueberry compote; orange-Drambuie ice cream with wild honey–cabernet sauce; Seasons chocolate marjolaine.

Other recommendations: Lunch: Maine lobster salad with Southwestern flavors; seared ahi tuna salad with cooling papaya-ginger relish; steamed Atlantic salmon fillet on cucumber semolina; beef vinaigrette; scaloppine of chicken on fennel-potato pancake with spring morel-port wine sauce; grilled prime minute steak, Dijon mustard béarnaise, and shoestring fries. Dinner: Roast Casco cod fillet with smoked cod-scallop hash; roasted free-range chicken and pearl barley–sweet corn pilaf; prime rib-eye steak, rustic onion baked potato, and garlic-mustard and rosemary grits; Atlantic salmon fillet braised in chardonnay with fennel-herb risotto and shallot-wine reduction.

Entertainment & amenities: Jazz from the adjacent Seasons Lounge Friday and Saturday evenings can be heard in the dining room.

Summary & comments: Seasons specializes in innovative American cuisine made from fresh—often unusual—regional ingredients served in a simple style. Executive chef Mark Baker, who is from Boston, loves working with New England seafood, and it shows. He completely changes the menu the first day of spring, summer, and autumn, and changes it partially mid-winter to utilize the freshest local products. Seasons has worked with the Department of Agriculture in several different states to hand pick the highest caliber regional suppliers. The restaurant also offers alternative cuisine which is low in calories and cholesterol. Baker's cooking overall avoids rich sauces; his creations evolve with richness of flavor from prime ingredients cooked together and from reductions and vinaigrettes. One of the most splendid hotel dining rooms anywhere. Try Seasons Cafe for lighter fare for any meal at lower prices.

Honors/awards: Three and one-half stars from *Chicago* magazine; three stars from *Chicago Tribune*; recently recognized by *Food and Wine* and *Forbes* magazines.

Shaw's Crab House and Shaw's Blue Crab Lounge & Oyster Bar

Seafood	
★★★★½	
Moderate	
Quality 95	Value C

Zone 4   The Loop
21 East Hubbard Street
(312) 527-2722

Reservations:	*Main dining room*: highly recommended; *Blue Crab Lounge:* not accepted
When to go:	Any time
Entree range:	$16–36; Blue Crab Lounge, blackboard items à la carte and a bit cheaper
Payment:	All major credit cards
Service rating:	★★★★
Friendliness rating:	★★★★
Parking:	Valet, $7
Bar:	Full service
Wine selection:	Largely Californian, several international; good selection by the glass; list chosen to be seafood-friendly
Dress:	Dining room, business casual; lounge, casual
Disabled access:	Wheelchair access
Customers:	Professionals, travelers, couples, singles
Lunch:	*Main dining room:* Monday–Friday, 11:30 A.M.–2 P.M.
Lunch/Dinner:	*Blue Crab Lounge:* Monday–Thursday, 11:30 A.M.–10 P.M.; Friday and Saturday, 11:30 A.M.–11 P.M.
Dinner:	*Main dining room:* Monday–Thursday, 5:30–10 P.M.; Friday and Saturday, 5–11 P.M.; Sunday, 5–10 P.M.

Atmosphere/setting: Two restaurants in one, with the main dining room (325 seats) reminiscent of an old New England seafood house, and the Blue Crab Lounge essentially a raw bar with high tables and stools, also serving the full menu from the dining room.

House specialties: Shaw's crab cakes; a great variety of oysters; sautéed sea scallops; Shaw's seafood platter.

Other recommendations: Lobster bisque; fresh seasonal specialties such as Maryland soft-shell crabs, Dungeness crab, stone crab, and other seafood. Daily desserts: popular refreshing key lime pie, fruit cobblers, crème brûlée, and pecan pie.

Shaw's Crab House and Shaw's Blue Crab Lounge & Oyster Bar *(continued)*

Entertainment & amenities: Blue Crab Lounge, jazz or blues, Tuesday and Thursday, 7–10 P.M.

Summary & comments: Pristinely fresh products, a variety of preparations, an extensive list of seafood-friendly wines, and knowledgeable service make Shaw's one of the best seafood places around. An on-staff seafood buyer constantly monitors products and storage temperatures. Oyster, Swedish crayfish, and other promotions keep the crowds coming. Overall, simple preparations fare better than the more elaborate dishes. Chef Yves Roubaud's crab cakes rate as the best. The bread basket items are addictive.

Honors/awards: *Forbes* magazine voted it among top six oyster bars in the country; *Chicago Tribune,* three stars.

Shaw's Seafood Grill

Zone 11   Northern Suburbs
660 West Lake Cook Road, Deerfield
(847) 948-1020

Seafood	
★★★	
Moderate	
Quality 80	Value C

Reservations:	Suggested
When to go:	Any time
Entree range:	$10.95–32.95
Payment:	All major credit cards
Service rating:	★★★
Friendliness rating:	★★★
Parking:	Lot
Bar:	Full service
Wine selection:	Most selected for seafood; largely Californian, several international; good by the glass selection, from $4.25; about 10 featured wines
Dress:	Casual or business
Disabled access:	Wheelchair accessible; call first
Customers:	Mostly professionals, travelers, couples, singles
Lunch:	Monday–Friday, 11:30 A.M.–2:30 P.M.
Dinner:	Early evening menu, Sunday–Friday, 5–6 P.M.; Monday–Thursday, 5–9:30 P.M.; Friday and Saturday, 5–10:30 P.M.; Sunday, 4:30–9 P.M.

Atmosphere/setting: Resembles a 1940s East Coast seafood house with seating for 260. A live lobster tank has been added.

House specialties: Maryland-style crab cakes; New England clam chowder; Shaw's Caesar salad; assorted grilled fishes; grilled seafood salad; regional oyster specials; grilled flatbread with various toppings (as an appetizer for dinner or as a main course for early dinner and lunch); Lake Superior whitefish, garlic crusted. Key lime pie, crème brûlée, and pecan pie.

Other recommendations: Seasonal specialties such as Maryland soft-shell crabs, grilled Copper River king salmon (available only two or three weeks each summer), grilled Pacific halibut. Daily desserts: sorbet, cheesecake, and cobbler.

Summary & comments: Although similar to Shaw's Crab House in Chicago, this place, which started two years later in 1986, has some menu differences and is fashioned more like Blue Crab Lounge in the city. The same care is given to pristinely fresh products prepared in a variety of ways. With knowledgeable service and a good, seafood-friendly wine list and casual atmosphere, this is one of the best seafood restaurants in the suburbs. Look for seafood promotions such as the August Lobster Fest.

Sher-A-Punjab

Zone 1   North Side
2510 West Devon Avenue
(773) 973-4000

Indian
★★★
Inexpensive
Quality 82   Value B

Reservations:	Recommended
When to go:	Any time
Entree range:	$8–11.75; lunch buffet, $5.95; dinner buffet, $7.95
Payment:	VISA, MC, D, DC, CB
Service rating:	★★
Friendliness rating:	★★★½
Parking:	Two city lots nearby
Bar:	None, BYOB
Wine selection:	None
Dress:	Moderately casual
Disabled access:	Yes
Customers:	Diverse, many ethnic families
Lunch/Dinner:	Daily, 11 A.M.–11 P.M.

Atmosphere/setting: Clean and modern with pink tablecloths, plastic covers, candles, and plants.

House specialties: Saag panir (homemade cheese cooked in spiced spinach); dal (spiced lentil dip); mixed vegetable curry; chicken tandoori (not on buffet); delicate chicken biryani; lamb curry.

Other recommendations: Butter chicken; bharvan kulcha (stuffed bread); panir jalfrazie (cheese cubes sautéed with vegetables and spices); eggplant bhartha cooked in spicy yogurt.

Summary & comments: The extensive buffet here is a nice way of sampling the menu, except for certain items such as the tandoori specialties, which must be made to order. The buffet is replenished frequently and includes two breads. Spiced tea settles all. Service can have lapses. The proprietor also owns Bundoo Khan, a Pakistani restaurant on the same block. This restaurant is small, casual, and cozy, and it's also a very good value.

Shilla

Zone 1 North Side	Korean/Japanese
5930 North Lincoln Avenue	★★★½
(773) 275-5930	Moderate
	Quality 86 Value C

Reservations:	Recommended, especially weekends
When to go:	Any time; Thursday and weekends busier
Entree range:	$7.95–28.95
Payment:	VISA, MC, AMEX, D
Service rating:	★★★
Friendliness rating:	★★★
Parking:	Free lot
Bar:	Full service; Asian brands, such as the Korean beers OB, Cass, and Nex
Wine selection:	International; house wine by the glass; sake and sweet plum wine; Korean soju
Dress:	Casual
Disabled access:	Yes
Customers:	Koreans, families, professionals
Open:	Daily, 11–2 A.M.; lunch buffet, 11 A.M.–3:30 P.M.; dinner buffet with 50 items and unlimited sushi, 5:30–10 P.M.

Atmosphere/setting: Large and upscale; an attractive 50-seat main dining hall with 7 rooms surrounding it. Smaller private dining rooms (a few are drab), some with grills in tables, are popular with professionals.

House specialties: Chap chae (pan-fried shredded pork, vegetables); mung bean noodles; nakji bogeum (stir-fried octopus, vegetables); kalbi (broiled short ribs); doenchang jige (spicy beef, vegetable, rice, and bean paste casserole—the bean paste takes six months to ferment); Korean barbecue, meats and chicken grilled at the table—wrap them in lettuce with bean paste; shik hae (off the menu), a punch drink of honeyed cinnamon broth with sweet rice and pine nuts.

Other recommendations: Pajun (scallion pancake with chopped octopus); buffets.

Summary & comments: Experience this place with several people if possible; it's fun to share specialties. The Korean menu is the least exotic Asian cuisine for the American palate, since it's based on grilled meats and barbecue-style sauces. A flotilla of side dishes is served with dinner. Dessert comes with dinners.

Honors/awards: 1996 Silver Platter; 1996 first-place winner, *Hard Kort* magazine.

Siam Cafe

Zone 1   North Side
4712 North Sheridan Road
(773) 769-6602

	Thai
	★★★
	Inexpensive
	Quality 84 Value A

Reservations:	Accepted
When to go:	Any time; evenings and lunchtime can be busy
Entree range:	$4.75–8
Payment:	VISA, MC, AMEX, DC
Service rating:	★★★½
Friendliness rating:	★★★½
Parking:	Street
Bar:	Beer and wine
Wine selection:	American
Dress:	Casual
Disabled access:	Yes
Customers:	Locals
Lunch/Dinner:	Wednesday–Monday, 11:30 A.M.–9 P.M.

Atmosphere/setting: Attractively decorated with Thai furnishings; dressier than many Thai places.

House specialties: Hot and spicy seafood soup (one version is just shrimp; another is beef and chicken); spring rolls; mee krob (crispy rice noodle, fried tofu, shrimp, and sweet-and-sour sauce); yum nam tok (beef-onion salad with hot-and-sour sauce); pad thai (rice noodles, peanuts, bean sprouts, egg sauce); curry fried rice with choice of meat or shrimp.

Other recommendations: Kai yang (marinated charcoal chicken); kra tiem prik Thai (chicken, beef, or pork with garlic) without rice; red snapper with ginger or hot sauce.

Summary & comments: Large menu with many good choices for rock-bottom prices. Hot items on the menu are starred, and one column of dishes is called "original hot and spicy." Some of the ingredients include red and green curry paste, red chili sauce, jalapeño pepper, and red-hot spicy sauce! These are for the veteran hot food lovers—novices beware. There are numerous intriguing rice dishes and variations without rice.

THE SIGNATURE ROOM
AT THE 95TH

Zone 3   Near North
875 North Michigan Avenue, atop the
  John Hancock Center
(312) 787-9596

New American	★★★★
Moderate/Expensive	
Quality 90	Value C

Reservations:	Recommended
When to go:	Any time
Entree range:	$21–30; Sunday brunch buffet, $29.95
Payment:	All major credit cards
Service rating:	★★★★½
Friendliness rating:	★★★★½
Parking:	Self-park garage
Bar:	Full service
Wine selection:	Award-winning, all-American list with over 150 selections; most are moderately priced, from $25 a bottle to expensive vintages at $250 a bottle; several good selections by the glass
Dress:	Chic casual, business, semiformal to dressy; at dinner, jackets suggested but not required
Disabled access:	Yes
Customers:	Locals, professionals, couples, tourists
Brunch:	Sunday, 10 A.M.–2 P.M.; extensive buffet of hot and cold foods, large assortment of desserts
Lunch:	Monday–Saturday, 11 A.M.–3 P.M.; cold and hot buffet available for $8.95
Dinner:	Sunday–Thursday, 5–10 P.M.; Friday and Saturday, 5–11 P.M.

Atmosphere/setting: The view from the top of the city on the 95th floor of the John Hancock Center is spectacular on a clear day. The breathtaking panorama is a beautiful, majestic backdrop for dining. Elegant, contemporary, sleek interior with wrap-around windows and a wrap-around mural depicting Chicago through the eyes of artists. The large chandeliers have been removed for a more modern look.

House specialties: Cured salmon appetizer; signature soup; roasted vegetable antipasti; honey-and-ginger-glazed salmon with napa cabbage, shiitake mushroom, and daikon salad, with ginger-lime vinaigrette; sautéed linguini with

(continued)

rock shrimp and bay scallops, mushrooms, spinach, roasted tomatoes, garlic, and herb-infused olive oil; roasted Colorado lamb chops; homemade ice cream.

Other recommendations: Appetizers: Roasted portobello mushroom glazed with goat cheese, sun-dried tomatoes, and black olives, with basil pesto; chilled Gulf shrimp with avocado-tomato salsa and gazpacho sauce. Signature tiramisu cake; chocolate crêpe cannoli.

Entertainment & amenities: Live music (often piano, violin, or saxophone) Saturday, 7–11 P.M.; Sunday, 11 A.M.–2 P.M. and 7–10 P.M.

Summary & comments: Healthful, contemporary American cuisine based on organically grown produce and chemical-free ingredients overall. The light cuisine is flavored a great deal with infused oils. The greatest 360-degree panoramic view of Chicago and its lakefront is from this restaurant, atop the John Hancock Center. The management, in its vision statement on the menu, makes its commitment to excellence in products, service, and atmosphere with an environmental conscience. It donates 10% of profits to a chosen charity each month.

Honors/awards: Silver Platter Award; Top Ten Most Distinguished Restaurants in North America; Restaurant of the Year by Food and Beverage Equipment Executives, 1996; *North Shore* magazine, Most Romantic Restaurant.

Skadarlija

Zone 1   North Side
4024 North Kedzie Avenue
(773) 463-5600

Serbian/Continental
★★★
Moderate
Quality 84   Value B

Reservations:	Accepted
When to go:	Dinner
Entree range:	$10.95–15.95
Payment:	AMEX, MC, VISA
Service rating:	★★★★½
Friendliness rating:	★★★★½
Parking:	Street
Bar:	Full service, including slivovitz (plum brandy)
Wine selection:	Limited; Californian and Serbian
Dress:	Casual, but no shorts; dressy, depending on time
Disabled access:	Yes
Customers:	Local, Europeans, Americans, families, couples
Open:	Wednesday–Sunday, 6 P.M.–2 A.M.; Saturday, 6 P.M.–3 A.M.; Monday and Tuesday, closed

Atmosphere/setting: Restaurant has two levels of seating, outdoor terrace, bar area, and dance floor. Dimly lit, comfortable dining room; seats about 100.

House specialties: Ajvar (appetizer spread of green and red sweet peppers with oil and vinegar); kjamak (fermented milk spread); Serbian cold plate (mixture of homemade sausage, cheese, olives, and peppers); a special appetizer of batter-fried, cheese-stuffed sweet peppers; raznici (shish kebab); roast veal.

Other recommendations: Homemade cheese strudel appetizer; cevapcici (well-garnished ground veal and beef, sometimes cheese-filled); gypsy plate (combination of several specialties for two); karadjordjeva (veal steak wrapped around Bulgarian cheese, lightly breaded and baked). Desserts: Palacinke (crêpes with preserves, chocolate, and walnuts) and apple strudel. Serbian tea (flambéed slivovitz).

Entertainment & amenities: Live music every night—violinist who plays variety of music, including classical, Russian, and gypsy.

Summary & comments: Skadarlija is a well-known street in Belgrade frequented by musicians, artists, and writers, and paintings of this street are on the walls. Appropriately, an evening at this namesake restaurant is a cultural experience. Traditional Serbian fare is prepared well here and served in a gracious style by the owners Nina and Zvonko Klancnika. Meat is dominant in this cuisine, especially pork and veal, but a couple of fish items are offered. The atmosphere is warm and friendly, and the authentic entertainment enlivens the evening.

Soul Kitchen

Southern
★★★
Inexpensive/Moderate
Quality 84   Value C

Zone 2   North Central
1576 North Milwaukee Avenue
(773) 342-9742

Reservations:	No
When to go:	Avoid peak dinner hours (7:30–9 P.M.)
Entree range:	$11–19; prix-fixe early dinner, $21.50–26, including wine or cocktail
Payment:	VISA, MC, AMEX
Service rating:	★★★
Friendliness rating:	★★★
Parking:	Valet available
Bar:	Full service; specialty cocktails such as Soul Martini, Dixie Margarita, and the Barry White
Wine selection:	International; $18–125 a bottle; $3.50–6.50 a glass
Dress:	Casual
Disabled access:	Yes
Customers:	Diverse; all ages; some restaurant owners
Brunch:	Sunday, 10 A.M.–2 P.M.
Dinner:	Sunday–Thursday, 5–10:30 P.M.; Friday and Saturday, 5–11:30 P.M.

Atmosphere/setting: Vibrant and colorful decor: orange chairs; multicolored tiles; murals depicting city scenes; faux cheetah and reptile skin tablecloths.

House specialties: Coconut shrimp; pecan-coated catfish; shrimp and grits with tasso ham; two berry buckle (blackberry and raspberry buckle with lemon ice cream); ice creams and sorbets; and truffles (Frangelico, Kahlúa, or Bailey's).

Other recommendations: Wasabi-grilled calamari with Asian slaw; smoked free-range chicken; fire and spice lamb; toasted coconut flan.

Entertainment & amenities: Energetic soul and funk background music.

Summary & comments: Soul Kitchen's motto is "Loud food, spicy music." This funky Wicker Park neighborhood restaurant on the border of Bucktown features eclectic flavors of the South, including soul food, along with infusions of Caribbean, Latin American, and occasional Asian touches. Chefs Monique King and Michael Clark have created a constantly evolving menu, and they see their kitchen as a culinary playground. The assertive cooking and soulful music make this one of Chicago's cutting-edge and dynamic eateries.

Honors/awards: *Bon Appetit*, Best New Chicago Restaurant, October 1996; *Chicago* magazine, Pick of the Week, February 1996.

SPAGO

Zone 3 Near North	American
520 North Dearborn at Grand Avenue	★★★★½
(312) 527-3700	Moderate/Expensive
	Quality 94 Value B

Reservations:	Required
When to go:	Avoid peak mealtimes unless you have a reservation
Entree range:	Lunch, $12.50–18.75; dinner, $15.50–25.50
Payment:	All major credit cards
Service rating:	★★★★½
Friendliness rating:	★★★★½
Parking:	Valet, $6
Bar:	Full service
Wine selection:	Mostly American and European, with some representations from other countries; good selection by the glass, but a bit pricey starting at $6
Dress:	Jackets and ties preferred
Disabled access:	Yes
Customers:	Locals and travelers, mixed couples, families
Lunch:	*Grill:* Daily, 11:30 A.M.–2:30 P.M.
Dinner:	*Dining Room:* Sunday–Thursday, 5–10:30 P.M.; Friday and Saturday, 5–11 P.M.
	Grill: Monday–Thursday, 5–10:30 P.M.; Friday and Saturday, 5 P.M.–midnight; Sunday, 5–9:30 P.M. Bar open every day, 11:30 A.M.–2 A.M.

Atmosphere/setting: Spago's $5-plus-million, 20,000-square-foot multi-level space in River North was designed by Adam D. Tihany of New York (who also did Spago locations in Las Vegas and Mexico City). This location has a clubby look, with fluid design, and features a casual grill and a dining room, both with open kitchens. The sophisticated nonsmoking dining room, with a huge vase of flowers at the entry, is decorated with patterned carpet and upholstery and subdued colors and lighting. The curved staircase leads to the second floor club room bar and lounge with a fireplace and leather couches and chairs. The top level has three private party rooms with views of the skyline. The custom-made look includes lovely wood, terrazzo, and intricate lighting. Robert Rauschenberg paintings are here, plus local artists' works.

(continued)

House specialties: Menu changes seasonally. Pizzas baked in wood-burning ovens; homemade pastas; mesquite-grilled fish and meats; Spago homemade charcuterie plate. Examples: stir-fried spicy lamb with garlic, chile, cilantro, and ginger-sesame glaze, served with radicchio leaves; tuna tatki with marinated seaweed and cucumber salad; leek and artichoke ravioli with sautéed black bass and young garlic–porcini sauce. Granny Smith apple tart with cinnamon ice cream; chocolate tart with vanilla ice cream and orange glaze.

Other recommendations: Sautéed foie gras with sweet potato chips and apple chutney; Maine scallops with pad Thai noodles and spicy coconut sauce; roasted Cantonese duck with star anise, grapefruit, and a sesame bun; almond butter crunch tart (not much crunch, however) with maple-walnut ice cream.

Summary & comments: After several delays, Spago finally opened in autumn 1996, and immediately received a lot of media attention. Chicagoans are glad that this Spago has been tailored to them. Superstar, Austrian-born chef Wolfgang Puck, who is credited with recreating California cuisine with his Spago on Sunset Strip (1982), said in a private interview that all his restaurants are like children; each is individual. He loves Chicago and is very pleased to be here. Wolfgang's brother Klaus and wife Amanda, with degrees from the Cornell School of Hotel Administration, are co–general managers. Managing partner Tom Kaplan has spent 14 years involved with Spago restaurants in Los Angeles, Tokyo, Las Vegas, and Mexico City. Executive chef François Kwaku-Dongo headed the kitchen at Spago in West Hollywood for five years before coming here to serve American cuisine with European and Asian influences and many midwestern ingredients. Puck gives his executive chef a lot of flexibility, and the food has been innovative and flavorful on all visits. Some of the signature dishes have been transplanted, but there are many new items in the repertoire. The Grill and bar area have a separate menu.

Spago Grill

Zone 3 Near North	American
520 North Dearborn	★★★★
(312) 527-3700	Moderate/Expensive
	Quality 94 Value B

Reservations:	Accepted
When to go:	Early dinner less crowded
Entree range:	$15.50–27
Payment:	VISA, MC, AMEX, CB, O, D, DC
Service rating:	★★★★
Friendliness rating:	★★★★
Parking:	Valet
Bar:	Full service
Wine selection:	American and European; several by the glass; a bit pricey
Dress:	Casual
Disabled access:	Yes
Customers:	Mixed; mostly professionals at lunch; evenings, familiess, couples, tourists, locals
Lunch/Dinner:	Sunday–Thursday, 11:30 A.M.–11 P.M.; Friday and Saturday, 11:30 A.M.–midnight

Atmosphere/setting: Spago and Spago Grill are housed together. To the left of the entrance is the cafe and bar area with its own menu. Open kitchen.

House specialties: Menu changes with what's seasonally available. Famous pizzas and calzones baked in wood-burning ovens; homemade pastas, such as François' angel hair pasta with tomato, basil, and garlic; mesquite-grilled fish and meats. Desserts may sometimes be the same as those offered in the dining room, such as Granny Smith apple tart with cinnamon ice cream. Others might be vanilla crème brûlée and tiramisu parfait.

Other recommendations: Pizza with duck sausage, shiitakes; oven-roasted Sonoma lamb with garlic potato puree and niçoise olive jus; roasted vegetable sandwich. Blonde brownie sundae; ice creams, sorbets, cookies.

Entertainment & amenities: Club room bar on second floor; retail shop.

Summary & comments: Austrian-born, superstar chef Wolfgang Puck shows his innovative culinary stuff here in Chicago at his Spago Grill as well as in his more sophisticated dining room, Spago. Executive chef François Kwaku-Dongo's American cuisine has European and Asian influences and a healthy portion of midwestern ingredients. The cooking is boldly flavored, a trademark of Wolf's. Children are welcome here at the grill, and booster seats and highchairs are provided; early reservations are suggested.

Spiaggia

Zone 3 Near North	Italian
980 North Michigan Avenue	★★★★½
(312) 280-2750	Moderate/Expensive
	Quality 95 Value C

Reservations:	Recommended
When to go:	Any time
Entree range:	$8.95–29.95; per person total, $50–60
Payment:	All major credit cards
Service rating:	★★★★
Friendliness rating:	★★★½
Parking:	Valet, garage
Bar:	Full service
Wine selection:	Extensive; Italian; $25–125 a bottle
Dress:	Business, some semiformal and formal
Disabled access:	Yes
Customers:	Local, national, international, business travelers, suburbanites, celebrities from entertainment and political arenas
Lunch:	Tuesday–Saturday, 11:30 A.M.–2 P.M.
Dinner:	Monday–Thursday, 5:30–9:30 P.M.; Friday and Saturday, 5:30–10P.M.; Sunday, 5:30–9 P.M.

Atmosphere/setting: Newly remodeled dining room with a contemporary, chic setting overlooking Lake Michigan and Oak Street Beach.

House specialties: Rags of fresh pasta with mushrooms; ricotta ravioli filled with sweet Tuscan pecorino cheese; seafood risotto; wood-roasted veal chop with smoked pancetta and vodka-cream sauce; fillet of salmon with asparagus, basil, and white wine sauce; wood-roasted guinea hen with Savoy cabbage, pancetta, and porcini mushrooms.

Other recommendations: Specials; mascarpone torte; homemade ice creams.

Summary & comments: This very chic restaurant, one of the Levy Restaurants, has had ups and downs in the past. For many years under the talented direction of chef Paul Bartolotta, the food has been elevated to a new plateau. He's rescued it from the earlier experimental and creative Italian fare and brought it back to regional roots. And the sometimes inconsistent, reserved service appears to have gotten on track.

Honors/awards: Chef Paul Bartolotta is the recipient of the James Beard Award; *Chicago* magazine's Critics Choice Award; Insegna del Ristorante Italiano del Mundo (for overseas Italian restaurants showing superior culinary achievement), June 1997.

SPRUCE

New American
★★★★½
Inexpensive/Moderate

Quality 94   Value B

Zone 3   Near North
238 East Ontario
(312) 642-3757

Reservations:	Recommended
When to go:	Early or late, Monday through Thursday
Entree range:	Three course prix fixe menu $45, with $28 à la carte entrees; five course prix fixe menu $85; paired with wines, $115
Payment:	MC, VISA, AMEX, DC, D
Service rating:	★★★★½
Friendliness rating:	★★★★★
Parking:	Valet, dinner; self-park
Bar:	Full service, but no seating
Wine selection:	Extensive, intelligent list of American, French and Italian wines, $25–100 per bottle; 20 by the glass, $7–14
Dress:	Business casual to dressy
Disabled access:	Yes
Customers:	Professionals, downtown shoppers, guests
Dinner:	Monday–Thursday, 5:30–10 P.M.; Friday and Saturday, 5:30–11 P.M., Sunday 5–9 P.M.

Atmosphere/setting: The action takes place in a large dining room that some see as "very New York;" hardwood floors, fresh flowers, warm lighting, and original art lend an intimate feel that enhances Spruce's casual elegance. A private room partitioned off the main dining area can seat parties of up to 45 guests. Several steps down from street level with windows.

House specialties: Menu changes to reflect what's seasonally available. The three course prix fixe menu features starters such as succulent crisp sweetbreads, earthy with wild mushrooms, cranberry beans, and garlic chips. Entrees to try: tender pepper-seared venison striploin with salsify, dried pears, balsamic vinegar with green beans and a wrap filled with fruit; pan-roasted pheasant enhanced with black currants, foie gras sauce, with creamy polenta and hedge hog mushrooms; sautéed striped bass with little neck clams, prosciutto, and champagne sauce. Vegetarians will enjoy root vegetable ragoût with jasmine rice spring rolls and warm wasabi vinaigrette. Desserts: Spruce bananas, a warm flourless chocolate banana cake (almost a soufflé) with roasted banana ice cream on a slice of banana bread with two sauces; warm pear hazelnut tart with Earl Grey ice cream.

(continued)

Other recommendations: Appetizer of pan-roasted quail with dried cranberries in port vinaigrette. Dishes on earlier visits have included herbed rabbit "chops" on crisp risotto cake with baba gannoujh and chipotle oil (somewhat spicy). For dessert, seasonal offerings such as citrus Napoleon; papaya and lime consomme with tropical fruit sorbets; house-made brioche bread pudding with roasted mango and Tahitian vanilla bean ice cream.

Summary & comments: This is one of the most exciting fine dining restaurants in downtown Chicago for the sheer pleasure of the food. One professional from Vancouver Island said, "My lunch was one of the ten best meals I've had in the United States, including New York and San Francisco." (Sadly, Spruce no longer serves lunch.) Executive Chef Cesar Reyes took over the kitchen in 1998. Managing partner Dan Sachs also brings great credentials to this restaurant (Spiaggia, New York's Tribeca Grill, and London's Kensington Palace). The food here is innovative, flavorful, and made from great ingredients, such as heirloom tomatoes, veggie chips, and artisan cheeses.

Honors/awards: *North Shore* magazine, Number One Readers' Favorite, 1997; AAA, four diamonds, 1994–1996; *Esquire*, Best New Restaurant, 1996.

STANLEY'S KITCHEN & TAP

	Southern
Zone 1 North Side	★★½
1970 North Lincoln Avenue	Inexpensive
(312) 642-0007	
	Quality 79 Value A

Reservations: For 8 or more
When to go: Any time
Entree range: $5.95–8.95
Payment: AMEX, VISA, MC
Service rating: ★★★
Friendliness rating: ★★★★
Parking: Street, lot nearby
Bar: Full service; over 120 kinds of American bourbon
                   and whiskey
Wine selection: All American; everything available by the glass
Dress: Casual
Disabled access: Yes
Customers: Locals, couples, families, some professionals
Open: Monday and Tuesday, 5 P.M.–2 A.M.; Wednes-
                   day–Friday, 11:30–2 A.M.; Saturday, 11 A.M.–
                   3 A.M.; Sunday, 11–2 A.M.

Atmosphere/setting: Entryway through 100-seat saloon with 32-foot mahogany bar. Very homey; wooden porch where you can play checkers, chess, dominoes, or backgammon in rocking chairs; 80-seat dining room resembles a stage set depicting a 1940s family kitchen. Downstairs dining room recently renovated.

House specialties: Kentucky-fried tomatoes; blackened catfish, tender and coated with Cajun seasonings; Stan's vegetarian lasagna; chicken-fried steak made with pounded sirloin, preferred over the usual cube steak; creamy chicken short-cake (on sourdough biscuits); mashed potatoes and macaroni and cheese.

Other recommendations: Fried catfish strips, blackened or buffalo-style; black bean chicken chili (thick with chicken); jalapeño Jack sticks. Suppers are served with side dish of choice. Exceptional side dishes: southern spaghetti (tossed) and wet fries (with gravy). Nightly specials such as shrimp Creole. Apple pie with cinnamon ice cream; bread pudding with warm vanilla sauce.

Summary & comments: This fun restaurant offers what our fast-paced lives make us yearn for—comforting food in a nurturing atmosphere. This is a home away from home and as close to Mom's cooking as you can get. The food is simple and good, served in generous portions in a caring environment, and the bargain prices add to the comfort factor.

Stir Crazy

Zone 9   Western Suburbs
105 Oakbrook Center, Oakbrook
(630) 575-0155

Pan-Asian	
★★★½	
Inexpensive	
Quality 88	Value B

Reservations:	For 8 or more weekdays
When to go:	Weekdays and Sunday evenings less busy
Entree range:	Small, $6.45–9.45 (lunch); large, $7.95–11.95
Payment:	AMEX, D, DC, MC, VISA
Service rating:	★★★½ (partly self-serve)
Friendliness rating:	★★★★½
Parking:	Free mall lot
Bar:	Full-service; wide variety of specialty drinks
Wine selection:	Japanese, American; $3.50–4.50 a glass; $15–19 a bottle
Dress:	Casual
Disabled access:	Complete
Customers:	Mixed; locals, professionals, families, couples
Lunch/Dinner:	Sunday–Thursday, 11 A.M.–10 P.M.; Friday and Saturday, 11 A.M.–11 P.M.

Atmosphere/setting: The name suggests casualness and whimsy, and the vibrant, contemporary decor echoes that tone. Colorful market bar; display kitchen.

House specialties: The create-your-own stir-fry has over 20 fresh vegetables; chicken, beef, pork, shrimp, salmon, and other seafood, which are topped off with three ladles of one of the eleven distinctive sauces and one ladle of a spice. White or brown rice and noodles; banana won tons with white chocolate; vanilla ice cream and caramel sauce; lemon-ginger sorbet.

Other recommendations: The "big and crazy platter" (imperial rolls, fried chicken and vegetable egg rolls, chicken satay, plum chicken); pineapple curried fried rice; wok-prepared garlic chicken and spicy kung pao chicken; Shanghai noodles and Vietnamese pho soup; Asian tiramisu; fruit-topped cheesecake.

Summary & comments: Stir Crazy has a special dual menu that gives customers the option of creating their own stir-fry or choosing from prepared dishes on the menu. This differentiates it from others in the "cook-your-own" Asian restaurant flock. This Oakbrook prototype embraces Asian cuisines, including Chinese, Japanese, Thai, and Vietnamese. The servers assist in recommending sauces. Then you're on your own to create your bowl full of ingredients.

SZECHWAN EAST

Zone 3   Near North
340 East Ohio Street
(312) 255-9200

Chinese
★★★★
Moderate

Quality 92   Value C

Reservations:	Recommended
When to go:	Any time
Entree range:	$7.95–13.95; $24.95 per person for Imperial dinner or $31.95 per person for Emperor's dinner (2 person minimum for both)
Payment:	All major credit cards
Service rating:	★★★★
Friendliness rating:	★★★★★
Parking:	Validated adjacent McClurg Court Garage (indoor walkway)
Bar:	Full service, including Mandarin cocktails and imported beers
Wine selection:	Regular list: about 24 international selections, including Harvest Moon chardonnay private label and several Oriental choices; mostly affordable; most bottles, $12–22, with several in $30s, and Dom Perignon for $120; several by the glass
Dress:	Casual
Disabled access:	Yes
Customers:	Mixed, professionals, couples, locals, celebs
Brunch:	Sunday champagne buffet, 11:30 A.M.–2 P.M., $15.95
Lunch:	Monday–Saturday, 11:30 A.M.–2 P.M.; 30-item lunch buffet, $8.95
Dinner:	Daily, 5–10 P.M.

Atmosphere/setting: Attractive, spacious dining room in tasteful Chinese decor divided into sections; recently renovated and expanded to include a second bar and indoor cafe and outdoor sidewalk cafe in summer.

House specialties: Appetizers: Fire pot satay beef; crab claws stuffed with minced shrimp and water chestnuts; Shanghai pot stickers filled with chicken and cabbage. Entrees: Governor's Chicken (chicken sautéed with sliced bell peppers, minced ginger, and garlic), a best-seller; steamed fillet of Chilean black sea bass

(continued)

with ginger root and scallions; black bean salmon (fillets); steamed fish (fillet—the orange roughy is great!) with rice and wine-ginger–black bean sauce; Peking duck (now available in half-duck portions, enough for two entrees; no advance order required). Vegetable dishes: Szechuan string beans; festival of mushrooms; steamed vegetable delight with tofu and garlic dipping sauce. Other items include three delicacies in a nest (scallops, escargot, and filet mignon chunks with Chinese vegetables, in a potato bird's nest); vegetable tempura; Hwa Shee Jeer Surprise (chicken and escargot in spicy hot sauce with mushrooms and vegetables); walnut chicken. Expanded lunch/brunch buffet, including fried wonton and calamari-peapod salad.

Other recommendations: Assorted hot appetizers, including the daily special vegetarian and the Suchow pot stickers; Taiwanese escargot rice (healthier than fried rice); moo shi crêpes with chicken, vegetables, shrimp, beef, pork, or duck; dim sum trio (shrimp, pork, chicken dumplings in mini steamer). Desserts: rich Chinese crêpes with dates; banana in flaming rum; light almond tofu; Chinese cakes.

Summary & comments: This is the reincarnation of one of Chicago's long-time top Chinese restaurants (considering current owner Alfred Hsu managed the predecessor Szechwan House at its previous Michigan Avenue location since 1981). While managing Szechwan House, Hsu, together with the legendary restaurateur Austin Koo, opened 17 other Chinese restaurants. When Szechwan House had to relocate in 1995 because the building was razed, Hsu opened Szechwan East on his own with the same staff and actually improved an already excellent restaurant. He and his master chef, Hu Xiao Jun, a Szechuan native, expanded the comprehensive, 120-item menu and increased the dining options, including half orders of most entrees. There is a trio of "healthy options" (steamed vegetables solo or with chicken or shrimp) and vegetarian dishes, "Chef's Specials," and multi-course set-price dinners. The restaurant is capable of turning out some impressive banquets. Excellent cooking and attentive service from the friendly staff continue. The food is exciting and the ever-changing menu tempts return visits. Carryout, dinner delivery, lunch boxes, and catering are available.

SZECHWAN RESTAURANT

Zone 3 Near North	Chinese
625 North Michigan Avenue	★★★
(312) 482-9898	Inexpensive/Moderate
	Quality 83 Value C

Reservations:	Recommended
When to go:	Any time
Entree range:	$6.95–19.95
Payment:	All major credit cards
Service rating:	★★★½
Friendliness rating:	★★★½
Parking:	Discount parking available
Bar:	Full service
Wine selection:	Mostly Californian, French; some Chinese;
	$14–26 a bottle; several by the glass, $4.50
Dress:	Casual
Disabled access:	Yes
Customers:	Diverse
Lunch/Dinner:	Daily, 11:30 A.M.–10:30 P.M.

Atmosphere/setting: Modern Chinese; spacious, handsome, comfortable interior; one level below sidewalk level.

House specialties: Dim sum available all day (e.g., steamed shrimp dumplings, vegetarian dumplings, pot stickers, shrimp toast, stuffed bean-curd rolls). Stuffed crab claws (Hunan appetizer); imperial honey ham (with lotus seeds in sweet laurel bloom flower sauce); empress sizzling lamb with leek; crispy chicken.

Other recommendations: Roast Peking duck (available with no advance notice); chrysanthemum fish sweet-and-sour; lobster with ginger and tomato sauce; peacock pork; stuffed banana with red bean paste (for two).

Summary & comments: This is one of the only places to get dim sum downtown and perhaps the only Chinese restaurant serving it all day long. Make a meal from the dim sum special menu, or start with dumplings and select one of the many unusual entrees. It's even possible to order Peking duck at the last moment here, unlike most other places, which request a day's advance notice. Hot and spicy dishes are starred.

Tallgrass

<table>
<tr><td></td><td>New French</td></tr>
<tr><td>Zone 8   Southern Suburbs</td><td>★★★★★</td></tr>
<tr><td>1006 South State Street, Lockport</td><td>Very Expensive</td></tr>
<tr><td>(815) 838-5566</td><td>Quality 98   Value C</td></tr>
</table>

Reservations:	Necessary
When to go:	Dinner
Entree range:	$45 (4-course) or $55 (5-course) prix fixe menu
Payment:	Personal checks (local), MC, V
Service rating:	★★★★★
Friendliness rating:	★★★★
Parking:	Street
Bar:	Full service
Wine selection:	Fairly priced; several by the glass
Dress:	Upscale casual to dressy; jackets required for men
Disabled access:	Partially accessible; not bathrooms
Customers:	Diverse; upscale, sophisticated diners
Dinner:	Wednesday–Sunday, 6–9 P.M.

Atmosphere/setting: Victorian, eclectic setting in a historic building. Downstairs dining room: copper-hued lavolier walls and ceilings; the chef's Aubrey Beardsley–inspired paintings. Smoke-free; smoking permitted in hallway.

House specialties: Appetizer trio of crab cake, lobster lasagna, shrimp timbale; crispy brie with oyster mushrooms, mixed greens; potato sandwich of duck breast; foie gras and coddled eggs; mint-crusted spring lamb loin; walnut-sorrel pesto–coated rack of lamb; grilled Atlantic salmon and jumbo prawn; soufflé of Belgian dark chocolate and cherry puree. Signature dessert: Tallgrass chocolate and raspberry tower with two sauces.

Other recommendations: Asparagus pierogis on wild mushroom duxelle; lobster, mango, basil salad, and Parmesan tile; coconut-crusted sea scallops with pineapple risotto, curry beurre blanc; chèvre and baby watercress with walnut oil; veal sweetbreads Provençal; savoury of poached pear, spiced nuts, blue cheese; lemon mousse between almond wafer cookies with raspberries, almond cream.

Summary & comments: Co-owners J. Thomas Alves and chef Robert Burcenski embellished this 1895 Victorian building in the charming town of Lockport. Chef Burcenski masterfully mixes his special culinary techniques and quality ingredients to create deliciously unique, beautifully presented dishes. Portions are ample. Salads are listed and served after the main course. Service here is first class. One of the greatest dining experiences in the Chicago area.

Honors/awards: DiRoNA; *Condé Nast*, four diamond award; *Wine Spectator* Award; one of five Best of the Year restaurants, *Chicago* magazine.

TANGO SUR

Zone 1   North Side
3763 North Southport
(773) 477-5466

Argentinian	
★★½	
Inexpensive/Moderate	
Quality 78	Value B

Reservations:	For 6 or more
When to go:	Monday, Tuesday, Wednesday, or Sunday
Entree range:	$7.90–16
Payment:	AMEX, MC, VISA
Service rating:	★★★
Friendliness rating:	★★★★
Parking:	Street
Bar:	None; BYOB
Wine selection:	None
Dress:	Casual
Disabled access:	Yes
Customers:	Professionals, theatergoers, locals, suburbanites, Argentinians, Peruvians, Colombians
Dinner:	Monday–Thursday, 5–10:30 P.M.; Friday and Saturday, 5–11:30 P.M.; Sunday, noon–11 P.M.

Atmosphere/setting: Simple storefront colorfully decorated.

House specialties: Matambre (Argentine specialty of veal rolled and cooked with vegetables, served cold); empanadas stuffed with beef, chicken, ham, and ricotta cheese, or just spinach and ricotta cheese; pastas with Argentinian tomato sauce; noqui (potato dumplings topped with beef stew); parillada (barbecue) featuring a variety of meats; traditional flan with Argentine caramel.

Other recommendations: Entradas: berenjena en escabeche (marinated sliced eggplant); bife de chorizo (grilled boneless strip steak); suprema à la napolitana (chicken breast breaded, topped with baked ham, mozzarella, tomato sauce); entrana (grilled outer skirt); vacio (grilled flap meat). Postres: pionono (Argentine pound cake rolled, filled with caramel).

Entertainment & amenities: Live folk or tango music and all-you-can-eat nocquis for $7.50.

Summary & comments: This new restaurant's timely arrival is in step with Argentina's higher profile, due mainly to the growing popularity of the tango (highlighted in the successful "Tango Forever" performance), and the recent release of the Alan Parker–directed *Evita*. Although the dance is sultry, this place is not; it serves straightforward Argentinian fare with lively native music that is often too loud for the small room. The staff is friendly, and the recommended items are quite good. This is a beef-oriented cuisine, and servings are large.

302 WEST

Zone 9   Western Suburbs
302 West State Street, Geneva
(630) 232-9302

Reservations:	Recommended
When to go:	Any time
Entree range:	$21–25 (perhaps slightly higher)
Payment:	All major credit cards
Service rating:	★★★½
Friendliness rating:	★★★★½
Parking:	Street
Bar:	Full service; premium labels
Wine selection:	Extensive American; unique styles; French champagnes; several $18–30, but most more expensive; many by the glass
Dress:	Casual; no dress code, but most guests are chic
Disabled access:	Yes
Customers:	Professionals, couples, wine lovers
Dinner:	Tuesday–Thursday, 6–9 P.M.; Friday and Saturday, 6–10 P.M.

Atmosphere/setting: Elegant, spacious restaurant on the second level of a historic bank building. High ceilings and 30-foot palladium windows. Relaxed fine dining; never intimidating.

House specialties: Menu changes daily. Examples: appetizers of roasted beefsteak tomato stuffed with goat cheese on angel hair; grilled, sliced southern-style barbecue rabbit tenderloin with corn pancakes; spicy Louisiana turtle gumbo; lightly smoked swordfish "tubetti" filled with tomato, cantaloupe, and pine nuts. Entrees: grilled Hawaiian moonfish steak; grilled, tequila-honey-lime-marinated half free-range chicken on spiced red beans; roasted sablefish fillet in smoked salmon cream; excellent hickory-roasted pork loin. Desserts: homemade mascarpone ice cream with dark mocha sauce; malted-milk chocolate mousse cake; peach-almond ice cream cake; pear-vanilla sorbet; granita of wildly fruity Barbera wine.

Other recommendations: Appetizer of grilled jumbo sea scallops tossed with baby lettuces and chardonnay vinaigrette. Entrees: fresh Canadian walleye fillet sautéed; grilled buffalo rib-eye steak with horseradish mashed potatoes; roasted, sliced pork tenderloin with Cajun gravy and southern-style "goober

(continued)

peas." Desserts: fresh mission figs marinated in sweet Muscat wine with mascarpone cheese; Key lime cheesecake.

Entertainment & amenities: Regularly scheduled piano, harp, and vocal music.

Summary & comments: The daily menu is a single page, whereas the wine list is 13 pages (not counting the extensive list of ports, sherries, and Madeiras, and an additional list of wines by the glass). Truly a wine-oriented restaurant, and the list is well worth scrutinizing before ordering, since this is a chance to try some very unusual selections. If you're waiting for a table at the upstairs bar, sip an apéritif wine and peruse the menu and wine list, which takes a bit of reading. Chef-owner Joel Findlay's personality definitely shines through his menu and wine lists. His wife, co-owner Catherine Findlay, warmly greets guests and oversees the front of the house. An ambitious dessert list with about 20 daily specials—some quite sweet, especially those with caramel sauce or brown sugar.

Honors/awards: *Wine Spectator* Award of Excellence; Best Seafood Chef Award from Illinois Seafood Association; DiRoNA.

Topolobampo

	Mexican
Zone 4 The Loop	★★★★½
445 North Clark Street	Moderate
(312) 661-1434	
	Quality 95 Value C

Reservations:	Required
When to go:	Tuesday, Wednesday, or Thursday
Entree range:	$14–25
Payment:	All major credit cards
Service rating:	★★★½
Friendliness rating:	★★½
Parking:	Valet, $7; street, public lots
Bar:	Shares a common bar with Frontera Grill; good tequila and Mexican beer list
Wine selection:	Quite extensive; very international
Dress:	Tastefully casual, no sneakers or jeans
Disabled access:	Yes
Customers:	Mixed, locals and travelers, professionals, couples
Lunch:	Tuesday–Friday, 11:30 A.M.–2 P.M.
Dinner:	Tuesday–Friday, 5:30–9:30 P.M.; Friday and Saturday, 5:30–10:30 P.M.

Atmosphere/setting: Formal and elegant; comfortable.

House specialties: Menu changes every two weeks. Appetizer samplers might offer crispy, smoky-flavored pork carnitas, guacamole with tomatillos, cactus salad, and more. Fish gets unusual treatment, such as succulent pan-roasted sea bass with roasted garlic, sweet plantains, toasted pecans, wine-marinated prunes, and olive oil, with red chile rice. Another sampler plate might offer chicken enchiladas in green pumpkin seed mole; griddle-baked quesadilla of cheese, duck, and peppers; tostada of marinated cactus salad and black beans.

Other recommendations: Sopa Azteca with chicken breast, avocado, and cheese; cod empanadas; tamale of fresh masa with pheasant; roasted capon breast stuffed with squash blossoms and wild greens.

Summary & comments: Owners Rick Bayless (chef) and wife Deanne (manager) lived in Mexico and co-authored a cookbook, *Authentic Mexican,* which was published about the time their Frontera Grill restaurant opened several years ago. Both the book and restaurant received good reviews. Service could be friendlier and more accommodating at times.

Honors/awards: Recognized as the best-researched Mexican restaurant offering regional dishes; chef Rick Bayless won Best Chef of the Midwest in 1994 and the International Chef of the Year Award, James Beard Foundation 1995. Julia Child Best Cookbook of the Year 1996.

Trattoria Gianni

Zone 1   North Side
1711 North Halsted Street
(312) 266-1976

Italian
★★★★
Inexpensive/Moderate

Quality 91   Value C

Reservations:	Requested
When to go:	After-theater crowd leaves at 7:30 P.M.
Entree range:	Pastas, $8.95–12.95; entrees, $10.95–16.95
Payment:	VISA, MC, AMEX, DC, CB
Service rating:	★★★★
Friendliness rating:	★★★★★
Parking:	Valet in front of restaurant
Bar:	Full service; all Italian beers
Wine selection:	All Italian regional wines; thoughtful list; several excellent choices by the glass
Dress:	Chic casual
Disabled access:	Yes
Customers:	Appeals to all ages, including families
Brunch:	Sunday, noon–3 P.M., Italian buffet brunch
Lunch:	Tuesday–Friday, 11:30 A.M.–2:30 P.M.
Dinner:	Tuesday–Thursday, 5–11 P.M.; Friday and Saturday, 5–11:30 P.M.; Sunday, 4–11 P.M.

Atmosphere/setting: Typical authentic Italian trattoria setting—warm, friendly, and bright. Recently expanded.

House specialties: Antipasti: portobello alla griglia (summer item: whole mushroom marinated in olive oil, garlic, rosemary, and balsamic vinegar, then grilled); polpo (grilled octopus); calamari vino blanco; insalata Variopinta (summer item: mixed baby lettuces, sliced apple and pear, arugula, caramelized pine nuts, goat cheese, Gorgonzola); rigatoni Nocerina (sun-dried tomatoes, mushrooms, olive oil, garlic, and basil in cream sauce); conchili del mercante (crumbled Italian sausage, mushrooms, fresh tomato sauce, scamorza cheese, peas); spaghetti Portofino (scallops, scampi, cherry tomatoes); vitello alla Gianni (scaloppine sautéed in brandy sauce with mushrooms, cherry tomatoes, artichoke hearts); pollo Toscana (boneless chicken breast marinated with fresh herbs); salmone al vino bianco (fillet of fresh Norwegian salmon grilled first, then sautéed); lombata (veal chop) Vesuvio. Desserts: housemade cannoli; tartufo; mandarino (sorbet inside frozen orange shell); tiramisu.

Other recommendations: Insalata alla Lipare (mixture of lentils and grilled and marinated calamari on a bed of arugula with chopped plum tomatoes)—not

(continued)

on the menu; gamberi alla Napolitana (mussels in marinara sauce and grilled vegetables); costolette d'agnello alla griglia (summer item: lamb chops marinated, grilled, and served with sautéed escarole and grilled potatoes); tonno alla griglia (summer item: fresh grilled tuna steak topped with cold sauce of chopped plum tomatoes, celery, green olives, green onion, olive oil, balsamic vinegar, with grilled vegetables); saltimbocca al sorrentina (tender veal scaloppine topped with prosciutto and mozzarella, sautéed with white wine and tomatoes).

Entertainment & amenities: Special wine dinners and other promotions.

Summary & comments: Chef Gianni Delisi established this, his first restaurant, in 1988, fulfilling his dream. When he first arrived here from Italy, he learned English and worked at the Italian Village and then at Trattoria Roma. He has woven into this place everything he considered important, including true Italian cuisine featuring family recipes. Some items are Delisi family creations, retained from his family's restaurant in Italy. The restaurant is comfortable and caring, and it offers some high-quality, innovative cooking at fair prices. This is one of the best trattorias around without the high noise level and crowds of some "in" spots. It's possible to have a relaxed dinner here even on a busy night. Buon appetito!

TRATTORIA PARMA

Zone 3   Near North
400 North Clark Street
(312) 245-9933

Italian
★★★★
Inexpensive/Moderate
Quality 89   Value B

Reservations:	Recommended
When to go:	Less busy before 6 P.M.
Entree range:	$7.95–16
Payment:	Major credit cards except D
Service rating:	★★★★
Friendliness rating:	★★★★½
Parking:	Limited street (lunch); valet (dinner), $6
Bar:	Full service
Wine selection:	Largely Italian, from $5 a glass and $20 a bottle
Dress:	Casual
Disabled access:	Yes
Customers:	Diverse; professionals, families, locals, tourists
Lunch:	Monday–Friday, 11:30 A.M.–2 P.M. Carryout menu, 11 A.M.–2 P.M., 2 hours notice requested; delivery ends at 2 P.M.
Dinner:	Monday–Thursday, 5:30–10 P.M.; Friday and Saturday, 5:30–11 P.M.; Sunday, 5–9 P.M.

Atmosphere/setting: Rustic and comfortable ambience of an Italian country home; wood chairs and floors, weathered green shutters, and lace cafe curtains. The beautiful large bar with a frescoed ceiling is from the 1930s.

House specialties: Antipasti parma (prosciutto di Parma with olives, giardiniera, and Parmigiano-Reggiano); eggplant parmigiana; rigatoni stuffed with chicken, wild mushrooms, ricotta; grilled shrimp and calamari; sautéed veal chops Milanese; panna cotta with raspberry sauce; chocolate cake topped with caramelized bananas.

Other recommendations: Fried calamari; tagliatelle Bolognese; penne carbonara; farfalle with vegetables, goat cheese; cannoli with ricotta cream filling and pistachios.

Summary & comments: This new Trattoria Parma, named for the gastronomic center of Italy (home of Parmigiano cheese), was launched in June 1997. This reincarnation of the former Mare, in the same location, is more casual with a completely new decor and authentic, Italian trattoria-simple dishes. Chef Paul LoDuca felt the River North area needed a friendly trattoria for a gathering spot. It has the right appearance and food combinations to make it successful. Carryout available.

Trio

Zone 11 Northern Suburbs	Fusion
1625 Hinman Avenue, Evanston	★★★★★
(847) 733-8746	Expensive/Very Expensive
	Quality 98 Value C

Reservations:	Highly suggested; weekends often booked weeks in advance; accepted up to 3 months in advance
When to go:	Tuesday–Thursday
Entree range:	$17–30; some specialties are higher; 8- to 10-course degustation, $75; vegetarian version, $65
Payment:	VISA, MC, AMEX, D, DC
Service rating:	★★★★★
Friendliness rating:	★★★★★
Parking:	Valet, $7
Bar:	Full service; international beers; extensive single malt scotches; infused grappas
Wine selection:	Fairly extensive; French, American, Italian, and several other international, from $30 a bottle; 10–12 by the glass; wine flight tastings (e.g., 4 half-glasses); reserve list, sommelier to assist
Dress:	Jackets suggested; dressy overall
Disabled access:	Yes; need assistance up 2 steps for rest rooms
Customers:	All types, all ages
Lunch:	Friday, seating noon–1 P.M.; 4-course prix fixe ($26)
Dinner:	Tuesday–Thursday, 5:30–9:30 P.M.; Friday and Saturday, 5:30–10:30 P.M.; Sunday, 5–9 P.M.

Atmosphere/setting: Housed in The Homestead, a hotel designed in Williamsburg Inn–style. Country estate–type living room is a waiting lounge. Welcoming entryway with display of kitchen-made specialty items; wine rack room dividers. Comfortable, warm main dining room and a brighter, more intimate porch room overlooking a garden. A subtle, rustic courtyard decor with antique weathered wood paneling and carved alabaster wall sconces, with earthy purples and greens and dried flowers. The kitchen, with one table in an alcove, is a bit more than half of the 3,500 square feet of restaurant space.

House specialties: Appetizers: porcini (roasted winter corn) "cappuccino" with Parmesan tuille; wild mushroom and Parmesan risotto with white truffle

(continued)

oil; mirrored mosaic (fish changes: one example was great ginger-cured gravlax, Pacific oyster, and Szechuan tuna sashimi); caviar service on a painter's palette (domestic); seared Hudson Valley foie gras (used lavishly here) with mango, or with roasted Granny Smith apple, black lentils, vanilla, and saké-infused veal reduction. Main courses: potato-crusted Columbia River sturgeon, Mt. Walden smoked trout, and lobster bordelaise; pomegranate-glazed pheasant breast, caramelized salsify, and swiss chard in a bittersweet tangerine sauce. Specials such as lobster bisque; grilled veal chop and crispy sweetbreads with three-bean ragout, escarole, and pearl onions, in a rosemary-infused veal reduction. Desserts: lemon tart Nico with white pepper ice cream, blackberry compote, dried apricots, and golden raisins; the Great Pumpkin crème caramel; and Valrhona chocolate bliss (Della's decadent mélange that once included a chocolate hazelnut tart, a spun sugar cup holding chocolate mousse, a chocolate meringue cookie dipped in pistachios with fudge sorbet, berries, and more).

Other recommendations: Circle Ranch buffalo carpaccio, tempura tiger shrimp, and horseradish aïoli; hazelnut-and-herb-crusted rack of lamb with foie gras hummus, ratatouille; the Vegetarian is a daily celebration of seasonal market vegetables and grains; crème brûlée. Buy a box of Trio's truffles to take home.

Summary & comments: By far one of the finest, most spectacular restaurants to open here in some time. Shawn McClain, sous-chef since 1993, was promoted to executive chef when the original "trio" split in 1995. Trio was named for the three cuisines the restaurant represents and for the original talented partnership including proprietor Henry Adaniya. Current pastry chef Della Gossett creates desserts as delicious as they are beautiful. The cooking is built on classic French and Italian foundations with Asian influences, and the finished dishes are avant garde. Stunning presentations—some whimsical—are arranged on unusual surfaces such as marble, granite, and mirrors. A complimentary sorbet arrives as an intermezzo during dinner. An entire dinner parade of such spectacular menu items is definitely culinary theater. Informed servers anticipate diners' needs, but are never doting. The joy of dining here has rejuvenated even the most jaded, worldly diner. The degustation menu is a great spontaneous tasting opportunity. Kitchen table must be reserved weeks in advance.

Honors/awards: *Chicago Tribune* and *Chicago Sun-Times,* four stars, 1996; *Gourmet* magazine rated it among the nation's top restaurants, 1996; *North Shore* magazine, Top 30 in the City, 1996.

Tufano's (Vernon Park Tap)

Zone 5 South Loop	Italian
1073 West Vernon Park Place	★★½
(312) 733-3393	Inexpensive/Moderate
	Quality 76 Value C

Reservations:	Not accepted; walk-ins wait about half an hour on weekends
When to go:	Weekdays
Entree range:	$6–12
Payment:	Cash, personal checks (local); no credit cards
Service rating:	★★★
Friendliness rating:	★★★★
Parking:	Valet
Bar:	Full service
Wine selection:	Limited, mostly Italian
Dress:	Moderately casual
Disabled access:	Limited; ladies' rest room is handicap accessible
Customers:	Diverse
Lunch/Dinner:	Tuesday–Thursday, 11 A.M.–10 P.M.; Friday, 11 A.M.–11 P.M.
Dinner:	Saturday, 5–11 P.M.; Sunday, 3–9 P.M.

Atmosphere/setting: Casual and cozy.

House specialties: Lemon chicken; eggplant Parmigiana; Tufano special salad.

Other recommendations: Other pasta dishes (e.g., lasagna; mussels with angel hair, your choice of red or white sauce; tortellini Alfredo); veal Marsala.

Summary & comments: Also known as Vernon Park Tap, this is a cornerstone of the old Taylor Street Italian neighborhood, founded by the Tufano family over 60 years ago. It's hidden among a row of older buildings, and the restaurant is behind a bar room. This is no-frills decor with blackboards listing the daily selections. The menu offers choices of red or white sauce, charges a bit extra for meatballs or sausage, and has the old traditional Friday fish specials. The place is a time warp, and that's why it's especially fun. Chef Joey Di Buono turns out respectable versions of the old-guard Italian fare in large servings. Everyone who eats here seems to walk out happy.

TUSCANY

Zone 5 South Loop	Italian
1014 West Taylor Street	★★★
(312) 829-1990	Moderate
	Quality 84 Value C

Reservations:	Recommended; walk-ins wait about half an hour on weekdays, 1–2 hours on weekends
When to go:	Any time
Entree range:	$15–30; average dinner of appetizer, entree, and dessert is $30
Payment:	All major credit cards except DC
Service rating:	★★★
Friendliness rating:	★★★½
Parking:	Valet
Bar:	Full service
Wine selection:	American and Italian
Dress:	Moderately casual
Disabled access:	Yes
Customers:	Local, diverse
Lunch:	Monday–Friday, 11 A.M.–3:30 P.M.
Dinner:	Monday–Friday, 5–11 P.M.; Saturday, 5 P.M.–midnight; Sunday, 2–9:30 P.M.

Atmosphere/setting: Cozy Italian decor with green and white tablecloths.

House specialties: Eleven dinner specials such as macaroni cippriani (freshly made square noodles with light cream-tomato sauce); rotisserie chicken; stuffed veal chop (a special now). All items are deftly prepared rustic-style.

Other recommendations: Mainstream antipasto and pastas with good sauces.

Summary & comments: One of the newest restaurants in Little Italy on Taylor Street. Owned by restaurateur Phil Stefani, this location has an open kitchen with a wood-burning oven and grill to produce typical Tuscan fare. Very popular and bustling. He owns several restaurants, including Stefani's Tuscany in Oak Brook and Riva on Navy Pier (see profile).

Honors/awards: 1993 Silver Platter Award.

Twisted Lizard

Zone 1   North Side
1964 North Sheffield Avenue
(773) 929-1414

Southwestern/Mexican
★★★½
Inexpensive

Quality 87   Value B

Reservations:	Not accepted
When to go:	Less crowded before 7 P.M. and after 10 P.M.
Entree range:	$6.75–12.75
Payment:	VISA, MC, AMEX, DC
Service rating:	★★★½
Friendliness rating:	★★★★½
Parking:	Street
Bar:	Full service; 8 types of margaritas; good selection of beers, including Mexican
Wine selection:	Small list: Spanish, Chilean, Mexican, Californian
Dress:	Casual
Disabled access:	Yes, call first
Customers:	Diverse; many young professionals
Brunch:	Sunday, 11 A.M.–3 P.M.
Lunch/Dinner:	Sunday–Wednesday, 11:30 A.M.–10 P.M.; Thursday, 11:30 A.M.–11 P.M.; Friday and Saturday, 11:30 A.M.–midnight

Atmosphere/setting: Cozy, subterranean cantina with bar. Rustic white cedar furniture; copper-top bar; colorful, wooden lizards; collection of dolls strung across the walls.

House specialties: Seafood queso fundido (sautéed shrimp and scallops baked and broiled with Chihuahua cheese, served with homemade flour and corn tortillas); barbecue chicken wings sprinkled with sesame seeds; flautas (three crispy corn tortillas rolled with choice of chicken or beef, topped with guacamole, sour cream, and Anejo cheese); Key lime pie; flan; good coffee.

Other recommendations: Enchiladas (three corn tortillas filled and baked with choice of meats, topped with choice of sauce and Chihuahua cheese); barbecue chicken breasts; fajitas (sizzling peppers, onions, and tomatoes with beef, chicken, or seafood with guacamole, pico de gallo, sour cream, rice, and beans).

Summary & comments: This is one of the best places for flavorful, top-flight southwestern and Mexican food, prepared by Mexican-born co-owner and chef Sergio Sanchez. The kitchen is so small that daily deliveries are essential, ensuring freshness. The interior is charming—although some people can't accept the lizard motif and are turned off by the name. Thriving catering business and carryout.

Va Pensiero

	Italian
Zone 11 Northern Suburbs	★★★★½
Margarita European Inn,	Moderate
1566 Oak Avenue, Evanston	
(847) 475-7779	Quality 96 Value C

Reservations:	Recommended
When to go:	Any time
Entree range:	$15.50–21.95; trattoria menu (early and late), 4-course dinner, $22
Payment:	VISA, MC, AMEX, DC
Service rating:	★★★★½
Friendliness rating:	★★★★★
Parking:	Valet, Monday–Saturday evening
Bar:	Full service, including grappas
Wine selection:	Recently expanded cellar inventory of more than 100 selections; all-Italian regional list; $18–148; excellent selections; about 12 by the glass, $5–8.50
Dress:	Moderately casual, business, dressy
Disabled access:	Yes
Customers:	Mostly upscale North Shore Italian food lovers; city professionals, couples
Lunch:	Monday–Friday, 11:30 A.M.–2:30 P.M.
Dinner:	Monday–Thursday, 5:30–9 P.M.; Friday and Saturday, 5:30–10 P.M.

Atmosphere/setting: Housed in the historic Margarita European Inn. Very Romanesque portico. Dining room has a Tivoli Garden look with plasterlike reliefs, peach-hued walls, candelabras, and white tablecloths. More casual cafe, the Verdi Room, open weekends. In spring 1997, quaint outdoor terraced roof garden was added.

House specialties: Antipasti: sautéed shrimp on crispy onion risotto cake, topped with pistachio pesto; insalata di calamari (warm); great house salad. Entrees: signature fazzoletti imbottiti (delicate white wine pasta filled with ricotta-spinach blend, with Parmesan and roasted tomato sauces); chicken breast stuffed with fontina cheese and prosciutto; crespelle al formaggio caprino (thin parsley crêpes rolled with creamy mild goat cheese, baked and topped with ragoût of wild mushrooms, cannellini beans, red wine, spinach); roasted Atlantic salmon with a mustard-mascarpone glaze. Desserts: budino al cioccolato (sensu-

(continued)

ous warm bittersweet chocolate cake with a creamy center, served with an almond milk sauce); silky cappuccino custard; their version of tiramisu (rich butter cake soaked in espresso and liqueurs, layered with whipped mascarpone).

Other recommendations: Homemade pastas (e.g., parsley ravioli stuffed with slow-roasted butternut squash and ricotta cheese); pan-browned veal tenderloin medallions; slow-roasted lamb shank. Desserts: rhubarb ice cream (in season); spumoni (trio of flavors of gelatti).

Summary & comments: Va Pensiero means "think freely" in Italian, and is the name of the composition a chorus sings in the opera *Nabucco*. It's an appropriate name for this restaurant, and the staff is living up to it. Chef-owner Peggy Ryan's refined, earthy cooking sings out in harmony now with her new chef, Jeff Muldrow, who was Ryan's sous chef in the early days of Va Pensiero and then executive chef at Vinci and Avanzare. His skills and her overall culinary vision combine with a new, energetic management staff to inject more vibrancy into this fine North Suburban Italian restaurant. The quiet, rather formal dining room has lightened its image; the male managers now wear attractive white shirts instead of jackets. The restaurant is more active with special events, as listed in their newsletter; they hold regional dinners every second Tuesday of the month; dinners featuring certain wines; holiday dinners; and festivals (in May they hold a Po River Festival, the best of Northern Italy, and a spring artichoke festival). Chef Ryan has conducted cooking classes, which have been repeated on popular demand. People often ask her how a chef named Ryan can cook Italian so well. Her instincts in combining Italian flavors and textures have been on target in all the dishes sampled on several occasions. The upscale setting in the vintage building is charming—a soothing environment with good jazz background music for enjoying fine Italian cuisine and regional wines.

Honors/awards: *Wine Enthusiast* magazine 1996 Restaurant Award (for excellence in service, storage, and wine list creativity); 1995–96 Silver Platter Award: Number One Favorite Italian Restaurant (voted by Chicagoland Restaurateurs); 1996 Silver Platter Award: Peggy Ryan voted Top Five Favorite Chefs.

VIA VENETO

New Italian
★★★½
Inexpensive

Quality 85   Value B

Zone 1   North Side
3449 West Peterson Avenue
(773) 267-0888

Reservations:	Recommended weekends
When to go:	Any time; weekdays less busy
Entree range:	$6.95–14.95
Payment:	Major credit cards
Service rating:	★★★½
Friendliness rating:	★★★½
Parking:	Street, small lot in rear
Bar:	Full service
Wine selection:	Mostly Italian, Californian, French; many affordable at $16 a bottle; Riserva and champagne, $52 a bottle; several by the glass
Dress:	Casual, business
Disabled access:	Yes, including rest rooms
Customers:	Diverse; locals, professionals, couples
Open:	Monday–Friday, 11:30 A.M.–10 P.M.; Saturday, 3–11 P.M.; Sunday, 3–10 P.M.

Atmosphere/setting: Cozy, bright, rather elegant with white tablecloths; Italian-style with display case of food; a sit-down bar and sidewalk cafe.

House specialties: Antipasto: melenzane stuzzicante (eggplant with tomato, garlic, olive oil, and mozzarella); shrimp sautéed with garlic and oil; grilled octopus with balsamic vinegar. Pastas: pumpkin ravioli in tomato–goat cheese sauce; penne Bolognese with rich meat sauce. Fish of the day; vegetarian dishes made from home-grown vegetables.

Other recommendations: Stuffed calamari; risotto with porcini mushrooms or four cheeses; the namesake chicken breast with mushrooms in white wine; tiramisu.

Summary & comments: Several years ago this was a hidden gem on the Northwest Side; it has since grown in popularity. Chef-owner Tony Barbanente's penchant for healthy, light dishes results in fresh, cooked-to-order items. The care shows both in the attentive cooking and accommodating service. An excellent value off the beaten restaurant path. Barbanente has also opened La Donna Nord, serving regional northern Italian cuisine (1001 West Golf Road, Hoffman Estates, 60195, (847) 843-8620), and La Donna, serving Roman cooking (5146 North Clark Street, Chicago, 60640, (773) 561-9400).

Viceroy of India

Zone 1 North Side	Indian
2520 West Devon Avenue	★★★
(773) 743-4100	Inexpensive/Moderate
Zone 9 Western Suburbs	Quality 84 Value B
19 West 555 West Roosevelt Road, Lombard	
(630) 627-4411	

Reservations:	Required on weekends
When to go:	Any time; weekends are busy
Entree range:	$6–13; lunch buffet, $6.95
Payment:	Major credit cards
Service rating:	★★★
Friendliness rating:	★★★
Parking:	Street, lots nearby
Bar:	Full service plus 3 Indian beers
Wine selection:	Limited
Dress:	Casual
Disabled access:	Yes
Customers:	Locals, ethnics, tourists
Lunch:	Daily, noon–3:30 P.M.; buffet available
Dinner:	Sunday–Thursday, 5–10 P.M.; Friday and Saturday, 5–10:30 P.M.

Atmosphere/setting: Formal, large dining room; dim lights and breezy sitar music; part of the wall is carved to resemble the intricate Mughal art often seen in ancient Indian Muslim architecture. Separate carryout and casual dining room; large private party room.

House specialties: Chicken tandoori is deliciously juicy; butter chicken is rich and creamy; light peas pulao (with fried long-grain rice) has the perfect taste balance with spicy bhuna gost (lamb cubes, tomato-onion gravy) and tender shish kebab (lamb).

Other recommendations: Chutneys are heartier than most; appetizers such as the steam cheese pakora (steam cheese fritters in graham flour batter) and samosa (flour patties stuffed with delicately spiced potatoes and peas) are light, golden, and crisp; onion kulcha (bread stuffed with onion, dry mango, spices); kulfi, an Indian-style pistachio-and-saffron ice cream; the mango lassi (an icy yogurt-mango drink).

Summary & comments: This is one of the nicest Indian restaurants on famed Devon Avenue, which has a string of Indian shops, cafes, and restaurants. Banquet facility for up to 400 people; restaurant can seat up to 150.

Vivere (Italian Village)

Zone 4   The Loop
71 West Monroe Street
(312) 332-4040

Italian	
★★★★½	
Moderate	
Quality 95	Value C

Reservations:	Recommended always
When to go:	Any time
Entree range:	Lunch, $9.95–22.95; dinner, $12.93–28.95
Payment:	Major credit cards
Service rating:	★★★★★
Friendliness rating:	★★★★★
Parking:	Valet, $7
Bar:	Full service
Wine selection:	Extensive (about 16) and well balanced; wines by the glass, changes daily; mostly Italian; good American and French selection; award-winning, 36-page, 950-selection reserve list
Dress:	Chic casual, dressy
Disabled access:	Yes
Customers:	Diverse, professionals, couples, operagoers, theatergoers
Lunch:	Monday–Friday, 11:30 A.M.–2:15 P.M.
Dinner:	Monday–Thursday, 5–9:30 P.M.; Friday and Saturday, 5–10:30 P.M.; Sunday, closed.

Atmosphere/setting: Award-winning decor is a unique "modern Italian baroque," a blend of the elements of a Medieval castle with futuristic fantasy—burgundy velvet chairs mix with peach hues and black accents, mirrors, and marble and shell-shaped light fixtures. Intimate open mezzanine area.

House specialties: Appetizer: Duck proscuitto with fresh mâche, with blueberries and lemon viniagrette. Tortine di funghi misti (garlic-infused mushrooms in an onion-thyme cream sauce); carpaccio, fava beans, truffle oil mayonnaise, and spinach soufflé; roasted butternut squash–filled pasta in Amaretti biscotti-pear-pecan sauce; braided lobster-filled tomato pasta with a lobster–light cream sauce; duck breast, sliced and fanned on a plate with zucchini puree, crisp leeks, and celery root, and a red wine–balsamic vinegar sauce; veal tenderloin in a porcini-pancetta-gin cream sauce with seasonal vegetables. Seafood of the day, such as Atlantic salmon in artichoke tomato sauce (charcoal-grilled or ai ferri—seared on a hot iron griddle).

(continued)

VIVERE (ITALIAN VILLAGE) *(continued)*

Other recommendations: Pheasant-filled pasta with butter, sage, and Parmesan; eggless pasta with four-cheese filling in cherry tomato–basil sauce (a special); daily risotto; oak-grilled lamb chops; roasted artichokes in a white wine-Mandarin-basil sauce. Desserts: mango sorbetti with tuille; gelati; a chocolate-truffle cake creation; panna cotta (timbale of sweet cream, caramel sauce, and nougat).

Summary & comments: Vivere means "to live" in Italian, and indeed, this is the way to do it Italian-style. After celebrating its 73rd anniversary in 2000, the Italian Village is a city landmark. Vivere is part of a triad of restaurants that make up the Italian Village, launched in 1927 by Alfredo Capitanini and now run by his sons, Ray and Franco, and Franco's three children. Chef Marcelo Gallegos prepares exciting contemporary, regional Italian food. The wine lists are dazzling and the prices overall spell good value. The heart-of-downtown location makes this a perfect place for an early dinner before the opera or theater. Vivere is on the main floor; the Village, upstairs (a charming re-creation of a town in Italy); and Cantina Enoteca (a great Italian seafood restaurant), downstairs. Italian Village holds an annual Garlic Festival in March. The same wine lists are available in all three, and they are organized by co-owner Ray Capitanini and Wine Consultant Robert Rohden.

Honors/awards: Wine list has received a *Wine Spectator* "Grand Award" annually since 1984. *Interiors* magazine award for design. In 1997, Vivere tied for second place in *Wine Spectator's* award for Best Italian Restaurant in the United States.

VONG

Zone 4   The Loop
6 West Hubbard Street
(312) 644-VONG (8664)

Thai/French	
★★★★½	
Moderate/Expensive	
Quality 97	Value C

Reservations:	Accepted; recommended weekends and large parties
When to go:	Anytime with reservation
Entree range:	$18–35
Payment:	All major credit cards
Service rating:	★★★★½
Friendliness rating:	★★★★½
Parking:	Valet
Bar:	Complete service
Wine selection:	Savvy international list
Dress:	Business; dressy; chic casual
Disabled access:	Yes
Customers:	Sophisticated palates of all types; professionals; couples; locals; travelers
Lunch:	Monday–Friday, 11:30 A.M.–2 P.M.
Dinner:	Monday–Thursday, 5:30–10 P.M.; Friday and Saturday, 5–11 P.M.; Sunday 5–10 P.M.

Atmosphere/setting: Stunning, elegant, Asian-inspired, sleek design with serene earth tones and celadon green. Materials selected for rich textures include a natural bamboo wood floor, sycamore, Kirkstone, and silk, which add warm tones. Zen-like atmosphere includes a torchiere wall of flickering lights (based on candles on walls in Buddhist monasteries) and a spice wall (teak shelf holds a selection of some of the fresh spices used in Vongerichten's cooking). Architect David Rockwell, who designed the original Vong in New York, and Vongerichten agree, "A great design must prepare the diner for the culinary experience they are about to enjoy."

House specialties: Appetizers: Signature "Black Plate," a selection of five seasonal creations. I tried some of the best: crab spring rolls, prawn satay with sweet-sour sauce, lobster daikon roll with rosemary ginger dip, quail rubbed with Thai spices, crunchy cress salad, and raw tuna and vegetables wrapped in rice paper. Charred lamb salad with aromatic herbs. Chicken coconut milk soup with galangal and shiitake mushrooms. Entrees: Muscovy duck breast, rare, spicy tamarind-sesame sauce; lobster with Thai herbs; monkfish baked with special

(continued)

spices and seeds with potatoes and asparagus. Desserts: "White plate," a selection of five signature desserts. I've tried warm Valrhona chocolate cake; fruit satay with passion fruit seeds; mango-wrapped fruit sushi; pineapple-wrapped white chocolate and peanut ganache; rice crêpe with crushed raspberries and coconut cream; banana spring roll.

Other recommendations: Appetizers: Warm asparagus salad, avocado and enoki mushrooms; grilled squid, sweet chili dressing, lime leaf crème fraîche. Entrees: "Fish," wok-fried Napa cabbage, water chestnuts, and chilies; spiced cod, curried artichokes; King salmon, morel mushrooms, turnips, and cardamom broth.

Entertainment & amenities: Browsing the creative menu. Private party areas designed for semi-private dining accommodating up to 20 each.

Summary & comments: This fusion restaurant is a merger between Lettuce Entertain You Enterprises president Richard Melman and French-born Chef Jean-Georges Vongerichten, whose dazzling cuisine at his bistro Jo Jo in New York (1991) won him awards. There he introduced his vibrant and spare cuisine, with intense flavors and seductive textures achieved with fruit essences, light broths, and herbal vinaigrettes His next restaurant was Vong (1993), which paid tribute to the spices of Orient, where he worked three-and-a-half years. He was so influenced by the cuisine in Asia that he developed his own unique Thai-inspired French cuisine at Vong, using over 150 different herbs and spices. In 1995 he opened a second Vong in London, and in 1997 a third in Hong Kong in The Mandarin Oriental Hotel. The same year he opened Jean-Georges in the Trump International Hotel and Tower and in 1998 Prime, a steakhouse in the Bellagio Hotel in Las Vegas. He continues expanding, and now Vong is here. His vibrant cooking with numerous spices, herbs, vinaigrettes, and oils yields explosively flavorful dishes, and leaves diners speechless. One critic/food writer said it took his breath away. One Chicago chef said his book, *Simple Cuisine,* changed her cooking—it so influenced her. This new restaurant, with an ever-changing menu, has a dynamic energy that creates immediate attention and lasting memories. After one meal here, it's easy to become a fan. One food-loving friend said, "Lunch at Vong was the best lunch of my life!"

Honors/awards: Too many to list, but several include Best New Restaurant of the Year (Jo Jo) by John Mariani, *Esquire;* Best Restaurant in the World (Vong, Hong Kong), Robb Reports.

Walker Bros. Original Pancake House

American
★★★
Inexpensive
Quality 88   Value B

Zone 11   Northern Suburbs
153 Greenbay Road, Wilmette
(847) 251-6000

Zone 10   Northwest Suburbs
1615 Waukegan Road, Glenview
(847) 724-0220

Zone 10   Northwest Suburbs
825 Dundee Road, Arlington Heights
(847) 392-6600

Reservations:	Not accepted
When to go:	Breakfast, brunch
Entree range:	$3.75–6.50
Payment:	VISA, MC, D
Service rating:	★★½
Friendliness rating:	★★★
Parking:	Free lot
Bar:	None
Wine selection:	None
Dress:	Casual
Disabled access:	Yes
Customers:	Locals, families
Open:	Sunday–Thursday, 7 A.M.–10 P.M. (10:30 P.M. in Wilmette); Friday and Saturday, 7 A.M.–11 P.M.

Atmosphere/setting: Comfortable and casual with stained-glass decor. The original place in Wilmette was the set for the film *Ordinary People.*

House specialties: Huge baked German pancake—the apple version is great; puffy omelet; French crêpes with strawberries and cheese.

Other recommendations: Waffles; spinach crêpes; corned beef hash.

Summary & comments: This is an old standby in several Chicago-area locations. The newest outlets are in Highland Park (with an expanded menu serving soups, salads, and sandwiches) and Lincolnshire (also serving salads and sandwiches). The quality of food exceeds the sometimes uneven service. A great family place for breakfast or brunch, and a fine place for a light supper—or late snack after a movie.

Wild Onion

Zone 1   North Side
3500 North Lincoln Avenue
(773) 871-5555

American/Italian/French
★★★½
Inexpensive/Moderate

Quality 85   Value B

Reservations:	Accepted
When to go:	Any time
Entree range:	$9.95–17.95
Payment:	All major credit cards
Service rating:	★★★
Friendliness rating:	★★★½
Parking:	Street (ample)
Bar:	Full service
Wine selection:	American West coast, French, and Italian
Dress:	Casual
Disabled access:	Yes
Customers:	Locals, professionals, couples
Brunch:	Sunday, 10:30 A.M.–2:30 P.M.
Lunch:	Monday–Saturday, 11:30 A.M.–3:30 P.M.
Dinner:	Monday–Thursday, 5–10 P.M.; Friday and Saturday, 5–11 P.M.; Sunday, 2:30–9 P.M.

Atmosphere/setting: Loft-style building with high ceilings, exposed brick walls, hardwood floors, lovely outdoor patio dining area. Recently remodeled.

House specialties: Grilled shrimp; crab cakes; duck enchiladas with mole sauce; grilled chicken salad, peanut dressing; smoked chicken chili. Four vegetarian entrees at dinner, and patrons can request other dishes to be made without meat or seafood. New pasta items.

Other recommendations: Baked artichoke hearts with blue cheese; seafood dill angel hair with garlic-tarragon cream sauce; crème brûlée; flourless chocolate cake.

Summary & comments: Out of the way in an unlikely neighborhood, this place, named for Chicago (the Indian name for "wild onion"), has always been rather creative with its food. The chef has a penchant for artichokes, and the menu has been expanded with more Italian and French infusion. The food is well prepared, portions are ample, and the service and atmosphere are pleasant—and the bonus is the pricing. Well worth a visit.

Wildfire (Russell Bry's)

Zone 3   Near North
159 West Erie Street
(312) 787-9000

American	
★★★	
Inexpensive/Moderate	
Quality 84	Value C

Reservations:	Recommended
When to go:	5–6:30 P.M. and 9:30–11 P.M.
Entree range:	$6.95–20.95
Payment:	All major credit cards
Service rating:	★★★
Friendliness rating:	★★★★
Parking:	Valet, $7; pull into garage next door to valet
Bar:	Full service; a dozen local microbrews; martinis; single-malt Scotches; small-batch whiskeys; and signature cocktails, such as Fired Up!
Wine selection:	Mostly Californian, a few Italian; several by the glass, $3.95 and up; bottles from $18
Dress:	Casual
Disabled access:	Yes
Customers:	Diverse; all ages, families, young urban professionals
Open:	Monday–Thursday, 5–10 P.M.; Friday and Saturday, 5–11 P.M.; Sunday, 4:30–9 P.M.

Atmosphere/setting: Rustic yet sophisticated; chestnut wood, lush carpeting, dim lighting; large bar area overlooks the dining room and open kitchen.

House specialties: Maine crab-and-shrimp cakes; house salad; woodland mushrooms oven-roasted pizza (shiitake, cremini, and portobello mushrooms with three cheeses); barbecued chicken house-smoked over maple and hickory; oak-planked Pacific salmon.

Other recommendations: Wildfire chopped salad; smoked chicken oven-roasted pizza; double-cut pork rib chop; and roasted fish of the day.

Entertainment & amenities: Special promotions; winemakers' dinners.

Summary & comments: Talented chef-proprietor Russell Bry prepares simple, hearty-flavored American cuisine in the oldest tradition of cooking—over a natural wood fire in an open wood grill, wood-fire oven, or on the rotisserie. The grill's amazing 1,000° F heat seals in flavors and obviously cooks food very quickly. Sounds like a hot kitchen job! Diners can see Bry's unique roasting and smoking methods first hand through the open kitchen near the dining room.

Honors/awards: Chef Russell Bry named 1997 Celebrated Chef by the National Pork Producers Council.

365

Woo Lae Oak

Zone 3   Near North
30 West Hubbard Street
(312) 645-0051

Korean
★★★★
Inexpensive
Quality 94   Value C

Reservations:	Accepted
When to go:	Weekdays (less crowded)
Entree range:	$8–16
Payment:	VISA, MC, DC
Service rating:	★★★★
Friendliness rating:	★★★★
Parking:	Free valet
Bar:	Full service; sake; Korean and Japanese beer
Wine selection:	Limited; mostly domestic and French
Dress:	Casual; many in business attire
Disabled access:	Yes
Customers:	Professionals
Open:	Daily, 11 A.M.–10 P.M.

Atmosphere/setting: Upscale decor with tables separated by frosted glass partitions and half walls of natural wood allowing for privacy. Ancient Korean pottery and classical music add to the elegance.

House specialties: Goo jul pan (Korean hors d'oeuvres of nine various ingredients wrapped in a pancake); mo doom jun (combination of pan-fried meatballs, shrimp fillet, fish fillet, and green peppers stuffed with ground beef, all coated with egg and flour); bul go ki (thin slices of marinated, grilled tender beef); jun gol (sukiyaki); buh sut jun gol (variety of mushrooms, thin slices of beef, and other vegetables; available without meat); dol sot bi-bim-bap (grilled, marinated strips of beef and vegetables topped with fried egg, hot paste sauce).

Other recommendations: Se wu tui gim (deep fried battered shrimp and vegetables); dak gui (lightly marinated, grilled boneless sliced chicken); yeon aw gui (fresh broiled salmon); chap chae (vermicelli noodles and vegetables sautéed in seasoned sauce); sik hee (sweet rice-flavored Korean punch).

Summary & comments: Each table has a built-in gas grill so diners can cook their own food. All main courses are served with kim chee (pickled and spiced cabbage), as well as side dishes such as spinach and spicy daikon radish. Opened in 1996, 50 years after the Jang family founded their first restaurant in Seoul, the Chicago venue of Woo Lae Oak is the eighth restaurant opened by Jin Keun Jang. His intention is to introduce Korean culture through high-quality food.

Honors/awards: Chosen by *Chicago* magazine as a "Pick of the Week."

Yoshi's Cafe

Zone 1 North Side	New French/Japanese
3257 Halsted Street	★★★★
(773) 248-6160	Inexpensive/Moderate
	Quality 94 Value B

Reservations:	Recommended, especially for weekends
When to go:	Weekend nights are busiest
Entree range:	$6–18
Payment:	All major credit cards except DC
Service rating:	★★★★½
Friendliness rating:	★★★★½
Parking:	Valet, $6
Bar:	Full service; bar/lounge adjacent to main dining room
Wine selection:	About 80 selections, mostly American and French, some international; $25 and up per bottle; 15 available by the glass, $4.50–6
Dress:	Casual
Disabled access:	Yes
Customers:	Diverse, local, visitors, Europeans, couples, professionals, families
Dinner:	Tuesday–Thursday, 5–10:30 P.M.; Friday and Saturday, 5–11 P.M.; Sunday, 5–9:30 P.M.; Monday, closed.

Atmosphere/setting: Very romantic, airy dining room with peach and beige walls, white linen tablecloths, and lots of silver; recently expanded to seat about 130 patrons, more than double its original size.

House specialties: Menu has an emphasis on seafood, with some unusual items, such as domestic fugu (blowfish—the Japanese type is poisonous if not prepared properly, but rest assured that domestic fugu is nonpoisonous). Items change due to availability. Tuna tartare with guacamole and toast; varied Japanese sushi and sashimi (spicy tuna roll; squid with tiny asparagus; rolled salmon with crab meat); salad of tomato, green beans, and cucumber with basil-infused oil vinaigrette; homemade buckwheat pasta (soba) with Oriental vegetables; veal scaloppine with mushroom Calvados sauce and risotto garnish. Specials such as grilled half duck, boned, with fresh persimmon sauce. Homemade desserts are worth the calories: dark chocolate pecan cake; velvety crème brûlée of the day (orange-ginger, coffee); refreshing lemon tart; thin sliced apple tart.

(continued)

Other recommendations: Grilled seared tuna with red wine–garlic–honey sauce; tofu steak with shrimp and shiitake mushrooms, sweet sake, soy sauce, and sesame oil sauce; grilled beef tenderloin with zinfandel sauce; veal with curry port wine sauce; rotisserie of chicken with rosemary au jus and mashed potatoes.

Entertainment & amenities: Viewing the artistic food plate presentations.

Summary & comments: Yoshi Katsumura and his wife, Nobuko, have operated their Franco-Japanese fine dining gem on Halsted for about two decades. In 1995, they renovated and enlarged the dining room to turn it into more of a true cafe; they also revamped the menu and lowered prices dramatically. About a fifth of the menu changes daily, and it changes completely every two months; there are daily specials. While an occasional dish might lack seasoning, Yoshi's French food with Asian influences is still mostly superb and beautifully presented, often on colorful Japanese plates. The professional, accommodating service remains as unwavering as before, but the feeling is more casual, set by the jazz and other music. A big bonus is that the prices make this affordable fine dining.

Honors/awards: DiRoNA Award (distinguished restaurant in North America since 1992, four diamonds); *Chicago Tribune* and *Chicago Sun-Times,* three stars; *Gourmet* magazine's readers' poll, America's Favorite Chicago Restaurant, 1996.

YVETTE

Zone 3   Near North
1206 North State Parkway
(312) 280-1700

New French	
★★★½	
Inexpensive/Moderate	
Quality 85	Value C

Reservations:	Recommended
When to go:	Any time; weekdays less busy
Entree range:	$12–20
Payment:	VISA, MC, AMEX, DC
Service rating:	★★★½
Friendliness rating:	★★★★½
Parking:	City lot across the street (discounted)
Bar:	Full service
Wine selection:	American, French, and Italian wines, ranging from $24–150 per bottle
Dress:	Informal, tastefully casual, some dressy
Disabled access:	Yes
Customers:	Upscale, largely professionals, couples; all ages
Brunch:	Saturday and Sunday, 11 A.M.–3 P.M.
Dinner:	Monday–Thursday, 4:30 P.M.–midnight; Friday and Saturday, 4:30 P.M.–1 A.M.; Sunday, 4:30–11 P.M.; 365 days a year

Atmosphere/setting: Sophisticated cabaret ambience in cafe area up front, set to accommodate musicians; dining room in back is comfortable. Chic Gold Coast bistro with a sidewalk cafe.

House specialties: Grilled trout with tomato concasse, garlic, and olives; French onion soup au gratin; seared bay scallops with spinach and diced tomatoes over fusilli and mushrooms; roasted filet of lamb with rosemary couscous, grilled ratatouille, and natural jus; salmon Yvette, smoked to order and served over angel hair pasta with vegetables and beurre blanc.

Other recommendations: Fruit and cheese plate with glass of port; a daily selection of homemade desserts.

Entertainment & amenities: Every night, live music (jazz, cabaret) and dancing; no cover.

Summary & comments: Unique French bistro with a cabaret atmosphere and nightly entertainment and dancing. Owner Bob Djahanguiri's hallmark is designing restaurants himself and blending live music with good French food and ambience. Yvette is a very romantic place for a special occasion or any time you're yearning for a taste of France.

ʌfANdEl

Zone I   North Side
59 West Grand Ave.
(312) 527-1818

American Ethnic (Folk)
★★★★
Moderate

Quality 91   Value C

Reservations:	Accepted
When to go:	Weekends less busy; anytime; try monthly special menus
Entree range:	$15.75–17.25; specials might be higher
Payment:	AMEX, DC, MC, VISA
Service rating:	★★★★½
Friendliness rating:	★★★★
Parking:	Valet, $8
Bar:	Complete
Wine selection:	Outstanding; diverse and intelligent list, especially featuring their namesake varietal; mostly affordable; many by the glass
Dress:	Casual
Disabled access:	Complete
Customers:	Varied, locals and travelers of all ages; sophisticated food and wine lovers; jazz lovers (Jazz Showcase is in the same building)
Brunch:	Saturday, 10:30 A.M.–12:30 P.M.
Lunch:	Monday–Friday, 11:30 A.M.–2:30 A.M.
Dinner:	Monday–Thursday, 5–10 P.M.; Friday and Saturday, 5–11 P.M.

Atmosphere/setting: Contemporary and colorful; whimsical with folk art; decorative screens; attractive and inviting bar/lounge area; murals; wall sculptures including one with beads and shells; curved bannister with curtains sets off upper level dining area. Wooden tables with candles.

House specialties: Appetizers: crayfish cakes/balls, crispy outside with carrots, greens with mustard sauce; warm Lovetree Farms sheep's milk cheese with arugula, black walnut salad, and maple mustard dressing. Main courses: Vegetarian portobello and green and yellow squash creation; banana leaf-steamed Hawaiian moonfish "lau lau" with shiitake mushrooms, ginger, and lobster curry sauce (special Hawaiian soul food menu); braised Illinois venison with posole, dried cherries, dark chile sauce, grilled flat bread. Dessert: devil's food cake with mint, chocolate sauce; gelatin with blackberries, blueberries, raspberry sauce.

(continued)

Other recommendations: Starter: Oak-smoked sunburst trout; spicy crawfish escabeche; crispy goat cheese–stuffed squash blossoms. Main courses: corn husk-smoked duck with double corn tamale, saffron piñon sauce, and wild sage pesto; goat cheese-stuffed artichoke with Hoja santa, whole grain "pilaf," raisins, and lemon.

Entertainment & amenities: Viewing the folk art.

Summary & comments: Chef Susan Goss, aided by a degree in anthropology, produces wine-friendly cuisines that reflect the regional and ethnic richness of America, such as those of the Hopi, Navajo, and Pueblo peoples. The restaurant features regional-folk menus that change monthly, for example: in March, Creole/Acadian month, and in October the emphasis is on the Pacific Northwest. Drew Goss, "husband of the chef" and resident wine expert, has selected some appropriate wines to complement this exciting food. He is on hand to greet diners and his warm hospitality adds special charm.

Honors/awards: Much media attention since opening several years ago, including *Chef* magazine; *Chicago Tribune; Chicago Sun-Times; Nation's Restaurant News.*